Cassette Culture

PETER MANUEL

Cassette Culture

Popular Music and Technology in North India

The University of Chicago Press · Chicago and London

Peter Manuel currently teaches at John Jay College (City University of New York).

The University of Chicago Press, Chicago 60637
The University of Chicago Press, Ltd., London
© 1993 by The University of Chicago
All rights reserved. Published 1993
Printed in the United States of America

02 01 00 99 98 97 96 95 94 93   1 2 3 4 5 6

ISBN (cloth): 0–226–50399–2
ISBN (paper): 0–226–50401–8

⊗ The paper used in this publication meets the minimum requirements of the American National Standard for Information Sciences—Permanence of Paper for Printed Library Materials, ANSI Z39.48–1984.

Library of Congress Cataloging-in-Publication Data

Manuel, Peter Lamarche.
Cassette culture: popular music and technology in North India / Peter Manuel.
p. cm.
Includes bibliographical references (p.)
1. Popular music—India—History and criticism. 2. Sound recording industry—India. 3. Mass media and music. 4. Music and society. 5. Audiocassettes.
ML3502.I4M36 1993
306.4′84—dc20   92–27626
                                                            CIP
                                                            MN

To Beth, Sophia, and Liliana

Religious madness catching hold of the nation

Politicians' gladness, their manipulation, children's sadness

They cannot understand why mother hates, why father kills,

Killing in the name of love, killing in the name of God

Killing in the name of a language,

Killing in the name of a temple, killing in the name of a mosque

Killing in the name of a gurdwara, killing in the name of a church

Killing in the name of Krishna, killing in the name of Allah

Killing in the name of the Saint, killing in the name of Christ

O stop, in the name of man, in the name of man, stop.

Remo Fernandes

Contents

Contents

Contents

Preface

This volume is a study of the impact of cassette technology on popular music in North India. It explores the nature and ramifications of the changes cassettes have wrought on the structure of the Indian music industry, on popular music itself, and on the meanings and effects that mediated music has for its audiences. As media theorists have come to speak of "media cultures," with their own conventions and codes, this book ultimately aims to posit and describe a North Indian "cassette culture," and to situate this phenomenon historically within the broader framework of Indian society. This study, then, does not purport to be an exhaustive survey of North Indian popular music, since it contains no musicological analysis and deals only secondarily with film music, which remains the single most widespread popular-music genre. It does, however, explore the structure, content, and social significance of most of the major styles of popular music that have emerged in close connection with cassettes, as well as of diverse preexisting genres—particularly folk and devotional styles—that have come to be disseminated on a mass basis through cassettes. The underlying intent of the descriptions of these genres is to illustrate how such musical styles and developments have been conditioned by a technological, and in a broader sense, a socioeconomic development, namely, the dramatic decentralization of access to and control of the means of production of recordings. Inevitably, a study of this sort must also confront broader issues relating to the diverse and often competing ideologies, aesthetic values, and material interests within different segments of Indian society.

There should be little need to argue the importance of popular music and popular culture in modern Indian society. Many Indians are considerably more familiar with commercial popular culture—especially film culture—than with their traditional arts and customs. Cinema idol Amitabh Bachchan is a far more significant and familiar name to most North Indians than is Subhash Chandra Bose, Surdas, or Shah Jahan; similarly, the thousands of songs recorded by Lata Mangeshkar have a much wider audience than the music of Ravi Shankar, or the Punjabi ballad of Hir and Ranjha. Further, much of the traditional culture that many modern urban Indians apprehend comes via the medium of the commercial entertainment industry—particularly films, but increasingly, music cassettes.

In 1972, Milton Singer coined the terms "Great Tradition" and "Little Tradition" to point out the distinction between mainstream, pan-regional, Sanskritic Hindu culture, and the panoply of discrete, localized, regional cultural heritages that abound in South Asia. In its pan-regionality and mass dissemination associated with cultural elites, mainstream popular culture—and particularly film culture—has come to constitute a new "Great Tradition," influencing the lives and worldview of several hundred million South Asians, in villages as well as towns and cities. To study this popular culture is not necessarily to celebrate it, but to acknowledge its pervasive influence throughout India, and in Indian emigrant communities.

The advent of cassettes has had a dramatic effect on the music industry and popular music throughout most of the developing world. In the industrialized West, sales of prerecorded cassettes now surpass those of records and CDs. However, relatively few recordings are issued in cassette format only, and cassette technology has had little influence on the structure of the music industry in general. In general, cassettes have come to be primarily a convenient alternative format, useful for home taping, and for automobiles and portable playing machines.

By contrast, in most of the developing world, cassettes have largely replaced vinyl records. The reasons for this development are obvious. Cassettes and cassette players are cheaper and more durable than records and turntables, and their power requirements are more easily met. Further, the mass production of cassettes is incomparably simpler and cheaper; on a small scale, commercial duplication can even be done with two cassette machines and a patch cord. The low expense of cassette consumption renders the medium accessible to rural and lower-income groups. At the same time, the lower costs of production enable small-scale producers to emerge around the world, recording and marketing music aimed at specialized, local, grassroots audiences rather than at a homogeneous mass market. The net result is a remarkable decentralization, democratization, and dispersal of the music industry at the expense of multinational and national oligopolies.

Motivations and Predispositions

While this volume aspires to the empirical objectivity of the best scholarship, it would be disingenuous of me to pretend that it is not tinged by my own personal interests and ideological perspectives. In pursuing this study I have been motivated less by a love for the music involved than by an interest in the sociocultural issues that it presents, and a conviction that popular music embodies and reflects important sociopolitical conflicts and contradictions. In a general sense, I am interested in the way in which the mass media can serve either to promote or inhibit progressive social awareness and change. I approach the subject with a profound mistrust of media that are controlled by dominant elites rather than by grassroots democratic communities themselves. Such mistrust extends not only to authoritarian state apparatuses but also to corporate networks, whose ideological messages may be more obliquely disseminated, and hence in many cases even more effective. I regard the mass media in my own country as playing a significant role in distracting the public from crucial issues and directly or indirectly serving to legitimize a status quo characterized by class polarization, ecological destruction, and imperialist foreign intervention. I share the opinion of other critics, who in this country might be dubbed "radical," that the media industry's reduction of all content to the level of entertainment, its glut of wanton violence, and its postmodern overload of media messages tend to leave consumers in a state of confusion and apathy, wherein significant political activism and discriminating critical thought are effectively discouraged (see, e.g., Lazere 1987:12).

Insofar as the mass media appear to contribute to this situation, I share the interest of many progressives in alternative forms of mass media characterized by democratic, participatory, grassroots control, a lack of social distance between producers and consumers, and a decentralized structure affording a responsiveness to community values and aesthetics. At the same time, I am painfully aware that grassroots media content is only as enlightened as the people who control the media, and that freedom and autonomy, in the form of media control, open up enhanced possibilities for abuse and subversion of the very potential for liberation and democracy that decentralization can bring. In India, the tendency of cassettes to promote social fragmentation, and most disturbingly, to foment religious bigotry and violence, raises fundamental questions about the merits of popular control of the mass media.

Until very recently, much of the attraction of a democratic vision of the media has derived from the absence of existing models whose merits and shortcomings could be empirically appraised. The cassette revolution in India, however, has provided many of the basic prerequisites for such a democratic restructuring of media control and content, at least in relation to popular music; my study, then, aims to explore the nature of the transformation of the Indian popular-music scene wrought by cassettes, focusing on the relation of these developments to the criteria and issues discussed below.

Scope and Orientation

Interpretive media-theory issues of alienation, authenticity, hegemony, and uses and abuses of media control constitute theoretical subtexts throughout this volume. The first chapter outlines these themes explicitly, suggesting their relevance to the advent of cassette technology, and to the emergence of a set of interactive, accessible new media capable of "democratic-participant" patterns of media use. Chapter 2 explores aspects of homogeneity and diversity within the international recording industry before and after the advent of cassettes, with brief sketches of selected representative music cultures. The following chapter reviews the development of the music industry in India before the cassette vogue, stressing its relation to film culture and the monopolistic nature of its control. Chapter 4 discusses the emergence and internal structure of the cassette industry in India. The two subsequent chapters are devoted to two music genres, *ghazal* and devotional music, whose commercialization has been inextricably associated with cassettes; as suggested above, my aim in these chapters is to analyze these genres as media content rather than to provide a descriptive style survey. Chapter 7 explores the phenomenon of tune-borrowing in popular music and its aesthetic implications. The next chapter surveys the emergence of regional folk-popular musics in the wake of the cassette boom, while chapter 9 focuses on the Braj region as a representative case study of the changes that can occur in a traditional folk genre under the impact of cassette-based commercialization. Chapter 10 examines the important and controversial role that cassettes have come to play in sociopolitical movements, and particularly in the militant Hinduism currently besetting the subcontinent. In the concluding chapter I return to some of the contentious issues raised in chapter 1.

The term *popular music,* as used in this book, is intended to mean music which is produced and marketed as a mass commodity, and whose style can be seen to have evolved or changed due to close association with the mass media. Thus it is the connection with the media—rather than any subjective qualitative criteria—that distinguishes popular music from other genres and conditions its production, dissemination, meaning, and, in often subtle but significant ways, its style.[1] In North India, many of the newly emergent music forms disseminated on cassettes, and in the media in general, fall clearly within the category of popular music as defined here. At the same time, the diversification of the music industry caused by cassettes has led to the widespread marketing of many music genres which resist facile classification as popular, folk, or classical. Such ambiguities are especially clear in the case of regional folk musics—that is, traditional musics which lack written theory and are associated with dominated classes. Many such kinds of music have recently come to be disseminated on cassettes, whether in stylized or purely traditional forms. In such cases, the application of labels "popular" or "folk" may be somewhat arbitrary, as the influences of commodification and the media upon style may be difficult to assess. This volume, despite its title, does not purport to restrict itself rigidly to the more overtly commercialized forms of mass-mediated music in India, but rather includes in its focus various kinds of folk and devotional music which have come to be widely marketed on cassette.

Methodology

Most of the research for this volume was conducted in India during an extended stay in 1989–90, and during a shorter visit in winter 1990–91. Given the novelty of the Indian cassette boom, the ephemerality of pop music, and the general paucity of studies thereof, I found relatively little in the way of scholarly literature on any aspect of the topic. Journalistic articles in the popular press about commercial music and the entertainment industry proved useful in their own way, as did *Playback and Fast Forward,* a *Billboard*-type trade magazine about the music industry. Reviews of popular music by journalists provided one particular set of emic perspectives, although representative of only a certain sector of the public. Most of my research consisted of interviews with various people—producers, musicians, folklorists, aficionados, etc.—who were connected in one way or another with the cassette boom or the musics affected by it. The reader will note that I include many quotations from various informants, as well as from Indian journalists and critics. I have done so not with the intent of rendering my own style journalistic, but rather to let Indians speak for themselves as much as possible, in accordance with contemporary ethnographic trends.

As the format of this book suggests, I combined general research into the industry with superficial coverage of major North Indian regions and more detailed investigation of one area, the Braj region south of Delhi. I based myself in Delhi, which is the center of the cassette industry in north-central India, and is home to large and musically active migrant populations from other North Indian regions. It is also conveniently close to the Braj region. I have chosen not to extend my study to South India, due to the glut of North Indian data, the discrete nature of the North and South Indian cassette industries, and my own continued general ignorance of South Indian culture and languages. I strongly suspect, however, that many of the processes and phenomena described in this text have closely similar counterparts in the South.

Transliteration

Indian-language words have been transliterated in this volume in the standard romanizations used in most Indian English-language publications. For more precise transliteration with full diacritical marks, the reader is requested to consult the glossary, wherein words are rendered according to the system used by Platts (1968).

Acknowledgments

This book could not have been written without the prodigious kindness, hospitality, and openness of the Indian friends and informants who assisted me in so many ways. As time passes, I grow increasingly aware of the debt I owe to such people, and the impossibility of returning such favors in kind. My friend, dramatist and literary critic Zahir Anwar, provided many insights, introduced me to the Calcutta *qawwali* world, and together with his wife, Ghazala, undertook tedious translation of difficult literature for me. As always, my teacher and friend, sarodia Kalyan Mukherjea, was an invaluable resource and host. Shubha Chaudhuri at the Archive and Research Center for Ethnomusicology, and her colleagues Ragini Deshpande, Maya Kothari, Kalpana Bandiwdekar, and Shalini Bhatnagar, were particularly helpful and made their institution a useful and friendly resource. My research into Braj music was greatly facilitated by the hospitality of Pt. Shrivatsa Gosvami of Jai Singh Ghera, Brindavan, the encouragement of Dr. Braj Vallabh Mishra, and the companionship of M. H. Zaidi. The assistance of folklorists Usha Banerjee and Shaka Bandopadhyaya was particularly gracious and useful. Special thanks are also due to Umesh Pandey and Mudit Tyagi, who assisted me in translating Braj Bhasha songs and proved to be excellent informants regarding Braj culture in general. Jagdish Ojha's help in getting me started in Delhi was invaluable.

I am especially grateful to the informants who tolerated my tedious interrogations and idiosyncratic Urdu with patience and indulgence. In particular I should mention Jagdish Arora (producer), Vidha Babu (*rasiya* vocalist), Mohan Swarup Bhatiya (folklorist), Anil Biswas (composer and vocalist), Olvin Brown, Suresh Chaturvedi (folklorist), Anil Chopra (editor of *Playback*), Shamsur Rahman Faruqi (Urdu scholar and poet), Laxmi Narayan Garg (of Sangit Karyalaya), Chhanvarlal Gahlot (producer, folklorist), Radha Bihari Goswami (AIR producer), Subhash Goyel (Punjabi vocalist), Mohan Guruswami (scholar and Janta Dal activist), Pushpa Hans (Punjabi vocalist), Sirajul Haq (producer), A. S. Jaiswal (scholar of Punjabi culture), Harbans Jaiswal (producer), Mohan Jhala (Rajasthani vocalist), Sharad Chandra, Ajit Kohli (T-Series A & R manager), Komal Kothari (folklorist), Fateh Krishna (*rasdhari*), Chandu Lala (vocalist), Kusum Lata (vocalist), Gurdas Maan (vocalist and composer), Sailesh Mathur (of Yuki Cassettes), Barin Mazumdar (music critic), Ram Narain Agarwala (folklorist), Swami Kalyan Prasadji (*ras-dhari*), Vinayak Purohit (historian), Mudra Rakshasa (author), Ashok Ranade (musicologist), V. A. K. Ranga Rao (music critic and archivist), Sevaram "Tanatan" Sharma (poet and composer), Pradeep "Pappu" Sharma (*rasiya* vocalist), Hoti Sharma (*rasiya* poet), Vijender Sharma (*rasiya* vocalist), Pamela Singh (vocalist), Smt. Vidhya Bindu Singh (folklorist), Govind Vidyarthi (of IPTA), and H. L. Vir (of Saraswati Recording). Correspondence with Michael Kinnear and Fran Pritchett, and conversations with Philip Lutgendorf, Amelia Cuni, Nalini Delvoye, Shyam Das, Assim Shapiro, Susan Wadley, and Laurie Eisler were stimulating and enlightening. I am particularly grateful for Daniel Neuman's insightful feedback. In writing chapter 2, I relied heavily on conversations with Gage Averill, John Cohen, Andrew Kaye, Deborah Pacini, Thomas Turino, and Chris Waterman. Most of the research for this book was financed by a Senior Fellowship from the American Institute of Indian Studies in 1989–90; Pradip Mehendiratta was instrumental in facilitating and extending my stay. Special thanks are due to my editors, and especially to T. David Brent. Finally, my wife Beth Robin and our daughter Sophia Rosa played significant supportive roles in their own ways.

1

Introduction: Theoretical Perspectives

The cassette revolution in India has engendered a dramatic restructuring and reorientation of the music industry itself, of the quality, quantity, and variety of popular music disseminated, and of consumption and dissemination patterns. Given such diverse effects and ramifications, the advent of cassette technology may be approached from a number of different and complementary perspectives: as a primarily musical development, as a specific instance of the international information revolution, as a mass-media phenomenon, or even as a socioeconomic development representing the demonopolization of the music industry. Accordingly, a holistic study of the cassette phenomenon in India should comprehend all these aspects and draw from the theoretical perspectives appropriate to each, including ethnomusicology, economics, and media studies, situating these in the context of North Indian culture and international commercial entertainment as a whole.

On a foreground level (as noted in the preface), much of this volume is devoted to empirical description of the rise of the cassette industry and the musical developments associated with it. At the same time, these descriptions are informed and framed, whether implicitly or explicitly, by an underlying theoretical perspective which is intended to integrate the data presented while offering a basis for cross-cultural comparison.

As the title of this volume suggests, it is the analytic perspectives of communications theory which have been most productive for the study undertaken here, and, correspondingly, it is to that field that the findings of this research may be most significant. In particular, the discussion of North Indian cassette culture may be taken as a case study of the development of new forms of mass media that have arisen in recent decades. More specifically, it is intended as a case study of the advent of a grassroots-based, decentralized, pluralistic, "democratic-participant" micro-medium in a given region, whose negative and positive ramifications may have broader implications for the spread of such technologies elsewhere.

Cassettes and the New Media Technologies

One of the major sociotechnological developments of recent decades has been the spread of new forms of media whose patterns of control, production, content, and consumption differ dramatically from those of older forms of mass media. Internationally, the most important of these new media are video, photocopy machines, personal computer networks, cable television, fax, satellite communications, and last but not least, cassettes. These media, although diverse, share many features, both in terms of their internal technologies and their implications for the broader issues discussed below (McQuail 1987a:16, 25, 40, 75–77, 275). Technologically, several of them involve similar features of miniaturization, transmission, display, and of storage and retrieval. More importantly, they constitute a challenge to the one-way, monopolistic, homogenizing tendencies of the "old" media (especially cinema, television, and radio). The new media tend to be decentralized in ownership, control, and consumption patterns; they offer greater potential for consumer input and interaction, and heighten the user's control over the form of consumption and over the relation to the media sender. Their emergence highlights the manner in which oppositional or affirmative tendencies or potential may lie less in the specific *content* of the media than in the *means* of production of that content. On the whole, they accompany the evolution toward postindustrial societies wherein information of one kind or another is the most valuable resource and product; further, as McQuail observes (1987a:76–77), in their weakening of "old" media which formerly operated at national levels, their emergence accompanies what appears to be the contemporary decline of the nation-state itself. In effect, the new media render the Orwellian vision of monolithic consciousness control a possibility of the past rather than the future; 1984, indeed, has come and gone.

Several of the new media in question are expensive, high-technology products whose widespread use and impact remain confined to developed countries or affluent elites within poor societies. Video and, to a lesser extent, computers have already had significant effects among the Indian bourgeoisie, which is often likened to a large (about eighty million), developed, affluent country in its own right, as opposed to the remaining impoverished 90 percent. The impact of cassette technology, however, is by no means limited to the wealthy sectors of society. Like some of the other new media, cassettes and tape players constitute a two-way, potentially interactive micro-medium whose low expense makes it conducive to localized grassroots control and corresponding diversity of content. Cassettes, unlike films, can be used at the owner's convenience and discretion; they thus resist various forms of control and homogenization associated with the capital-intensive, monopolistic "old" media of television, cinema, and radio. The emergence of cassette culture in India thus must be seen in the context of a new world information order with new potentialities for decentralization, diversification, autonomy, dissent, and freedom.

Cassette Technology and "Democratic-Participant" Media

Many of the negative features associated with the mass media—manipulation, deculturation, monopolization, and homogenization—are to some extent inherent concomitants of large-scale, one-way, expensive, centralized forms of mass media. In the case of state-run media in authoritarian dictatorships, the negative characteristics are likely to be transparently obvious. Due to market pressures, elite control, and concentration of ownership, commercial corporate media in "free" societies can often be seen to exhibit the same sorts of manipulative and homogenizing tendencies, however subtler their techniques and effects may be. Public control of the media (particularly broadcast media) can avoid commercial pressures, but may exhibit the same or similar defects because of its typically centralized bureaucratic control and its freedom from direct accountability to public interest. Thus, from one perspective, the only significant alternative to such pitfalls may be the spread of various forms of inexpensive, grassroots-based micro-media, which provide dominated social groups with an unprecedented degree of access to, representation in, and control of mass media. These media would include some of the new technologies mentioned above, and especially the cheaper and more accessible media, such as underground presses, posters, pirate radio stations, video, and cassettes. The resistance of these media to authoritarian state control has been well demonstrated and exploited in recent decades by oppositional political movements, which will be discussed below.

McQuail (1987a:121–23) and Enzensberger (1970) have succinctly described the ways in which such "democratic-participant" forms of mass media present new possibilities for alternative forms of control, content, and effects. Benjamin's well-known essay "The Work of Art in the Age of Mechanical Reproduction," written in the 1930s, spoke optimistically of the mass media as potentially liberating forces; in subsequent decades, most critical theorists found the manipulative and stupefying aspects of the mass media far more apparent. With the advent of new forms of media more open to reciprocity and subaltern control, Benjamin's optimism might seem considerably more credible and prescient today. Enzensberger, for example, writing from a neo-Marxist perspective, hails the revolutionary and subversive power of the new media and their potential for mobilizing masses to empower themselves. Of course, it could be noted that a grassroots revolution utilizing the mass media might well have a different goal than the establishment of democratic socialism; the use of cassettes in the Iranian Revolution is an obvious example. Nevertheless, whether seen as vehicles of political mobilization or of com-

munity identity and aesthetics in general, the liberating and empowering potential of the new media stands in marked contrast to the monolithic control
associated with the "old" media. Enzensberger's dichotomization of media
also fits those uses characteristic of "old" media and "new" media such as
cassettes (adapted from 1970:26):

Repressive Use of Media	Emancipatory Use of Media
Centrally controlled program	Decentralized program
One transmitter, many receivers	Each receiver a potential trans-mitter
Passive consumer behavior	Interaction of those involved, feedback
Production by specialists	Collective production
Control by property owners or bureaucracy	Social control by self-organization

If we interpret "emancipatory" to refer not necessarily to socialist revolution,
but to more modest goals of local identity reassertion, the spread of interactive, grassroots media could ideally revitalize community values, enhance local sociopolitical participation, offer greater diversity and richness of media
content, and, in general, address the needs of small-scale communities, interest groups, and taste cultures. Conversely, however, it could exacerbate antagonisms, weaken desirable forms of intergroup solidarity, and promote reactionary beliefs and oppressive practices by backward minorities.

As will be explored below, many of these contradictory tendencies, in fact,
are already visible in the form of developments associated with the advent of
cassette technology. Cassette culture in North India thus presents a unique
opportunity for the study of the spread of a democratic-participant mass medium. On the surface level, its effects are most evident in the realm of music,
but as this volume aims to show, the impact of cassettes often quite clearly
involves broader fundamental issues of autonomy, freedom, and national integrity. It is in this sense that this text is presented as a case study in the
development and evaluation of a democratic-participant mass medium, whose
musical and extramusical ramifications may constitute a contribution to communications and social theory in general, as well as to an appreciation of
Indian music and culture.

Theoretical Approaches: Ethnomusicology and Media Theory

Ethnomusicology, to its credit, has always been too diverse a field to adhere
to any small set of identifiable research models. Such flexibility is fortunate
for the study of non-Western popular music, as the analytical models which
have been the most influential in ethnomusicological studies of music in cultural context have marked limitations in dealing with complex societies, es-

pecially where the mass media are involved. The approach associated with Alan Merriam, regarded as paradigmatic by many scholars in the 1960s and even later, was oriented toward the study of music in isolated, classless societies. A competing model (advocated by Gourlay 1978), stressing the act of performance, reflects the same limitations in its applicability to popular music. A more influential paradigm in culture theory and ethnomusicology since roughly the mid–1970s has been the interpretive anthropology propounded and articulated most cogently by Clifford Geertz. Advocating a holistic "thick description" which treats a given social phenomenon as an iconic embodiment of culture as a whole, Geertz suggests analyzing a given text, be it a folk tale, a cockfight, or a ritual, as "a tale a culture tells about itself." The use of such a model posits that the consumers of or participants in a given cultural text are essentially the same as its producers—or at any rate, that there is no significant difference between the two groups. Such a model, like that of Merriam, can be seen to work best in cultures that are relatively closed, coherent, homogeneous, and self-contained. Accordingly, the most successful ethnomusicological studies applying this analytical framework (especially Feld 1982) have been those dealing with small, autonomous, and classless societies.

An analysis based on the thesis that participants and producers of cultural phenomena are one and the same, that "man is an animal suspended in webs of significance he himself has spun" (Geertz 1973:5) becomes problematical when complex cultures are involved. Such an approach has considerable difficulty addressing social antagonisms, contradictions, and, most notably, ideological hegemony of any sort.[1] The shortcomings of a paradigm assuming social uniformity and cohesion become even more obvious when the mass media are involved—as they are in almost every society today. With the rise of entertainment industries based on the mass media, the producers and consumers of culture may be quite distinct from each other, and their power relationships may be profoundly asymmetrical. The values and aesthetics of the North Indian film industry constitute a case in point. Many aspects of these values do influence lower-class culture, from the use of film tunes in folk genres to the preference, among many, of cinema over folk theater. Yet lower-class Indians have no direct hand in creating film culture, which is generated largely by an oligopoly of corporate producers in Bombay. Film culture may be produced to some extent *for* lower-class Indians, but it is certainly not produced *by* them (nor, for that matter, *about* them). It would be naive, if not grossly distorting, to regard commercial Hindi films as "tales lower-class Indians tell about themselves."

It should be clear that a holistic analysis of popular music in a complex culture must in some fashion address the operation of the media and their content, and, on a broader level, fundamental issues such as those pertaining to dualities of hegemony vs. pluralism, uniformity vs. diversity, authenticity vs. alienation, and the like. Such issues, inherently polemical and potentially subjective as they are, are essentially unavoidable in media studies, and thus call for special care to distinguish authorial value judgments from hard data and the substantive conclusions generated by them (McQuail 1987a:309). Within media studies, greater emphasis has naturally been placed on subjects such as news reporting, whose ideological orientation is more tangible and concrete than that of most entertainment forms, and especially of the more "abstract" realm of music.

Nevertheless, such normative issues are ultimately as inescapable in the study of popular music as they are in media studies in general. Music may be inherently oblique and subtle in its meanings and effects, and it may be enjoyed by some of its audiences precisely because it seems to provide an escape from sociopolitical polemics. At the same time, popular music in most of the world remains embedded in powerful commercial enterprises linked to dominant classes with their own ideological agendas; popular music is inseparable from notions of social identity, and derives much of its appeal from the ways it embodies, however obliquely, encoded ideologies that may be all the more pervasive for their ambiguity and subtlety. Indeed, popular music may be equally pervasive and influential, if not more so, than explicit, prosaic forms of persuasion, for an ideology is most effective when it is invisible and taken for granted, shaping the opinions especially of those who do not cultivate an active interest in politics. Thus, however dispassionate and objective scholarly communications literature or popular-music studies may attempt to be, they must ultimately confront fundamental evaluative questions relating to power, freedom, authenticity, and alienation. Does popular music enrich or alienate? Is it an expression of grassroots values and sentiments, or a manipulative fabrication of a self-interested, elitist entertainment industry? Does popular music promote homogeneity and conformity, or social fragmentation and diversity? What are the negative and positive ramifications of these tendencies? In many cases, such questions can only be answered by addressing other issues, relating to the nature of the mass media, the form of its control and ownership, the nature of media content, and the patterns and effects of media consumption and reception.

Several ethnomusicological studies in recent years have explored the manner in which diverse popular musics serve as vehicles for social identity, including among dominated minority groups.[2] A few short articles have addressed the impact of cassettes in Indonesia, Egypt, and in passing, other countries.[3] The most significant and relevant study of the music industry outside the West is Wallis and Malm's informative, insightful, and original *Big Sounds from Small Peoples: The Music Industry in Small Countries* (1984). This volume surveys the music industries in selected countries, offering some data on cassettes from the vantage point of the early 1980s, and emphasizing the competition of hegemonic Western pop music and indigenous national genres. In a literal sense, *Big Sounds* is not directly relevant to this study, since

India is not exactly a small country, and, further, since Western popular music has played a relatively limited role in the Indian music scene. Nevertheless, the analytic approach of Wallis and Malm's volume does relate to that of this text, especially in the sense that the interaction *Big Sounds* portrays between Western music and that of developing nations parallels, in some senses, that between dominant mainstream Hindi film music and regional folk/pop musics; thus *Big Sounds* constitutes an important precedent for this study.

Given the limited applicability of favored ethnomusicological and anthropological models to media studies, it is not surprising that *Big Sounds* draws more from communications theory than from those fields. Similarly, the analytical approaches of communications studies, more than any other approach, have informed the present work. Since popular music, as defined for the purposes of this volume, is inherently and inextricably associated with the mass media, it can in many respects be more productively analyzed as a commodity, and as a form of media content, than solely, or even primarily, as an art work to be judged by aesthetic criteria. Hence it may be appropriate to outline the aspects of media theory which have proven most intrinsic to this study.

Popular Music, Alienation, and Hegemony

Mass-media dissemination of music, and especially of popular music, introduces fundamental changes in traditional patterns of musical production, consumption, and meaning. Before the advent of recording, a singer could no more be separated from his song than could a dancer from his dance. Recording technology effected such an alienation, presenting a fixed rendition of a performance as a tangible, salable entity. Acquiring commodity status, the recording takes on a social life of its own, subject to new dimensions of economics relating to commercial mass-market pressures and incentives. As recording technology and the mass media in general spread, they can be seen as inherently alienating insofar as they can promote passive consumption of culture rather than active creation of social and artistic life. In the classic neo-Marxist analysis of commercial popular culture, music-making ability is taken from people and returned in the form of a commodity. Individuals and communities are thus alienated from their own creative talent, and deprived of the warmth and solidarity reinforced by communal music-making. Instead they become increasingly dependent on the media for their musical needs, which are exploited and manipulated by entertainment industries which fetishize stars and songs.

While this theoretical scenario has been justifiably criticized as simplistic and overgeneralized, to a certain extent it may well be applicable to urban India. There is little doubt that in urban North India, and increasingly in small towns and villages, the spread of mass-mediated music genres—especially film music—has contributed to the decline or even extinction of once-vital

7

folk genres. The replacement of collectively performed musics by mass-mediated commercial products implies the alienation of individuals from their potential as performers, and of communities from their ability to exercise direct influence on professional forms of entertainment (e.g., folk theater). More palpably, perhaps, it is a sense of community—whether of neighborhood, class, region, gender, religion, or taste—that may be undermined by the mass media and commercial entertainment, whose impersonal oral culture may replace a traditional oral culture wherein communication, reception, and personal interaction are inseparable. Thus, if individuals cease to perform together, or to share and indirectly shape collective events like folk theater, they become alienated not only from themselves but from each other. At the same time, a rich network of community social life based around religious institutions, folk drama and music, tea-stalls, evening strolls, and the like may be increasingly replaced by a fragmented society of atomized families passively imbibing the impersonal, unidirectional media of video, television, cinema, and radio. While such transformations are more visible in the developed world, the spread of inexpensive micro-media—above all, of cassettes—in societies like India enables us to witness and document the effects of one kind of mass mediation in transforming traditional cultures.

While the negative features of such transformations are often quite evident, the mass media can and often do enrich as well as alienate, exposing audiences to a broader awareness of ideas, art forms, and culture in general. If the peasant from an isolated hamlet becomes disenchanted with the crude and unpretentious folk music of his area, he may also apply the higher technical standards of the professional music he hears on the radio to improving his own traditions. Moreover, the media can immensely broaden the worldview and learning of audiences otherwise limited by the proverbial "idiocy of village life." Such an alienation is not without its positive side, which at least partially justifies the spread of modern technology, urbanization, and development in general. The expense, of course, is the destruction of insular, cohesive traditional societies.

Further, as I shall attempt to illustrate below, the traditional Marxist indictment of mass mediation should be fundamentally qualified by the recognition that the relations between a media text, on the one hand, and experience, on the other, are not pregiven or fundamentally determined by the nature of the text. Rather, as Stuart Hall and others have stressed, the uses, effects, and interpretations of the text are the ongoing product of people's attempt to represent their own experiences, and to speak in their own voices instead of hegemonic codes.

Short of nuclear or ecological catastrophe, the mass media and class society will remain with us, and folklorists lamenting the decline of traditional folk performance must reconcile themselves to the irreversible spread of the mass media. The structure and orientation of the mass media, however, are theoretically within the control of men and women as active historical agents, even if aspects of their form and control may be conditioned by social structure in general. Thus, while the media are here to stay, there are different kinds of media with different effects, and it is natural that many countries have adopted explicit policies designed to control, for better or worse, the nature of media development and content within their borders. The advent of new forms of mass media—again, cassettes are the most outstanding example—offers new possibilities for transformation and heightens the importance of understanding the impact of mass mediation on sociocultural life.

A fundamental issue in the study of the mass media involves the extent to which the media function as instruments of manipulation, whether through prosaic persuasion or through subtler forms of indoctrination, for example, through music. Whether the media educate or mislead, serving as mirrors or filters, they may naturally tend to promote the ideologies and aesthetic values of certain groups—typically, those that own or directly control the media—at the expense of others. While the manipulative goals of mass-media content in authoritarian dictatorships are often readily apparent, the media can be seen to exercise a crucial role in free societies as well, by filtering and distorting public discourse in favor of a dominant ideology.

Marx and Engels provided an initial theory of hegemony in the seminal, but rather crude and extreme form of their oft-quoted opening to *The German Ideology* (1964:60):

> The ideas of the ruling class are in every epoch the ruling ideas, i.e., the class which is the ruling material force of society, is at the same time its ruling intellectual force. The class which has the means of material production at its disposal has control at the same time over the means of mental production, so that thereby, generally speaking, the ideas of those who lack the means of mental production are subject to it.

A more complex body of thought on the mass media and popular culture was generated by the Frankfurt School, notably, Marcuse, Adorno, and Horkheimer. Seeking to explain fascism and the failure of Marxism in the West, Frankfurt theorists argued that modern capitalism operated through the acquiescence of a depoliticized, alienated, and generally stupefied public. The mass media (and in Adorno's thought, popular music) played essential roles in legitimizing the status quo by stultifying critical consciousness, commodifying and disarming oppositional art, and promoting consumerism and the myth of a classless society. The media are seen in this view as manipulative instruments which by their very nature tend to exclude the voices of dominated groups in favor of those who, by virtue of their power and resources, not only control the media but are least likely to criticize existing power relations. Thus media contents evolve into reified dream worlds promoting escapism, commodity fetishism, and low levels of community solidarity and participation.

In recent decades, scholars such as Stuart Hall, Simon Frith, and Richard Middleton, deriving initial inspiration from Antonio Gramsci, have found an approach to be more fruitful which treats public culture, including popular music, neither as pure corporate manipulation nor as grassroots expression, but as contested territory where hegemonic and oppositional values symbolically or explicitly engage each other. Popular music and the mass media themselves are thus best seen as sites of negotiation, mediation, and "rearticulation" of these and other dialectics, such as, traditional/modern, young/old, male/female, city/countryside, and regional/pan-regional.[4] Such an analytical approach employs neo-Marxist principles of hegemony, alienation, and cultural materialism as means of linking the cultural and ideological superstructure with its socioeconomic base; at the same time, it extends the application of these concepts to encompass contradictions pertaining to region, ethnicity, religion, race, gender, and other factors, as well as class. Further, it clarifies the nature of hegemony as not dependent on the explicit and conscious biases or conspiracies of key individuals in the media, but rather as the natural and inevitable product of the system of relations involved in a given media situation. The advent of a new medium, such as cassettes, with dramatically different characteristic patterns of ownership and control, presents remarkable possibilities for new, diverse forms of expression.

Of course, in attempting to apply such approaches to non-Western popular culture, one must naturally be careful to distinguish general heuristic universals from concepts and analyses relevant only to the West. While Indian popular culture shares many features with its Western counterpart, it also exhibits some fundamentally distinct characteristics, which are particularly visible in the realm of commercial music.

First, one may note that Indian popular-music styles have not evolved in connection with alienated youth and class subcultures. As stressed in the work of Hall and others, a central component of the emergence of contemporary Western popular music (primarily rock and its subgenres) has been the appropriation of stylistic and aesthetic features from black proletarian or lumpen subculture and its music (blues, rhythm and blues). Such subcultures have had no comparable counterpart in India, where the specific features which conditioned and precipitated the emergence of rock in the 1950s—for example, a generational counterculture and a two-decade baby boom—did not obtain. Indeed, some of the syncretic musics now marketed on cassette in North India are more likely to be consumed by elders than by young people.

Secondly, in accordance with the uneven and incomplete development of capitalism and modern technology in India, Indian musical culture as a whole is far less permeated by market relations, corporate influence, and, to some extent, mass media penetration than is music in the West. The postmodern media saturation so evident and influential, for example, in rock video, has yet to become widespread in India outside of the urban bourgeoisie. Cassette-based musics are entirely free from corporate sponsorship, and have only loose and indirect ties with the other mass media. Indian popular musics lie on a continuum illustrating close links to folk musics with origins in the pre-capitalist past; the continuing vitality and adaptability of such musics provides popular music with raw material for syncretism, and prodigious potential for creative rearticulation. A concomitant of the folk affinities of much cassette-based popular music in India is the emphasis on the text, which stands in contrast to the oft-noted stress on vocal timbre, style, presentation, and gestural nuance in rock, which often overshadow the inconsequential lyrics. Among other things, the importance of the text in Indian folk/pop musics conditions the degree to which songs, or elements thereof, can be reappropriated and resignified by consumers. In general, it may be stated that the penetration of the mass media, and particularly of cassettes in India, is more extensive and advanced than the spread of consumerism, capitalist values and practices, and mass culture as a whole.

Popular Music as Agent of Homogeneity or Diversity

We have touched on one of the persistent questions in media studies and, to some extent, in literature on popular music, having to do with whether, and in what way, the media tend to promote cultural unification and homogenization or, alternately, decentralization and fragmentation (McQuail 1987a:59–60, 304–5). A related issue is whether the given tendency is to be regarded as positive or negative. Insofar as music often constitutes a potent symbol of social identity, the competing tendencies toward homogeneity or diversity are often highly visible in parameters of musical style and content, as well as in text content.

Popular musics and the mass media in general often function as unifying, centripetal entities, promoting a cosmopolitan, universalistic consensus of values and taste. Such uniformity, indeed, is a natural outcome of the desire of entertainment industries to seek economies of scale by orienting their products toward a mass, homogeneous audience rather than toward diverse minorities with specialized interests. Alternately, the media, particularly if they are decentralized in control and ownership, may address themselves to more localized communities or special-interest groups, thereby promoting fragmentation and diversity.

An examination of the centrifugal or centripetal tendencies of a given medium or media product is inevitably obliged to address conceptions of what constitutes a desirable social formation—are the given unifying or diversifying tendencies good or bad? On the one hand, homogenization, whether of political ideology or musical taste, can be seen as a prerequisite to nation-building and modernization, a means toward achieving group solidarity, and a valuable tool for integrating diverse people into an otherwise impersonal and anonymous modern society. The uniformity and consensus promoted by the mass media can contribute to prosocial behavior and collective mobilization toward shared goals. From this perspective, media decentralization could reinforce provincial isolation and backwardness and facilitate use of the media for hate-mongering, provocation, and petty factionalism. Such fragmentation could thus be associated with the atomization of individuals and the isolation of backward communities, and the dissolution of society into narrow and antagonistic special-interest groups.

On the other hand, homogenization, as promoted by the media, could be regarded as the deculturating, stupefying effect of corporate or state manipulation, which tends to exacerbate the dissolution of communal, grassroots social life, weaken the individual's sense of community and belonging, and promote a mindless conformity and acquiescence. Accordingly, diversification and decentralization, as promoted by the media, can be seen in a positive light, as conducive to individual freedom and choice, and to the vitality of specialized communities (whether based on class, gender, ethnicity, etc.). For example, the emergence of democratic-participant media forms in India could revitalize rich regional forms of subcultural expression—including music—which have been weakened by an alienating, monolithic film culture; on a broader level, it could empower dominated groups and promote solidarity among peoples—specifically, the poor and oppressed—who have traditionally enjoyed little access to or representation in the mass media.

Such questions are of particular importance in the present, when so many countries worldwide are wracked by such vicious internal divisions that the very concept of the nation-state is being questioned. While Western attention has focused more on fragmentation in the former Soviet bloc, India faces equally fissiparous and violent conflicts, whether based on class, religion, region, or ethnicity. Since the late 1970s the country has been torn by Sikh and Kashmiri separatism, Hindu-Muslim (in Indian usage, "communal") riots, ferocious agitations by Gurkhas and Assamese directed against unwelcome Bengali migrants, and a variety of caste-related riots and massacres. In such conditions, the ability of the media, as well as such important identity symbols as music, to promote either unity or diversity is not of merely academic concern. Thus, for example, it has often been observed that the Bombay film industry has served to promote Hindi-Urdu as a lingua franca, as well as common cinematic and musical tastes, and perhaps even a shared worldview in its vast and diverse audience. Indeed, it could well be argued that fondness for Hindi cinema and the music associated with it is perhaps the single most prominent consensual value among North Indians, given the weak sense of nationalism, the diversity of traditional regional and religious cultures, and the increasingly violent antagonisms between them.

A consensus which legitimizes an unequal social order, however, is not an unqualified good. Commercial Indian cinema (along with capitalist entertainment industries in general) has been accused of promoting consensus largely by distracting its audiences with escapist common-denominator products, while benumbing their creative and critical faculties in the process. The oligopolistic control of Indian film industry and the music associated with it can be seen to illustrate how elite ownership of the media can lead to the promotion of values favorable to the dominant groups; many Indian intellectuals argue that the products of such media may serve to distract audiences with escapist fantasies and promote a consumerist, alienated false consciousness which can itself be manipulated toward communal antagonism rather than, for example, solidarity among the poor. Further, the "community" of mass-entertainment consumers may turn out to be an intangible and shallow one, wherein audience members are united only by their shared devotion to a media star or image; meanwhile, the media may continue to alienate them from forms of traditional or potential social and cultural life based on grassroots customs and direct interaction with other community members. One must ask, then, if the order and consensus promoted by the homogenizing mass media are genuinely in the interests of audiences, and—even if they are deemed to be so—if they justify the alienating effects of the media.

Control of the Media

A basic axiom of studies in popular culture is—or should be—that holistic interpretation of commercial cultural products lies not in the analysis and reading of reified "texts," but in contextualizing such entities in the processes of production, dissemination, consumption, uses, re-uses, and varying idiosyncratic popular interpretations. In addressing fundamental questions relating to consensus, diversity, alienation, and freedom, a holistic analysis of media culture must examine three distinct but interrelated realms of inquiry: the nature of control of the mass media, the content disseminated therein, and the effects of these on, and uses by, audiences. Of these, the form of control of the means of media production is the most accessible to empirical analysis, and is a crucial, if not primary, determinant of the social character of an art form. Corporate monopolies, public ownership, authoritarian state domination, and grassroots participatory control of the mass media may all serve different class or community interests and engender distinct forms of content and effects.

In traditional society, it is the social position of the consumer that ultimately conditions the nature of art. Thus, for example, the elite and esoteric nature of classical music in the Mughal courts was determined by the aristocratic status of its clientele; the class background of court musicians themselves had but a secondary impact on the nature of the music. Similarly, an

Indian folksinger tailors his style and content to the demands of his audience, with which he is in direct, face-to-face contact, and which may reward him on the spot with immediate approbation and honoraria or, alternately, with indifference or criticism. As for collectively performed genres, the performers and consumers, naturally, are one and the same. Such a coherence between consumer taste and performance content is typical of precapitalist societies, where persons and their products are seen as intermeshed.

The presence of the mass media distances producers from consumers, and invariably enhances the conditioning influence of the former at the expense of the latter. Bourgeois ideology assumes that the nature of the competitive free-enterprise system obliges producers to tailor their products to consumers' tastes, and even Marx quipped, "He who pays the piper calls the tune." Yet in the case of art forms such as popular music, which tend to be dependent on and associated with unidirectional mass media, the consumers can be seen to forfeit a considerable degree of control to the producers. Such factors as economies of scale, concentration of media ownership, radical socioeconomic differences between producers and consumers, and the lack of direct input from the public can make the relation between production and consumption far more complex and unequal than in traditional, face-to-face forms of communication and performance. Thus, with the advent of the mass media and capitalist entertainment industries, the producers of a professional art form may come to exercise extensive and unprecedented control of the means of artistic production, enabling them to manipulate media content and, to an extent, public taste. Such, I shall argue, has been essentially the case with the production of Indian film music, which has been generated by a handful of corporate cinema directors and superimposed on a mass listening audience. And it is precisely this aspect of Indian popular music that has changed so dramatically with the advent of cassettes, which have allowed diverse smaller producers to usurp the dominance formerly enjoyed by multinationals (particularly EMI [Electrical and Musical Industries Ltd.]) and the corporate film industry.

Popular opinion, as articulated in journalism and everyday discourse, generally assumes the congruence of media content and public taste in the capitalist "free" world; allegations of manipulation are commonly, if justifiably, associated with Marxism and with cynicism about the merit of the free enterprise system as a whole. In the realm of scholarly literature, however, one finds fewer sustained, explicit expressions of faith in the authenticity of media product. One relevant articulation of this perspective is presented by Kakar (1989:28–29), who argues that the Indian cinema audience is not only the reader, but also the effective "author" of Hindi films; the "ostensible creators"—producers, directors, actors, and scriptwriters—are essentially incidental editors who merely transmit and realize the collective fantasies of their audiences. Films not corresponding to these popular fantasies fail at the box office, and thus the audience preferences effectively serve to shape and, ulti-

14

mately, to create the cinematic products. The mass media and their owners and directors, in this view, are essentially neutral, passive vehicles for the transmission of authentic popular aesthetics and art forms. With this premise Kakar then proceeds to analyze Indian films as texts which are representative of basic, fundamental aspects of the Indian psyche.

While Kakar does not discuss music, his approach should, in theory, apply to music in an identical manner, implying that Indian film music—or popular music in general—has evolved as a direct product and reflection of popular demand and aesthetics, relatively uninfluenced by such matters as the nature and control of the mass media. If this viewpoint is taken as a general thesis about the effective neutrality of the mass media and the irrelevance of its owners and producers, its fundamental shortcomings may well be illustrated by the topic of this book—the dramatic transformation of Indian popular music since the late 1970s. In this period, film music—whose dominance might previously have been assumed to indicate its exclusive popularity—fell from roughly 90 percent of the recorded-music market to around 40 percent (as will be discussed below). A vast and diverse body of regional, pan-regional, devotional, and secular genres arose as new, mass-mediated popular musics. If, as Kakar's approach would imply, the media and their owners and directors are merely "incidental" editors and transmitters of popular taste, then we must assume that a spontaneous and unprecedented revolution occurred in the realm of musical aesthetics throughout the subcontinent. It should be clear, however, that the transformation of popular music was not due to any such revolution, but rather to the emergence of a new mass medium—cassette technology—that brought with it new patterns of ownership, control, access, and production. Whatever changes in taste and aesthetics that ensued can be seen to a large extent as ramifications of the new media technology, and the change in the control of the means of musical production. The inextricable association between cassettes and changes in Indian popular music should clearly illustrate how a holistic analysis of mass-mediated products must never isolate them from their means of production, which are far from neutral, incidental, or invisible.[5]

Media Content

The nature of media control is important primarily for the influence, direct or indirect, that it exerts on media content itself—in this case, popular music. Music itself, not surprisingly, has been the primary focus of traditional musicological and ethnomusicological studies, and it is only in recent decades that the academic community has recognized the need for a more holistic, contextualized approach. However, the musical text itself will always remain a central aspect of popular-music studies. Approaching popular music as media content does not imply ignoring its aesthetic dimension, but involves exploring how it functions as a commodity and a component of media culture, whose aesthetics are subject to the constraints and conventions of that culture and involve the ideological issues discussed above. In many cases, media content—including popular music—may be seen to recapitulate or encode specific features of its context, including the nature of its disseminating medium. Thus, the study of Indian popular music as media content may illustrate how features such as style, language, and text content, while significant in their own right, are conditioned by the medium with which they are associated. Analysis of popular music as media content may also question the locus of a given text's meaning—as residing in authorial intent, in the text itself, or in its interpretation by audiences.

Walter Benjamin noted decades ago how media dissemination serves to divorce art from its traditional, obliquely or explicitly ritualistic performance contexts. In the process, artistic production of entities designed for mass reproducibility becomes but a marginal aspect of a much greater and more significant productive dimension (1968:223–27). An analysis of popular music which concentrates only on the phenomena of composition and studio performance thus runs the risk of distorting reality by means of a sentimental and nostalgic reification of creative processes which are of secondary importance in media production as a whole.

As mentioned, the mass media may tend to weaken grassroots community social life and values by promoting passive domestic consumption rather than collective production of sociocultural life. In the case of music, the decline of community values is reflected not only in consumption patterns but in the nature of the music itself. In India, this process has been particularly apparent, as folk songs sung in local dialect and style, abounding in topical, contemporaneous references to regional lore and events, are replaced by film songs using a lingua franca, produced in faraway studios, aimed at creating a mass, common-denominator audience. Thus, the qualitative differences between regional folk songs and Hindi film songs are conspicuous in the songs themselves, while embodying, at the same time, characteristics of the specific media (mass or traditional) with which they are associated. The cassette boom, by diversifying and democratizing ownership of popular-music production, has altered not only the structure of the music industry, but the nature of popular music itself. Corporate-produced film music now competes with a panoply of new genres which have either become mass mediated only recently, or else have actually evolved largely as a result of the cassette boom. The many stylized versions of regional folk musics are the most prominent examples of this development. Differing from film music in style, text content, and often language, the new cassette-based, stylized versions of regional folk musics have significantly altered the character of the North Indian popular-music scene. As music genres, they merit discussion in themselves, and are the subject of chapters 8 and 9 in this volume; at the same time, as media content, their form, content, and meanings are strongly conditioned by and inseparable from the advent of cassettes, and hence they must be holistically understood in that perspective.

Reception Theory: Effects and Audience Interpretations of Media Content

Along with studying the nature of media control and the content of media output itself, a holistic study of the mass media and their effects must also incorporate the meanings that media content has for its audiences, the uses to which it is put, and its impact upon consumer behavior and attitudes. These matters are in many respects the most significant aspects of media and popular music studies. At the same time, they may also be the most intangible and unquantifiable. Their study—reception theory—commences with the acknowledgment that media content is not necessarily identical to media impact and meaning. Indeed, as Marx noted, an object does not become a "product" until the act of consumption.

Audience interpretation of media content is an initial issue. Media dissemination often inherently invests a given entity with distinctive meanings and associations. A regional folk genre may acquire prestige from being marketed on cassettes or broadcast on the radio. Alternately, or simultaneously, some listeners may be embarrassed by the public dissemination of, for example, erotic songs traditionally sung by villagers amongst themselves. Further, audience interpretation of media content is often highly variable and unpredictable. Consumers may resignify mass-disseminated material, especially ideologically ambiguous entities like popular songs. The importance of the relatively intangible parameters of style, melody, and rhythm in musical meaning renders analysis of consumer interpretation particularly difficult. Texts, although less abstract, can be equally malleable. Listeners may interpret or use popular songs in ways which are irrelevant or even contradictory to their producers' intentions, as, for example, in the extremely common North Indian practice of borrowing film melodies for use in folk genres and even political songs. An innocent, nursery-rhyme song like the early 1980s film hit "Chal chal chal meri hathi" (Go, go, go, my elephant) can become lewd if accompanied by erotic gestures; or an erotic tune (such as the *rasiya* hit "Meri chhatri ke niche a jao" [Come under my umbrella]) can be used in a musical political debate to portray members of one party beckoning to a wavering rival to join them. Children throughout much of North India play a game called *antakshari* wherein the catch line (*mukhra*) of a song—usually a film song—is sung, and the next child must sing another *mukhra* beginning with the last letter of the previous line (Chandavarkar 1990:22). Similarly, when folksingers recycle film melodies with new texts or meanings, they can be seen as actively enriching their own melodic repertoire and resignifying pop-

17

ular tunes through a process of creative appropriation and reproduction. Recognition of such phenomena implies that Adorno's portrayal of audiences as passive consumers deftly manipulated by corporate producers is itself a one-dimensional approach which must be complemented by the study of reception patterns. (Similarly, much of the music criticized by Adorno was intended to accompany dance, which is hardly a passive mode of consumption.)

At the same time, there may be limits to the ability of audiences to exercise creative control over the meanings of the music they consume via the media. First of all, audiences cannot resignify music they have not heard, and the media—especially gatekeeping monopolistic music industries such as that prevailing in India until recently—may offer only a relatively standardized and homogeneous fare. Further, the possible multiple readings of popular music may be strongly conditioned or constrained by aesthetic and ideological subtexts which are encoded or embedded in the music itself, whether overtly or obliquely (Hall 1973). Because of such encodings, for example, it could be argued that the usage of film melodies in a folk or devotional genre may represent less creative resignification than the further intrusion of an alienating and inappropriate *filmi* aesthetic into community culture, and the displacement of traditional repertoire as well.

Further, mediated music can be used in a variety of ways, of which "passive" recreational listening is but one type. For example, it may often be the case that commercial recordings of hymns or prayers (e.g., Hindi *bhajans* and *artis*) replace collective singing, leading to an atrophy of musical ability among former amateur participants who now passively listen. In other contexts, however, such recordings may be used to accompany and guide group or family singing, in which case they may expand repertoire and raise performance standards. Such factors must be considered in any holistic appraisal of popular music and the mass media.

Base and Superstructure in an Integrated Cultural Materialism

This study is devoted to illustrating the relationship between a technological mode of production—cassettes—and cultural phenomena—developments in the realm of popular music. While Marxism is no longer the only analytical approach attempting to link economy and culture, it is various forms of neo-Marxism and Marxist-informed cultural materialism that have proven particularly useful in such projects, and that inform this work. In orthodox forms of Marxist analysis, mode of production and culture are relegated to two relatively discrete, albeit interrelated spheres—base and superstructure. "Mode of production," in such a perspective, is used to denote a general prevailing economic system. Such a "vulgar" Marxist approach, simplistic, schematic, and restrictive as it is, could be applicable in some senses to the study of cassette culture in India. The advent of cassette technology has not precipitated a fundamental revolution in basic modes of production in India, which remain capitalist, semicapitalist, or in various stages of transition and mixture of capitalist and feudal. However, insofar as cassettes have engendered an exponential expansion of the capitalist music industry, they have served to extend capitalist relations of production to various regions and folk genres still characterized by precapitalist norms and values. Thus, when a Rajasthani folksinger freely sells his wage labor to a cassette producer, instead of or in addition to performing, out of custom or duty, for his feudal patron (*jajman*), one may speak of a fundamental change in mode of production, though in a very limited sphere.

Ultimately, however, a "vulgar" Marxism which sharply dichotomizes and, indeed, reifies economic base and cultural superstructure, proves artificial and limited in its usefulness. Raymond Williams (esp. 1977) has argued most articulately for a conflation of the two realms in an analytical approach that recognizes culture itself as constituted and pervaded by material processes. "Mode of production," accordingly, is best conceived of not as denoting solely obvious tools and systems of economic organization, but a broad range of specific forms of technical and industrial production as well as the social relations and bodies of knowledge and belief associated with them. As Richard Middleton observes:

> Thus the structure of relations responsible for the making, circulation, and use of, say, a piece of recorded music cannot be mapped entirely onto the structure responsible for other kinds of commodity, "cultural" or otherwise, still less onto those constituting an abstract model of capitalist production as such—even though, obviously, important links, similarities and pressures exist. It is precisely the degree of disparity which indicates the opportunities for independent reorganization of music apparatuses (that is, without a general social upheaval), and at the same time which sets their limits. (1990:92)

The impact of cassette technology on popular music in India provides a particularly clear illustration of the effectiveness of such an approach. Cassette technology, as this book aims to show, constitutes a particular mode of production which is itself conducive to particular forms of control, and which has had profound effects on the production, distribution, consumption, and content of popular music in India. Cassette technology engenders specific kinds of cultural-commodity production which are not necessarily identical to other kinds of cultural-commodity production—such as, for example, those associated with cinema. Nor, for that matter, are they identical to any particular general model of prevailing commodity production, which, in the case of India, would have to be so all-encompassing (e.g., "semicapitalism") as to be of little analytical value. It is most fruitful, then, to recognize cassette technology as constituting and engendering a set of modes of production, which themselves not only influence but constitute cultural phenomena, from the social relations of musical production and consumption to musical style itself. Furthermore, in postindustrial societies, or postindustrial sectors of countries such as India, information, media content, and aspects of the "consciousness industry" themselves acquire increasing economic importance, thus embodying many of the characteristics of the "economic base" of orthodox Marxist analysis (Middleton 1990:92).

Conclusions

The dualities of homogenization vs. diversity, grassroots expression vs. elite indoctrination, and alienation vs. authenticity remain at the heart of media studies and popular-music research. In the United States, where regional and linguistic diversity is relatively limited in comparison with other large countries, and where the myth of classlessness has been so successfully purveyed, it is easy to dismiss persistent scholarly rehashing and rebashing of Frankfurt School polemics as dated and quaint. Nevertheless, not only do the questions initially raised by Marcuse, Adorno, and their colleagues remain pertinent to American culture, but their applicability should be particularly evident in a country such as India, with its extreme class polarization and its unusual diversity of regional cultures. The monopolistic, undemocratic nature of the music industry in the precassette era, as I shall discuss in chapter 3, would seem to provide an archetypical example of the standardization and homogenization portrayed by Adorno in his denunciation of Western popular music in the 1940s. Cassette technology, by decentralizing and diversifying the control and products of the music industry, has rendered Adorno's pessimistic criticisms less applicable. At the same time, however, the impact and ramifications of cassette technology are most apparent in the realm of the conceptual dualities mentioned above, which were intitially posed by Frankfurt School theorists. Thus, the spread of inexpensive micro-media like cassettes at once illustrates the obsolescence of Orwellian pessimism, as well as the necessity of examining recent developments from the perspective of the now-familiar questions relating to autonomy, freedom, and control of the means of production.

2

The Impact of Cassettes on the International Recording Industry

As I have suggested, the advent of cassette technology can have significant effects on the structure of a given music industry, on the musical content disseminated, and on patterns of reception and consumption. The remarkable cassette-based demonopolization and diversification of the Indian music industry constitute an extreme case of change induced by new technology and attendant forms of control of the means of musical production. Since the contrast between the pre-cassette and contemporary periods is so dramatic in the Indian music industry, the Indian case provides a fertile area for the study of the relationships between technology, control of the music industry, musical content, and the degree to which they promote diversity and fragmentation, or, conversely, homogeneity and integration. At the same time, the Indian case is in some ways unique, particularly in the degree of monopolization and standardization in the pre-cassette era. A brief look at aspects of the international recording industry elsewhere may serve to contextualize India's situation and illustrate both the ways in which it is distinctive and the ways in which it is representative.

A fundamental theme of the preceding chapter, and of this study as a whole, is that control of the means of music production is a key determinant of variety, responsiveness, and creativity within a music industry. It has been extensively argued, for example, by Bagdikian (1985), that diversity of media ownership is the only means of obtaining diversity of media content, and that concentration of ownership inexorably leads to standardization and, by extension, to the sort of self-censorship and narrowness decried in Marcuse's classic, *One-Dimensional Man* (1964). In some cases, such conclusions can be seen to be overgeneralizations, as under certain conditions oligopolistic recording industries have in fact provided an impressive diversity of product. Nevertheless, the *tendency* for decentralized ownership to serve as a precondition for diversity of content is amply illustrated in many regions worldwide, including South Asia.

In reference to recording industries, the dichotomy between concentration and diversification of ownership is generally framed in terms of the competition between the "majors" which are vertically integrated corporations which control their own distribution, production, and marketing, and the independents, or "indies," which generally market their product via separate distribution networks, or, very often, by arrangements with the majors. The indies tend to be small companies catering to specialized markets, with which they are more in touch on a grassroots level than the majors are willing or able to be. The majors can afford to take risks, but generally avoid doing so; rather they prefer to wait until a group or artist has made a name on an indie label, and then they acquire that act from the indie, thus letting the indies bear the cost of research and development. Artists themselves often prefer to work with majors, which offer superior marketing networks and greater reliability in terms of royalty payments. In general, the majors enjoy advantages of greater capital reserves, extensive distribution networks, and incomparably greater promotion capacity, for example, through exerting pressure on radio programming. Indies survive by filling niches and margins in the recording market, often producing records inexpensively, with small projected sales (two thousand copies). On the whole, the indies tend to be rooted in their specialized audiences, whether these be distinguished by ethnicity, region, language, class, or taste culture. Many indies are operated by enthusiasts motivated by love of music rather than commercial incentives. Thus for example, in the United States, indies have played essential roles in the recording and marketing of minority musics like blues, jazz, Latin music, and early rock music.

Indies are often portrayed as creative, dynamic, and responsive to audience tastes, in contrast with the majors, which are faulted for their commercialism, manipulative tendencies, and alleged promotion of standardization in the attempt to produce common-denominator products for homogeneous audiences. Frith (1987:69–72) correctly notes that this dichotomy is often overstated, and that the relationship between indies and majors is more often symbiotic than competitive. Similarly, as Wallis and Malm observe (1984:85), the indies' common dependence on majors for distribution renders the term *independent* a bit of a misnomer. Further, the indies have such a variety and multiplicity of labyrinthine collaborative arrangements with the majors that it is often difficult and artificial to dichotomize the two. Nevertheless, there is general agreement that indies can and often do differ substantially in their orientation and operation, and in the nature of their contribution to music industries; indies are particularly important in the promotion and marketing of minority musics or those associated with small countries, language areas, or ethnic communities (Wallis and Malm 1984:88, 92, 109, 119). However, the interaction between indies and majors in the international record industry is complex, diverse, and in many ways resistant to generalization.

Several aspects of the relationship between indies and majors can be seen as being replicated, on a larger scale, by that between indigenous and multinational recording companies, in the complex combination of competition and symbiosis, and of assistance and exploitation. Historically, the development of the international record industry has followed the general pattern of monopoly capitalism and domination of the third world by the Western powers. Graham notes,

> By the 1930s, with international financial interests in both radio and records, the world's major music companies had largely succeeded in rationalising the industry and dividing the world market into distinct spheres of interest and control. By this time, the music majors had assumed a corporate identity, far removed from folk culture and with the ability to manipulate taste and exploit musicians on a truly global scale.
> RCA, GEC, ITT and Westinghouse controlled the entire American market, both north and south; Decca and EMI controlled not only the British market but that of the entire British Empire; while in France, a single company, Pathe-Marconi, enjoyed unrestricted access to French and French colonial markets. Finally, although based in the Netherlands, Philips dominated the markets of north and central Europe. (Graham 1988:13)

In the decades after World War II, the tendency toward oligopolization continued, with the concentrated dominance of the "Big Five": CBS, RCA, WEA (these three based in the United States until Sony's purchase of Columbia Records); EMI (Great Britain, now a subsidiary of Thorn); and Polygram (based in the Netherlands and heir to Philips and Deutsche Grammaphon Gesellschaft). These companies were able to monopolize control by virtue of their experience, superior resources and technology, vast marketing and distribution networks, and in a more general sense, by the workings of world monopoly capitalism, which has favored concentrated economic control by large corporations based in the former colonial powers. Wallis and Malm (1984:49) note that the Big Five accounted for roughly 60 percent of record sales in the mid-1970s.

The Big Five, like major record companies and multinationals in general, have often been targets of criticism. While introducing advanced technology and distribution systems to underdeveloped countries, the multinationals have been denounced for extracting prodigious profits from poor countries, and for stifling competition in their domains. Most relevantly for our purposes, they have been accused of supporting homogeneity and standardization by promoting Western international pop or local common-denominator genres rather than trying to respond to diversified, local taste groups.

The development of the music industry in India prior to the cassette boom epitomizes many of the potential faults of multinational hegemony. For seventy years the Gramophone Company of India (GCI) enjoyed a virtual monopoly in India, superimposing a homogeneous, studio-produced, pop music on a vast and diverse audience numbering in the hundreds of millions. While expatriating profits, GCI stifled or absorbed indigenous competitors. It was only with the advent of cassettes that the music industry was turned on its head, as hundreds of small and medium-sized regional competitors dethroned GCI and introduced an unprecedented degree of diversity and responsiveness to the popular-music scene.

Contrasting Patterns of Development

While we shall explore the development of the Indian music industry in greater detail in the following chapters, at this point it may be useful to sketch the dichotomies of popular musical diversity and homogeneity in a few contrasting regions, in order to contextualize the Indian case, and to illustrate the ways in which it is representative, or alternately, unique.

The United States

We may start by outlining some aspects of the patterns of development within the dominant (or once-dominant) metropole itself, the United States. Until the early 1940s, the American recording industry was controlled, in classic monopoly capitalist form, by four majors (RCA, Victor, Columbia, and Decca), which tended to promote mainstream bourgeois musical genres. The majors marketed only enough minority or regional musics to stifle any genuine competition in those fields. During World War II, however, a variety of factors contributed to the emergence of a set of dynamic indies. Wartime shellac shortages led the majors largely to abandon minority musics, while the lowered costs of production and the rising purchasing powers of ethnic and racial minorities facilitated the establishment of minority-oriented indies. Further, in a confrontation between the two associations of professional musicians, BMI (Broadcast Music Inc.) turned to nontraditional (mainly black and Latin) popular musics when ASCAP (American Society of Composers, Authors, and Publishers) banned broadcasts of its own recorded repertoire in the early 1940s. As a result, a host of indies emerged which were able to serve specialized markets in a more responsive and energetic way. Such labels as Sun, Phillips, Chess and Atlantic played crucial roles in the marketing and evolution of Afro-American styles (rhythm 'n' blues, rock), while indies like Tico and Alegre gave new vitality to the emergent urban Latino styles on the east coast (Manuel 1992:162; Robinson et al. 1991:43ff.).

The subsequent decades were characterized by fluctuating, intricate jockeying between the majors and indies. Majors reestablished dominance in the late fifties, while independents enjoyed another surge in the middle to late sixties. As the majors reasserted themselves after 1970, they tended to con-

tract many of the creative aspects of music recording to independent producers, absorbing indies or setting up joint ventures with them (Garofalo
1987:78). The diverse and byzantine relationships established between the
indies and majors resist simple description, although one can generalize that
the ongoing arrangements have enabled concentrated regional and ethnic minorities to sustain several local or specialized indies. While many of these
companies tend to produce records (and CDs) rather than only cassettes, the
United States is sufficiently affluent that record-pressing technology has been
available to a relatively broad spectrum of producers. In the field of rock music, the majors themselves have sought to target increasingly fragmented and
specialized audiences. In other cases, however, they have tended to promote
common-denominator pan-ethnic musics. In the field of Latin music, for example, the majors have energetically pushed international-style romantic soft-
rock ballads, leaving the indies to market grassroots-based, regional-audience
genres like salsa, *merengue, cumbia,* and Tex-Mex music (Manuel 1992).

The North American case thus well corroborates many of the critiques of
the majors and the praise of the indies. At the same time, it illustrates that in
a society sufficiently affluent that minorities can own independent recording
companies, the music industry may come to offer a relatively satisfactory balance and coexistence between dominating, homogenizing majors, and
smaller, marginal indies.

Africa

While it would be unnecessary, if not impossible, to summarize the history of
the music industry throughout Africa in a few pages, it may be useful to point
out some of the diversity of developmental patterns in the continent. As noted
above, by the 1930s, the international record industry had come to be dominated by a handful of multinationals, operating largely within their respective
colonial domains. In Africa as elsewhere, musicians often were paid paltry
fees, copyright was nonexistent, and vast profits were extracted from the continent; in the years 1979–83, for example, the Big Five extracted more than
one billion dollars' worth of profits from Nigeria alone (Robinson et al.
1991:95). In the postwar decade, as most African countries gained independence, a number of contrasting and contradictory patterns emerged. Graham
notes:

> Thus in countries like Ghana, Nigeria, and Zaire, the music industry
> was steadily brought under national control—albeit in private hands.
> Other countries, most notably Tanzania and Guinea, opted for social-
> ism and in time brought the music sector under direct state control,
> paying musicians and owning the recording facilities. However, in
> other countries, like Kenya, South Africa, and Côte d'Ivoire, the music

multinationals were able to strengthen their grip, hindering the growth of a local industry. (Graham 1988:18)

Different forms of music-industry development afforded different sorts of diversification. Countries lacking any recording industries, such as Rhodesia until the mid-1970s, were subject to inundation by foreign musics (in this case, Congolese, Western, and South African—Zindi 1985:8ff.). Recordings of indigenous traditional and syncretic musics flourished in some regions where the industry was locally controlled, as in Ghana in the 1960s. Multinational domination had mixed effects elsewhere. In Nigeria, multinationals came to coexist with, and in many cases, collaborate with dozens of small local companies, all of which collectively recorded and marketed a wide diversity of genres (Waterman 1990:90–92, 117; Graham 1988:24).

Meanwhile, in Kenya, the multinationals were able to thoroughly dominate the field until the late 1970s (Wallis and Malm 1984:93–95, 113–17, and elsewhere). Graham has suggested that multinational domination in Kenya and elsewhere inhibited local businesses and the development of an "authentic national sound," while promoting Western pop instead (1988:18). Yet such criticisms may not be entirely accurate. Graham himself notes that the multinationals "recorded a great deal of local music" (1988:17), while Collins observes that as early as 1939, HMV (His Master's Voice)/Zonophone had marketed over 80,000 regional-language records (out of a total of 200,000) in East Africa (1985:115). Moreover, John Storm Roberts, an authority on popular music in Kenya and elsewhere, flatly denies that the Big Five promoted homogenization, recalling how during his residence in Kenya in the sixties and seventies, multinationals energetically marketed a wide variety of local and regional musics (personal communication, June 1991). (A more significant homogenizing factor, notes Roberts, was the replacement of 78-RPM records, which could be played on spring-driven turntables, by 45s and LPs, which required electric power unavailable to most villagers.) Waterman (1990:91–92) also attests to the diversity of regional musics marketed by multinationals as well as local companies in Nigeria. Similarly, Wallis and Malm note that different multinationals operate in different manners (1984:317); in particular, CBS has been especially constructive in aggressively promoting all manner of local musics, marketing regional musics internationally and allowing local producers considerable leeway and initiative (1984:283). Accordingly, Stapleton and May cite one East African industry producer who recalls, "We used to go out with the ferrograph machine into the bush and record all different dialects. We'd call some bloke over and he'd sing right there by the side of the car, with the machine running off the car battery" (1987:271).

These glimpses of the recording industries in Africa, while hardly exhaustive, do illustrate some significant differences from the music industry in India. The Indian record industry was never brought into the public sector, as was that of Guinea; nor was it nationalized in private hands, as was the case in Ghana and Zaire. Nor, for that matter, did it coexist with a variety of significant competing foreign and domestic companies, as happened in Nigeria and elsewhere. Most significantly, GCI, unlike any multinational in Africa, succeeded in promoting a single genre—the Hindi film song—using a lingua franca, which marginalized all other regional styles and languages in North India. While GCI did record a wide variety of regional styles, these constituted, according to informed estimates, less than 10 percent of its output. In Kenya, by contrast, CBS and other multinationals marketed a broad spectrum of regional genres. Swahili, although familiar as a lingua franca, was not used as the medium for a common-denominator popular music.[1] Thus, the pre-cassette Indian music industry was relatively unique in the thoroughness of its monopolization, and the pervasive dominance of a single mass popular music.

The Andean Region

The Andean highlands of Bolivia, Ecuador, and especially Peru present another contrasting picture of the structure of a music industry. The mountain highlands have long constituted a somewhat distinct, albeit internally diverse musical and cultural region, with certain song and dance genres—above all, the *huayno* (Bolivian *huayño*)—popular throughout the area. While the *huayno* is rural in origin, it has always been widely popular among the several millions of migrants from the mountain highlands who reside in Lima and other urban centers, and who retain fondness for their traditional culture.[2] Forms of stylized, syncretic, commercial *huaynos* have come to coexist with traditional rural *costumbrista* or *típico* genres and styles.

The Andean regions have constituted a lively market for commercial records since the 1940s. Multinationals have been active in the region, but they have tended to market only international pop genres (*cumbia,* ballads, Western pop, etc.) aimed at urban elites; thus, recording and marketing of *típico* highland musics have remained in the hands of small and medium-sized indigenous labels. By 1949, four of these were thriving, specializing in stylized or straightforward renditions of traditional genres, especially the *huayno,* sales of which surpassed all other genres combined until the mid–1970s. While two of these companies have since disappeared, a host of smaller ones emerged in the subsequent decades. Many of these producers have been grassroots-oriented businesses recording specialized genres associated with particular festivals, regions, dialects, and the like. Several of them came to own their own record-pressing machinery, often obtaining secondhand equipment from the United States or elsewhere. These companies routinely purchase air time on local, early-morning radio programs to promote their products. While the

Andean region is hardly affluent, it has evidently been wealthy enough—and sufficiently unfettered by multinational monopolies—to sustain a significant number of indigenous record companies with their own pressing facilities.

Again, the contrast with India is remarkable; as we shall see in the next chapter, GCI succeeded in absorbing or eliminating most of its rivals in India during its many decades of virtual monopoly. Even its fledgling competitors were obliged to have their records pressed in Germany or Japan, as GCI had the only pressing plant in the country.

These brief vignettes of selected international recording industries have been presented partly in order to illustrate some of the complexities, ambiguities, and qualifications needed in the notion that diversity of ownership is a prerequisite to diversity of media content. We have seen, first of all, that the variety of collaborative ties between indies and majors often renders it difficult to ascertain who owns or controls a given entity within the music industry. Secondly, the Kenyan example, and the operation of multinationals such as CBS, illustrate that dominating corporations can, in some cases, actively promote musical diversity. Thirdly, it is clear that the degree of homogeneity or variety represented by a music industry is conditioned by several factors, including the composition and ideologies of linguistic and ethnic groups, and the nature of the technology employed, along with the particular forms of media ownership and control. Such considerations oblige us to qualify our paradigm that diversity of ownership is a prerequisite to diversity of content, and to recognize that other factors must also be considered in explaining music-industry patterns. At the same time, the operation of multinational oligopolies in India and other countries does make it clear that concentration of control and ownership can, in certain cases, lead to homogeneity and streamlining of content.

The International Impact of Cassette Technology

In the 1960s, a new dimension was introduced into the international music industry with the advent of silicon chips and integrated circuits, leading to the emergence of cassette technology. Cassettes were initially designed by Philips for use in Dictaphones and other professional purposes, but were successfully developed and marketed by Japanese companies for use as an alternative consumer format to vinyl (Robinson et al. 1991:53). By 1970, cheap, compact cassette recorders were coming into common usage in the developed world and, increasingly, elsewhere. Cassettes are currently estimated to account for over half of current sales of prerecorded music worldwide (Fisher 1991:61).

Cassette technology offers many advantages over vinyl record format. Cassettes are a two-way medium, which can record as well as play. Cassettes and cassette players are cheaper, more durable, and more portable than records and phonographs. Recorders and players have simple power requirements and are repaired relatively easily. Most important, mass production of cassettes is incomparably easier and cheaper than pressing records, thus enabling diverse lower-income groups to enjoy access to both production as well as consumption of recorded music.

In general, as we shall see, cassette technology has been conducive to the decentralization, diversification, and marked expansion of recording industries. At the same time, its impact has not been entirely uniform throughout the world, but has to some extent been conditioned by the same sorts of factors which distinguished music industries in individual regions during the pre-cassette period.

First of all, we may note that there remain a few areas, even within the developed world, where cassettes have not become widespread, or did not become so until relatively recently. Most notable in this category is the former Soviet bloc, where cassettes and players have spread only as imported, parallel-market luxuries. While some have suggested that Soviet-bloc governments were consciously reluctant to promote a medium so resistant to control and censorship, it seems more likely that the paucity of cassettes has been due to protectionist restrictions which limited imports, the failure of phlegmatic state-run industries to capitalize on silicon chip technology, and the low importance placed by planning committees on consumer electronics.[3] Infant-industry protectionist policies also limited or delayed the spread of cassettes in a few capitalist countries, most notably India, where, as we shall see, state regulations limited both the importation and the indigenous manufacture of cassette technology until the late 1970s. Finally, there remain countries such as Colombia and the Dominican Republic, where vinyl is still the preferred format (perhaps due to established cultural preferences) so that cassettes constitute a secondary medium without a dramatic effect on the music industry per se (Deborah Pacini, personal communication, April 1991).

The developed countries of the West constitute a somewhat distinct set of cases. Cassettes have certainly been influential in these countries; in the United States, they have come to be the most popular recording format, outselling records by 30 percent in 1989 (Pollack 1990). At the same time, cassettes cannot be said to have precipitated any dramatic revolution within the structure of the recording industry. As mentioned, the affluence of these countries had already enabled a certain number of independent recording producers to flourish, using record pressing or, more recently, CD-manufacturing technology. Recording companies producing only cassettes remain a relatively marginal phenomenon, although, as we note below, they are emerging as significant vehicles for certain specialized genres, as in Hawaii. Meanwhile, efficient law enforcement has limited commercial piracy, and the potentially destructive effects of widespread home taping have been mitigated, at least for the majors, by vertical integration, such that the majors manufacture and thus profit from the sale of blank cassettes, even if such tapes are used to dub rather than purchase recordings.

Cassette Piracy

It is in the developing world that cassettes have had the most marked impact. In most cases, the most conspicuous, dramatic, and controversial development associated with the advent of cassettes has been the endemic spread of piracy, in the form of commercially marketed pirate cassettes, and the proliferation of dubbing shops which duplicate requested hits for individual consumers. For many musicians and recording producers, cassette technology is seen not as a blessing but as a curse which has bankrupted legitimate music industries throughout much of the developing world. Wallis and Malm note that as of 1984, for example, the rampant cassette piracy in Tunisia had effectively prevented the rise of any significant indigenous recording industry (1984:84). In other countries, extant flourishing record industries have been crippled by piracy.

African countries have been hit particularly hard, especially since their governments have been largely unable, and in some cases unwilling, to enforce copyright laws. Cassette piracy is generally cited as one of the main factors which, together with general economic decline, effectively destroyed the formerly lively Ghanaian record industry, inducing multinationals like HMV and Decca to abandon the country altogether (Andrew Kaye, personal communication, 1991). Ghana, formerly a center of commercial highlife recording, now instead hosts over 2,700 dubbing shops, while some two million pirate cassettes are allegedly sold there every year.[4] In Uganda and Tanzania, where indigenous recording industries were negligible to begin with, essentially all cassettes sold are pirates. Pirate cassettes made in Hong Kong, Singapore, Taiwan, and South Korea are said to constitute 70–80 percent of the market in Nigeria, Morocco, Algeria, Zambia, and Guinea.[5] Kenya, the former center of the East African music industry, fares no better, with piracy accounting for 80–90 percent of sales. It is little consolation to legitimate Kenyan industry personnel that indigenous piracy is now rivaling the Asian and Middle Eastern producers who dominate pirate-cassette production elsewhere in the continent (de Vries 1988). Cassette piracy has contributed to the wholesale migration of much of the legitimate African music industry to Europe, where recordings are made and marketed for emigrant Africans and European enthusiasts.[6] Consumers in countries like Kenya complain that record producers have abandoned them, and especially production of local music, because of the inability to compete with pirates, who, of course, pay no taxes, recording fees, or royalties (Stapleton and May 1987:273, de Vries 1988).

From one perspective, such countries can be regarded as representing an initial stage in the transition from vinyl format to a flourishing local cassette industry. When cassettes are first introduced, they enjoy a free rein because of outdated, nonexistent, or poorly enforced copyright laws, and can effectively ruin a local music industry. At the same time, their ability to do so is dependent on the spread of cassette players, which subsequently come to replace record players throughout the country. The spread of cassette players lays the foundation for the possible development of an indigenous cassette-based recording industry. India, as we shall see, constitutes a model in this respect; there, pirate cassettes came to account for some 90 percent of sales in the early 1980s, but now, with a revised and more rigorously enforced copyright law, piracy constitutes only some 30–40 percent of an otherwise flourishing and lively cassette-based music industry. There is reason to believe that some African countries will be able to effect this transition. In the late 1980s, despite rampant piracy, numerous indigenous legitimate cassette producers have emerged in Ghana, Nigeria, Kenya, Benin, and several other African countries.[7] Organizations of musicians and legitimate producers, such as the Nigerian musicians' union PMAN, have vehemently clamored for copyright protection (Collins 1985:119), and if India and Indonesia have learned to keep piracy within manageable limits, relatively developed African nations like Nigeria should eventually be able to do the same.

The Emergence of Legitimate Cassette Industries

There are several countries in the developing world where, despite widespread cassette piracy, we see the growth of small, grassroots cassette producers, recording and disseminating genres whose commercial markets were in many cases too localized and specialized for multinationals and even regional record companies to service. Nigeria, indeed, could be included in this category, although other countries appear to represent a more advanced stage of the healthy transition to legal-cassette domination. In the Andean region, the diversity of the music industry has been intensified by the spread of cassettes, which are in the process of altogether replacing vinyl. While piracy there has bankrupted many record companies, cassettes have emerged as a legal medium for various specialized regional genres neglected by the record producers, and, most visibly, for the increasingly popular *chicha* music. *Chicha* is an urban syncretic genre which is stylistically derivative of the *huayno* and Colombian *cumbia,* and whose texts are rooted in *ambulante* urban street life. *Chicha,* like many other proletarian hybrid genres in recent decades, has come to be closely associated with cassettes, rather than records,[8] and its emergence illustrates how cassettes can be a crucial vehicle for the evolution and dissemination of grassroots genres ignored, for various reasons, by record companies oriented toward middle-class consumers.

The impact of cassettes is most striking in countries where, piracy notwithstanding, an extant record industry has been entirely replaced by a vibrant and flourishing cassette scene. Indonesia, whose transition to cassettes occurred a decade before that of India, constitutes one such case. With its relatively lax import policies, and the limited scale of its record industry (in comparison to India's), Indonesia was hosting small cassette companies as early as the late 1960s, some of which, as Sutton notes (1991:207), consisted of little more than a dozen cassette decks and a technician running dubs all day. Sutton also observes that while vinyl records generally sold for the equivalent of around $5.00 in the 1960s, cassettes cost as little as $0.60, and seldom more than $1.50. As inexpensive cassettes and players spread throughout Indonesian villages and cities, they precipitated, as elsewhere, an exponential expansion of the recording industry as a whole. Thus, as Yampolsky observes (1987b:2–5), the output of the state record industry, Lokananta, grew from 41,508 vinyl discs in 1970, to 898,459 cassettes (and 290 records) in 1975. Many of the several dozen private cassette companies that emerged in the seventies and eighties specialized in regional musics, rather than lingua-franca (i.e., Bhasa Indonesian) genres such as *kroncong* and *dangdut*. The market share of the latter genres subsequently fell from 44 percent in the 1960s, to 13 percent by 1986. (As we have noted above, cassettes led Hindi film music to suffer an even greater proportionate decline in India, while its sales expanded in real terms due to the growth of the market as a whole.) Aside from recording and marketing various regional genres which had been neglected by Lokananta, which now concentrates on Javanese *gamelan* music, the cassette companies were instrumental in the emergence of at least one indigenous pop genre, the Sundanese *jaipongan* (Manuel 1988b:213–19; Manuel and Baier 1986). Cassettes have also come to permeate consumption and dissemination of traditional genres like *tembang sunda,* leading to new forms of commercialization, increased demand for novelty, and the emergence of a "star" system in a once genteel, elite genre (Williams 1990:182–203).

Sutton's summary of the effects of cassette technology in Indonesia (1991:209–15) is representative of many other countries as well. The emergence of cassettes of regional musics, as produced by small, local entrepreneurs, lent a new legitimacy to regional musics, especially those which had never been commercially marketed before. Local "stars" subsequently arose, and new standards of professionalism came to be adopted. The proliferation of regional cassettes at once precipitated a degree of cross-fertilization, stylistic borrowing, and homogenization, while at the same time sharpening awareness of local traditions, and effectively crystallizing their image through mass-media dissemination and preservation. While the marketing of rustic regional musics alongside hoary Solonese gamelan music to some extent leveled out the differences in status between such genres, sharp divisions in prestige emerged between those performers who had commercially recorded and those who had not.

Cassettes have had a similarly fundamental impact on the music industry in Egypt, where they have entirely replaced vinyl records and have turned the state-owned Sono Cairo (Saut-al-Qahira) from a recording monopoly into a slightly stodgy, if prestigious minority concern. El-Shawan (1987) notes that Egyptian open import policies and easy licensing procedures had contributed to the emergence, by 1984, of over four hundred cassette companies, recording a wide variety of genres, some of which had not been previously marketed. Cassettes effectively replaced records in many other countries as well, from Thailand to Sri Lanka (Wong 1989–90; Siriyuvasak 1990; Wallis and Malm 1984:147). I noted in my own travels that cassettes had become the exclusive commercial format in Pakistan and Afghanistan by 1978, although a few vinyl records could be found gathering dust in music stores.

The advent of cassettes has precipitated a number of interrelated effects in these and other countries. As mentioned, the low cost, portability, and durability of cassettes and players have led to a vast expansion in the size of the recorded-music market. Records have become collectors' items, and once-dominant state companies or multinationals have found themselves competing with innumerable smaller cassette companies. While obscure, specialized traditional genres have come to be marketed on cassette, new syncretic styles have also emerged in close association with cassette dissemination. Such genres have been able to bypass the disapproving or indifferent control of state bureaucracies and/or formerly dominating majors.

In Israel, *rock misrahi* associated with Oriental Jews, although scorned by Ashkenazis and the state radio stations, has enjoyed ample dissemination by cassettes (Manuel 1988:169–70). Similarly, while air play on the Egyptian state radio was once a prerequisite to any sort of musical renown, singers such as Ahmad 'Aduwe have become stars via cassettes, in spite of being shunned by radio gatekeepers (el-Shawan, personal communication). The Turkish state music bureaucracy, although contemptuous of the Arab-influenced pop genre *arabesk,* has been unable to curb its popularity, as cassettes of it abound. Sri Lankan pop *baila* has similarly flourished almost exclusively on cassettes, with taxi drivers playing essential roles as disseminators via their car stereos (Wallis and Malm 1984:255–56). Even in the United States, cassettes have established niches as vehicles for regional syncretic genres; one example is "Jawaiian," a Hawaii-based fusion of reggae and Hawaiian pop music. As a local journalist notes:

> Vinyl records are history, gone with the '80s . . . and compact discs are still too expensive for specialized markets. Enter the cassette tape, sounding better than ever, priced competitively and completely portable. (Burlingame 1991)

"Jawaiian" musicians have discovered that they can produce their own cassettes for as little as one thousand dollars, dispensing with exploitative recording managers and production agents; tapes are then duplicated overnight in accordance with market demand (Burlingame 1991:E3).

In several countries, cassettes have served to disseminate genres that have been formally banned or discouraged by authoritarian governments. Tapes of sentimental pop music from Taiwan and Hong Kong (especially the music of Deng Li-chi/Theresa Deng) have spread widely in China despite official sanctions (Kristof 1991a); cassettes also disseminate the music of dissident rock star Cui Jan, which is banned from the state-run media (Kristof 1991b:56). In the erstwhile Soviet Union, Western rock music, regarded with dour ambivalence by the state, became familiar throughout the country via informal cassette networks (Engelberg 1991). Cassettes have proven to be an invaluable medium for the spread of otherwise repressed protest musics. Such tapes have served to popularize the music of Palestinian singer-poet Marsal Khalifeh, possession of whose recordings has been treated by Israeli police as a crime (Langer 1988:116–17). In the closing years of the Duvalier regime in Haiti, foreign-produced tapes of protest songs by Ti-manno and Frère-Barent circulated widely in Haiti (Gage Averill, personal communication). In Chile, smuggled cassettes of progressive musicians like *nueva trovador* Silvio Rodriguez helped inspire hopes for reform during the seventeen-year rule of the CIA-installed dictator Augusto Pinochet.

Cassettes have also been used as vehicles for overtly political speeches. The CIA circulated tapes in Iraq denouncing Saddam Hussein in 1991 (Wines 1991:9), while in neighboring Saudi Arabia, cassettes of fundamentalist Muslim tirades against the pro-American government have spread through the country (Fandy 1990; Ibrahim 1992). However, by far the most extensive and effective use of cassettes in political movements has been in the Iranian Revolution of 1978, documented by Sreberny-Mohammadi:

> Tape recorders in the rented Paris house recorded all of Khomeini's speeches and pronouncements and duplicated them for transmission or transportation. Using international phone lines, a tape-player in Neauphle-le-Château could "speak" to one in Tehran; his followers in make-shift studios worked around the clock to reproduce cassette tapes in large quantities, and within hours Khomeini's latest pronouncements and instructions were available from street-vendors on sidewalks in Tehran. Music stores slipped a religious tape in with the purchase of a music tape. Supposedly blank tapes were found to contain Khomeini's messages. Tapes were duplicated by the thousands and distributed along with other goods through the bazaar system inside Tehran and out to other cities and towns; they were also carried by migrant building workers and youths to remote villages where collective listening and discussion ensued. These tapes were Khomeini's electronic pulpit, a switched-on *minbar*. For a population with 65% illiteracy, in a cul-

tural milieu where oral communication is still the preferred means of communication . . . this electronic pulpit was a powerful channel . . . Other factions of the opposition also utilized tapes in what at times can only be described as a propaganda war of the tapes. (1990:357–58)

In subsequent years, Afghan rebels made similar use of cassette technology.[9] As we shall see below, cassette technology spread later in India than it did in Iran and Indonesia. Its eventual impact, however, was in many respects even more dramatic than in those countries, restructuring the music industry, engendering new forms of popular music, and generating its own propaganda tape wars.

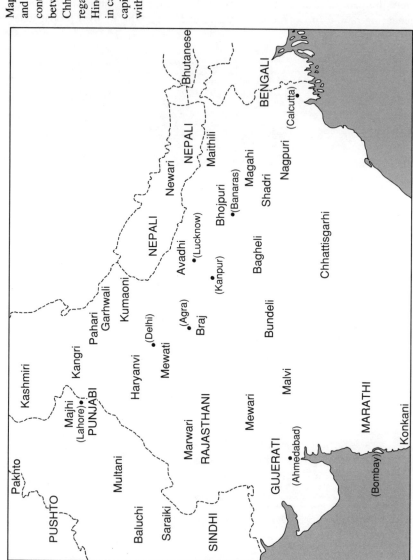

Map showing major languages and dialects in the northern sub-continent. Note that all dialects between Marwari, Maithili, and Chhattisgarhi, inclusive, are regarded as members of the Hindi language group. Names in capital letters = languages; in capital and lower-case = dialects; within parentheses = cities.

3

The Music Industry and
Film Culture up to 1975

The impact of cassette technology in India can only be properly understood when seen in the context of the development and form of popular music and the Indian entertainment industry over the course of the twentieth century. The most remarkable feature of this development is the dramatic contrast with the period before the advent of cassettes—a contrast marked enough to enable one to speak without exaggeration of a cassette revolution, which has fundamentally restructured the commercial-music industry and the nature of Indian popular music in general.

This chapter focuses on those aspects of pre–1980 popular music and the music industry that have been most overtly altered by the advent of cassettes—namely, the highly concentrated control of the music industry, its tendency toward stylistic homogeneity and standardization, and its distinctive ideological and aesthetic orientation.

The Growth of the Indian Record Industry

The record industry got off to an early start in India, with commercial records being marketed as early as 1902—only a year after the invention of wax recording. In 1908 the British-owned Gramophone Company of India (GCI) established a pressing factory in Calcutta, and by 1910 had released over four thousand recordings, competing with smaller local subsidiaries of Odeon, Beka, Nicole, and Pathe. Nicole and an indigenous competitor, Binapani, folded shortly thereafter, while another Indian company, Ramagraph, prospered in Western India. Competition was earnest due to the early saturation of the market, which consisted of those few who could afford such luxuries.

Thus in the early decades of the century, while around a dozen smaller competitors eked out niches in the market, the recording field was dominated by GCI, most of whose repertoire was marketed after 1910—quite appropriately, given the company's colonial character—under the label name His Master's Voice (HMV). GCI was able to maintain its dominance by establishing exclusive distribution arrangements with most retailers, and by owning the only record-pressing factory in the country. Rivals like Beka were obliged to have their discs pressed in Germany or, as in the case of the indigenous Viel-o-phone Company, in Japan. By the mid-1920s GCI's only competitors were Viel-o-phone and Ramagraph (which issued around five thousand releases), with Odeon perpetually struggling to establish a foothold. Sales of records and players increased considerably in the 1930s due to the import of cheaper Japanese phonographs, the construction (in 1929) of a larger GCI factory at Dum Dum, and the continued growth of the urban middle class (Joshi 1988, Gronow 1981). In 1931, HMV was acquired by EMI, which subsequently became the largest recording company in the world.

In order to establish an appearance of competition in India, GCI, under EMI's control, started issuing records under the labels of various subsidiaries, while also pressing records for over two hundred smaller independent producers.[1] These latter accounted for only a small fraction of the record market; indeed, GCI enjoyed an almost complete monopoly, whose only significant challengers were Viel-o-phone, the classical-music label Broadcast Records, and the more overtly nationalistic Young India (founded in 1935). GCI's effective monopoly persisted until the entrance of Polydor in the late 1960s. The absence of effective competition enabled GCI to pay many of its artists poorly, and to pursue conservative and in many ways phlegmatic marketing practices (Joshi 1988:149–51).

Confronting the regional and linguistic diversity of the Indian population, GCI, from its very inception, faced the alternatives of catering to specialized, distinct markets, and/or trying to unify the purchasing audience by promoting common-denominator products accessible to a broad spectrum of the populace. Classical instrumental music posed no linguistic problems, but had too limited an audience to constitute a solution. Before 1940, GCI—especially through its smaller subsidiaries like Marwari and Megaphone—produced a considerable amount of recordings of regional musics. Old GCI catalogs reveal what appears to be an impressive variety and number of regional-music releases. At the same time, the regional musics produced by GCI were limited both in genre and in audience. The purchasing audience was largely confined to the urban upper class. In the 1960s and 1970s, for example, phonographs cost around five hundred rupees (around sixty-six dollars at that time), and LPs (produced since 1964) retailed at thirty-five to forty-five rupees apiece (around five dollars). Such luxuries were well beyond the means of all but the bourgeoisie. Most villagers—80 percent of the population—appear to have had little exposure to records, save the occasional visit by an itinerant entrepreneur who would charge a few paisa to play discs on his portable machine. Records became even less accessible to villagers when 78s, which could be played on spring-driven machines, were replaced by 45s and LPs, which required electric power largely unavailable in rural areas. Accordingly, GCI essentially ignored many rural folk genres, such as *rasiya,* the most popular genre of the extensive Braj region south of Delhi. Further, many of the most popular rural folk genres consist of lengthy narrative songs sung strophically over the course of many hours; 78- and even 45-RPM records could not begin to do justice to such genres, and, as a result, GCI largely neglected such essential folk forms as Braj *Dhola,* Bundelkhandi *Alha,* and many other epics and tales sung in Rajasthan, Haryana, and the Punjab. Finally, GCI appears to have entirely neglected regions like Kummaon which were evidently deemed too inaccessible or linguistically too fragmented to merit investment.

From the perspective of economies of scale, there were clear advantages to marketing records which could appeal to a broader, pan-regional audience. Accordingly, from the very start of recording in India, it was natural that a plurality of records consisted of genres sung in Urdu or, to a lesser extent, Hindi (the two overlapping sister languages serving as the lingua franca in the North).[2] Particularly well represented in the early decades were *ghazal,* an Urdu poetic form sung in light-classical style, most typically by courtesans, and *qawwali,* an Urdu Muslim devotional genre generally sung by male professionals. These genres were more popular than high classical music, and their lyrics were understood and enjoyed by educated Hindus and Muslims throughout the North. The emerging Hindi-Urdu film music—to be discussed below—presented greater opportunities for homogenizing the market, and by 1940 came to dominate commercial record releases.

Radio

Indian radio broadcasting began in 1927 with the establishment of private transmitters in Bombay and Calcutta. In 1930 the British took over these operations and banned private broadcasting. Colonial and independent national radio policy has confronted the same demographic diversity as did the record industry, although its goals have been shaped by political and cultural parameters rather than commercial ones. The British colonial administrators, although generally regarding Indian music as monotonous and primitive, allotted it some seven-eighths of broadcast time. The Imperial government established nine stations by 1947, with the goal of providing news and music in as many regional languages as possible.

With the advent of Independence, the Indian government, like those of many other developing nations, maintained the monopoly on radio broadcasting. In 1952 radio fell under the direction of B. V. Keskar, who served as Minister of Information and Broadcasting until 1960. Keskar, a nationalist and moderate Hindu chauvinist, largely banned the broadcast of film music on All-India Radio (AIR), regarding it as vulgar, excessively Westernized, and too steeped in Urdu (rather than Hindi). In its place he sought to promote art music and a standardized sort of orchestral light music which was to form the basis for a new national folk music (Keskar 1967:7, Lelyveld n.d.). In

1957, however, film music was reinstated on a new AIR channel (Vividh Bharati) after it was discovered that listeners were tuning in to powerful Ceylonese and Pakistani stations in order to hear film songs. Since then, most Indian radios have remained tuned to Vividh Bharati.

While AIR's orchestral light music (Vadya Vrind) is largely ignored, its broadcasts of folk music have come to play a certain role in musical life. As the number of regional stations has expanded to eighty-six, many rural listeners do take interest in regular folk-music programs, while artists regard radio performances as prestigious and useful for publicity, if only minimally remunerative. Although adhering to state goals of promoting secular nationalism and pan-regional integration, regional radio stations do not hesitate to broadcast folk musics in local dialects and styles. At the same time, aside from the reifications involved in disassociating folk music from its ritual and collective contexts, radio and television broadcasts do not always represent folk traditions in ideally authentic manners. Producers often add nontraditional instrumental accompaniment, particularly *tanpura, sarangi,* and *tabla,* which traditionally only accompanied classical and light-classical music; critics of this policy allege that as audiences become accustomed to such instrumentation, they become dissatisfied with and alienated from the traditional folk styles of rendition.[3] Performers complain that they are requested to sing the same favorites time and again. Some of the better performers avoid AIR out of exasperation with its bureaucracy. Meanwhile, producers often prefer to hire urban middle-class amateur singers rather than genuine folk musicians; most of those who sing folk music on Delhi television and radio are of bourgeois backgrounds (Parmar 1977:66–67, Louden 1986:53–58). New songs are commissioned on government-promoted themes, especially birth control. As a result of such policies, some critics have assailed radio-produced folk music as artificial and sterile (Ranade 1984:60–61; Parmar 1977:64–65).

Radio has long constituted the most widespread mass medium in India; most villages have at least one radio, and many rural folk spend a certain amount of their leisure time listening to film music on the radio of a friend or in a tea-stall. At the same time, few poorer villagers own radios (Hartmann, Patil, and Dighe 1989:56, 131), and the impact of radio in many rural areas may be quite limited. There are only 4.4 radios per hundred persons throughout the country (Yadava 1986), and it may be assumed that most of these are owned by city-dwellers, leaving many villagers without access to radio.

Film Music and Film Culture

Since the 1940s, film culture, in which music plays a large role, has become one of the most pervasive features of Indian culture as a whole, influencing the musical tastes, fashion, speech, and worldview of a few hundred million viewers. Accordingly, within a decade of the introduction of the sound cinema in 1931, film music had come to be the predominant popular-music idiom in India, and remained virtually unchallenged in that capacity until the advent of cassettes in the late 1970s. Thus, for roughly forty years, commercial popular music was virtually synonymous with film music, which dominated record output and Vividh Bharati, marginalizing all other forms of mass-mediated music in the process.

The expansiveness of film culture, and its dominance over other mass media, derive from distinct features of Indian society. The print media are naturally weak in a country where some 65 percent of the populace is functionally illiterate. Televisions and even radios have remained expensive investments for indigent masses who can, nevertheless, afford occasional cinema tickets. Further, by offering mass viewing through an extensive network of theaters and traveling screen shows, cinema easily co-opted the popularity of traditional folk theatrical genres. Purohit (1988:2:897) notes that from the investor's perspective, cinema constituted the only non-print mass medium open to indigenous capital, since the recording industry was until recently a closed monopoly or duopoly, while the broadcast media were state-run. Such conditions contributed to the phenomenal growth of the Indian film industry, which has for many years been the world's largest, producing over seven hundred feature films annually. It is commonly estimated that every day over fifteen million Indians attend cinemas.

Music has played an integral part in Indian cinema since the advent of sound film. With the exception of a few art films and eccentric experimental failures, virtually all commercial Indian movies have been musicals. In the first decade, actors and actresses themselves sung their musical parts, but by the mid-forties, the songs came to be recorded separately by "playback" singers, and the screen actors merely mouthed the words in lip-sync. While the early films resembled traditional theater forms in their constant alternation between spoken dialogue and sung verses, the postwar movies settled into a standardized format of more or less naturalistic acting, enlivened by five or six songs and three dance interludes. These musical segments typically portray two lovers cavorting in a mansion, park, cabaret, or some bucolic setting. The song scenes may be dramatically functional, for example, by compressing the portrayal of "falling in love" into a few minutes; more often the songs are more-or-less gratuitous insertions into the plot, to be enjoyed for their own sake. Their importance, nevertheless, is reflected in the fees charged by top music directors, and by the success of many otherwise indifferent movies with hit songs. (In recent years, the films *Tridev* and *Tezaab* are oft-cited examples.)

The importance of music in Indian film is due to more than a simple national fondness for music. In cinema's early years, movies drew heavily from Marathi and Parsi urban theater, and from folk dramatic forms like *nautanki* and *jatra,* all of which interspersed dialogue and action with song and dance.

Secondly, by emphasizing music, filmmakers were able to transcend linguistic barriers and reach broader audiences; thus, many Hindi-Urdu films have enjoyed considerable popularity in South India because of the appeal of the songs, in spite of the fact that most South Indians are ignorant of, and in some cases actively hostile to Hindi. Finally, just as GCI and state monopolies on records and broadcast media, respectively, channeled private entertainment investment into cinema, so did film emerge as the only mass medium for commercial popular music open to Indian capital (Purohit 1988:2:897).

To some extent, Indian film music assumed a life and significance of its own that was independent of cinema. Now as in the past, many Indians—especially villagers and women—attend movies infrequently or not at all, but are nevertheless familiar with film music via the radio. Moreover, film songs have always been marketed independently as records, acquiring their own commodity status (see Ranade 1984:77). Nevertheless, for many, if not most consumers, the significance of film songs remains allied to their cinematic context. As we have noted, many Indians—particularly those too poor to own radios—hear film music primarily when attending movies; other listeners view the same movies repeatedly for the pleasure of experiencing the songs with their visual picturization. Covers of cassettes and records of film music invariably portray the actors and actresses of the film, never the musicians. Further, cinema culture is so pervasive and distinct that it may color the associations and meaning of film songs even for those who seldom or never attend movies. Finally, it may be assumed that, from the producers' perspective, the aesthetics and evolution of film songs are naturally oriented toward their paying consumers—cinema audiences—rather than toward those who hear them for free on the radio. Film culture itself thus merits some discussion in order to provide a context for a holistic appraisal of film music.

Assessing Indian cinema is inevitably contentious, as the gap between popular sentiment and intellectual opinion is even wider than with most forms of popular culture. Opinions towards commercial cinema vary greatly even among educated middle-class Indians, some of whom enjoy it while others regard it as beneath contempt. Evaluations are further complicated by the contradictions embedded in cinema culture, and the inherently subjective nature of the issues involved. At the same time, Indian films tend to be so stereotypical in their plots, style, and structure that they do lend themselves to careful generalization fairly readily.

First of all, there is no doubt that Indian cinema has come to be associated with a certain sort of modernity. While "mythologicals" have in the past constituted an important category of Indian films, most movies have been domestic melodramas set in modern times.[4] Similarly, although the themes and plot outlines of many films correspond to traditional models (e.g., love vs. parental constraints), the morals tend to be in many respects liberal, celebrating romantic love over family, dowry, class, and caste constraints, and often contrasting the virtues of the poor with the venality and corruption of the rich and powerful. Inflammatory communalism (such as having heroes and villains of opposite religions) is generally avoided. Most overtly, non-mythological films are invariably set in Westernized, modern backgrounds, where protagonists frequent cabarets, drive sport cars, drink liquor, and wear chic Western clothes. Further, despite strict censorship of kissing, Indian films manage to be quite sensual, with their erotic dances, obligatory "wet sari" scenes, and romantic themes.

Consequently, the association of films with modern, nontraditional life-style and mores is quite explicit for many Indians. Elders often deprecate film culture as vulgar, corrupting, and immoral, and attempt to discourage their children (especially girls) from attending (Hartmann, Patil, and Dighe 1989:203–4). Meanwhile, many youths, and particularly urban young men, identify profoundly with film culture, mimicking the stars' dress and manner-isms, spouting snatches of film dialogue, and heckling passing women with excerpts of suggestive songs. In most towns and cities, there are clear distinc-tions between such snappily dressed, film-oriented rowdies, and others who, whether out of poverty, preference, or parental coercion, wear Indian dress, prefer traditional forms of entertainment, and shun the movie theaters (Kumar 1988:109). Thus Hartmann, Patil, and Dighe suggests that the symbolic sig-nificance of film fashions and music may carry with it an openness to change and a means of asserting opposition to traditional restrictive village values for many Indian youths (1989:262, 203–6, 212).

As noted above, Indian cinema could also be regarded as promoting na-tional unity. Since the early 1980s India has been wracked by vicious ethnic and religious conflicts in Kashmir, Punjab, and Assam, while during the 1989 elections many hundreds of Muslims and several Hindus perished in com-munal riots. Given the weak sense of national identity, cinema could be ar-gued to constitute one of the major culturally unifying features in Indian so-ciety. Hindi films dominate cinema in North India, accounting for between 55 and 72 percent of North Indian films from the 1950s to the 1980s (see Purohit 1988:2:1240–41); furthermore, Hindi films generally have larger audiences than regional-language films, as they are screened throughout the country rather than only in specific linguistic areas. By being aimed explicitly at a mass, pan-regional audience, Hindi films thus serve to spread Hindi as a lin-gua franca.[5] More importantly, commercial cinema in general, it could be ar-gued, promotes a unified worldview and taste culture in a situation otherwise characterized by regional, class, and religious antagonisms. In many ways, cinema mediates and bridges some of the social and ideological distance be-tween village and city; one Lucknow folklorist notes, for example, that an urban type of Lucknow-area wedding song, *jaymal git,* has spread throughout rural Avadh after being popularized on films (Smt. Vidya Bindu Singh, inter-view, September 1989).

Nevertheless, a conception of Indian cinema as progressive and consensus-building would be incomplete, if not highly arguable. The profoundly asymmetrical power relationships between the producers and consumers of commercial cinema naturally tend to privilege the views of the former at the expense of the latter. Thus, many Indian intellectuals charge that commercial films, while distracting and entertaining audiences, manipulate and alienate them, obscuring class consciousness and the mechanisms of dominance, and promoting a combination of neo-feudal values with the most reactionary aspects of bourgeois ideology. "Popular cinema," writes progressive filmmaker Mani Kaul, "is extremely conservative, extremely orthodox . . . it reinforces the social institutions of society and makes them more oppressive" (Shahani, Kaul, and Karnad 1981:100). Hartmann, Patil, and Dighe (1989:262) note that despite the celebration of Western fashions, "in the *denouement*, traditional values tend to be reaffirmed, or at least not fundamentally undermined." Problems besetting communities are solved by the intervention of the hero rather than through collective action. Women are generally portrayed as passive victims or self-sacrificing martyrs rather than meaningful, realistic, progressive role models. From the 1950s to the early 1970s, the standard heroine was, in the words of one critic, "a feather-brained glamour doll who exists only to highlight the hero's masculinity" (Rao 1989:452). The action-oriented films popular in recent decades (e.g., *Coolie*) have often featured liberated, leather-clad Amazons who are as realistic in the Indian context as Santa Claus. Meanwhile, rape scenes for the titillation of the predominantly male, working-class audience have become common features since the mid-1980s (Pratap 1990). Most importantly, commercial films dogmatically avoid any portrayal of the grinding poverty which afflicts most Indians; instead, most movies take place in a fantasy world of sumptuous mansions, lush gardens, discotheques, and European spas. Implicit in such a determined avoidance of reality is a contempt for the poor, who, if they are occasionally portrayed, tend to appear as menials, passive wretches, or laughable fools. Lower-class society itself, whether in its material indigence or its cultural vitality, is utterly absent. ("Poor" heros and heroines are generally recognizable as such only by the plot, as they invariably appear well-fed, well-groomed, and, in the case of men, well-dressed in Western, if slightly rumpled, attire.) Such a perspective is natural, given the fact that the poorest Indians generally cannot afford film tickets, so that the films are naturally not oriented toward their worldview. In Purohit's assessment, the cinematic language of glitter and Westernized luxury creates

a dream world of unattainable riches for the man in the contemporary street; similarly *Mughal-e-Azam* [a classic historical melodrama] projects this backwards into the past, wherein palatial mansions and medieval paraphernalia recreate the same awe, alienation and fascination. The common man is to be enticed, overwhelmed and reduced to a non-entity.

The implicit sociopolitical message, he argues, is far from progressive:

> The elite are entitled to rule and reside in the never, never world; and the creator of communal wealth, the average labouring man must be brainwashed into feeling that extraction of surplus value from him is entirely voluntary and justified. (Purohit 1988:2:1081)

From such a perspective, the portrayal of Westernized modernity promotes not a progressive reformism, but a consumerist and voyeuristic alienation which legitimizes social inequality, obscures real injustices, and breeds contempt and indifference toward poverty, or—in the case of the poor themselves—self-hatred.[6] Similarly, the depiction of tradition and modernity in cinema, it has been argued, reflects not a sensitive cultural mediation, but the fragmented identity of an alienated society determined to ignore the intense contradictions besetting it (U. Banerjee 1985). Far from avoiding taking stances toward social inequities, such films could be said to exhibit a remarkably consistent political stance—namely, evasion and denial.[7]

The fundamentally escapist nature of Indian commercial cinema is nowhere more explicit than in the statements of its producers. Manmohan Desai, one of the most successful filmmakers, asserts:

> I want people to forget their misery. I want to take them into a dream world where there is no poverty, where there are no beggars, where fate is kind and God is busy looking after his flock. (Gill 1983)

Producer and actor Raj Kapoor is even more revealing:

> The best entertaining film is a film that does not raise any controversy. In a democracy of ours . . . one has to be very careful as to what kind of fare to present and how much of truth you can present along with that. (Marre and Charleton 1985)

While Kapoor's statement is somewhat ambiguous, it naturally suggests that the Indian masses cannot be trusted to make intelligent or desirable decisions based on accurate portrayals of reality by the mass media; the fact that India is a democracy—and that the poor have the electoral power to unite and rule the country in their own interest—makes their stupefaction, distraction, and depoliticization all the more essential to the dominant classes who produce films.

Fantasy, comforting myths, social amnesia, and voyeuristic displays of wealth have natural appeal, and perhaps even important roles in India. Indian films serve their own functions, providing entertainment, relaxation, and escapist diversion which may constitute a significant aid to psychic survival under the adversities of Indian life. When for most people, reality means toil, poverty, harsh climate, and rigid socioreligious restrictions, cinema may be valued precisely because it provides an alternative. Indeed, escapism can be said to be one of the fundamental functions of much art and entertainment throughout the world. Even when presentable alternative forms of art are present, it may be natural for people in adversity to seek refuge in fantasy. Hence, for example, a journalist writes of contemporary Bengalis:

> Young people, they themselves will confide, are sick of the social realist pretensions of Bengali films. They do not want to be told of their wretched conditions. For a brief couple of hours, they want to escape, to surrender themselves to vacuity. (Mitra 1986)

Still, the escapist nature of mainstream Indian cinema cannot be attributed entirely to the preferences of audiences or the inclinations of its producers. Nor can it be attributed to the conservative nature of commercial sponsorship, since cinema (unlike commercial television or radio) is largely free from advertisements. Government censorship, however, has been a significant factor in inhibiting confrontation of genuinely controversial issues. The British colonialists narrowly circumscribed film content, and the subsequent independent government enacted a censorship code proscribing such features as "accentuation of class distinction" and encouragement of "subversive activity," effectively ensuring the triviality of most films (Purohit 1988:2:964ff.). Moreover, state governments have levied onerous taxes on movie halls, ranging up to 150 percent of ticket prices in Uttar Pradesh (Awasthi 1987:15), which have further discouraged experimentation and controversial subject matter.

The conservative escapism of Indian cinema may also be related to the film industry's marked concentration of production. Until the late 1940s, the industry was dominated by a triopoly consisting of Prabhat, New Theatres, and Bombay Talkies. After the war, these firms were largely replaced by a host of new corporations, but the oligopoly persisted in a new form, that of the "star system" dominated by a handful of producers, stars, and music directors. Fewer than seventy such individuals can be said to have dominated cinema production since the 1940s (Purohit 1988:2:1078, 1053, 996–97). Such is the conviction that stars are needed for success that fees for leading idols can often account for up to 65 percent of a film budget, and films often take over three years to produce because the stars are involved in as many as fifty films at once (Kaye 1988). Meanwhile, the reliance on a handful of top directors results in these individuals themselves often being involved in dozens of films at once, with some directors even reputed to direct scenes via telephone from another studio. In general, the oligopolistic organization of the Indian film industry—which may be said to be typical of third-world neocolonial economies—encourages homogenization and standardization, inhibits genuine competition, and renders the audience captive consumers of an idiom into whose production they have little or no direct input.

It is a recurrent finding in media studies that the content of media with the largest audiences tends to legitimize social norms, focusing on elites and avoiding challenges to the prevailing system (McQuail 1987a:285). Accordingly, the mass audience and oligopolistic control of Indian film production could be seen as contributing to the escapism of Indian cinema, since the producers belong exclusively to a corporate class with a vested interest in preserving the status quo and obscuring working-class interests.

Radical filmmaker K. A. Abbas's assessment is representative of a certain school of Indian intellectual opinion:

> With a limited number of cinemas, and those too being monopolized by the producers of commercial glossies, there is an exhibition bottleneck which makes it virtually impossible for any off-beat, no-star, low-budget picture to get playing time. This is called free trade, according to the law of supply and demand that governs the market in cement, steel—or cinema entertainment. The public comes to accept and demand what it is fed on, and no wonder the commercial interests have decided that there is no demand for anything but their star-studded blockbusters. (Abbas 1977:71)

The implicit argument is that film culture, by replicating and idealizing a capitalist, unequal, and consumerist status quo, serves to prevent viewers from grasping the structures of domination, promoting a false consciousness which can be manipulated to elite advantage.

Film Music: Context and Content

I have undertaken this digression into film culture in order to be able to situate film music in its cinematic context. For not only is the aesthetic and social meaning of film songs allied to the movies they are embedded in, and the ethos of Indian cinema in general, but film music itself can also be seen to embody and reflect some of the same patterns of media organization and ideological values as film culture. The diverse cassette-based musics discussed in subsequent chapters at once replicate and challenge these patterns and values, which thus merit some attention here.

An initial point to be made about Indian popular music in the pre-cassette era is its relatively unique association with cinema. Of course, popular music in other cultures has at various times been associated with movies, such as those featuring Carlos Gardel (Argentina), Mohammad al-Wahhab (Egypt), Fred Astaire and others (United States), Jorge Negrete (Mexico), and Rhoma Irama (Indonesia). Musicals were particularly popular in the 1930s and

1940s, when movie tickets were more accessible than audio-playback equipment. In subsequent decades, popular music in most countries became independent of cinema, as consumer audio technology became more affordable, and as spreading bourgeois aesthetics of verisimilitude made musical sequences seem artificial. In India, however, most filmgoers remained too poor to afford record players, and were familiar enough with folk theatrical forms that they did not find musical interludes disturbingly unrealistic. The change that did occur in India in the 1940s was the advent of playback singing, and the bifurcation of the roles of singing and acting.

As a result, the relationships between radio, cinema, and the recording industry in South Asia are quite different from those in most other countries. In the United States, for example, commercial music, as produced by a recording industry, is a means to sell records (or CDs or cassettes). Commercial radio stations use music to attract audiences for their sponsors, while in effect offering supposedly free promotion to record companies. MTV (Music Television)—the closest American equivalent to Indian musical films—functions like radio in programming music (videos) to garner audiences for its commercials; for the record industries which produce the videos, MTV serves as another means of promotion; the music videos themselves are not commodities or commercial entities, but function as advertisements and entertainment.

In India, by contrast, radio, film, and record industries are technically discrete. The radio is state-controlled, and, while Vividh Bharati accepts advertisements, its goal is not profit, but public service. The production of film music is actually in the hands of the film producers; they are the ones who stand to profit most directly from a successful score, which will attract audiences to buy their product—i.e., film tickets (or, more precisely, rental copies of the films). Indian films, unlike MTV music videos, are commercial entities in themselves. Indian recording companies, on the other hand, simply purchase the rights to the scores from the film owners; their profits, like those of record companies elsewhere, derive from the sale of recordings. The largest profits from film music, however, are derived from the music's original function in cinema.

A significant ramification of the association with cinema—and a feature relatively unique to India—is the fact that singers and composers of Indian popular music are not stars themselves. There is no aura of fantasy and glamor woven around the leading singers, who remain invisible voices singing for the actors. Thus, the portly and plain-looking Lata Mangeshkar is not a pop-culture idol; rather, the personality cults are promoted around the actors and actresses, who are the subjects of fan clubs and magazines. Accordingly, extramusical values and associations of popular music are explicitly present in the cinematic contexts, rather than being intimated from a cluster of pop cultural norms, modes, and ideologies woven around the music and musicians themselves, as in the West. Likewise, the musicians (composers, singers, and instrumentalists) are essentially cogs in a system oriented primarily toward the production of films. If American rock musicians have complained about the loss of creative control over their image when music-video production is directed by industry personnel, the Indian film musicians' lack of freedom and control is even more complete, since they are even further removed from the visual picturization and cinematic context. It could be well be pointed out, of course, that the ideal of artistic freedom implicitly invoked here is a purely Western bourgeois notion (Appadurai, Korom, and Mills 1991:475); certainly, the Mughal court singer enjoyed no greater license. The difference here is in the degree and nature of control over a popular art form exercised by a corporate elite—quite uncharacteristic of folk music, traditional or modern. The ability of a musician to make any sort of oppositional statement is thus practically nil, since his or her own contribution is so deeply imbedded in a capitalist production network. None of this, of course, is to imply that film music cannot be aesthetically beautiful and expressive, but rather suggests that its role in popular culture, as in the films themselves, is overdetermined by the function and needs of a corporate production system ruled by the demands of capital.

Another important feature of Indian film music is, that, unlike most commercial popular musics worldwide, it does not emerge from an extensive base of amateur and professional live performance. Rock music is much more typical of world popular musics in this respect; the style itself was nurtured and molded collectively by a broad continuum of amateur and professional performers, from whose ranks the leading artists emerged. For every successful rock group on the mass media there have been dozens of grassroots, neighborhood bands playing at a wide variety of locales. Such is not the case with Indian film music, which, while drawing liberally from traditional folk and light-classical genres, is a studio-bred art to which live performances are unimportant. It is true, of course, that folk musicians (as will be discussed in chapter 7) often borrow film melodies, but on the whole, only elaborate "orchestras" playing for upper-class festivities even attempt to reproduce the ensemble timbres and style of film songs. Further, while top singers like Lata Mangeshkar do give occasional live performances, these are but secondary sources of income; moreover, these singers do not cultivate stage presence, but tend to stand motionless before the microphone, often with head buried behind a notebook from which they are reading the lyrics.

It has been pointed out that rock music itself has evolved to a considerable extent as a recording art, insofar as so many commercial recordings are conceived, produced, marketed, and appreciated as aesthetically independent entities rather than as mere versions of live performances. As Clarke observes (1983), such recordings are better regarded not as performances or scores, but as "aural compositions," with their own aesthetic criteria, and their own sorts of "spontaneity," "improvisation," and the like. If such a description is partially true for rock music, it is even more appropriate for Indian film music, which lacks the broad base of live-performance contexts which have always constituted an important aspect of the rock scene. In this sense film music differs even more dramatically from folk music, or from Indian folk-music cassettes, which essentially constitute frozen reproductions of live performances, with relatively little adaptation to the studio environment. Thus, Indian film music, more than any other prominent popular music, has been a studio art form, disseminated by the mass media, and lacking a direct source and counterpart in grassroots performance.

Nevertheless, film music, like Indian cinema in general, can be said to reflect in its own way the dialectic interaction of tradition and modernity, city and countryside, and national identity and the West. Most film songs combine Western and indigenous elements. Imported instruments like congas, synthesizers, horns, and especially violins are used alongside *tabla* and *dholak* drums and melodic instruments like sitar and *sarod*. Instrumental accompaniments typically contain nontraditional features like chordal harmonies and sectional ensemble passages in contrasting orchestral timbres. Such elaborate arrangements reflect a precomposed and notated (i.e., written) approach to music composition and performance which is quite distinct from most forms of Indian folk music, which remain thoroughly oral in their transmission and orientation, relying on variation and repetition of strophes and melodic cells. While many melodies are quite Western-sounding in their tonal organization, most are distinctly Indian, using characteristic modes and melodies akin to those of folk or light-classical music. Cuban and disco rhythms are not uncommon, but far more typical is a quadruple meter essentially equivalent to the *kaherva tal* ubiquitous in North Indian folk and light music. However, the most conspicuously indigenous feature, as with most non-Western popular musics, is the vocal style, which exhibits characteristically South Asian ornamentation and timbre.

Many film-music producers consciously endeavor to produce songs whose melodies are accessible to the broadest common denominator. Music director Kalyanji (of Kalyanji-Anandji) explains:

> We try to write songs so simple that they can be hummed by every-
> body. Every song should be as simple as a nursery rhyme. (Marre and
> Charlton 1985:142)

In actuality, the ensemble accompaniment to film songs is sometimes quite complex in terms of harmony and orchestration, even if the "nursery-rhyme" aesthetic does pervade many melodies. Similarly, while some film-song texts are sophisticated and clever productions of respected poets, most are simple verses written by lyricists who regard accessibility as the prerequisite of a good text.[8]

Film-music production exhibits the same "star-stranglehold" and concentration of media control that characterizes Indian cinema in general. For the last several decades, the vast majority of film scores have been produced by seven or eight music directors, who are each generally involved in several pictures at any given time. One result is an oft-criticized "conveyor-belt" mass production of songs, with modern composers like Bappi Lahiri boasting of scoring thirty or more films in a year.[9] Even more notable than the oligopoly of music producers is the almost exclusive reliance on only five or six playback singers. From the 1940s until the late 1980s, these consisted of Mukesh, Talat Mahmood, Mohammad Rafi, Kishore Kumar, and above all, Lata Mangeshkar and her sister Asha Bhosle. Kishore Kumar is estimated to have sung in around 60 percent of all Hindi-Urdu film songs in the decades before his death (Rahman 1987:81). Lata Mangeshkar is claimed to be the most recorded voice in the world, being featured on several thousand film songs in the course of her career.[10] South Indian films have been similarly dominated in recent decades by S. P. Balasubramaniam.

The concentration of film-music production in the hands (or throats) of such a limited number of artists naturally affects the degree of stylistic diversity within the genre. Indian films in general exhibit a marked degree of standardization in plot and cinematography, with most movies containing a formulaic package of obligatory fights, chases, songs, dances, rapes, erotic scenes, and recurring story devices (love triangles, conflicts between love and arranged marriages, separation and eventual reunion of lovers or family members, etc.). In the case of film music, the tendency toward stylistic homogeneity is even more clear, and affords its producers the advantages, mentioned above, of offering a standardized product to a mass audience rather than catering to smaller, specialized markets.

Given the vast output of film songs, a certain degree of stylistic and regional variety has naturally been evident, as has been stressed by Arnold (1988). Some of the examples of diversity cited by Arnold—such as the imitation of Chinese music in *Nai Dulhana*—are clearly marginal, atypical eccentricities; on the other hand, she is quite correct in observing that film producers have drawn freely from a palette of art music, Western and Latin pop, and diverse regional folk styles of India, and furthermore, that the "mainstream" style itself is inherently eclectic. Regional cinema (films made in languages other than Hindi-Urdu) naturally contains songs redolent of local traditions. More importantly, film composers have often employed melodies from their native regions; Hemant Kumar, S. D. Burman, Salil Choudhury, and Anil Biswas all borrowed songs from their native Bengal, while Ghulam Haider popularized Punjabi-style music. In some cases, and particularly in regional cinema, the use of regional music was intended to provide local color. In the dominant Hindi-Urdu films, however, the borrowed tunes were generally of a generic North Indian character, or were altered in such a way that they shed their regional flavor and thus could appeal to a pan-Indian audience. Anil Biswas, for example, stated that he would not use a Bengali tune in Hindi cinema unless he could "color it so much that it lost its Bengali provinciality" (interview, 1990). On the whole, film composers have avoided using melodies that would be recognizable as regional, both because of the remoteness of the film milieu from the rural folk ambience, and because of their goal of producing a style that would be popular on a pan-regional level (Chandavarkar 1987a:8). As a result, a clearly identifiable "mainstream" style coalesced, adhering to the general norms described above, and serving to homogenize the musical tastes of a vast audience of formidable heterogeneity. As one music critic observed, since the mid–1940s, "You could not hope to record any song that did not have a typical orchestral accompaniment, characteristic harmony, characteristic voices" (Chandavarkar 1987b:22). While achieving the economies of scale desirable in monopoly capitalism, the film-music industry thus, as Arnold blithely puts it, "succeeded in minimising India's cultural diversity" (1988:187). (Nevertheless, however Bombay music directors may have attempted to make Hindi film songs into a national syncretic music, it remained unlikely that regional minorities like the Tamils would ever accept any music with Hindi texts as their own.)

The homogeneity of Indian film music is most evident in the uniform vocal style, as perpetuated by the half-dozen aforementioned singers, and especially by Kishore Kumar and Lata Mangeshkar. Lata, as claimed, may indeed have sung in eighteen different languages, but she cannot really be said to have sung in more than one style. Furthermore, vocal style (aside from language) is often the single most important marker of aesthetic identity in music, as evidenced in the emergence of numerous non-Western popular musics, from Vietnam to Turkey, which employ standard Western instrumental accompaniment but distinguish themselves as local solely through the parameter of vocal style (Manuel 1988b). The uniformity of film music's vocal style contrasts markedly with the stylistic variety found in North India. Several North Indian regional musics have distinctive vocal styles, from the intense shouting of Haryanvi men's songs, to the nasal timbre of Garhwali singing and the classicized coloratura of Rajasthani Manganhar and Langa music. Even if the major North Indian regions are less easily differentiated by vocal style, individual genres within these areas are often clearly distinct in this parameter, such that an untrained ear can easily distinguish the strained, high-pitched Hathrasi *rasiya* from the rippling, lavishly ornamented Punjabi *Hir-Ranjha,* or plain, straightforward women's work songs from the tense projection of Bhojpuri *khari birha.* Further, individual performers naturally have their own idiosyncratic vocal styles, and it may be mentioned that Hindustani classical singers make no attempt to standardize their vocal timbre as do Western vocalists. Such varied vocal styles, however, are utterly absent in Indian film music. Indeed, the one vocal style that is difficult to find in North Indian folk music is the shrill falsetto of Lata Mangeshkar and her imitators.

Lata's distinctive, girlish voice has become one of the most characteristic features of Indian popular music and film culture in general. Anil Biswas claims that although never enamored of her voice, he and other composers eagerly relied on her from the 1940s on because she was the only professional singer on the Bombay commercial scene who could learn songs so easily (interview, 1990). Music critic Raghava Menon (1989) writes that Lata's style subsequently became

> the ultimate measure of sweetness in a woman's voice. Its chief characteristic was the skillful use of a particular kind of falsetto which did not exist in quite the same way before her coming . . . Lata brought this curiously stupefying voice into our light music. And the technique narcotised all forms of light music. Even the folk genre seems to have tried out this technique. Down South in the land of Tyagaraja, where the prevailing female voices always had a chesty timbre, Lata clones sang shrieking into the night in every language. Even Bengali voices, which only a few years earlier reflected the honeyed textures of Kanan Bala, abandoned their inheritance and joined the Lata bandwagon.

As a result, a film-music critic could recently write, "Today it is difficult to imagine a female voice that is not Lata Mangeshkar's" (Chandavarkar 1987b:22).

The dominance of the Lata-Kishore style can hardly be attributed to popular demand, but rather to the creation of film music as a common-denominator mass-music style, produced in corporate, urban studios and superimposed on a heterogeneous audience; this audience has no active role in the creation of this music, and can exercise only indirect influence by choosing among the songs and styles proffered by the industry. Thus, for example, the film-music listener from Nainital region could choose from several thousand songs in one style by Lata, but would be unable to find a single film song rendered in the style of his or her native Garhwal. Ranade describes how the music industry, and particularly film-music producers

> fail to do justice to the variety, topicality, and finished quality of the popular variety of music . . . If one remembers that till recently there was only one gramophone company in India, the crushing power of the monotony of musical soundscape can be easily felt. In this way the media dominate and create a situation where popular music is forced into narrow and repetitive grooves . . . It is therefore difficult to conclude that passive exposure to the fare provided can be construed as endorsement or approval of its quality. With no alternative available to users it is unfair to interpret the tolerance of the *culturally cornered people* as their voting in favour of the quality of music they are inundated with. (Ranade 1984:64–66)

The tendency of film songs to promote an amorphous, homogeneous, root-less sense of identity rather than an affirmation of local community values and regional cultures is most explicitly evident in the parameter of song texts. It can well be argued, of course, that commercial songs about sentimental love fulfill certain functions in a society—whether in Asia or the developed West—where many individuals lead unsatisfying emotional lives, or are too embarassed or otherwise inhibited to express their feelings. Nevertheless, one cannot but be impressed by the contrast between the limited range of topics in film songs and the breadth of subjects in folk songs, which are directly created by the masses themselves. Aside from employing local dialect, folk-song lyr-ics abound in references to local customs, mores, names, and sociopolitical events. Even, for example, in a repetitive women's song form wherein the singer requests her husband to bring various objects from the market, local culture is often affirmed by the very naming of particular kinds of fruits, jew-elry, garments, and spices characteristic of that area. Folk-song texts are one of the most important arenas in which a given community asserts, dramatizes, and constructs its own distinct subculture.

A music industry designing a standardized product for a mass audience naturally avoids such region-specific references, and it is not surprising that such expressions of local color are seldom found in Hindi film music. Rather, the vast majority of film songs deal with sentimental love—a topic of no small import and appeal, but one which hardly compares in variety with the broad spectrum of emotional and social issues one finds in Indian folk music.

In assessing the extent to which the Indian music industry superimposed mainstream lingua-franca Hindi-Urdu film music on an ethnically diverse au-dience, it would naturally be of interest to examine statistics regarding the quantity of film-music record sales as compared with sales of regional musics. Unfortunately, no such statistics exist. HMV evidently made little attempt to maintain documentation of its output, and the extant data, in the form of sur-viving annual catalogs, list titles of releases but give no indication of numbers of sales of individual items. Thus, for example, Ojha (1985:29–30) cites fig-ures showing that in the period 1974–84, film music accounted for 58 percent of record releases; GCI historian Michael Kinnear estimates that the number of film and nonfilm music releases were roughly equal during most of the film era (personal communication, 1991). The actual percentage of film-music *sales,* however, is undoubtedly much higher; classical and folk-music record-ings are considered successful if they sell a few thousand units, while hit film recordings may easily sell over a million. Kinnear, who has conducted the most extensive and detailed studies of the Indian recording industry, accord-ingly notes that production reruns of film-music releases generally ran on the order of ten times larger than those of nonfilm releases. Hence, discographer V. A. K. Ranga Rao may well be accurate in estimating that over 90 percent of GCI's output consisted of lingua-franca film music in mainstream style (personal communication, September 1989), suggesting, indeed, an over-whelming domination of the market by a single homogenizing genre. Even if such an estimate were grossly exaggerated, documentation of record sales would only begin to suggest the extent of the dominance of mainstream film music, since most popular music was accessed through cinema and radio rather than through records. Phonographs, after all, were owned only by a tiny percentage of Indians, whereas movies disseminating lingua-franca film music have been widely influential even among the lower classes since the 1940s. When consumption of film music via cinema and radio are taken into account, it becomes clear, even with the lack of statistical data, how exten-sively Bombay-produced film music dominated the realm of mass-mediated popular music—until the advent of cassettes.

The Impact of Film Music on Folk Music

The incorporation of certain elements and melodies of regional folk music into film music has been noted above. The converse influence—from film music to folk song—is equally evident, and reflects how the interaction of the two realms, although in some cases symbiotic, often works to the detriment of folk song. Film culture, with its enormous capital resources, its mass dis-tribution networks, and its appeal of glamor and spectacle, enjoys prodigious advantages over folk forms of entertainment, and it is not surprising that many folk genres have either disappeared or survived only by compromising with film culture.

The decline of many genres of folk music and entertainment in twentieth-century India has been well documented. In many respects, it may be difficult to attribute such developments to any one factor such as cinema, since the extinction of an art form is more likely to be overdetermined by a set of inter-related changes. The advent of capitalist modes of production may make genres celebrating feudal values seem archaic. News services on the mass media may render obsolete traditional oral songs and verses which offered information as well as entertainment. Work songs accompanying a particular activity (e.g., grinding wheat) may naturally disappear when that form of la-bor is mechanized. Increased transportation facilities make people less depen-dent on the art forms of their immediate locality. The eclipse of a certain social class—such as feudal landlords and princes—may naturally lead to the de-cline of art forms dependent on their patronage. Finally, the mass media in general may weaken local art forms by providing alternatives to villagers who had never before been exposed to any music other than that of their own com-munity or of the occasional itinerant ensemble.

Nevertheless, many scholars, as well as performers themselves, tend to single out cinema as a primary culprit in the decreasing vitality of folk enter-tainment and music forms. Hartmann, Patil, and Dighe (1989:213) note how cinema has usurped the popularity of *Dhujari, Bhanumati gan* and other genres among young Bengali villagers. Tewari (1974:18) blames films for the decline of many Uttar Pradesh folk genres, and observes that many folk minstrels have abandoned their traditional repertoire to join groups playing film songs. Kumar (1988:151) attributes the dramatically decreased popularity of Banaras-region *kajli* to film influence. Henry (1988:112) and Slawek (1986:21–22) both observe how Banarsi and Bhojpuri village women often abandon singing wedding songs due to the competition from loudspeaker systems blaring film music at marriages. Penurious snake-charmers complain that they are increasingly unable to compete with cinema (Chandra 1989:188). Folklorists note the transformation, and in some cases, the loss of traditional Punjabi folk-song repertoire under the influence of film music (Bedi 1971:107). Traditional forms of music theater like *sang* (*swang*) have particular difficulty competing with cinema (Vatuk 1979:26). The tradition of North Indian urban beggars reciting Urdu couplets is long dead, replaced to some extent by snippets of film songs rendered by itinerant musical mendicants.

Many folk genres survive only at the expense of incorporating film songs into their repertoire. While the use of film melodies (with new texts) may incur the displeasure of elder listeners (and ethnomusicologists), it has become extremely common in most Indian folk music genres except in the most isolated regions. Its presence has been noted in Meerut-area *sang* (Vatuk 1979:28), Haryanvi *ragini* (Sharma 1983:273), Bengali *jatra* (Mullick 1985), Rajasthani Bhopa renditions of the Pabuji epic (Louden 1986:65), Manganhar performances (Jairazbhoy 1977:58), *nautanki* of western Uttar Pradesh (Awasthi 1977:29), Gujerati *garba* (Mahurkar 1990), and Muslim devotional *qawwali* and *na't* (Marcus, in Manuel 1988b:187). Informal women's singing sessions may now include film songs or newly composed "folk" songs (such as childbirth *sohar* songs) using film melodies (Henry 1988:34, 112; Tewari 1988:269). Bhojpuri *birha* thrives as never before, but only at the expense of becoming a medley of tunes, most of which derive from films (Marcus 1989:99). Bengali *jatra* also seems to be enjoying unprecedented popularity, partly through the incorporation of film tunes and other cinematic effects (Das Gupta 1987:108–9). I have personally noted the use of film tunes in *Ramlila*, Hindu *bhajans*, and Braj-area *lavni* and *rasiya*, while anyone who has encountered snake-charmers (*jogis*) has undoubtedly heard their rendition of the theme song from the 1950s film *Nagin*.[11]

While the practice of borrowing film melodies reflects the spread of corporate-produced music, it may be difficult to generalize about other ramifications of this trend (which will be discussed in greater detail in chapters 6 and 7). The common usage of film tunes in devotional *bhajans* is often deplored as introducing inappropriate associations.[12] Nita Kumar notes that in Banaras *qawwali*, "The efforts of artists to be creative tend in the direction of imitation of the latest and the best in films rather than towards spontaneity and inspiration from everyday life" (1988:153). In many cases, however, it is unclear whether film tunes are actually replacing or merely supplementing folk melodies. The use of sophisticated film tunes could be argued to constitute an enrichment of some folk genres, especially those text-oriented genres whose traditional melodies are plain and monotonous; on the other hand, it could be regarded as indicating a loss of creativity and an alienating intrusion of inappropriate *filmi* aesthetics. Similarly, film influence has been seen to inculcate higher standards of intonation and professionality among some folk musicians (Louden 1986:101); but such influence could also be regarded as homogenization and deculturation. Finally, it should also be mentioned that film music can popularize and disseminate folk music insofar as film composers borrow folk melodies so liberally. In some cases, film music has served to preserve obscure and otherwise forgotten folk melodies; a noteworthy example in the classic hit film *Awara* is the melody of "Ghar aaya mera pardesi," which derives from a now largely forgotten *sohar* (child-celebration song) of eastern Uttar Pradesh.

In assessing the allegedly detrimental impact of film music, and of any commercial popular music on folk music, it is important to note that the two sets of genres may have significantly different functions. In India, as in most traditional societies, many folk genres are associated with particular performance contexts, be they religious festivals, life-cycle events, seasonal occasions, or various kinds of work and household chores. Many such genres remain familiar and vital, but are not represented on commercial recordings, which present more secular entertainment musics not associated with specific occasions. Similarly, in the United States, for example, there are many of us who are not averse to hearing or even singing Christmas carols in December, but few of us are likely to purchase a recording of such music. From one perspective, then, the fact that Christmas carols and Indian wedding songs are poorly represented on commercial recordings does not in itself necessarily imply cultural decline; further, just as middle-class Westerners—including intellectuals and aesthetes—are more likely to cultivate interest in contemporary popular (or even classical) music than in their own folk music, so, similarly, the fascination young Indians have for pop music should not necessarily be lamented. One may counter, however, that there are alternatives between a homogenizing popular music and "Little Brown Jug," and it is still possible for a community to create or nourish a syncretic popular music that is at once modern and affirmative of many of the best values of their traditional culture. Such responsive kinds of grassroots music genres do seem to have arisen in connection with cassettes, as we shall discuss, and many of them differ dramatically from mainstream film music in their representation of specific community aesthetics. Further, when the media contribute to a situation where a community forsakes all kinds of music-making in preference for mediated music, one can certainly speak of a decline of musical energy and a degree of creative alienation as well.

Conclusions

Despite the rather pejorative tone of the preceding assessment of films and film music, I have deliberately attempted to avoid making subjective value judgments about the quality of the music itself; in passing, I would not hesitate to opine that many commercial films are to be credited with slick and professional production, effective acting, and heartrending plots, and similarly, that many film songs are memorable and evocative works of art (of which I am quite fond). Moreover, it would hardly be appropriate for a Western writer such as myself to publicly question the aesthetic merit of a music cherished by hundreds of millions of South Asians. At the same time, I have not attempted to avoid contentious issues pertaining to homogeneity, responsiveness, and alienation insofar as they are suggested by the nature of the data themselves, and by the opinions of Indian intellectuals—which are clearly at odds with popular taste. Further, if I have highlighted certain negative features of the music industry—oligopolistic structure, standardized content—it is because these are the very aspects which have been most palpably changed by the advent of cassettes.

Given the subjective and potentially controversial nature of the arguments presented above, it may be appropriate to recapitulate them, reiterating the distinctions between empirically verifiable data and subjective interpretation. First of all, this chapter has illustrated the fact that control and production of the commercial music industry during the period in question have been concentrated in the hands of a corporate oligopoly consisting of GCI and a handful of film-music directors. Accordingly, in spite of a degree of linguistic diversity and stylistic eclecticism, most film songs since the 1940s have been produced and sung by a small handful of artists. On the whole, this corporate and professional elite has endeavored to market a standardized, common-denominator music to a broad, pan-regional audience. In their uniformity of vocal style, text content, and language, film songs differ markedly from the diverse folk musics with which they compete. Further, film music is embedded in and closely associated with a cinema culture whose production is similarly oligopolistic, and whose orientation (in the words of its producers as well as critics) is openly escapist.

The nature of Indian cinema has inspired predominantly negative interpretive appraisals by Indian scholars, whose writings have tended to criticize its escapism, implicit elitism, obscurantist conservatism, and its alienating effects. Similarly, folklorists have accused film music of usurping the popularity and patronage of folk-music forms. I have argued here that film music, regardless of its merits, has flourished at the expense of a sense of community, and that one should well question whether and in what manner it responds to or, alternately, manipulates popular taste. Such criticisms, of course, have been articulated most visibly by members of educated elites (including this author) rather than by lower-middle-class Indians, for whom most Indian films and film songs are produced. Nevertheless, the extent to which musical demand was unsated by film song has become glaringly apparent in that as soon as Indians were presented with significant mass-mediated alternatives (via cassettes), film music's share of the commercial market plummeted to less than half of all sales.

Film music, I would contend, can be seen as a "people's music" insofar as it is cherished by hundreds of millions of Indians, and is widely incorporated into all manner of live folk performances. At the same time, imitation, reproduction, and passive consumption are different from the actual creative production that would distinguish a genuine, grassroots "people's art" from a corporate-produced mass art. Any interpretive assessment of film music must note its stylistic homogeneity, absence of topical contemporaneity, and the entire undemocratic, unidirectional structure of the industry producing it. It is precisely these aspects of the music industry that have been overthrown by the cassette boom, to which we may now turn.

4

The Advent of Cassettes:
New Alternatives to His Master's Voice

Cassettes Come to India

Until 1978 India had pursued economic and political policies designed to provide autonomy and self-reliance. One of the few genuinely nonaligned countries, India studiously avoided joining either of the rival superpowers' camps. On the economic front, India pursued a path of controlled capitalist development, mitigated by a large public sector and extensive bureaucratic regulation of the private sector. This regulation was the primary, though not exclusive, factor which delayed the spread of cassettes within the country. After Independence, India established a protectionist policy in order to promote indigenous infant industry. The rupee was declared inconvertible, foreign multinationals had either to sacrifice majority ownership or leave the country, and imports of goods were allowed only in special circumstances approved by the state bureaucracy. Such policies promoted industrial development—particularly of large-scale sectors like steel, trucks, and railroads—such that India became one of the world's larger industrial powers; they also insulated India from inflation and kept the foreign debt at low levels in comparison to most developing countries. At the same time, infant-industry protection promoted a degree of inefficiency and sloth, limiting exports and obliging Indian consumers to contend with inferior products and limited variety. Restrictions on imports also stifled the growth of the consumer-electronics industries, which required at least some foreign-made components. On the domestic front, economic policies designed to promote small-scale industry and discourage luxury consumption also inhibited consumer electronics and other sectors, by overtaxing products, hindering licensing of companies, and administering prices of some commodities.

By the late 1970s cassette players had begun to appear in noticeable quantities throughout much of the country; most of these were Japanese "two-in-ones" (radio cassette recorders) brought by the tens of thousands of guest workers returning from the Gulf states; the numbers of such workers had by this point reached such levels that their remittances, as well as their hand-carried imports, were having noticeable effects not only in Arabian Sea areas like Kerala, but throughout much of the hinterland as well. Accordingly, in 1979 GCI had started issuing cassette releases, while offering duplication services to other companies. By this time, pirate cassettes of film-music records became commonplace in bazaars, stimulating demand for players. Nevertheless, the cassette boom, as well as the consumer-electronics industry in general, cannot really be said to have taken off until slightly later, due to broader changes in the Indian economy.[1]

In 1978, the slow growth of the economy and the increasing dissatisfaction of middle-class consumers led the government to liberalize the economy; these policies have been perpetuated, with some tinkering and negotiation, by subsequent administrations. Whether regarded as an Asian Reaganomics or a latter-day Leninist New Economic Policy, the new course was designed to stimulate growth, demand, exports, and product quality. Import restrictions on many items were liberalized, and many regulations and controls were eased.

The results of the policy changes were mixed. On the one hand, because of inflation, the condition of the poor remained roughly the same or, by some indices, worsened, while the rupee was devalued by half, and foreign debt tripled,[2] exposing India for the first time to the danger of falling into the classic third-world trap of foreign dependency, mounting fiscal deficit, and widening income disparities. On the other hand, exports, foreign investment and the economy in general expanded dramatically. A middle class equal in size and affluence to the whole of France has come to flourish as never before,[3] exercising unprecedented purchasing power and enjoying a lively business climate and a plentiful variety and quality of luxury consumer goods. Television, videocassette recorders, stereos, cameras, vacuum cleaners, blenders and other modern gadgets have become commonplace in middle-class and even working-class homes, as the annual growth rate in demand for such goods has ranged from 10 to 20 percent since the late 1970s. Consumerism in general has spread and matured, with the growth of an ambitious and materialistic bourgeoisie, half-liberated from caste and tradition, and worshiping at the new temples of conspicuous indulgence, the opulent five-star hotels. The boom in consumer spending has spread to rural areas as well as cities,[4] and to lower-middle-class buyers as well as the bourgeoisie.

The economic liberalization policies, together with other related developments commencing in the middle or late 1970s, led to the phenomenal, if slightly belated, spread of cassette technology in India. The purchasing power and increasing consumerism of the flourishing bourgeoisie stimulated demand for audio and visual entertainment systems. While tariffs on foreign televisions, tape players, and stereos remained over 100 percent, many middle-class Indians felt affluent enough simply to pay the high import duties on foreign electronics goods. Aside from the thousands of "two-in-ones" brought by Gulf guest workers, many Japanese tape players and televisions also found their way illegally into Indian markets. The Indian consumer-electronics industry also flourished as a result of the increased demand and other factors. After years of protection, the industry had by the mid-1970s grown in size and sophistication. Reduced duties on certain items finally enabled Indian manufacturers to import selected components for the local manufacture of cassettes and players.[5] Further, the new policies enouraged foreign collaborative "tie-ins," notably Bush-Akai, Orson-Sony, BPL-Sanyo, and Onida-JVC in the realm of cassette-player manufacture, and, in 1990, Sinkyong-Modi, Du Pont-Hindustan Magnetics and others in magnetic-tape production.[6] Onerous excise taxes have continued to be imposed and rescinded by the state, but the general trend has been toward deregulation.[7] Music-industry journalist Anil Chopra observes:

> The real cassette boom has happened mostly since 1984 or '85, especially because tape coating has started in India in a huge way . . . The big boom has been because the costs of these raw materials has become dirt cheap—available all over the country. The molded shell [of the cassette], the hubs, the rollers, the whole thing is available dirt cheap. There wasn't so much easily available before that. Then from '82 to '85 the record dealers switched to cassettes, and the *pan-walas* [lit., betel-nut vendors] started selling them. (Interview, April 1990)

As a result, the Indian consumer-electronics industry, and the cassette boom, which had commenced in earnest around 1980, expanded exponentially in the next five years. Sales of recorded music—almost entirely cassettes by the late 1980s—went from $1.2 million in 1980 to $12 million in 1986, and to over $21 million in 1990 (Swamy 1991).[8] Exports of Indian-made recorders leapt from 1.65 million rupees' worth in 1983 to 99.75 million in 1987 (Muralidharan 1988:1661). By the late 1980s, Indian consumers were buying around 2.5 million cassette players annually (while the entire number of phonographs in the country is estimated at well under one million) (Gopal 1987:32). Philips, the largest local maker of cassette recorders in the early 1980s, sold 72,000 units in 1983, and 395,000 in 1986, introducing seven new models in the mid-eighties (Chengappa 1987:113). As the consumer-electronics industry annually doubled in size throughout the latter 1980s (Bhargava 1991:58), it came to be recognized by the state as one of the more dynamic sectors of the economy. As of 1989, around five hundred companies (not including cassette producers) were involved in the industry, of which around four hundred were small-scale (Sarkar 1989:73). Most remarkably, in the space of a few years India has become the world's second largest manufacturer of cassettes, as of 1991 marketing some 217 million cassettes, surpassing China (125 million) and Great Britain (83 million), and thus trailing only the United States (ca. 446.2 million) (Swamy 1991; Bhargava 1991:58).[9]

Television played a significant part in the consumer-electronics boom, accounting for roughly two-thirds of its output. Television's vogue was spurred by some of the same factors that spurred the cassette vogue, together with deliberate encouragement by the state since 1982, and marked improvement in the popularity of Indian programming—notably, the appearance of domestic soap operas and ongoing serial renditions of the *Ramayan* and *Mahabharat* epics. The Sunday-morning broadcasts of the epic serials became national events in the late 1980s, bringing life throughout the country to a halt as viewers crowded before televisions in bazaars, friends' shanties, or bourgeois living rooms. Cheaper portable black-and-white televisions selling for around 3,500 rupees (ca. $210) have become the fastest-growing part of the television market, as urban areas became saturated and poorer rural buyers began purchasing in large numbers (Rajan 1989:23). Despite increases in excise taxes in the latter 1980s, over 120 Indian television manufacturers have emerged since 1980. Many Indians, it should be noted, save up for extended periods in order to buy televisions, skipping audiocassettes altogether. I have noted, accordingly, that in some villages there are as many televisions as cassette players; studies have also revealed that in middle-class homes, televisions are only slightly less common than cassette players. The spread of television and videocassette recorders has also contributed to the marked decline of cinema-industry revenues since the mid-eighties, precipitating the closure of hundreds of cinema halls throughout the country (Kaye 1988).

The flourishing of cassette technology effectively restructured the music industry in India. By the mid-1980s, cassettes had come to account for 95 percent of the recorded music market, with records being purchased only by wealthy audiophiles, radio stations, and cassette pirates (who prefer using them as masters) (Kaye 1988). Relatively little commercial music was even released in record format. The recording-industry dominance formerly enjoyed by GCI dwindled to less than 15 percent of the market, as over three hundred competitors entered the field. While sales of film music remained strong, film music's share of the dramatically expanded market dropped from roughly 90 percent of the total to less than 40 percent (Sayani 1988:37). The remainder now consists of diverse forms of regional folk music (40–60 percent of the market),[10] devotional music, and other forms of non-*filmi*, or in industry parlance, "basic" pop music.

In effect, the cassette revolution had definitively ended the hegemony of GCI, of the corporate music industry in general, of film music, of the Lata-Kishore duocracy, and of the uniform aesthetic which the Bombay film-music producers had superimposed on a few hundred million listeners over the preceding forty years. The crucial factors were the relatively low expense of the cassette technology, and especially, its lowered production costs, which enabled small, "cottage" cassette companies to proliferate throughout the country. As mentioned above, the small labels tend to have local, specialized, regional markets to whose diverse musical interests they are able and willing to respond in a manner quite uncharacteristic of the monopolistic major recording companies, which prefer to address and, as much as possible, to *create* a mass homogeneous market. As one journalist described the majors,

> They all operate on a high cost and high overhead environment. And in their preoccupation with the national market, they began losing out on regional music, which turned out to be the backbone of the industry.[11]

In the process, the backyard cassette companies have been energetically recording and marketing all manner of regional "Little Traditions" which were previously ignored by GCI and the film-music producers. Rather than being oriented toward undifferentiated film-goers, most of the new cassette-based musics are aimed at a bewildering variety of specific target audiences, in terms of class, age, gender, ethnicity, region, and in some cases, even occupation (e.g., Punjabi truck drivers' songs). The smaller producers themselves are varied in terms of their region, religion, and insofar as many are lower-middle class, their class backgrounds as well. Ownership of the means of musical production is thus incomparably more diverse than before the cassette era. As a result, the average non-elite Indian is now, as never before, offered the voices of his own community as mass-mediated alternatives to his master's voice.

In the following pages I will examine some of the leading and representative smaller cassette producers, the relevant aspects of the Indian consumer-electronics industry, some financial aspects of cassette production, and piracy. Before doing so, however, it may be appropriate to point out the difficulty, and in many cases, the impossibility of obtaining remotely accurate statistics on many key aspects of the industry. There is, of course, no shortage of relevant and interesting statistics to be found in trade journals, corporate reports, government surveys, tax and duty summaries, and executives' statements. Unfortunately, these are in many cases widely inconsistent, representing educated or uneducated guesses, and, occasionally, deliberate distortions.

An initial problem is the existence of a vast pirate or "unorganized" sector of the music industry, which naturally defies being measured and studied statistically, especially on macro levels. Secondly, members of the electronics and music industries often have strong incentives to conceal or misreport aspects of their operations. Small and large companies may hide aspects of their business which involve the use of illegally obtained components, whether they be smuggled from abroad or indigenously manufactured by unlicensed companies.[12] A company importing large quantities of magnetic tape, for example, may seek to evade the heavy import duty by obtaining smuggled tape;

similarly, a tape producer may underreport the extent of his production in order to avoid excise and sales tax. Thus, the sale of prerecorded cassettes in the early 1980s was several times larger than the sum of cassettes officially produced or imported in India, implying a vast usage of unreported production and smuggling (Nair 1986:52). Other companies are alleged to falsely claim that they are exporting cassettes, thereby avoiding excise taxes on domestic sales.[13] It is also common practice for companies to report inaccurately small incomes, or even losses, in order to avoid income tax. Government bureaucracies are often quite unable to spot such misrepresentations. The absence of reliable statistics, as we shall see, impedes various aspects of a holistic study of the cassette industry, but also constitutes, in its own way, a distinctive feature of the Indian music scene.

Cassette Producers

By the mid-1980s certain aspects of the Indian music industry had come to resemble counterparts in the West. In India as in the United States, for example, the market has become divided between a handful of large corporations, and a considerable number of smaller ones with more specialized audiences and repertoire. But whereas records, compact discs, and cassettes all compete for customers in the West, Indian commercial recordings now consist almost entirely of cassettes, with records constituting not more than 2 percent of the market, and CDs, at this point, remaining novel curiosities for the rich. In accordance with the relative ease and low cost of cassette duplication, the record-industry distinction between "majors" (who own their own pressing and distribution systems) and "independents" (who generally do not) is not so clear or significant in India. A small company, or even an individual entrepreneur, may duplicate his own cassettes and even assemble the components, while some larger companies may contract out such aspects of their operations. Only a few music producers actually manufacture their own cassette components.

It is difficult to estimate the precise number of cassette producers in India. In 1986 *Playback* magazine estimated their number at "more than 200."[14] A survey conducted around the same time by Venus Records and Tapes counted 256 producers (Khosla 1987:25). *Playback* editor Anil Chopra estimates their number at around 500 (interview, April 1990). In 1989–91 I enumerated around 170 in North India, but my survey was incomplete. Many small producers of regional musics are unknown outside their limited environs; further, there are unregistered cassette producers consisting of sole individuals who record music and sell masters out of their residences, dubbing copies on one-to-one setups on request; some artists also engage in such activities to promote their own music. In such a situation, it is virtually impossible to ascertain the number of producers. Furthermore, the precise figure may not be entirely significant, as the producers vary so greatly in size, from T-Series, with several thousand releases, to New Delhi's Chandrabani Garhwal Series, whose series, as of 1990, consisted of a single cassette. Nevertheless, excluding pirates and unregistered producers, based on my own research I would hazard an estimate of some 250 producers in North India.

Due to the aforementioned factors, it is difficult to estimate the relative shares of the market. In 1986 former HMV director Anil Sud claimed that small regional producers had captured 75 percent of the billion-rupee ($60 million) legitimate (non-pirate) market, with HMV retaining only 13 percent.[15] A survey of legitimate cassette sales in 1985 estimated market shares as follows: HMV 32 percent, Music India 16 percent, CBS 12 percent, and others 40 percent (Nair 1986:53).

His Master's Voice

The most prominent and, by some indices, the largest company in the music industry remains HMV (by far the largest and most important label of GCI), whose early history has been outlined in the previous chapter. Due to its virtual monopoly until the late 1960s, and its duopoly for the subsequent decade, HMV has by far the largest back catalog. It continues to enjoy the most prestigious reputation, and attracts many of the top singing artists. HMV was one of the two companies which rode the crest of the *ghazal* boom in the late 1970s and early 1980s. It is one of the few producers that usually pays royalties rather than flat payments to artists; its tapes, although more expensive, are generally presumed to be of higher quality (although such is not always the case). HMV has the largest repertoire, not only of classical music, but of popular music as well. Since being taken over by the R. P. Goenka group (RGP Enterprises) in 1985, it has lost some of the stigma of being a subsidiary of a foreign multinational.

At the same time, HMV has been in a state of clear decline since the early 1970s, such that its logo of a terrier listening to an antique gramophone strikes many consumers as more pathetic than prestigious. HMV has had several problems, including, according to some, phlegmatic habits acquired through decades of monopoly, which have rendered it ill-equipped to face the harsh winds of competition that accompanied cassette technology. Myopic government restrictions also inhibited its expansion in the early years of the cassette boom; in particular, HMV was not allowed to manufacture tape until 1978, at which point it was allowed a quota of only 1.2 million cassettes, with the absurd stipulation that 80 percent of that had to be exported (Mohideen 1989:8). Just as cassettes were coming into vogue, HMV was investing heavily in a new record-pressing plant. Because the company had neglected to keep masters or even copies of much of its old repertoire, it has had difficulty reissuing evergreen hits still in demand; a warehouse fire in 1983 exacerbated problems (Alison Arnold, personal communication). Due to such factors, HMV has been quite unable even to keep up with demand for its products, filling only some 30 percent of its orders; as a result, pirates have feasted on its repertoire. HMV's share of the market plummeted after the advent of cassettes. Current film music—still the single most popular commercial music—is now thoroughly dominated by the rival upstart label T-Series, while aggressive smaller producers have entrenched themselves in the regional markets, which now account for around half of all recorded-music sales.

As of 1986, the company's finances were strained by a "headcount headache" of some twelve hundred surplus workers. Fear of annoying the songstress Lata Mangeshkar allegedly inhibited the company from experimenting with new singers (Bhargava 1991:59). The company claimed overall losses throughout most of the 1980s. Failure to pay royalties on their international product in the late 1980s resulted in a legal sanction on releasing their foreign repertoire—again allowing pirates to monopolize sales. By 1987 HMV's outstanding royalty debt exceeded fifty million rupees.

Since being acquired by the Goenka group, the company appears to be getting back on its feet. It currently produces about one hundred thousand cassettes a day. In 1989–90 it registered a profit for the first time since 1982, fueled to a large extent by the hit film score *Mainne Pyar Kiya,* which sold over five million cassettes in the legitimate market alone.[16] The success of HMV's Hindi pop singer Alisha Chinai and of Punjabi vocalists Gurdas Mann and Malkit Singh also contributed to HMV's revival, although the company will never enjoy the comfortable dominance of its monopoly days.

T-Series

In 1979, twenty-five-year-old Gulshan Arora, together with his brother Gopal, an electronics buff, took time off from manning their father's fruit stall in Delhi to tinker with radio repairs and a fledgling cassette hobby. Within eight years he and Gopal had built their enterprise into one of India's most dynamic new industries, with a plant and investment worth over $120 million (Badhwar 1987:110). T-Series, with its sister concern Super Cassettes (SCI), now constitutes the most important company in the cassette boom, having outstripped HMV in several key aspects of the business through a remarkable combination of skill, energy, and, by most accounts, an elastic conception of law and ethics. The story of T-Series' ascent itself illustrates some of the dynamism and ruthless entrepreneurship animating the cassette industry in general.

The Arora brothers allegedly started with a small studio where they recorded Garhwali, Punjabi and Bhojpuri songs, attempting to tap the emergent market for regional folk-pop musics. Gopal borrowed money to visit Japan, Hong Kong, and Korea to learn about cassette technology. As cassette sales soared, the Aroras expanded into related sales of magnetic tape and silicon paper, and built their own cassette plant which offered duplication services to other smaller regional cassette producers. T-Series rode the crest of the cassette boom, establishing itself as the current industry leader by the mid–1980s. One particularly innovative and shrewd strategy of Arora's (to be discussed in chapter 6) was the phenomenally successful production and marketing of cover versions of HMV's classic film songs, which HMV itself was proving unable to reissue. Arora also promoted the marketing of cassettes in small, unconventional distribution outlets like betel-nut stalls, groceries, and other street vendors (Bhargava 1991:91). In spite of largely avoiding the South Indian market, T-Series has usurped HMV's position as the dominant film-music producer, and now releases music for 70 percent of current films. Through manufacturing its own cassettes (twenty-five million a year, as of 1991) and enjoying considerable economies of scale, T-Series is able to undersell most competitors in the audio market. Its sales of prerecorded cassettes have surpassed those of HMV (Bardhwan 1987), and it now exports some fifty million rupees' worth of cassettes a year.[17] The company has since expanded into manufacture and export of televisions, cassette recorders, toothpaste, detergent, blank audiocassettes and videocassettes, and other products. In 1990, T-Series began producing feature films, reversing the prior norm of film companies producing soundtracks. In 1991, partly due to the increasingly exorbitant prices of promising soundtracks (up to four million rupees), T-Series ceased purchasing rights to film scores by other companies, preferring to concentrate on its own production.

Much of T-Series' remarkable success is clearly due to Arora's shrewd entrepreneurship, good labor-management relations, and his energetic and prescient development of new markets such as cover versions and regional music. Arora takes a strong personal interest in all aspects of his business, frequently monitoring and overseeing recording procedures in the studios. Arora himself attributes his fortune to his patron Vaishno Devi, a goddess whose shrine in Jammu currently enjoys great renown. An eccentric who still occasionally mans the family fruit stall, Arora has constructed temples to Vaishno Devi, produces several cassettes of devotional music to her, and donates prodigiously to charities in her name. However, many of those involved in the music industry, while not denying Arora's skills, attribute his success in large part to another factor: piracy (to be discussed in greater detail below). T-Series is widely alleged to have flourished in its early years by issuing pirate releases of film music and of stars like Gurdas Maan, capitalizing on HMV's problems and the absence of copyright enforcement before the mid-1980s. One T-Series employee told me:

What people say about our activities in the early years—it's mostly true. But I tell you that back then, the big *ghazal* singers on HMV were privately coming to us and asking us to market pirate versions of their cassettes, for their own publicity, since HMV wasn't nearly able to keep up with demand.

While T-Series' piracy is believed to have decreased in recent years, pirate cassettes with T-Series labels (i.e., of recordings legitimately released under other labels) still abound in bazaars. Arora is credited with various particularly devious and unscrupulous practices; for example, when his own "Tony" blank cassettes were competing in the market with a popular Singapore-made brand, "EHF," Arora is said to have purchased massive amounts of the latter, inserting his own inferior Tony magnetic tape in the EHF shells, and vice versa, in order to discredit EHF and confuse the public. (Indian makers of razor blades are rumored to have engaged in similar practices with Gillette imports.) Arora is also accused of surreptitiously obtaining film scores before the films were even released, so that his pirate recordings would be the first on the market.

Such allegations, and the extent of T-Series' piracy, are difficult if not impossible to verify. T-Series sources claim that they themselves are in fact the largest victims of piracy, and that illegitimate cassettes with T-Series labels are not produced by them but by pirates seeking to capitalize on T-Series' prestige.[18] In fact, given T-Series' vast catalog, its considerable prestige among the public, and the persistence of audio piracy, there is little reason to doubt that T-Series has been and continues to be a prime victim of piracy. It is also quite possible that many pirate cassettes with T-Series labels might be produced by other illegal entrepreneurs. The music-industry organization IPI (Indian Phonographic Industry) has considered Arora's shenanigans verifiable enough to blacklist T-Series from membership. Still, piracy allegations notwithstanding, T-Series is now the single largest producer of commercial music in the country, enjoying a reputation among artists for fairness, competent production, and excellent distribution.

Other Large Producers

Following T-Series and HMV in size, by most indices, is Music India Ltd. (MIL—formerly called Polydor), which is a subsidiary of Polygram, the Dutch-British multinational which inherited, among other entities, Philips and Deutsche Grammaphon (DGG). The company entered the Indian market in 1969, building its own record-pressing plant in Bombay and being the first to challenge HMV's monopoly successfully. In 1980 it began producing cassettes. Despite the rapid expansion of the market during this period, MIL, along with the other majors, registered losses during 1982–84, due primarily to piracy and, to a lesser extent, competition from smaller producers. MIL's problems were compounded by labor-union opposition after the company closed its record plant and laid off workers. By 1985 MIL was the only major to register a profit. MIL's growth, and its ability to weather difficulties, has been primarily due to its dominance, along with HMV, in the realm of *ghazals*—a romantic song form which, as discussed in the next chapter, was the first commercial genre to flourish with the advent of cassettes.[19] *Ghazal* crooners Anup Jalota and Pankaj Udhas continue to be the biggest breadwinners for the company, although it has also enjoyed a market for its own international repertoire in India.

CBS, the dominant multinational in the world, established a presence in India in 1982, in partial collaboration with the Indian conglomerate Tata. In the next few years, however, facing the same piracy as the other majors, CBS lost money, although soon establishing itself as one of the top four companies (along with HMV, MIL, and T-Series). Like MIL, CBS's main asset is its international repertoire. Nevertheless, the Indian upstart label Magnasound, founded in 1989, has been able to capitalize on the difficulties of the other major labels and, lacking the debts resulting from piracy and the transition from record format, has been able to flourish, surpassing CBS-India in sales of international repertoire, and thus trailing only HMV in that category.[20] Magnasound has been particularly aggressive in publicity and promotion for its products.

Venus Records and Tapes, since its establishment in 1984 (under the name Jain Enterprises), has become one of the five largest music producers in India, and is in fact third in terms of turnover (Khosla 1987). Venus has a diverse catalog including film scores, a wide variety of regional musics, as well as *ghazals,* classical music, and devotional music. Another growing panregional producer is TIPS, which specializes in films and cover versions, including the especially successful English-language cover versions of Hindi pop hits.

A notable recent entry into the market is Music Today, a branch of India's newsweekly *India Today.* Music Today, in spite of the high price of its digitally mastered cassettes and their exclusive focus on classical music, has fared quite well since its establishment in 1990. Attractive packaging and aggressive promotion through its parent magazine have boosted sales, with a cassette of *tabla* solos by Zakir Hussein and Akka Rakha selling over a hundred thousand copies by early 1991.[21]

In the realm of smaller producers, one may distinguish a category consisting of around a dozen producers which, operating out of Delhi, Bombay, or Calcutta, have generated a thousand or so releases each, aimed at the linguistic-ethnic groups of the surrounding areas (and migrant communities in the cities themselves). In Delhi, for example, Max, Rama, Sonotone, and Yuki produce cassettes, in varying proportions, in Punjabi, Garhwali, Braj Bhasha, Haryanvi, Rajasthani, and Bhojpuri. In Bombay, the Trimurti and Oriental labels produce music in Marathi, Gujerati, and Konkani; in Calcutta, Gathani and Sound Recording generate repertoire for Bengali, Bhojpuri and Orissi (Oriya) listeners. All of these producers may also hold music rights to a few medium-budget films, and market product in the linguas francas of Hindi and Urdu.

Beneath this level are around two hundred still smaller producers, with repertoires typically ranging from fifty to a few hundred cassettes. Whether based in cities like Delhi, or provincial towns like Bulandshahr, they generally produce music for their specific, regional audiences, focusing on traditional folk genres, or newly composed songs in folk style, sung in regional dialect. Most of these companies started in the years 1983–86, when the large corporations were stalled, piracy was beginning to wane, excise taxes were declining, and the cassette boom was definitively flourishing. In some cases, their founders owned electronics-repair shops (e.g., Venus), or record and tape retail stores (Mainpuri's Rathor). Some (e.g., Yuki) were producers or wholesalers for HMV who struck out on their own. Others have been recording-studio owners, for whom cassette production has become a secondary business (e.g., Lucknow's Mamshar). In some cases (e.g., Delhi's Saraswati), the founders were folk-music enthusiasts for whom cassette production became a rewarding hobby, and an ancillary source of income. A few performers themselves, such as Goanese pop singer Remo Fernandes and Braj poet-vocalist Sevaram Tanatan, started their own small labels (both artists, as their popularity grew, went on to record for larger companies). Finally, there are entrepreneurs who, as a hobby or secondary business, record local singers in makeshift studios, and dub copies upon request for individual customers and cassette retailers (who then duplicate them). I encountered two such producers in Jodhpur, Rajasthan; one, Mohan Jhala, himself is a singer who records regularly for labels such as Yuki, and performs at *jagrans* (temple ceremonies) once a month or so, when not working at his daily job with the Border Security Police. The other (Chhanvarlal Gahlot), is a lyricist, promoter of folk music and dance shows, occasional folk dancer, and owner of a cassette-repair shop. It is difficult to estimate how many other such neighborhood producers exist in the North.

Financial and Technological Aspects of the Cassette Industry

Given the great variety of sizes and resources of the North Indian cassette producers, expenses on the various aspects of recording and production vary greatly. Cottage producers like Gahlot and Jhala may record for a pittance, by writing their own material, using makeshift studios at home, and hiring a local harmonium player and drummer to accompany a singer who may record for free in order to become known. For such producers, capital investment may consist of little more than two cassette recorders (for initial recording, and subsequent dubbing) and a microphone. The boast of one producer of Braj-

Bhasha folk-music tapes is not atypical among lower-end family businesses: "We only need to give the artist some booze and he will do the recording for us" (Tiwari and Ahmed 1991:166).

Most producers, however, operate on larger, more professional scales, although expenses may still vary considerably. On the lower end, a recording of Braj folk music might involve four or five accompanists, each paid about 300–400 rupees ($18–24) for a standard six- or seven-hour shift, and the singer, who might receive around 1,000 rupees; occasionally the entire ensemble might receive as little as 300 rupees. A producer, if present, might himself receive 1,000 rupees or so. A typical studio charges 1,000 rupees for an eight-hour shift, or 250 rupees per hour; some studios charge considerably less for folk-music recordings. Thus, for example, Saraswati Recordings' H. L. Vir lowers his standard rate of 250 rupees to 175 rupees for folk music, saying, "Otherwise these people will record in their own makeshift studios" (interview, January 1991). One or two reel-to-reel spools of tape must also be bought, at around 200 rupees for Indian brands, or 550 for an imported Maxell tape.[22] Many cassettes of folk music can be recorded in a single shift. In many cases, a freelance producer may initiate a project, persuading a cassette company to pay him a flat fee out of which he will pay for the artists and recording fees. For a recording of Braj folk music, a producer might receive 3,500 rupees, expecting to hire a lead singer for 1,000, accompanists for another 1,000, studio time for 600, and a master tape for 200—leaving himself a profit of 700. Designing and printing the cover typically costs around 2 rupees per cassette, with the remaining expense being that of the blank cassettes, which, in the late 1980s, cost from 5 to 7 rupees each, depending on the quality. Except for the larger companies, the labels on the cassettes themselves generally indicate the company, but not the particular item, allowing savings on printing costs. Retailers can thus return unsold cassettes for future use; while this practice is not routine, it does occur, especially, for instance, when releases of seasonal music (e.g., songs of the vernal Holi festival) arrive late due to transportation problems.[23]

Most professional recordings cost somewhat more. Expenses for a typical cassette of *qawwali* (Muslim devotional song) may run around 10,000 rupees, including fees for lyricist, musicians, studio, and producer. The cassette can then be marketed wholesale for 11.50 rupees, and retailed for 15 rupees; in some cases—such as with cassettes designed to be marketed at specific events like temple or shrine festivals—the producer will set up his own stall and dispense with middlemen.[24] A regional-music producer and studio owner in Lucknow estimated average recording expenses per cassette at around 14,000 rupees. Cassettes aimed at broader, pan-regional markets, with more elaborate production may easily cost considerably more. At Concord Records, a mid-level pan-regional producer, average recording and studio costs range around 40,000–55,000 rupees.[25] Expenses for some cassettes—even of regional folk music—may exceed even this. A renowned folk performer like Bhojpuri songstress Sharda Sinha may reportedly demand up to 50,000 rupees for a recording—although this still does not compare with Lata Mangeshkar and Asha Bhosle, who charge 25,000–30,000 rupees *per song* (Rahman 1987:82). Total production costs—especially of film music—may occasionally reach 200,000 rupees for a full-length recording.

On the whole, only the largest companies pay royalties; most musicians receive flat fees. Many artists keenly resent the large profits music producers sometimes make from cassettes for which they were paid a thousand rupees or so; on the other hand, performers are aware of the unreliability of royalty payments in India, where, as we have seen, even HMV failed to pay royalties for a number of years in the 1980s. Furthermore, profits recouped by smaller producers of folk music are often negligible. Performers complain of various kinds of mistreatment by the cassette companies. A prominent *katha* singer of Jodhpur claimed to have been paid with a bad check by Target Records. Another singer told me that he recorded ten songs, was told by the producer that only five were usable, and after being paid for those, later discovered that all ten had been released. A prominent but illiterate Rajasthani *manganhar* was cajoled into endorsing a contract forbidding him to sing any of his repertoire in public.[26]

A cassette of regional folk music made on a minimal budget may turn a profit with sales of only 100 pieces.[27] Most regional producers aim to sell more. Even in the relatively small, though active Konkani (Goa region) market, cassettes generally sell between 1,000 and 5,000 copies; while a few hit Konkani cassettes have sold larger amounts, 3,000 is considered to be a successful figure.[28] T-Series artist-and-repertoire manager Ajit Kohli regards sales of 5,000 cassettes as the minimum for a profitable cassette of regional folk music, while Hindi-language pop or folk releases (which cost more to produce) should sell around 15,000 in order to turn a profit (interview, December 1990). The producer of a tape of *qawwalis* dedicated to a particular saint may do brisk business at the saint's *'urs,* or death (lit. wedding) anniversary celebrated at his shrine, selling 1,000 cassettes for seventeen rupees each. As elsewhere in the world, most releases lose money, with the 30 percent or so that are profitable making up for the losses.[29] Customers for folk-music tapes include not only individual consumers, but also professional "loudspeaker-walas" who provide amplified prerecorded background music for weddings and other festivities. A producer in Lucknow estimates the number of such customers at over 40,000 in Uttar Pradesh, and regards them as a significant market (Harbans Jaiswal, interview October 1989). Moderately successful film scores generally sell more than folk-music titles, averaging around 40,000 pieces (Zuzart 1990:71). A 1989 version of the Punjabi-Pashto ditty "Tutuk tutuk tutiyan," which reportedly sold over half a million copies, illustrates that "rediscovered" folk songs can also enjoy hit status (Bhargava

1991:59). Meanwhile, film hits are reaching ever higher markets, with sales of the late-1980s hits *Lal Dupatta Malmal ka* and *Ram Lakhan* surpassing two million tapes, *Tridev* selling over four million units, and *Mainne Pyar Kiya* exceeding an estimated five million as of January 1991.[30] (For purposes of comparison, we may note that a record selling five million units in the United States in the 1970s would have constituted a significant hit; Michael Jackson's *Thriller,* representing an all-time extreme, has sold over 40 million copies.)

Recording studios vary from the regional producer's converted back room with boarded-up windows, to the spacious and modern film-scoring facilities; Bombay's new Golden Chariot studio is the product of several million rupees' worth of investment (Chopra 1991). Most studios, naturally, lie in between these extremes. Although small and generally lacking such luxuries as air-conditioning, most offer four- or eight-track mixers, a soundproof control room, and imported microphones and recorders (purchased with an import duty which has ranged from 100 to 250 percent over the last ten years). For example, by 1991 most of the six or seven Delhi studios, in natural competition with each other, had acquired Japanese eight-track mixers, digital effects processors, and recorders with half-inch tape capacity. Saraswati Studio's H. L. Vir was pleased to report, in 1991, that despite having had to spend two years' savings on the eight-track equipment, he was now attracting business not only from domestic musicians, but also from NRI (non-resident Indian) groups based in Great Britain, recording for the European market.

By Western standards most Indian studios would be rather threadbare, if acceptable in quality, and have been compared to "a good home studio in the West."[31] Nevertheless, they are quite adequate for most Indian recordings, where orchestration is minimal (especially since the advent of synthesizers) and little overdubbing is necessary. When recording regional folk music, the better studio engineers keep in mind that the recordings are more likely to be played on cheap and often decrepit two-in-ones than on high-fidelity systems; hence, they mix the bass at a low volume, and use two-track stereo with relatively little separation, so that presentable sound may still be obtained on a faulty machine whose playback head is reproducing only one channel properly (H. L. Vir, interview, December 1990). The most aggravating problem for the mid-level studios, as for most Indian small businesses and industries which lack their own generators, is the frequency with which power outages occur, especially in the summer. Musicians and engineers learn to take for granted that much of a given session may be spent sipping tea in a dark, candle-lit, stuffy, suffocatingly hot studio waiting for the neighborhood electricity to return.

Most cassette producers have their own duplicating facilities, which generally consist of more than the theoretical minimum of two Walkmans and a patch cord; indeed, a real-time one-to-four duplicator is regarded as the basic prerequisite—and the single largest expense—for a fledgling company (whether legitimate or pirate). In the late 1980s an unlicensed indigenous manufacturer was surreptitiously marketing one-to-five duplicators for around twelve thousand rupees. Most producers have ended up importing Japanese duplicators, attempting to persuade the state to reduce the standard 165 percent duty to 30 percent, and typically spending forty to fifty thousand rupees for a Sony high-speed one-to-five machine. By 1990 indigenous duplicators were available for this price. Larger producers use Japanese high-speed "loop-bin" systems; these dub master versions onto six or so recorders ("slaves") using large reels ("pancakes") of cassette tape, which are then cut up and inserted in the individual shells ("C-Os"). The typical small producer, however, may have a remarkably modest "factory." For example, I visited the production center of a medium-sized cassette producer in Calcutta, which consisted of two windowless rented rooms near Super Bazaar. Inside, one worker operated a generic, rickety one-to-four duplicator, while another sat at a desk assembling cassettes by hand, placing the small tape spools in the shells and screwing the top of the shell on—each cassette taking about a minute to assemble. An adhesive printed label—either that of the company, or else a fake "TDK" label—would then be applied.

Several larger and medium-sized companies, instead of owning their own duplicating facilities, rely on one of the several firms such as Kapco or Sagarika which specialize in duplication. With their loop-bin systems, these are able to produce large numbers of cassettes in response to sudden demand. Such facilities, indeed, have been among the key factors in the cassette boom (Zuzart 1990:69). The magnetic tape itself may be wholly imported, or may consist of imported polyester tape coated with magnetic oxide in India; T-Series manufactures its tapes with wholly indigenous products (Swamy 1991). While in 1986, roughly 70 percent of the tapes sold in India were of foreign origin, by 1990 only about 18 percent contained foreign components (Chopra 1986:66). At present there are some fifteen tape-coating plants in India, whose production of cassettes, as was noted, is now second only to that of the United States.[32] (As noted above, producers generally use imported reel-to-reel tape for masters.) The state has continued to impose and rescind heavy import duties and excise taxes—alternately regarding the consumer-electronics sector as a taxable luxury or as a dynamic employer and exporter—and in response to pressure exerted by different interest groups. Bourgeois consumers, for instance, want low duties and taxes in order to promote variety and affordability of products; smaller music producers and new companies also oppose such taxes, along with devaluations of the rupee. On the other hand, indigenous manufacturers of magnetic tape and other components want infant-industry protection, while larger established studios and producers support high import duties in order to stifle rival upstarts; such pressure exerted by the recording "mafia," for example, is alleged to have accounted for the 1990 duty hike on imported duplicators.[33]

Another sector to be considered is the manufacture of tape recorders. As mentioned above, the liberalized economic policies of the 1980s led to various foreign "tie-ins" like Orson-Sony, producing cassette players ranging from three hundred rupees to more expensive and elaborate models. Several wholly indigenous manufacturers have also flourished since the mid-1980s. A few of these use only Indian parts, but most import magnetic heads and micromotors; the remaining aspects of production—preparing and assembling the plastic shells and mechanical parts—are well within the capacity of Indian light industry. Indeed, the assembly process is so simple ("a silly, two-minute job")[34] that advocates of infant-industry protection have charged that such rudimentary and large-scale assembly of veritable "kits" are violating the spirit of Indian protectionism against imports. It has been estimated that there are around one hundred such producers in Delhi's Noida district alone, although this may be an exaggeration.[35] Whatever their numbers, these manufacturers and the "tie-ins" were producing some 2.5 million cassette recorders annually by 1987 (Gopal 1987:33).

Promotion and Publicity

In most countries, sales of commercial recordings are heavily dependent on promotion via radio broadcasts. Of course, radio airplay does not directly benefit recording companies, and indeed, companies may go to considerable expense—including payola—to get their product aired. Nevertheless, radio broadcast is generally regarded as the most effective and indispensable means of sales promotion. Radio networks, like other aspects of the large, capital-intensive "old" media, are in many cases largely controlled by corporate conglomerates or state bureaucracies, whose manipulative marketing strategies or official ideologies often leave broadcast content at odds with popular taste. In recent years in India, radio promotion of film music has been supplemented by cable television, video, and television programs such as "Chitrahar." As mentioned above, with the advent of cassettes, many commercial popular musics around the world have come to enjoy considerable sales and popularity without significant broadcast-media promotion. Sri Lankan *baila*, Sundanese *jaipongan,* and Israeli *rock misrahi* are notable examples. In India, music programming on radio, now as in the past, consists primarily of musics other than the non-*filmi* popular and folk musics disseminated on cassettes. Most primary AIR stations broadcast traditional classical and folk musics, while the more popular Vividh Bharati stations play primarily film music. AIR maintains a policy of refusing to broadcast from cassettes, using only vinyl records or reel-to-reel tapes. Moreover, many of the cassette-based modern-style *ghazals, bhajans,* and commercialized folk songs do not fit comfortably into the stylistic categories of AIR programs. As a result, the vast majority of non-

filmi musics disseminated on cassettes have come to flourish without any significant amount of radio airplay, relying instead on grassroots appeal and word-of-mouth popularity. In recent years, AIR has sold time to music producers, during which the latter may promote their own product by playing reel-to-reel masters of the current releases. Larger cassette companies, and several medium-sized ones, have taken advantage of this opportunity by offering regular programs during which they play recent recordings.[36]

The practice of selling air time to music producers outright is one which has been largely discontinued in the West, perhaps because it so clearly exposes the otherwise pervasive myth that the media are responsive primarily to popular demand, rather than corporate manipulation. In countries such as India, sale of air time does generate revenue for the state-run broadcast media; it also may prevent larger corporations from completely shutting medium-sized competitors out of the airwaves. Nevertheless, the majority of music producers, who also generate the majority of releases, cannot afford to purchase radio time and must rely on the intrinsic potential of their recordings to generate sales. Their recordings must and do sell without any form of advertisement.

Larger companies, however, do make significant investments in publicity, mostly in the form of billboards, posters, gala release functions, and promotional tours.

Music-Industry Organizations

The music industry, or parts of it, are represented by a number of organizations, the largest of which are the IPI and the IPRS. The Indian Phonographic Industry (IPI) claims to represent the producers of recorded music. Founded in 1936 by HMV, it is affiliated with the International Federation of Phonogram and Videogram Producers (IFPI), which has members in over sixty countries. IPI membership in India is limited to the largest producers; for many decades it consisted only of HMV and a few subsidiaries; by the late 1980s it had come to include around eight active major companies and a dozen or two smaller ones, together representing around 10 percent of the market; in 1991 its membership expanded to thirty-nine companies. The IPI, together with the IPRS, serves as a spokesman and lobbying organization for the recording companies. Its primary activities in India have been lobbying for reduction of excise duties and for a crackdown on piracy; the IPI was influential in persuading the state to revise the Copyright Act in 1984, and has instigated numerous police raids against pirates since then. At the same time, the organization has excluded most of the numerous smaller producers, who consequently tend to regard it with ambivalence or indifference. The IPI is thus criticized for representing only the interests of the majors,[37] just as the IPRS in general is regarded by many as a tool of the multinationals (Wallis and Malm 1984:49). As we have mentioned, the IPI also excludes T-Series because of piracy allegations.

The Indian Performing Rights Society (IPRS) is an organization complementary to, and in some respects competitive with, the IPI. It holds the mechanical and performing rights of the artists that are registered to it. Affiliated to the Performing Rights Society of London and the Mechanical Copyright Protection Society, the IPRS can also be seen as the Indian counterpart to ASCAP and BMI in the United States. As the supposed representative of artists and composers, the IPRS attempts to collect royalties for its members from recording companies that use their material, as well as from hotels, restaurants, cinema halls (who play taped music before films) and, ideally, performing groups that play such recordings. As of 1990 the IPRS had around six hundred members—mostly individual composers and lyricists involved in film music. In recent years the IPRS has been successful in persuading hotels and restaurants to pay royalties to them; in doing so, the IPRS found itself at loggerheads with the IPI, which unsuccessfully claimed rights to the royalties. Indeed, the IPRS claims substantial royalty dues from the IPI, which professes to be unable to pay.[38]

The expansion and effectiveness of the IPRS, and of legitimate royalty payments in general, are limited by a number of factors. In film music, most composers and lyricists sell their copyrights to the film producers, who then sell them to the music companies. Further, as mentioned above, most singers and musicians receive flat payments for their recordings, rather than royalties. Recording companies marketing Western music are supposed to pay royalties to the IPRS, but even some of the major legitimate companies fail to do so (Chopra, interview, April 1990).[39]

Different sectors of the music industry are also represented by smaller, more specialized organizations, such as the Cassette Manufacturers Association of India, founded in 1990, whose primary activity consists of lobbying for reduction of excise duties. A similar group, the Indian Music Companies Association (IMCA), representing around a dozen larger producers, promotes prosecution of pirate affiliates (e.g., those who print pirate labels) and lobbies for revision of the markedly lax copyright code.[40]

Piracy

Piracy has been the nemesis of the cassette industry from its inception. Indeed, the same factors that fueled the advent of cassettes—particularly, the ease of duplication—have facilitated the emergence of a vast, parasitic, "unorganized" sector of the music industry which has bled many legitimate producers to bankruptcy. Until the late 1980s, pirate producers dominated the industry in terms of turnover and profits, and they continue to claim a significant share of the market.

While piracy thus merits examination in a study such as this one, any detailed investigation of the nature and extent of piracy is inhibited by the natural secrecy of the pirates themselves, and, in many cases, by the misrepresentations and illegal activites of many of the "legitimate" producers as well. Pirate retailers are quite visible on Indian sidewalks, and small-scale pirate duplicators are easy enough to find. They seem to operate especially openly in the bazaars around Muslim shrines and mosques, specializing in sales of *qawwali*—particularly unauthorized copies of Pakistani cassettes which would otherwise be unavailable in India. I found some such producers to be quite frank about their activities. Clearly, however, such entrepreneurs represent only the tip of the pirate iceberg, which is presumed to include several large-scale operations as well as innumerable petty producers; data on the former are particularly hard to acquire.

Piracy in India, as in many other countries, has taken three forms: bootlegging, dubbing of select requested songs for individual customers, and, above all, unauthorized duplication of existing legitimate recordings for mass marketing. Bootlegging, denoting the marketing of an unauthorized recording of a live performance, did not exist in India before the advent of cassettes, although bootleg records of jazz and rock concerts did constitute a minor irritant to Western music industries in the pre-cassette era. Bootleg recordings are naturally most desirable in the case of oral-tradition, improvised genres where each performance is a unique event; several, if not most professionally performed Indian music styles are of this nature, and thus constitute a precondition for a certain market for bootleg recordings.

Since the 1960s, many aficionados of North Indian classical music have avidly collected live recordings of concerts. Before the cassette era, these had to be recorded on reel-to-reel machines, and were generally done so, in varied contexts, with the consent of the performer. With the advent of small cassette recorders, surreptitious concert recording became much more feasible, such that since the early 1970s, Indian audiences have grown accustomed to hearing clicking and clacking forty-five minutes into a concert as those making recordings flip sides. The market for art music is too limited for such tapes to be sold commercially. Nevertheless, from my own personal experience as a student of Hindustani music during this period, I can attest to the zeal with which such recordings were produced, exchanged, and enjoyed by collectors. By the early 1970s, musicians were having concert emcees explicitly request audiences not to tape performances; in doing so, I suspect, the artists were motivated both by the fear that they would be deprived of royalties from commercial sales, as well as from annoyance that music students would copy their compositions and styles without actually becoming disciples. Before the late

1970s, relatively few Indians had cassette players, so that unauthorized concert tapes were generally made by foreign students and upper-class Indian enthusiasts. Nevertheless, I knew a few Indian music students who did collect and study concert tapes, and it was occasionally heard that such-and-such a student had learned primarily from "Ustad TDK Khan." Cassettes have served to make it easier for aspiring musicians to study and imitate the masters, and have enhanced the tendency of young musicians to combine and mix styles other than those of their own teachers, and further, to rely on imitations of top artists rather than material learned personally from their teachers. In recent years I have encountered a few prominent Indian performers who are themselves avid, if belated collectors of concert recordings, and I have occasionally earned their gratitude by sharing some of the fruits of my own (long past) years of fetishistic acquisition.

On the whole, commercial bootleg recordings in India have only proliferated in connection with a few select genres. In the late 1970s, some bootleg tapes of *ghazals* were marketed in India and Pakistan (although it is possible that in some cases the performers may have agreed to be taped in exchange for some remuneration). Far more widespread have been bootleg tapes of *birha,* a folk-music genre which has thrived for several decades in Benares and the surrounding Bhojpuri area. *Birha* consists of a lengthy narrative tale sung to a series of melodic fragments, accompanied by harmonium and barrel drum. While many forms of Indian folk music have declined in the twentieth century, *birha* has flourished, incorporating film melodies and enjoying prodigious grassroots popularity among Bhojpuri speakers. Due to its length, *birha* naturally lends itself poorly to record format, and few of the predominantly rural peasant *birha* fans have ever owned gramophones. The legitimate music industry took relatively little interest in *birha* until the mid-1980s, and the absence of copyright enforcement left bootleggers with a productive and relatively unrestricted market. Hence, Scott Marcus, researching *birha* in the early 1980s, noted that during the frequent public performances of leading groups, various individuals would routinely set up microphones near the singers or, more typically, near the loudspeakers. Within days, commercial cassettes of these performances would appear in the market (Marcus 1989:108).[41] As of 1989, bootleg *birha* recordings were still marketed in Benares; major companies like T-Series were by this time actively producing legitimate *birha* cassettes, but the absence of any legitimate producer based in the Benares area left much of the market to bootleggers. (Curiously, bootlegging does not seem to have flourished in other genres such as Braj *rasiya,* where similar conditions prevailed.) While such bootlegs are parasitic to the legitimate cassette industry, on the whole they can be said to present a more "authentic" sort of product, directly taken from live performance, rather than being ornamented with commercial-style orchestration, or affected by time limitations and production effects that take place in studio recordings; there are undoubtedly some listeners who prefer the straightforward, unpretentious performances marketed on bootleg tapes.

The second form of cassette piracy in India consists of the dubbing of particular songs requested by individuals. This practice is conducted by various cassette retailers, electronics-repair shops, and dubbing kiosks that specialize in the business. Typically, an individual will provide the dubber with a list of eight or more songs—perhaps the hit, title songs from a number of films; the dubber, drawing from his own archive (which may consist primarily of vinyl records), will then duplicate these songs onto a cassette for a given fee—five to ten rupees in the hinterland, and as much as thirty rupees in New Delhi. Dubbing pirates in places like Madras have grown so familiar with the nature of such requests that they have for several years been releasing weekly tapes of compiled hits from various labels and films (Gopal 1987:34). It is essentially impossible to estimate the extent of this form of piracy, especially since the businesses specializing in it often do not advertise themselves as such, unlike, for example, the "cassette bars" throughout Sri Lanka. Many if not most cassette stores engage in such dubbing as a side business. The practice appears to be quite widespread, and there has been little organized attempt to eradicate it.

By far the largest and most influential form of piracy in India is the unauthorized mass duplication and sale of copies of extant commercial recordings. It is this practice which the term *piracy* generally—and henceforth in this work—denotes, and which has the greatest impact on the market and is of greatest concern to legitimate producers.

Cassette piracy in India, as elsewhere, can be said to have predated the legitimate cassette industry itself. In the mid-seventies, before any legitimate music companies were issuing cassettes, pirate (*naqli*) cassettes of Indian and foreign LPs were being marketed for purchase by the growing numbers of Indians who owned cassette players. By the late seventies, when HMV and others began introducing tapes instead of or in addition to LPs, the pirate sector was well-poised to prey on their releases. Still, the pirates required a few years to produce cassettes in such quantities as to dominate the market. In 1980, pirate tapes accounted only for an estimated 10 percent of sales, but by 1986 the pirate share had increased to around 95 percent (Dubashi 1986). In growing so exponentially, the pirates were aided by a number of factors. First of all, the demand for prerecorded music cassettes has in many cases been far in excess of supply, and continues to be so. I have noted above that HMV was unable, for various reasons, to issue sufficient numbers of its past film-music hits, or even of its contemporary releases. The vast and growing demand for HMV's catalog was thus met by the pirates, who enjoyed a virtual monopoly in the realm of film-music reissues. Even today, the frequent inability of producers to meet the sudden demand for hit recordings provides pirates with their best business opportunities. An example in the late 1980s was the comedy cassette hit *Sirippu Siripy,* produced by Sampath Recordings, whose personnel consisted of a college student, his wife, and a friend. As the cassette became an unexpected hit, the producers found themselves quite unable to meet the demand for five hundred cassettes daily on their home duplicating setup; pirates, however, quickly met the demand, garnering an estimated 250,000 rupees in profits.[42]

The second set of factors aiding piracy involves the natural economic advantages of illicit duplication. Pirate duplicators do not pay any recording or production costs, whether in the form of studio fees, promotion costs, or payments to artists. Nor need they waste resources on experimentation with new artists and repertoire, or unsuccessful recordings; rather, they may simply issue releases only of those recordings which are proving to be popular or can be assured to be so. Since all aspects of pirate production are surreptitious, pirates need not pay sales tax, and they avoid paying excise duties (e.g., for blank tape) by acquiring raw materials on the black market; unlicensed producers and importers of blank tape are naturally happy to find ways to sell their products to pirates without having to pay taxes themselves.

Until the mid-1980s, government regulations and taxes on the legitimate producers were so onerous as to virtually guarantee a huge pirate sector. Licensing procedures for new music companies involved aggravating red tape and crippling restrictions, especially for the larger corporations who were generally discriminated against in favor of small-scale business; companies were expected to export 75 percent of their product, while excise duties of 26 percent were levied on sales to dealers. A 15 percent sales tax, the excise duty, other local taxes, and standard 13 percent royalty to the copyright holder (in the case of film music) gave pirates roughly a 55 percent advantage in pricing.[43] For their part, the major cassette producers during this period myopically exacerbated the problem by overpricing their cassettes. The desire to avoid taxes is also believed to have encouraged many supposedly legitimate producers to collaborate with pirates, or to engage in piracy themselves.

Further, it may be said that many Indian consumers, especially in the early years of the cassette industry, were unaware of the disadvantages of buying a pirate cassette whose fidelity and durability were markedly inferior to that of the original (if it existed). Indian studios before the 1970s generally had rather inferior recording equipment, so that Indians were accustomed to hearing records with distorted timbres and did not always find the fidelity of pirate cassettes to be intolerably worse. One might also note that many cassette players in use have been and continue to be so mediocre, or in such poor condition, that the difference in sound quality between a crude pirate tape and a legitimate one is often inconsiderable. (Very few consumers clean or demagnetize their tape heads.)

The final factor abetting piracy was the virtually complete absence of legal penalties before 1984. As in many countries, India's copyright act dated from the colonial, pre-cassette period, when piracy was virtually nonexistent. While the cassette boom occurred fairly rapidly, the updating of copyright law took several years, especially with the initial indifference of the state to what it regarded as a frivolous, luxury sector of the consumer market. As a result, by the mid-1980s, as noted, pirates allegedly accounted for some 95 percent of the prerecorded-music market. All the major music producers registered losses during this period, and many smaller legitimate producers appear to have been forced out of the market—or induced into piracy—shortly after entering.

By this time recording companies and artists themselves were clamoring for reform. Classical and popular musicians took out full-page advertisements in leading newspapers demanding government action, and the large recording companies, especially via an antipiracy cell of the IPI, actively lobbied for reform. Their demands were: (1) abolition of the requirement that 75 percent of domestic production be exported; (2) abolition of the 26.75 percent excise duty; (3) amendment of the Copyright Act to enable it to contend with cassette piracy; and (4) vigorous state enforcement of the act.[44] Eventually the federal government realized that it was losing considerable tax revenues due to piracy, and undertook most of the requested reforms. By March 1984 the excise duty was ended, and a few months later the export requirement was scrapped. Most importantly, in October of that year a revised Copyright Act was promulgated, containing special provisions regarding tape piracy. It included the requirement that every commercial cassette must list the name and address of the producer and copyright owner, and the publication date of the product. Pirates could henceforth be imprisoned for up to six months and fined up to fifty thousand rupees, while the offense was declared non-bailable. While the police have been generally uninterested in conducting raids on their own initiative, they have frequently arrested pirate retailers and producers in tandem with IPI officials or industry representatives. In the late 1980s the International Federation of Phonograph Industries gave the IPI 4.3 million rupees to fight piracy.[45]

Recording companies, due to the reduced excise tax and the realization that they had been pricing themselves out of the market, lowered their prices significantly. Konkani cassettes previously sold at fifty rupees, for example, were reduced to twenty-five to thirty rupees.[46] Since this period, many consumers, increasingly aware of the disadvantages of buying inferior pirate tapes, have tended to opt for legitimate cassettes which, if available, are frequently only two or three rupees more expensive. Further, as we shall see in the next chapter, MIL and HMV deliberately promoted high-fidelity *ghazal* recordings aimed at middle-class consumers, who would avoid inferior pirate cassettes. As a result of these factors, together with increased police enforcement, piracy, although still open and widespread, has diminished considerably, at least in relation to the market as a whole. As usual, there are no precise figures as to its current extent, and I was given widely varying estimates by different informants in the music industry. A 1991 market survey commissioned by the IPI estimated that piracy accounted for about 40 percent of the domestic market.[47] On the basis of my own impressions of retail merchandise, I would regard this figure as quite credible, if slightly on the high side.

Among Indian music cassettes marketed abroad, pirates appear to outnumber legitimate cassettes; the leading producers appear to be the Apple and Double Apple labels from Singapore, the Australian H & R, and the Dubai-based Sahara (which, unlike the others, proudly lists its address on its covers). These retail in the West for as little as $1.25. Singapore piracy is abetted by the difficulty legitimate foreign wholesalers have in acquiring distribution rights for Indian-made cassettes.[48] Retailers say their customers prefer the pirate versions of cassettes because the tape is better quality (usually Sony or Maxell) than that used in legitimate Indian cassettes.

Pirate cassettes themselves are marketed in a variety of guises. Most easily recognizable, of course, are those whose inlay labels are either handwritten or else black-and-white photocopies of the original labels; such cassettes clearly make no pretense of being legitimate. More often, new inlay cards are photocopied or cheaply printed, whether as counterfeit versions of the originals, or bearing new designs. Such labels may bear either the logo of some known illegitimate producer (such as Midas), or perhaps of a genuine producer. Most common in the latter category are pirates featuring the T-Series logo, or a cheap reproduction thereof. As I have noted, T-Series has been widely accused of mass piracy, especially in its early years; at the same time, there is no doubt that many, and possibly most or even all, of the cheap pirate cassettes with crude T-Series logos that currently abound are not T-Series products in any sense, but instead are produced by pirates who apply the prestigious logo. The routine use of this logo as a mark of quality may explain the presence of "T-Series" pirate versions of recordings originally issued by HMV, MIL, or other companies, rather than by T-Series itself.

As buyers grow increasingly discriminating, pirates in some cases go to greater lengths to disguise the illegitimacy of their product. H. L. Vir, owner of Saraswati, a small Delhi-based company, showed me counterfeit versions of his more successful Garhwali folk-music tapes, whose inlay cards and adhesive labels could only be distinguished from the originals when compared side-by-side; the fake inlay cards, as well as others bearing logos of fictitious companies (e.g., Gulshan) were allegedly produced in nearby Lajpat Rai Market, the center of Delhi's cassette and consumer-electronics businesses. In general, however, pirates using fake inlay cards do not restrict themselves to the logo of the original copyright owner; in 1990, *Playback* magazine reported, for instance, that the hit soundtrack for *Mainne Pyar Kiya* was being marketed under twenty-three different labels by pirates, who were garnering 70 percent of the cassette's sales.[49] Several cassette-industry personnel assured me that many licensed, legitimate cassette companies are mere fronts for pirate operations.

Piracy seems to affect certain genres and certain regions more than others. Now as before, most pirate cassettes consist of film music, whether contemporary hits or classics of the past. *Ghazals* and successful folk-music recordings, however, are also widely sold in pirate form. To some extent, piracy appears to be more rampant in regions where there are no local producers. For example, there are some five or six small, legitimate producers in the city of Jaipur, producing and marketing regional folk music for local consumption. Three representatives of these firms assured me that piracy was no longer a significant problem for them, and I saw no pirate versions of their cassettes in the local bazaars. Pirate cassettes were more evident in Jodhpur, where there are no local mass producers to goad police into enforcement. Similarly, cassette piracy appears to be rampant in Garhwal, whose commercial music is produced primarily in Delhi by labels like Saraswati. Saraswati's Vir manages to eke out profits from his Garhwali tapes in spite of piracy, and feels powerless to oppose it, saying, "When justice takes so long and costs so much, it's not worth it."

Piracy is certainly not limited to regions lacking local producers. In Calcutta's Chandni Chowk, the owner of Sound Recording, a producer of Bengali music tapes, pointed out that cheap pirate versions of his own cassettes were marketed in the store adjacent to his own shop. Another producer, when asked why he could not organize police raids on the nearby sidewalk vendors selling pirate versions of his product, lamented, "Those retailers have their own arrangement which the police, which I won't go into." Even when the police are cooperative, small producers find the expense and difficulty of attempting to prosecute offenders to be prohibitive. Another Calcutta producer related,

> Sometimes the police at Lal Bazar even raid the pirates and seize the cassettes at our request, but then there is some bribery, some collusion, and by the time the tapes are brought to court the babu who sits and supposedly watches over all the various seized material has been bribed for 500 Rs. to pass a magnet over the tapes so that they are blank.

Most producers I interviewed seemed to accept piracy as an inevitable business loss which would persist due to the lower expenses and retail prices of the pirate competitors. Pirates also continue to enjoy an absolute monopoly in fields where there are no legitimate producers. The largest such repertoire is Western pop music. HMV, Magnasound, and Bremen (aside from CBS-India) have acquired rights to release some international product,[50] but most Western popular-music hits are not legitimately marketed by any producer in India. As a result, middle-class music stores openly sell pirate cassettes of Van Halen, Boney M, and other contemporary favorites.

Piracy is not regarded as an unmitigated evil in India, and it can be said to have had certain beneficial effects, at least in the short-term perspective. In cases where legitimate recordings (e.g., of Western pop, or classic film songs) are unavailable, pirate cassettes naturally meet consumer demand that would otherwise go unfulfilled. Pirate recordings of Western pop helped stimulate demand for such music, facilitating the success of legitimate companies like Magnasound which subsequently entered the field (Swamy 1991). Pirates have helped keep records financially remunerative, as pirate producers prefer records to cassettes for use as masters. Pirates also played a role in inducing legitimate producers to lower their prices. Moreover, as we have seen, bootleg cassettes provide a more authentic reproduction of live performance aesthetics than do legitimate studio-produced tapes. Further, in some cases, the pirate cassettes have actually been superior in tape quality to legitimate originals. Many pirate versions of Goanese music tapes are produced in the Gulf countries on tapes which are considerably better, in terms of fidelity and durability, to the Indian-made originals. Such tapes are preferred by Goanese workers in the Gulf states, as well as consumers in Goa itself, who purchase them locally.[51]

Similarly, the musicians' perspective on piracy may naturally be different from that of the producer. In most cases, artists are paid flat fees rather than royalties on sales, and thus do not suffer directly from piracy. More than one performer has told me that he does not mind seeing pirate versions of his recordings, and a singer of classical and light-classical music featured on a few cassettes told me she would be honored to be pirated. *Ghazal* singer and T-Series recording artist Pamela Singh aptly observed:

> Piracy has its advantages and disadvantages for the artist. The advantage is that you reach out to more people. The disadvantage is that the quality is not good; people who have not really heard you [i.e., in person] might think that your quality is substandard. But really, the cassettes only help you get more concerts. They give you more popularity, but in terms of money, I don't think anyone makes recordings with the royalties in mind, because it's very hard to keep track of sales. Even the big stars make more from concerts than from cassette sales. But you can't have concerts without cassettes, because first people have to know about you. (Interview, October 1989)

Finally, one could advance a nationalistic argument in favor of T-Series' alleged piracy of EMI recordings. Western multinationals, including EMI, have historically perpetrated all manner of unethical activities in order to achieve and maintain monopolies in the developing world. Coca-Cola, for example, has been widely accused of such tactics as buying out bottle supplies, and temporarily lowering prices well below cost in order to bankrupt local competitors in countries like Mexico. Coca-Cola itself is said to have suffered from similar cutthroat practices by the largest Indian competitor,

Thums-Up, and an opponent of the Coca-colonization of the third world might well sympathize with such forms of resistance, including T-Series' alleged early malpractices, which helped destroy the monopoly enjoyed by the multinational EMI.

Such considerations notwithstanding, the negative effects of piracy seem to far outweigh its benefits. Piracy naturally deprives income from artists who have royalty contracts with producers, and can be said to lower flat payments as well. Performers as well as legitimate labels acquire bad images from consumer dissatisfaction with counterfeit, low-quality tapes using their names. The state is deprived of revenues, and, above all, the legitimate producers suffer, often to the point of bankruptcy. The large corporations sustain the largest losses, but they are generally able to absorb them, while smaller producers are occasionally put out of business altogether.

The piracy network has in some situations worked in collaboration with the legitimate sector. I have mentioned the occasional symbiotic arrangements between, for example, sellers and buyers of Indian-made or imported tape who wish to avoid taxes. Occasionally, more direct forms of collaboration occur, in which legitimate producers who are unable to meet demand for a runaway hit persuade the larger pirate duplicators to raise their wholesale prices and pay a royalty to the producer. HMV is alleged to have made such a deal with pirates when it found itself unable to meet demand for its film hit *Mainne pyar kiya,* which as of July 1990 was estimated to have sold ten million copies (legitimate and pirate). Due to HMV's inability to produce more than three million cassettes, it is reported to have brokered an arrangement with pirates, under which the latter would increase their price from eleven to thirteen rupees, and pay HMV half a rupee in exchange for using the HMV label. One cannot but wonder how such deals were negotiated, given the obvious absence of legal controls and supervision. Other companies, including T-Series, are said to have made similar deals with pirates.[52] Producers are widely believed to collude with pirates in production and marketing, so that they can minimize their taxes and royalties by hiding the extent of their sales (Chopra 1988a).

Collaborations such as that alleged between HMV and pirate producers illustrate that the vast underground pirate duplication network could occasionally serve the interests of both the producers and consumers. Interestingly, the reports also imply that much of the so-called "unorganized" (i.e., pirate) sector is in fact quite organized, and may well share many features with the legitimate cassette sector. In particular, the pirate network, like its legal counterpart, appears to comprise, on the one hand, innumerable petty duplicators marketing regional music for local audiences, and on the other hand, large-scale corporate-like enterprises specializing in pan-regional film music and commanding such vast resources, distribution networks, and dominance of the field that they can occasionally collaborate with HMV and other legitimate producers. Pirates raided by police in spring 1991 included some substantial operations, such as Bombay's "Push and Rush" and "Dash and Dip" labels, whose confiscated machinery and product were worth millions of rupees.[53] Street vendors of pirate cassettes in Bombay have even established their own trade association, the Maharasthra Cassette Dealers Sena. This association is alleged to have the support of the Hindu Shiv Sena, which supposedly collects fees of eight thousand rupees in exchange for protection from police raids.[54]

Compact Discs

The desire to circumvent piracy has been one of the primary incentives for the development of compact-disc technology in India. In the developed countries of the West, CDs have all but replaced vinyl discs, such that some retail stores, such as certain branches of the United States–based Tower Records, no longer even sell records. In India, a prerecorded compact disc costs around 225 rupees, or twelve times as much as a cassette, and as much as many Indians earn in a month of labor. CD players themselves cost about 5,000 Rs., which would constitute a small fortune for most Indians. As a result, CDs naturally remain confined largely to the upper classes. Nevertheless, by 1991 they have come to merit more than a footnote in a study such as this one. For the music producers, the growth of the CD market is seen as a possible weapon against piracy, as the CDs cannot be duplicated (onto other CDs). By mid-1990, roughly 750 titles were already released on CD, by EMI, T-Series, MIL, and Weston. While these CDs were manufactured abroad, in early 1991 the government sanctioned the construction of four CD-manufacturing plants; Indian-made CDs are projected to cost around 150 rupees when they appear on the market (Swamy 1991). Foreign companies (Ocora, Sonodisk, Nimbus, Rykodisc, Oriental, India Archive, and others) have also been producing CDs of Indian music for NRI audiences.[55] Naturally, these have consisted largely of musics enjoyed by upper-class Indian and interested Western listeners— classical music, *bhajans, ghazals,* and sophisticated Hindi pop.

5

Cassettes and the Modern *Ghazal*

The Traditional *Ghazal*

The preceding chapter's overview of the contemporary North Indian music industry, and the role of cassettes therein, has stressed the features which distinguish the contemporary scene from the pre-cassette era. Foremost among these are the replacement of records by cassettes, the end of film-music dominance, the decentralization and diversification of ownership and control of the mass media, and the subsequent rise of a large number and variety of commercially marketed regional and pan-regional musics aimed at heterogeneous audiences. As may be expected, these changes did not occur overnight. While cassettes and players began appearing and having some limited impact in India in the early 1970s, it was not until around 1983–84 that the hundreds of small regional producers emerged and that the music industry assumed its present decentralized form.

We may regard the years 1977–82 as a sort of transitional period, in terms of both the nature of the music industry and the genres and styles it disseminated. The distinctness of this period, indeed, stands out quite clearly in retrospect, for it was during these years that commercial cassettes definitively replaced vinyl discs, and that the dominance of HMV, and of the cinematic playback singers and music directors, was shattered by the unprecedented emergence of a non-*filmi* mass commercial genre—namely, the modern pop *ghazal*. These developments were so closely related that it is in many respects difficult to distinguish cause from effect. The rise of the commercial *ghazal* merits discussion as the major musical development during this period, and as a concomitant of the cassette boom. At the same time, the *ghazal* vogue was equally conditioned by other factors (particularly the burgeoning of a consumerist bourgeoisie) which, though not unrelated to the advent of cassettes, have their own independent significance and origins. A thorough and holistic discussion of the development of the modern *ghazal* would thus involve some digression from the theme of this volume, and the interested reader may wish to consult other publications which explore the *ghazal*'s musical evolution in more detail (especially Manuel 1988a). Nevertheless, the contemporary *ghazal* played such a crucial role in the advent of cassettes that its emergence, even if overdetermined by other factors as well, must be given some attention here.

Properly speaking, *ghazal* denotes a poetic genre, though in India and else-where the term commonly also implies the musical form in which it is rendered. As a lyric genre, it originated in classical Arabic poetry, codified as a set of rhymed couplets in the form *aa ba ca da* etc., employing a double end rhyme (*radif* and *qafiya*) and set to strict poetic meters based on Arabic prosody (whose rules are observed faithfully even by illiterate poets). The couplets are united only by meter and rhyme, rather than by content; thus, each couplet is intended to constitute a discrete entity—like a pearl in a necklace, or a flower in a garland, to use familiar metaphors. While never achieving great significance in Arabic literature, *ghazal* was adopted and cultivated with great zeal by the Persians, and became the single most important genre of Persian literature. Reaching a classical zenith in the works of Sadi (d. 1292) and Hafiz (d. 1390), the Persian *ghazal* acquired formal and aesthetic characteristics which persist to this day in the *ghazal* as cultivated in other languages as well. These features include the use of a set of closely related themes: unrequited love, mystical devotion, philosophical rumination, ridicule of religious ortho-doxy, symbolic celebration of madness and intoxication, and a sort of self-abnegating, sometimes masochistic immersion in the pangs of longing and frustration. The reliance on these set themes, together with the usage of a set of standardized symbols and metaphors, compensates for the fragmentary nature of the *ghazal* as a poem and facilitates the epigrammatic condensation for which, among other qualities, individual couplets are prized.

The *ghazal,* with its extended end rhymes, constant meter, romantic themes, and often flowery diction, lends itself well to musical rendering, and has thrived, in various forms, as a musical genre in Turkey, Iran, Central Asia, and, last but not least, India. The persistence of its form, themes, and images contrasts with the remarkable variety of musical styles in which it has been and continues to be rendered. Indeed, it is this protean versatility which has enabled the *ghazal* to adapt to changing audiences and patronage forms and enjoy such extraordinary popularity in North India today.

While the Persian *ghazal* enjoyed a long and distinguished career in India, by the eighteenth century it was gradually giving way to the Urdu *ghazal,* which adhered largely to the form, imagery, and content of its ancestor. The Urdu *ghazal* continues to enjoy prodigious popularity in North India and Pakistan—a popularity, indeed, incomparably greater than that of any poetic form in the West. Although Urdu is, on the whole, a product of Indo-Muslim culture, the *ghazal* has traditionally been enjoyed and cultivated by Hindus as well.

Evidence suggests that the *ghazal* as a musical genre has thrived for several centuries in North India. *Ghazal* could be chanted in a semi-melodic *tarannum* style by poets at poetry readings, or it could be used as a text for Muslim devotional *qawwali* performed by professonal groups in shrines. Most commonly and importantly, however, *ghazal* was performed by courtesans and other trained vocalists as a genteel light-classical music style, which stressed interpretive melodic improvisation—*bol banao*—on the nonrhyming, first line of each couplet. Classical *rags* (modes) and accompanying instruments (*tabla* drum-pair, *sarangi* fiddle) were used, and a sophisticated aesthetic developed which evaluated *ghazal* songs on the basis of the poetry itself, the precomposed tune used for refrains (especially of the rhyming lines), and, above all, the singer's skillful, improvised *bol banao*.

Ghazal as a musical genre became particularly popular in the nineteenth century, when a proto-capitalist, incipient bourgeoisie began to replace the declining feudal, Mughal nobility as patrons of the fine arts. In the first half of the twentieth century, the light-classical *ghazal* continued to enjoy popular appeal among music aficionados and middle-class enthusiasts, although it was to some extent stigmatized by its association with the declining courtesan culture. On the whole, however, the light-classical *ghazal* successfully effected the transition from court and courtesan salon to the public concert hall, and from feudal to bourgeois patronage. This transition was personified in the career of the mid-century's most prominent singer, who commenced as courtesan Akhtari Bai, and then withdrew from singing for several years after marrying a respected barrister, to be reincarnated in her later years as Begum Akhtar (d. 1974), a singer of the concert-hall rather than the *mujra* (private courtesan performance).[1]

The Rise and Fall of the Film *Ghazal*

The *ghazal*'s popularity was aided by the advent of the recording industry in India in 1901. From the very start, *ghazals* constituted a significant part—and perhaps a plurality—of commercial recordings, largely because *ghazal* was the most popular music genre in Urdu, the lingua franca of North India. The recording industry naturally promoted *ghazal* as a one of the few genres with a pan-regional, potentially mass common-denominator market, unlike, for example, classical music or regional folk styles. With the advent of sound cinema, *ghazals* came to account for a large portion of the music of Hindi cinema, especially in the early decades. In the process of being transformed into a commercial popular music with mass appeal, however, the film *ghazal* underwent predictable changes which brought it stylistically in line with mainstream film music as a whole. Thus the improvisatory *bol banao* was eliminated, so that the genre became, essentially, a precomposed song, accompanied, like most film music, by varied ensembles of Western and Indian instruments. Improvised drum passages (*laggi*) traditionally rendered be-

tween couplets were replaced by precomposed ensemble instrumental interludes (referred to as "music" by native musicians). The film *ghazal,* as popularized by Talat Mahmood, Lata Mangeshkar, and others, retained some of the
exotic and romantic associations of the courtesan world and of Urdu verse in
general, while aiming at a contemporary and less sophisticated audience. The
Urdu lyrics cohered well with the diction of so-called Hindi films, most of
which were in fact in Urdu, in accordance with that language's "sweet" and
romantic ethos, as opposed to standard Hindi, which is perceived as a more
utilitarian tongue. Meanwhile, throughout the 1960s, the light-classical
ghazal, particularly as sung by Begum Akhtar, continued to enjoy a stable, if
limited degree of popularity among connoisseurs of classical music and Urdu
poetry.

By the early 1970s the film *ghazal,* although still relatively common, was
undergoing a marked decline. Aside from the retirement of Talat Mahmood in
1970, a primary factor was the reorientation of film music in general, toward
fast, rhythmic songs influenced by Western rock and disco, in place of the
traditional melodic, sentimental styles like *ghazal.* Western influence on the
tastes of urban middle-class youth was one factor in this development, but
critics, composers, and film producers generally agree that a more significant
cause was the increasing trend toward action-oriented *masala* (lit., spice)
films, rather than sentimental melodramas and "costume-drama" mythologicals. (In the mid-1980s, this trend itself appears to have been intensified by
the spread of video among the upper and middle classes, whose declining
cinema-attendance rates have obliged producers to orient films more toward
the lower- and lower-middle-class males who now predominate in movie theaters, prefer action and adventure films, and who often regard *ghazal* as elitist, dull, and overrefined.) Melodic, romantic song interludes are seen as less
suitable for the *masala* thrillers, which stress fisticuffs, car chases, and rapes
instead of leisurely love triangles (Rahman 1987:82). Although the *ghazal*'s
versatile formal structure could conceivably have been adapted even to disco
styles, the genre has remained too closely associated with its traditional subject matter of broken hearts, weepy lovers, and the stylized refinement of
Urdu culture in general.[2]

The other development contributing to the gradual eclipse of the *ghazal*—
in both its film and light-classical styles—has been the marked decline of the
Urdu language in India. Through the early decades of the twentieth century,
Urdu had been the primary literary language and lingua franca of North India.
Muslim rule and its legacy had promoted the use of Urdu throughout the
North, and the language had a much richer literary tradition (especially in the
form of *ghazal*) than did *khari boli* Hindi, the Meerut-Delhi dialect which
later became the mainstream lingua franca in the North. Hence educated Hin-
dus as well as Muslims had for generations avidly cultivated Urdu and even
Persian. The diction of commercial Bombay films, as we have noted, was

generally closer to Urdu than Hindi, and the language of *ghazal* was understood by most educated North Indians. With Independence in 1947, the situation began to change. Hindu-Muslim relations were embittered by the violence accompanying Partition and the concrete antagonism between India and the new nation of Pakistan. The Indian government came to be dominated by Hindus, with Muslims now constituting only 11 percent of India's population, rather than some 30 percent, as before Partition. The rising Indian bourgeoisie, furthermore, was even more predominantly Hindu (and, eventually, Sikh), so that Muslim culture in general, although retained as quaint and romantic in film music and dialogues, was seen as backward and suspect. With Hindi chosen as the national language, the Indian government largely defunded Urdu education, such that even most Muslim schoolchildren have failed to learn Urdu properly.

In public discourse and, to some extent, common speech, Sanskrit-derived Hindi words have increasingly come to replace Perso-Arabic Urdu ones, while common Urdu words, more than ever before, come to be mispronounced (i.e., by Urdu standards) with Hindi phonemes (e.g., *jauk* for *zauq*). Except for in special Urdu broadcasts, Urdu vocabulary (along with English loan words) has been systematically purged from national radio and television programs; the Urdu words have been replaced by obscure Sanskrit-derived ones, resulting in an artificial diction which is often unintelligible to many educated as well as uneducated Hindi speakers, not to mention Urdu speakers. The Sanskritized newspeak, however, has been promoted partially in order to communicate to educated South Indians, whose languages share many Sanskrit loan words. Meanwhile, Urdu has been promoted as the national language of Pakistan, but has been a first language only for the immigrant (*muhajir*) community, which has never constituted more than 10 percent of the population. Most other Pakistanis favor their native tongues (Punjabi, Sindhi, Baluchi, Pashto, etc.) and in some cases tend to resent the use of Urdu. Meanwhile, in Bengali-speaking Bangladesh (formerly East Pakistan), Urdu has practically disappeared, except in the relatively powerless Bihari community.

The result of these developments has been the marked decline of Urdu in its traditional homeland of Uttar Pradesh and Bihar, and its partial replacement by some form of Hindi as the lingua franca of North India. The decline of the *ghazal*, in both its commercial film and light-classical varieties, was an inevitable concomitant. Nevertheless, by the mid-1970s, certain broad social, aesthetic, and technological developments had emerged which paved the way for the revival of a modernized form of the *ghazal*. As we have noted, the action-oriented *masala* films, while satisfying cinema audiences, took film music in a direction contrary to the tastes of the many middle-class listeners, who continued to prefer tuneful, sentimental crooning to the disco-influenced modern film music. One may hypothesize that as the consumerist urban bourgeoisie grew in strength, numbers, and self-identity, a demand arose for a music which reflected its own self-image and aesthetic values. Such a music would have to be more genteel than the raucous and lowest-common-denominator film music, and yet it needed to be simpler and more accessible than classical music, constituting, in Birmingham School terms, a "rearticulation" of the elite semiclassical *ghazal*. As more middle-class consumers were able to afford phonographs, the potential began to emerge for a new pan-regional popular music which could be, for the first time, independent of films. A modernized, simplified pop *ghazal* was the ideal genre for such an audience, and it correspondingly began to flourish as such around 1977. Thus, one *ghazal* singer observed:

> The main reason for the current popularity of ghazal is the downfall of film music. A lot of people felt they didn't get satisfaction from film music, and classical music was too difficult to understand, so the ghazal was in between, especially the easy ghazals. (Pamela Singh, interview, October 1989)

In order to achieve a genuinely mass audience, however, it required a mass medium which was cheaper and more accessible than records, and yet still distinct from cinema. The spread of cassette players among the upper and middle classes in the late 1970s provided the essential catalyst for the flowering of the modern *ghazal* as the first pan-regional commercial genre to challenge the dominance of film music and its coterie of stars and producers.

The Modern *Ghazal*

The modern *ghazal* emerged in the mid-1970s with the rise of two Pakistani singers, Mehdi Hasan and, subsequently, Ghulam Ali. Both had some training in classical music; Hasan had also sung for Pakistani commercial films. Both possessed sweet, supple voices, and generally selected verses, whether classical or contemporary, which critics regarded as tasteful and effective song texts. Both singers recorded *ghazals* for commercial films, in a style not remarkably distinct from that of Mahmood and earlier film *ghazals*—avoiding improvisation, and using accompanying ensemble with Western and Indian instruments. On the whole, however, their popularity, especially with the new middle-class audience, rested on their live performance style, wherein, accompanied by harmonium and *tabla,* they rendered *ghazals* in a leisurely, relaxed style, crooning softly into the microphone, and indulging in langorous improvised *bol banao* on the non-rhyming lines. Classical musicians have tended to regard these improvisations as somewhat pedestrian, although the singers' courtly stage demeanor, sparse accompaniment, use of Urdu lyrics, and genteel (if tame) *bol banao* identified their music, for their growing bourgeois audience, as sharing some of the "serious" sophistication of art music, while remaining much more accessible.

Objective factors limited the initial popularity of Hasan, Ghulam Ali, and the new style of *ghazal* they had fashioned. As Pakistanis, they toured India infrequently, and performances in their own country were discouraged by heavy entertainment taxes imposed by Zia ul-Haq's orthodox Islamic regime. While they were thus largely dependent on the mass media, they received relatively little radio airplay, and the sale of their records was naturally limited by the continuing relative paucity of phonographs in the subcontinent. Indeed, it was only with the advent of cassettes that they achieved truly mass popularity.

By the late 1970s, as we have noted, cassettes and tape players had started to become commonplace in India and Pakistan. During this period, they were owned primarily by members of the upper and middle classes, and by emigrant Gulf workers. Due to Pakistan's relaxed import restrictions and higher percentage of guest workers, cassettes appear to have spread earlier in that country than in India, and by 1977, legitimate and pirate tapes of Mehdi Hasan, Ghulam Ali, and older singers like Farida Khanum and Iqbal Bano abounded in bazaars, by far outselling commercial vinyl records. The modern *ghazal,* however, was destined to achieve a much vaster audience in India, but in order to do so, it had to be further simplified, and it required expanded dissemination on cassettes.

The recording industry in India at this time continued to be dominated by film music, and by HMV, with some inroads being made by Polydor MIL. Film music itself, however, was increasingly regarded as being in a state of decline (Rahman 1987:82), because of the reorientation toward action films as well as curbs on cinema attendance due to entertainment taxes and competition from video. While music producers had started releasing commercial cassettes, piracy, especially of film music, had become a serious problem. Prescient executives in both HMV and MIL saw in the modern *ghazal* potential for a prodigious and largely untapped consumer market. Indeed, it is clear that the growing cassette industry, rather than passively responding to the rise of *ghazal,* played an active role in its popularization. The switch from record to cassette format was the first and perhaps most influential step, allowing cassettes and the *ghazal* to grow hand-in-hand, reinforcing each other as they spread; by 1982, annual sales of *ghazal* recordings were five times larger than in pre-cassette years (ur-Rahman 1982:122).

Moreover, cassette producers in the companies most closely associated with *ghazal*—namely HMV and MIL—saw in *ghazal* a means of overcoming piracy. Most pirate cassettes, as mentioned, consisted of film music dubbed on low-fidelity, low-durability cassettes aimed primarily at lower-middle-class consumers. Film-music audiences were already accustomed to hearing such songs on overloaded theater or sidewalk speakers, and the presence of distortion even on vinyl records leads one to suspect that it may actually be appreciated by Indian listeners.[3] The modern *ghazal,* however, was far less raucous in style and timbre; perhaps its single most distinctive characteristic, especially as the genre coalesced, was its silky, smooth, and nonpercussive timbres, achieved primarily by a reliance on soft, individual stringed instruments (especially *santur, surmandal,* and guitar)[4] rather than the standard screeching violins and rowdy congas and bongos of film music. The use of these timbres in the modern *ghazal,* indeed, has become so routine that it generally enables one to identify the genre immediately upon hearing it, without waiting to ascertain its identity from the diction and rhyme scheme. Cheap pirate cassettes were largely unable to do justice to the modern *ghazal's* distinctive timbre, and legitimate cassette producers (again, largely HMV and MIL) realized that the *ghazal* thus provided an opportunity to circumvent piracy, especially since the genre was oriented primarily toward upper- and middle-class listeners who were likely to own presentable playback systems. Thus, MIL's Vijay Lazarus remarked in 1986:

> We were successful in creating a new repertoire line, first the ghazal and then the bhajan—where the buyer is much more discriminating and looks for quality and legitimacy. Hence, we were able to totally take over the top end of the market not only from the pirates but also from our legitimate competitors.[5]

The further popularization of the *ghazal,* however, required that the genre become simpler and more accessible to the predominantly Hindu (and Sikh) bourgeoisie. Thus, while Mehdi Hasan and Ghulam Ali continued to enjoy renown, HMV and MIL (which by this time were rapidly switching to cassette format) turned to the promotion of a more populist, less demanding *ghazal* as sung by a new coterie of vocalists, notably Anup Jalota, Pankaj Udhas, and the duo of Jagjit and Chitra Singh (none of whom, it may be noted, is Muslim). In the hands of these artists, and especially Jagjit Singh, the modern *ghazal* assumed its definitive shape and style. This style has much in common with that of Mehdi Hasan and Ghulam Ali, and, to a lesser extent, with the earlier light-classical and film styles. Nevertheless, it is possible to speak of an archetypical, characteristic modern *ghazal* style—perhaps best exemplified by the music of Jagjit and Chitra Singh—distinguished by its instrumentation, slow tempi, diluted Urdu poetry, general absence of improvisation, simple melodies (cf. the aforementioned "nursery-rhyme" aesthetic) and an overall relaxed, epicurean sort of ambience.

"Pop" Goes the *Ghazal*

The modern *ghazal,* as we have seen, has emerged and, to some extent, was deliberately *created* by the cassette industry in order to appeal to a large sector of the pan-regional, Hindi-speaking North Indian bourgeoisie. In particular, it has been oriented toward middle- and upper-middle-class audiences who find film music too rowdy and plebeian, and yet who lack familiarity with pure classical music. The modern *ghazal,* as befits the composition and tastes of its audience, retains a distinctly aristocratic, courtly image (or, one might say, pretension). Singers appear on stage and on cassette covers dressed in fine Muslim-style *kurtas* and *sherwanis.* Cassettes often feature canned (artificially inserted) exclamations of "wah-wah!" (bravo!) intended to suggest the ambience of the genteel courtesan salon or *musha'ra* (poetry reading). In the use of *tabla* (as opposed to bongos, or folk barrel drum), occasional tame improvisations, *ghazal* form, and the Urdu language itself, the modern *ghazal* retains some of the mannerisms, if not the substantive content, of the traditional light-classical *ghazal* enjoyed by the Urdu-speaking nobility of previous generations. Thus the entire identity and core audience of the modern *ghazal* are quite distinct from those of the mainstream film song. Journalistic critics, for their part, are quick to deplore the occasional presence of *filmi* elements in the contemporary *ghazal,* such as the usage of borrowed film melodies.[6]

At the same time, the modern *ghazal* is clearly more accessible, in style, diction, and patterns of dissemination, than was its highbrow predecessor, the audience of which consisted primarily (though not exclusively) of aristocrats steeped in refined Urdu culture. Thus, for example, whereas the aesthetic substance of the light-classical *ghazal* was the *process* of textual-melodic improvisation (*bol banao*), cassettes of modern *ghazals* are aimed at musically less-educated consumers who expect singable, fixed tunes. Pamela Singh, an articulate and educated singer of *ghazals* whose practice and opinions may be taken as more or less representative of modern *ghazal* singers, notes:

> The whole performance in the recording is fixed. You have to know
> which line is going to be repeated twice, which one thrice, because a
> set pattern has to be there, so if you sing the mukhra, say, four times,
> and the second time you sing it only thrice, then the people will be
> expecting it the fourth time. So you have a format you have to follow.
> (Interview, October 1989)[7]

By contrast, a recording of *ghazals* sung in light-classical style would require little or no rehearsal, due to the sparse instrumentation, the use of informal *laggi* rather than precomposed instrumental interludes, and the overall reliance on improvisation rather than fixed compositions. On the other hand, a recording of a single old-style film *ghazal* (e.g., of Talat Mahmood), with its elaborate orchestral ensembles, would generally require up to two weeks. Again, we find the modern *ghazal* lying somewhere between these norms. Singh describes her procedure for commercially recording ghazals:

> Usually a cassette takes about three days. I meet the arranger earlier
> and give him an informal tape of my songs, showing the basic tunes.

Then he does his homework, and brings the notated sheets, using English notation to the studio for the different musicians. They hear me sing the whole song once, and the music is there, and they rehearse. Then we do one rehearsal all together, and then a take.

The absence of improvisation renders the modern *ghazal* fundamentally different in aesthetic content and import from its light-classical antecedent, and more akin to a *git* (*geet*)—literally "song," but, implicitly, a precomposed commercial song. Journalist critics tend to disparage this development, as in the following excerpt from a concert review:

Gone are the days of the expansive, free ghazal. Its difference from the circumscribed and hide-bound geet is being fast obliterated.[8]

Vocalist Sonali Jalota is one of the few singers to openly acknowledge this development, such that in concert she invariably announces such songs *git-numa ghazal* (*git*-style *ghazal*).

Modern vocalists, like their predecessors, tend to sing the works of contemporary poets as well as old favorites by past masters. Rather than indicating a decline, the preference for contemporary verses, even if often inferior to the classics, can be regarded as an indication of the continued vitality and evolution of the *ghazal* as poetry. As has often been observed, mediocre poems may make effective song texts, just as much as great poetry lends itself poorly to musical rendering. Nevertheless, aficionados of Urdu verse tend to regard the majority of verse sung by modern singers as markedly inferior when judged by past standards. While traditional themes, metaphors, and imagery are retained, many modern *ghazals* seem more sentimental than classical Urdu verse, which treats lover and beloved more as archetypes. Much of what is popularized by the contemporary stars consists of shallow, inconsequential, and hackneyed verse, reiterating tired cliches whose triviality, for annoyed connoisseurs, is only heightened by the artificiality of the canned "wah-wahs" following them on cassettes. Thus, for example, one critic complains:

Thanks to the influence of film songs, the temptation to choose compositions by poetasters and set them to cheap music and pass them off as ghazals is on the increase. (S. Banerjee 1976)

Of course, there have always been dozens of ordinary poets for each talented one—especially in a genre so widely cultivated as the Urdu *ghazal*. Perhaps what invites the purists' scorn is the modern *ghazal's* unprecedented mass dissemination, which popularizes otherwise forgettable verse among vast audiences.[9] Thus, it may be the ubiquity and mass popularity of ordinary poetry that leads a critic such as Shamsur Rahman Faruqi to opine, "In the past, perhaps thirty percent of what singers sang was bad poetry; now it is seventy percent" (personal communication, 1990).[10]

Connoisseurs of high Urdu also lament the extent to which Urdu diction has been simplified, or replaced with Hindi, in order to reach a broader, Hindi-speaking audience. As popular knowledge of Urdu declines, singers of pop *ghazals* increasingly avoid verse with unfamiliar Perso-Arabic diction, including many of the most famous *ghazals* of the great classical poets like Ghalib. Critics also point out that some modern singers—including some of the top stars—pronounce Urdu phonemes incorrectly, substituting Hindi phonemes for Urdu counterparts and misplacing unwritten elisions (*ezafet*).[11] A few vocalists have been known to confess in private that they themselves are unsure of the meaning of some of the couplets they sing.[12] Some of the most popular modern *ghazals* employ distinctively Hindi diction which would never be encountered in traditional Urdu verse. The use of the Hindi word *kathin* (difficult) in Ghulam Ali's popular recording of Ahmad Faraz's "Kathin hai rah-guzar" is a prominent example. Interestingly, both Ghulam Ali and Faraz are Pakistani Muslims, for whom the occasional use of colloquial Hindi ("*ganga-jamuni zaban*") may represent less commercial capitulation than the innocent interest in using, for variety's sake, a dialect which, especially in Pakistan, may sound quaint and even a trifle exotic. Nevertheless, the popularity of this and other Hindi-oriented *ghazals* clearly coheres with the general dilution of Urdu in the modern *ghazal*.

A curious development in the last decade has been the emergence of commercial cassettes of *ghazals* sung in different regional languages, especially Punjabi, Marathi, Gujarati, Bengali, Pashtu, and Hindi itself.[13] While these *ghazals* often use the standard imagery, rhyme scheme, and, to some extent, meters of their Urdu models, what distinguishes them more clearly as *ghazals* is their style, which imitates that of the contemporary mainstream *ghazal*. The appearance of regional-language *ghazals* is directly related to the rise of cassettes, with their crucial role in the *ghazal* boom in general, and in the emergence of commercial regional musics.

The dilution of Urdu in the mainstream *ghazal*, the rise of regional-language *ghazals*, and the dominance of Hindu vocalists could well be said to represent an unprecedented "Hinduization" of the *ghazal*, which constitutes the most prominent aspect of Urdu-based Indo-Muslim culture in general. Such a Hinduization may be seen as a natural consequence of the replacement of a predominantly Muslim feudal elite with a predominantly Hindu bourgeoisie in North India; this marked transformation in patronage of classical and light-classical music has led to other changes in the realm of Hindustani music.[14]

Changes in the text content and interpretation of the modern *ghazal* are not limited to diction and language. Some critics of the literary aspect of modern *ghazals* have also suggested that its lyrics, even when employing traditional themes and imagery, are interpreted in different, less refined ways than was the *ghazal* in earlier times. Couplets extolling wine and inebriation, for example, traditionally suggested an antinomian, nonconformist hostility to social orthodoxy, which was personified in the figure of the Muslim priest (*shaikh*). Such *sharabi* (wine-oriented) lyrics are highly popular today, and are even marketed in featured "mood" (i.e., thematically unified) cassettes, such as Bhupinder's *Taubah taubah,* or the HMV compilations dedicated to *jam* (flask) or simply *sharab* (wine). Disparaging critics, as well as more conservative, classicized singers, have suggested that the contemporary audiences' fondness for such lyrics represents less a principled commitment to unorthodoxy than a shallow, petty-bourgeois/yuppie hedonism, if not an outright glorification of alcoholism.[15] It is not, however, that contemporary lyrics themselves are more explicit and prosaic in their celebration of the grape, for such is not the case;[16] rather, the difference is that the pop *ghazal*'s bourgeois, relaxed ambience, its commercial packaging, its consumerist audience, and its absence of the light-classical *ghazal*'s rigor and *intensity* somehow fail to accommodate the bohemian, oppositional spirit of the traditional *ghazal*. In effect, the contemporary bourgeois audiences appear to have rearticulated the *ghazal*'s former oppositional licentiousness into a complacent sybaritism.

While the *ghazal* has now achieved an exponentially greater audience than it has ever enjoyed before in any form, the genre has changed dramatically in the process, now lying, in terms of sophistication and accessibility, somewhere between the old-style film *ghazal* and the light-classical *ghazal*. Pamela Singh articulates the orientation of the new *ghazal:*

> In a small *mehfil* [private concert for connoisseurs] you can sing the difficult poetry and take your time, singing a ghazal for fifteen or twenty minutes, with a lot of improvised variations, but in a concert hall program, you're singing to the masses, so you can't sing something difficult. It should be all easy tunes, easy lyrics, so that people can hum the song. That's very necessary for popularity, when you record as well. So I don't improvise on my recordings. I would like to sing like a layman, on cassette, so that I try to reach out to everybody. The moment you make it difficult, these days, the commercial value decreases.

When I noted that Begum Akhtar enjoyed considerable popularity in spite or because of singing difficult *ghazals* and improvising freely, Singh correctly observed:

> Begum Akhtar actually had quite a restricted audience, in the sense that in those days only those people who were fond of ghazals would listen to her. But today I think everybody knows who Anup Jalota and

Pankaj Udhas are, so that even people who don't understand the words well, like South Indians—they too like these singers, since they have made the ghazal so easy and popular. (Interview, October 1989)

Given its dramatic transformation in the interests of mass popularity, the modern *ghazal,* not surprisingly, is the subject of some controversy. On the one hand, lower-class music audiences still tend to prefer film or folk music, finding *ghazal* too elitist, too difficult to understand, or simply dull. On the other hand, many aficionados of the now-eclipsed light-classical style regard the modern *ghazal* as cheap, manneristic kitsch. Music critics writing for newspapers generally represent this latter perspective. A few excerpts from reviews may serve as representative:

Exuding the sick-sweet smell of decadence, the ghazal is irretrievably trapped in its feudal associations. Cultivated and practised in eternal leisure of the ivory towers of the rich, it cannot altogether rid itself of reactionary trappings. And yet, one must admit, it had, in those days, a classical aestheticism, epitomising the supreme pursuit of beauty amid refinement for its own sake. The modern ghazal has been pulled down from the coterie of refined aristocracy and brought to the masses, but at a stiff price. The so-called popular exponents of the ghazal have drastically devalued its form and content, substituting its refinement with obstreporous [sic] vulgarity, bringing it at par with the intelligibility of the masses . . .

A problem with the new commercial ghazal is that it's no longer a ghazal; it seeks to meet the "geet" halfway . . . One strains one's ears to catch anything of note, but the lyrics are dumb . . .

The ghazal has been so bastardized in the '80s that its filmi versions sound more unfeigned that the non-film exertions with their fakc feelings and canned "wah-wah"s . . .

This [Jagjit and Chitra Singh's *Desires*] is a mild, frivolous, and superficial cassette, lazy and languid, both without depth and substance. This is the kind of stuff . . . that ghazal-singers in five-star hotels churn out while you have your dinner. It's soft and fluffy, and it doesn't matter if the song gets lost in the clatter of cutlery . . .

It is a sad commentary on our [culture] that ghazal singers today demand to be accompanied by nothing less than a symphony orchestra . . .[17]

Urdu novelist and critic Qurratulain Hyder's eloquent appraisal of the contemporary *ghazal* is worth citing at length. The *ghazal,* she writes,

. . . went pop and was further debased in the potboilers [i.e., Hindi films] . . . This deterioration of the ghazal reflects the rapid socio-economic changes which are taking place in our multi-lingual society.

Urdu has, by and large, taken a back seat. Politically, it has become a
thorny problem and it has only reemerged as a kind of entertainment
industry . . . It must be remembered that [Urdu] was not only a language. It was a *culture,* denoting refinement and intellectual attainment
. . . At the same time it was not merely elitist, as it also represented
the broad-based *speech*-culture of the masses . . . But the ghazals have
come back as essentially Urdu exotica. The erotic pop variety is as hol-
low and crass as the video-cassette culture of the new rich in which it is
flourishing . . . Now the TV serials [especially a popular serial on the
19th-century poet Ghalib] have turned the resplendent history of the
Urdu ghazal into haphazardly-produced, shoddy soap operas. [The
Ghalib of the serial] speaks incorrect Urdu and cannot recite his own
verses correctly . . . [18]

The modern pop *ghazal,* as disseminated by cassettes, has been the most conspicuous manifestation of the transformation of refined Urdu culture into commercial kitsch. At the same time, while Hyder's trenchant indictment may be
accurate, it could to some extent be balanced by a more favorable perspective
on the modern *ghazal*—a perspective which should be seen as complementary
rather than contradictory. For if the commercialization of the modern *ghazal*
can be seen as a degradation of its light-classical predecessor, so, conversely,
can its mass popularization to some extent be seen as a classicization of the
film *ghazal,* reflecting and contributing to the refinement of millions of listeners who would otherwise be familiar only with film music, which is even more
populist and unsophisticated. Similarly, while the modern *ghazal*'s simplified
diction, flawed pronunciation, and predominantly Hindu audiences and singers can be said to reflect a decline of Muslim Urdu culture, they could also be
seen as *spreading* that culture on an unprecedented mass scale, even if in a
rather diluted form. Thus, for example, Urdu scholar and poet Shams ur Rahman Faruqi comments:

I hate the sort of *ghazals* people sing nowadays, and the way they sing
them, but in spite of that I think that this *ghazal* vogue is a good thing.
(Personal communication, October 1989)

Faruqi also opines that the predominance of non-Muslim singers and audiences can be seen as a healthy popularization of Indo-Muslim syncretism (albeit in a watered-down idiom) among Hindus and Sikhs, and should not be
regarded as an expropriation of a formerly Muslim art form. Indeed, one
could well argue that now, when Hindu-Muslim relations are more antagonistic than at any time since Independence, the pop *ghazal* represents perhaps the
single most prominent and overt symbol of Indo-Muslim creative collaboration and harmony. The *ghazal*'s very existence attests to the extent to which
North Indian culture is a syncretic product of both Hindu and Muslim contri-

butions, and the current mass popularity of this genre, in however simplified a form, may well constitute a unifying element in a period otherwise marked by religious bigotry, violence, and persecution.

Conclusions

The emergence of the modern *ghazal* represents an important stage in the history of Indian popular culture, and particularly of music and the mass media. The pop *ghazal* constituted a new genre, for a new mass medium, and, to some extent, a new audience. It was the first popular-music idiom to achieve mass popularity independent of cinema. Its leading performers had only incidental connections with film music; while some of them, like Talat Aziz, Anup Jalota, and Pankaj Udhas, sing and compose for films, their primary renown has always derived from their *ghazals*. Similarly, the audience for the pop *ghazal* is also to some extent distinct from that of film music, or represents the top end of that audience in terms of social class, education, and affluence. Finally, and most conspicuously, the modern *ghazal* has been the first popular music to be associated since its inception with a distinct new mass medium—cassettes.

As I have stressed in the preceding chapter, in the mid-1980s cassette technology came to serve as the vehicle and catalyst for the emergence of hundreds of smaller music companies producing regional genres for specialized community audiences. The advent of the modern *ghazal,* in diachronic perspective, can be seen as a transitional, initial phase in this process of decentralization. In 1977–82, the early years of the *ghazal* vogue, cassette-player ownership in India was limited largely to members of the urban middle class; this group was not certainly not as specialized a market as that of other more recent cassette-based genres (e.g., Punjabi truck-driver songs), as it was a large, pan-regional audience. Accordingly, the mainstream modern *ghazal* is sung not in regional languages, but in a simplified Urdu, which is understood by at least 100 million North Indians. Further, as we have seen, *ghazal,* unlike later cassette-based genres, has not been associated with small cottage cassette companies, but rather with the large corporations, especially, HMV, MIL, and more recently, T-Series. At the same time, the *ghazal* audience could be said to constitute, then and now, a more specialized group than the mass audience of Hindi films, with their common-denominator orientation. In terms of production, the *ghazal* differs from film music in its independence of cinematic contexts, of film singers and directors, and, to some extent, of HMV dominance. The extent to which the *ghazal* vogue has been declining since the mid-1980s reflects less a shrinking of its potential or real audience than the emergence of rival cassette-based musical genres.

The modern *ghazal,* seen in relation to its light-classical predecessor, has been the subject of much controversy, especially since the dilution and commercialization of the genre occurred so rapidly and is so well documented on recordings. Its emergence naturally invites evaluation in terms of the interpretive issues discussed in the first chapter—the extent to which it represents a triumph of diversity or homogenization, of commercialization or refinement, of corporate manipulation or consumer creativity. A balanced appraisal of the *ghazal* according to these criteria may well be ambivalent, in accordance with the transitional nature of the genre. The modern *ghazal* represents a sort of intermediate genre in terms of specialization of audience, sophistication of content, and relation to the corporate entertainment industry. Similarly, *ghazal* could be seen as promoting a minority language, insofar as high Urdu continues to decline; alternately, it could be regarded as promoting the North Indian lingua franca of Hindi-Urdu. Any negative appraisal of the "hegemony" of this language would have to be tempered by the fact that Urdu's traditional association with an increasingly persecuted minority makes the popularization of an Indo-Muslim genre a welcome and unifying cultural development.

6

Devotional Music

The closely linked emergence of cassettes and the modern commercial *ghazal* inaugurated a new stage in the development of South Asian popular music. Just as the *ghazal* constituted the first successful challenge to the dominance of film-music, so did cassettes offer a new alternative to the corporate-controlled cinema and the state-run broadcast media, thereby disrupting, at the same time, the near-monopoly of HMV and the corporate film music world. These developments paved the way for the emergence of other varieties of commercially marketed cassette-based musics, of which devotional musics were the next to flourish.

In many ways, the mass marketing of religious music in South Asia in connection with cassette technology has been a unique, if logical event in the realm of international popular music. At the risk of overgeneralizing, it may be said that in no other major culture outside India is there such a flourishing diversity of devotional musics, playing such central roles in cultural life. Due to the forms that modernization and commercialization have taken in the developed world, devotional musics—for example, Christian rock, gospel—have remained largely at the margins of the mass media. Other circumstances have limited the role of religious music in the mass media elsewhere. In most of the Muslim world, devotional music has always been stigmatized by a religious orthodoxy which regards the very concept of Islamic music as oxymoronic; thus, in the Arab world and Muslim Indonesia, religious musics constitute relatively peripheral phenomena in the mass media, which are dominated by secular music. The secularization of Chinese society that has accompanied the communist revolution has eliminated religious music from public culture, while in countries like Mexico, the generally somber and serious nature of the most characteristic forms of sacred music has limited their impact on and role in the more entertainment-oriented mass media. In India, by contrast, music has always played a central role in Hindu devotion.

While the unparalleled popularity and importance of devotional music in India make the popular-music scene there somewhat unique, the incorporation of these musics into the realm of popular culture involves many of the same themes and processes which characterize other forms of mass-mediated musics, and which inform much of this book. Thus, for example, a holistic comprehension of the mass-marketing of devotional musics in India entails the study of the relationships between mainstream, pan-regional genres and diverse "Little Traditions," between live performance and mass mediation, and between the emergent commercial subgenres and the dominant secular entertainment style, which is film music. This chapter is intended less as a survey of contemporary mass-mediated devotional musics than as a preliminary interpretation of the way the cassette-based emergence of these musics embodies these issues.

An initial problem arises in delimiting the scope of this discussion, for the distinctions between sacred and secular music in India, and especially in Hindu culture, are often arbitrary or nonexistent. Much of traditional and modern Hindu and Indo-Muslim poetry, song, and dance is characterized by an often deliberate ambiguity as to whether erotic or devotional passion, or both, are being depicted; the audience's interpretation is often variable and may depend on a variety of factors, including authorial intent, performance context, and the predispositions of the audience. Poetry and song texts in many secular genres may include references to deities or the supernatural. Music that is in other respects secular may be performed with devotional intent; thus, for a classical vocalist such as Onkarnath Thakur, the rendering of a *khyal* (the standard classical form) may constitute a form of worship. Moreover, all manner of essentially secular music, including the most worldly film songs, may be performed in temples (especially in nocturnal *jagran* celebrations), where such music is perceived as a form of worship by the very fact of occurring in temples, thereby entertaining the gods, attracting visitors, and constituting activity in general. Similarly, for example, Rajasthani *kathas* (extended sung stories) may be largely secular in content, but are generally performed in religious contexts—most typically, temple *jagrans*. However, for the purposes of this chapter, I shall restrict myself to genres which are explicitly religious in content; given the predominance of Hinduism in India, and the importance of Hindu devotional music in the cassette medium, most of the following discussion will concern Hindu genres, with Muslim *qawwali* subsequently examined as a distinct, and yet in other respects representative, case study. Similarly, while Hinduism and certain forms of Hindu devotional song are increasingly inseparable from political life in India, I shall postpone discussion of their political dimensions until chapter 10.

Music and *Bhakti* in Hindu Culture

Most Hindu religious music is associated, directly or indirectly, with the forms of worship characterized as *bhakti,* or, loosely, "devotion." Although often referred to as a cult or movement, *bhakti* comprises too ubiquitous, heterogeneous, and fundamental a set of beliefs and practices in Hindu culture to be circumscribed by such terms. In general, *bhakti* stresses devotional worship of a personal deity, rather than realization of an impersonal Absolute through meditation and esoteric knowledge (*jnan, gyan*). While the roots of *bhakti* can be traced to sixth-century A.D. Tamil saints, to texts like the *Bhagavad Gita* (possibly from the fourth century), and earlier theistic sectarian movements, *bhakti* did not come to occupy a central role in Hindu culture until around the eleventh century. In this period, influenced to some extent by Sufism, *bhakti* worship gained wide adherence as a reaction against the perceived sterility and elitism of Brahminism. *Bhakti* deemphasized sacrifices and Brahminic ritual in favor of a personal, emotional devotion that could provide an intimate relationship with one's god in the immediate present, rather than only in the *samadhi* attained after innumerable births and rebirths. While not attacking the caste system per se, *bhakti* worship circumvents socioreligious hierarchy by celebrating lower castes in its lore, offering non-Brahmins direct supplication of deities, and promoting intercaste forms of worship, especially collective song and prayer.

Most North Indian *bhakti* is associated either with Shaiva-ism or, more commonly, Vaishnavism, denoting the worship of the gods Shiva and Vishnu, respectively. Vishnu is most often celebrated in his human incarnations, Rama and Krishna. Goddess cults, especially those of Kali-Durga, Vaishno Devi, Santoshi Ma, and other popular deities, also play important roles in contemporary *bhakti*. To some extent, *bhakti* varieties may further be classified along regional tendencies and traditions. Maharashtrian *bhakti* centers around worship of the god Viththala, and the veneration of his saintly devotees, Jnanadev (Gyandev), Tukaram (b. 1598, of the lowly *shudra* caste), Eknath, Nandu, and others. The Bengali saint Chaitanya (b. 1485), a devotee of Krishna, is the central figure in Bengali *bhakti* and enjoys considerable following elsewhere as well. Tulsidas (d. 1623) is renowned above all for his *Ramcharitmanas,* a rendering in Awadhi (a dialect of Hindi) of the epic *Ramayan.* Of special importance is the *pushti marg sampradaya* (sect of the path of grace) founded by Vallabhacharya (1479–1531); this sect remains influential throughout much of North India.

Music has always played a central role in *bhakti* culture, where it has been regarded as a form of worship and a means of attaining direct communication and even mystical union with God. Tukaram and his followers explicitly stressed the efficacy of singing *kirtan* (devotional song) as a means of liberating the soul and achieving divine bliss.[1] Vallabhacharya's immediate disciples included several prominent vocalists who enshrined devotional singing at the core of *pushti marg* worship. Bengali *kirtan* occupies a similarly central role among Chaitanya's followers, while Tulsidas appears to have promoted the practice of singing *bhakti git* (devotional song) among Rama devotees in the eastern Gangetic plain and elsewhere.

The categories of *bhajan* and *kirtan* (both denoting devotional song) comprise a wide variety of styles and genres. Classicized styles associated with the archaic *dhrupad* (e.g., *vishnupad, haveli sangit*) have long been cultivated in temples, especially for the Vallabhacharya *sampradaya*. Simpler, typically responsorial forms of collective *bhajan* and *kirtan* continue to flourish in temples and other contexts, generally as performed by members of *bhajan mandalis* or clubs. Maharashtra and Bengal are each host to distinctive forms of *kirtan*. Since the early twentieth century, a polished, more soloistic style of *bhajan* has also arisen, loosely allied, during the colonial period, with the Independence movement. The preeminent figures in the popularization of this "stage *bhajan*" have been V. D. Paluskar (d. 1931) and his son D. V. Paluskar (d. 1955), who are regarded as models by older aficionados of the genre. Classical singers like Omkarnath Thakur (1897–1967), M. S. Subbalakshmi, Jitendra Abhisheki and Bhimsen Joshi have also cultivated a sophisticated, semi-improvised, *thumri*-style *bhajan;* Abhisheki is himself a priest of the well-known Mangesh temple in Maharashtra. As I shall suggest, the mainstream pop *bhajan* that emerged in the late 1970s can be seen to draw primarily from the stage *bhajan* tradition and, oddly, perhaps, from commercialized versions of the Indo-Muslim *ghazal*.

Devotional Music and the Mass Media

Hindu devotional musics had long enjoyed a secure, albeit marginal niche in the realm of commercially marketed music. Not surprisingly, recordings tended to represent relatively polished versions of *bhajans* sung by professional vocalists rather than the collective amateur song sessions more typical of popular worship. A few classical vocalists recorded *bhajans,* which subsequently became familiar to art-music audiences; particularly noteworthy in this regard were Bade Ghulam Ali Khan's "Hari Om Tatsat," and the several short recordings by D. V. Paluskar (accompanied by chorus), including favorites like "Raghupati Raghav." Devotional genres were more extensively represented in film music, in the form of *bhajans* and *artis* (chanted hymns concluding a *puja* or prayer ritual). These latter, as sung by popular playback singers or *bhajan* specialists like Juthika Roy and Manna Dey, were rendered more or less in standard film-song style—as precomposed songs accompanied by ensembles of Western and Indian instruments, using simple, tuneful melodies set to familiar meters. Many of the *artis* rendered in this style, while retaining the text content, devotional context (i.e., in the film), and in many cases, the traditional texts of temple *artis,* contrasted markedly with the simple, chant-like hymns actually sung in temples throughout the country. Nevertheless, a few film *artis* became so popular that they came to be widely sung in temple *pujas;* the most notable example was the *arti* "Om jay Jagdish

Hari" from the film *Purab aur Paschim*. Meanwhile, record companies (primarily, of course, HMV) had come to time new releases (of all genres) with the main Hindu festivals, especially the simultaneous Dussehra, Bengali Durga Puja, Gujerati Nauvratri, and Maharasthrian Ganesh Puja, during which the public customarily indulges in gift-buying sprees.

In spite of such precedents, it may be said that Hindu devotional music occupied a rather marginal role in commercial recordings. Devotees familiar with neighborhood *bhajan* sessions had no need to hear rowdy recordings of the same, while *bhajan* as a polished, professional genre did not really enjoy wide popularity before the mid-1970s. Film *bhajans,* even more so than devotional and mythological movies in general, tended to be marginalized by the prevailing glitter and romance of commercial cinema. Moreover, as we have noted, the state-run broadcast media, in accordance with the avowed secularism of the government, have effected some moderate limitations on the amount of devotional music presented on the air.

In the mid-1970s, playback singer Mukesh recorded an original rendition of Tulsidas's *Ramcharitmanas*. Mukesh's version, spanning seven LP records, employed sparser and more traditional instrumentation than mainstream film music, and retained a certain classicism in its use of *rag* and improvisatory flavor, and in its avoidance of harmony and Western instruments. The recordings became widely popular, especially once they were made available on cassette. As Philip Lutgendorf relates, they "became the Muzak-of-choice for broadcast at a wide range of religious functions" (1990:166). Mukesh's tapes were the first commercially marketed devotional recordings to achieve truly mass appeal, and thus constitute an important precedent for the commercial *bhajan* vogue that followed shortly thereafter.

Ghazal, Cassettes, and the Emergence of the Pop *Bhajan*

The emergence of the pop *bhajan* around 1980 was closely associated with two vocalists, Anup Jalota and Pankaj Udhas. The *bhajan* style that they popularized can be seen, from one perspective, as a commercialized continuation of the professional stage *bhajan* tradition of Paluskar and others. Although using larger accompanying ensembles than their predecessors, Jalota and Udhas avoid the large orchestras, shrill violin sections, and disco-influenced rhythms of mainstream film music. Their use of improvised passages, however tame and occasional, also links their style with the light-classical stage *bhajan* tradition.

In other respects, however, the primary antecedent and stylistic source for the pop *bhajan* was the modern commercial *ghazal*. As we have seen in the preceding chapter, *ghazal* was the first music genre to achieve mass popularity independent of cinema. Jalota and Udhas, we may recall, emerged in the early

1980s as the most popular Indian exponents of the modern *ghazal,* promoting a simplified, less classical version of the *ghazal* style Mehdi Hasan and Ghulam Ali had recently established. At the same time, Jalota and Udhas introduced their own versions of *bhajans* in their performances, and began releasing cassettes of *bhajans* as well. This trend was followed by most other leading non-Muslim *ghazal* singers, including Jagjit and Chitra Singh.

Stylistically, the pop *bhajan* bore close affinities to the contemporary *ghazal.* The instrumentation for each was essentially the same, so that singers could juxtapose the two genres in live programs. Both employed relatively simple diction that could be understood by most educated North Indians, whether native Hindi-speakers or not. While differing in text structure, use of Hindi rather than Urdu, and its explicit devotional content, the pop *bhajan* resembled the *ghazal* in its texture, tempi, vocal style, use of light improvisation, and other formal features. Most importantly, the pop *bhajan* employed the same new mass medium—cassettes—as did the modern *ghazal;* further, both genres targeted, in their initial stages, the same primary audience—the pan-regional North Indian middle class, much of which found classical music too demanding and film music too plebeian. That this class was predominantly Hindu made *bhajan* a natural alternative, or complement, to the pop *ghazal,* whose diction, although simplified, often taxed the comprehension of many Hindi speakers. The connection between the *bhajan, ghazal,* and cassettes was quite apparent to lay listeners and journalists; one cynical columnist noted,

> Perhaps the real reason for this manic following of bhajans was the spectacular rise of audio-visual electronic consumer goods and the rise of the ghazal . . . Since the *ghazal* boom *ghazalias* [*ghazal* singers] seemed to have cashed in on the arid *bhajan* lane and *bhajans* piggy-backed on the brand name as it were. (Lalitha 1988)

Despite the affinities of the genres, critics and aficionados have been quick to criticize vocalists who inject too much of the secular, sybaritic, and perceivedly self-indulgent mannerisms of *ghazal* singing into *bhajans.* Thus, one journalist, while praising film singer Anuradha Paudhwal's tasteful *bhajans,* remarks, "I am afraid some of our other notables of the *ghazal* scene just cannot live down the *ghazal andaz* [style] when they try their hand at *bhajans"* (Savur 1989).

As with *ghazal,* the music industry did not passively respond to an emergent popular demand for a new genre, but actively participated in stimulating demand in order to exploit the potential of the new medium and the new genre. While a certain sort of Hindu resurgence has been emerging since this period, the more fundamental precondition for the flourishing of the pop *bhajan* was the advent of a new, non-*filmi* medium, with a growing audience. Thus, for example, veteran *bhajan* singer Purshottam Das stated:

Bhajans have always been popular in certain segments of our society. But now the catchy tunes have been successful in attracting the youth. Essentially, it is the cassette medium which is responsible for the growing sales rather than growing interest. (in Upadhyay 1987:15)

Cassette producers themselves recognized that a successful devotional cassette could enjoy considerably longer "shelf life" than most other pop-music releases, whose sales generally dwindle after a few months. Thus, a Calcutta-based producer, referring to an elaborately produced, relatively expensive (twenty-five thousand rupees) cassette of Kali-Durga *bhajans,* observed,

This kind of tape takes more energy and expense to produce than a tape of Bhojpuri folk music, but it will sell forever. This is not an asset only for a month or two, but for a whole lifetime, because the devotees are not going to go away; they will always be there, increasing.[2]

Similarly, a South Indian producer (of the Sangeetha label) opined, "While the demand for film music dies down once the film is off the theatre, the demand for devotional songs keeps returning" (Shetty 1989). In the summer and fall of 1990, when cassette sales slackened because of communal riots and anti–affirmative-action agitation, several cassette producers, including T-Series, halted all new releases except for devotional musics, whose sales have been found to be sufficiently steady and reliable to withstand such disturbances.[3]

Executives of the larger cassette companies saw themselves as actively stimulating the demand for *bhajans,* just as they had done with *ghazals.* We may recall the statement of MIL's Vijay Lazarus (cited above), in which he described the strategy of promoting *ghazals* and *bhajans,* whose soft and subtle timbres, aimed at middle-class audiences, could not be adequately reproduced on cheap pirate cassettes, most of which consist of film music. As with the pop *ghazal,* the stylistic simplification of the light-classical stage *bhajan* was also an explicit strategy of the large producers, who saw a vast potential market for a less demanding, more populist, commercialized *bhajan.* HMV's A & R manager noted:

What became necessary . . . was to take ghazals and bhajans to a wider market, thus simplifying them and making them more universally accepted . . . Many such trends can be created.[4]

While it would be an exaggeration to attribute the *bhajan* vogue solely to music-industry strategies, it should be clear that the trend mushroomed not because of a spontaneous demand on the part of listening audiences, but primarily because of the spread of cassette technology, which enabled non-*filmi* music producers to emerge and created a new purchasing audience consisting of those with cassette players.

111

The Mainstream Pop *Bhajan:* Aesthetics, Ethos, and Commercialism

The mainstream pop *bhajan,* like the modern *ghazal,* can be regarded as an intermediate and, in some respects, transitional genre. It is intermediate in the sense that its primary audience consists of members of the pan-regional, over-whelmingly Hindu, North Indian middle class, who, for reasons of aesthetics, education, and social identity, prefer more refined-sounding musics than pop-ulist film music, and yet lack appreciation of classical music. This audience, although vast and pan-regional, can to some extent be considered a special-ized audience in comparison to the audience for common-denominator film music. Meanwhile, the mainstream *bhajan* and *ghazal* can be seen as transi-tional in the sense that while they still flourish, they were the first genres associated with the cassette medium and its unprecedented ability to cater to more diverse and specialized markets than commercial cinema.

While the affinities between *bhajan* and *ghazal* are remarkable, there exist significant differences between them. Perhaps least important among these are the overt, formal distinctions—that mainstream *bhajan* texts employ none of the stylized Urdu diction, standardized imagery, and specific formal structure of the *ghazal,* but rather are generally in Hindi, and are Hindu-oriented rather than Islamic/Perso-Arabic in their imagery and content. A more significant distinction is that *bhajans* are explicitly devotional, whereas *ghazals,* while occasionally accommodating mystical interpretation, are predominantly sec-ular, especially in their commercial forms. The difference is not merely one of text content, but of aesthetic, performer's image, and attendant extramusical associations.

Daniel Neuman has aptly suggested that in Hindustani (North Indian clas-sical) music, "there are two primary models from which cultural cues of stage presentation are involved: the courtly (*darbar*) and the devotional (*bhakti*)." Neuman, describing these models as "bipolar traditions of music as a way for and a way of life," suggests how a performer's stage presence may suggest one or the other of these models, or in some cases a third one—that of the courte-san. Such distinctions are also quite applicable to light forms of music, espe-cially semiclassical music and intermediate genres like the modern *ghazal* and *bhajan.* From this perspective, *ghazal,* having been somewhat sanitized of its courtesan associations, is strongly redolent of the *darbar* milieu which, Neu-man notes, may be intended to encourage bourgeois listeners to dream of an aristocratic past (1990:221–22). With its refined diction and imagery, its ro-mance and nostalgia, its cultivated virtuosity, and its historical roots in elite Indo-Muslim culture, the *ghazal* is ideally performed (as portrayed in numer-ous films) by the courtesan or court singer performing in the suavely sybaritic *mehfil* atmosphere for a handful of elegantly dressed noblemen reclining on cushions and smoking a hookah.

The *bhajan* model, by contrast, is that of devotion, which should characterize the singer's personal image, stage presence, and performance style. While commercial *bhajan* singers need not be ascetics or saints, their personal lives are expected to conform to certain standards. Thus, for instance, one devout Brahmin, a music director at AIR, commented on Anup Jalota's *bhajans,* "I don't mind his singing, but this business of him divorcing his second wife and marrying a third—it's not right." Such considerations would be essentially irrelevant for a *ghazal* singer, while a racy and libertine image would be considered acceptable, if not desirable, for a film star. For singers like Jalota who sing both *ghazal* and *bhajans,* complications may arise. Thus, it is easier for Hari Om Sharan, who sings only *bhakti* music, to maintain an unambiguously pious image, as on the cover of his most popular cassette (*Aaradhan*), where he is shown looking heavenwards as if in mystical communion; the male *ghazal* singer, by contrast, is typically depicted wearing a luxuriantly embroidered Kashmiri shawl, and singing to the camera, that is, to an implicit *human* audience (cf. Pankaj Udhas's *Aafreen*). As one music critic noted, "the impact of the bhajan rests entirely on the singer's personal character and approach. 'A devil cannot cite scriptures' so far as the rendering of a bhajan is concerned" (Wadhera 1986).

Bhakti sentiment is intended to pervade musical style as well. In the *bhajan* aesthetic, the devotional content of the text is paramount. Thus, the innovative and often eccentric modal experiments indulged in by *ghazal* singers would not be seen as appropriate in *bhajan*. More importantly, abstract improvisations should be kept to a discreet minimum, so as not to distract attention from the words. For many purists, the model remains D. V. Paluskar, who, according to one connoisseur, "knew just how much *bol banao* to introduce without distracting from the text." Unlike classical music, *bhakti git* is meant to be simple and accessible, and its appeal, in strictly musical terms, rests largely on the melodic setting, which must be tuneful, singable, and tasteful. One journalist praises Hari Om Sharan in such terms:

> His presentations of simple bhajans are ideal renderings that have an immediate and favourable impact on listeners. The extremely rich and devotional content affects the listeners with its straight simple style. There are no artificial frills attracted to his expositions and yet their impact on the listeners is soul stirring, marked with sincerity and an intense Bhakti element. (Joshi 1987:30)

Another critic notes:

> Bhajan, as a musical form, has a certain single-track melody with a certain simplicity and forthrightness of expression. To be effective, it does not stray, dilly-dally or seek to dazzle. It spurns over [sic] much ingenuity or cleverness and looks with disfavour on too many melodic variations. (Wadhera 1986)

The pop *bhajan*'s aesthetic of simplicity and accessibility, coupled with the inevitable effects of its mass commodification, naturally incline it toward the populism of film music. Accordingly, as with *ghazal,* one may note a continuum ranging from the cultivated, somewhat classicized *bhajans* sung by Hindustani vocalists (especially Kumar Gandharva, Bhimsen Joshi, and Pandit Jasraj) to others that are stylistically quite close to film music. The affinities of many pop *bhajans* with film songs are highly controversial. On the one hand, the conflation with film-music style vastly expands the pop *bhajan*'s audience to include many millions of film music lovers who would regard the more classicized *bhajans* of, say, Kumar Gandharva, as dry and plain. On the other hand, use of features typical of film music draws fire from purists who regard the film milieu, with its commercialism, hedonism, and meretricious glitter, as anathema to devotional sentiment.

The use of ensembles larger than the traditional light-classical contingent (*sarangi, tabla, tanpura*) is an initial subject of controversy. The instrumentation of the mainstream *bhajan* (e.g., of Jalota, Udhas, and Sharan) typically corresponds to that of the modern *ghazal,* using guitar, bass, harmonium, *tabla,* possibly synthesizer, and other traditional or Western instruments. One journalist wrote of Hari Om Sharan, "How could he ever think that the guitar accompaniment could go well with the devotional propriety of his numbers?" (Wadhera 1986). Another critic noted:

> What irks a lot of *bhajan* enthusiasts is the orchestration. Whereas
> once an ektara [one-stringed folk lute] or a rubab sufficed, today there
> is a whole new city of sound along with the vocalist. (Lalitha 1988)

Even more controversial than the expanded accompanying ensemble is the use of film melodies. The setting of new texts to borrowed melodies is one of the most common and fundamental features of most forms of Indian music, from stock folk tunes to classical compositions. The mass media have contributed greatly to this trend, so that film melodies have for decades been freely adopted for use in all manner of folk genres (as mentioned above in chapter 3). The leading exponents of the mainstream *bhajan* compose their own tunes, and their fame and popularity rest as much on their compositional skill as on their voices. Yet film tunes are widely used by lesser singers, and are particularly common on cassettes. As we have observed, the use of film tunes in *bhakti git* may naturally attract film-music lovers.[5] Purists, however, disparage the trend, which has been exacerbated by the commercial *bhajan* vogue. One music reviewer discusses the 1988 devotional cassettes:

> Mention must be made of the deplorable trend of so-called *bhajans* that
> are a travesty of traditional values. I refer, of course, to the ones that
> are based on plagiarised Hindi film hits of yesteryear . . . These are
> . . . an anathema on the devotional scene. (Savur 1989:43)

Critics note that the film melody may have strong associations for those who have seen the original film, or who are familiar with the original text, which, in many cases, may be quite erotic, if not vulgar.[6] Thus, for example, the use of film tunes in Sikh *kirtans* (devotional group songs) has been denounced:

> It has been observed that sometimes the singers sing the hymns in film tunes which distract the mind and bring to the listener's memory a recollection of the scenes in which the original film song was sung. That is why religious organizations like the Shiromani Committee have rightly banned the singing of *Shabads* [hymns composed by the Sikh gurus] in film tunes in the presence of *Guru Granth Sahib*. (Mansukhani 1982:77)

Since *bhajans* are addressed ultimately to the deities themselves, critics have often questioned whether the gods enjoy film music. A cassette of songs set to disco-oriented film tunes (by Bappi Lahiri and others) addressed to the Mother Goddess causes Subhash Jha to write, "I really can't imagine the Mataji jiving to Bappi's ramba-samba tunes . . . To make bhajan out of disco songs? What is it supposed to be? Disco-bhajans?! The endeavor is too ludicrous to be blasphemous" (Jha 1990a). Such *bhajans,* along with others set to advertising jingles, are also commonly blared from loudspeakers in temples. They are also performed, along with secular film songs, by bands that play in temple *jagrans* in Delhi and other cities; these groups, using synthesizers, electric guitars, and the like, play primarily film songs and filmi *bhajans,* and go to the extent of reproducing erotic dance scenes in which the female singer is drenched with buckets of water to simulate the obligatory "wet sari scene" of the original film (Mathai 1988). Even some film-music lovers deplore the use of film tunes in *bhajan;* such songs, one film-music buff told me, are for the "front-benchers"—the lower-class theater-goers who can only afford the cheap seats close to the screen.

From the perspective of many cassette producers, use of film tunes and other film-derived features in *bhakti git* is certainly desirable if it leads to greater sales, whether the customers are "front-benchers" or not. However, producers assured me that the use of film melodies does not necessarily enhance the market of a cassette. Sailesh Mathur, manager of Yuki Cassettes, noted that many listeners—such as rural, tradition-oriented Rajasthanis— often prefer devotional music in the traditional style and melodies of their own region (interview, October 1989); alongside such releases, Yuki thus markets separate cassettes where the use of film tunes is clearly advertised, to inform prospective customers. Producers also have noted that the more commercial and film-oriented cassettes are, the briefer their sales are. Thus, a Calcutta-based producer observed:

> No, we generally don't use film tunes in our *bhakti git*. First of all, I don't like it, and secondly, those cassettes don't last. People may buy it

for three or four months, as long as the film [from which the melodies have been borrowed] is popular, but then when the film fades away, people forget the tunes. You can take a pop song like "Hawa Hawa" and set new texts to it, and it will sell very well, but for a limited period, for a month or two. But these devotional cassettes we are making, they'll sell forever.[7]

"Great" and "Little Traditions" in Commercial Devotional Music

The mainstream Hindi pop *bhajan*, like the mainstream film song, can be regarded as a sort of commercial "Great Tradition" in the sense of enjoying a pan-regional audience. Like the modern *ghazal*, the commercial *bhajan* also bears a certain filial relationship with light-classical Hindustani music, which is less ambiguously regarded as part of the North Indian "Great Tradition." For the modern pop *bhajan* and *ghazal*, as noted, emerged at a time when cassette-based musics were developing in response to a new audience consisting primarily of middle-class owners or potential owners of cassette players. As cassette technology spread, ownership of cassettes and players spread to the lower-middle and even lower classes, while diversification and decentralization of the music industry accelerated, with the appearance of hundreds of small producers with specialized markets.

An inevitable consequence of this development was the recording and marketing of a vast variety of devotional subgenres, whose audiences, in terms of language, sect following, class, and taste culture were extraordinarily diverse. Whereas the mainstream pop *bhajan* remained largely in the hands of the larger producers (especially HMV, MIL, and T-Series), commercial versions of diverse, "lesser traditions" of *bhakti git* have been marketed largely by the small, grassroots-oriented producers which proliferated in the mid-1980s. The commercial marketing of dozens of different kinds of devotional music thus highlighted the dichotomy between the commercial "Great" and "Little Traditions."

The extraordinary diversity of devotional musics that have been commercially recorded since the mid-1980s reflects the richness of the folk traditions extant in India, and to some extent constitutes a representative cross-section of the various kinds of *bhakti git* flourishing in the subcontinent. A survey of these genres and subgenres is beyond the scope of this work, although it may be useful to indicate the variety of forms involved by suggesting some of the predominant categories into which they can be grouped, with a few representative examples of individual genres. No one classification scheme, however, can do justice to the panoply of genres involved, which are better regarded as belonging to a set of distinct, albeit overlapping taxonomies.

An initial distinction can be made between functional *bhakti git* and other varieties which are not allied to any specific rite or occasion. Many forms of devotional music, including those marketed on cassette, are intended to accompany or constitute a *puja,* or formal prayer session. A *puja* ritual generally concludes with an *arti*—a familiar prayer which is chanted or sung. As mentioned above, commercially marketed *artis,* whether in films or cassettes, are often as musically elaborate as film songs, but still might be used in domestic worship. Recordings often include chimes or group singing in order to simulate the temple atmosphere. Devotees might sing an *arti* they had learned from a film or cassette, or they might simply put on the cassette in place of singing. A common practice is to do both—to play the cassette and sing along with it.

Another class of functional musics comprises those associated with ritual fasts (*vrats*), which are often undertaken by housewives. Particularly common among these are the *vrats* dedicated to *Satyanarayan,* and to *Santoshi Ma,* a formerly obscure goddess whose cult mushroomed in the wake of a phenomenally popular 1975 devotional film. To perform a *vrat,* a woman will fast for a day, and either silently read the story of Satyanarayan, recite it, or, ideally, call a *pandit* to chant it.[8] In the latter case, the auspiciousness of the occasion, which might follow a wedding or some other event, would be enhanced by the presence of neighbors and passers-by, who would also be treated to some sort of *prasad* (food dedicated to a deity). The most important component of the *vrat* is the *hearing* (*sruti*) of the story—the devotee need not necessarily recite it himself or herself. In such a situation, cassettes have naturally come into common use (as had records, to a far lesser extent). Thus, one acquaintance related to me:

> My aunt used to fast and read the *Satyanarayan vrat* on Thursdays, but now she just puts a cassette player next to the picture of the god, and plays a tape of the condensed version. Then she goes about doing her housework. When the *arti* comes at the end, she'll stop and do the *puja.*

Another functional aspect of cassette usage involves their pedagogical potential and, often, intent. Many Hindus consider it meritorious to memorize and recite, whether silently or aloud, familiar prayers or extended mantras. The *Hanuman chalisa* is perhaps the most widespread of these, although there are many others. Hari Om Sharan's musical setting of the *Hanuman chalisa* has become one of the most popular devotional cassettes, and is commonly heard blaring from temple loudspeakers throughout North India. Reviews and advertisements for such tapes do occasionally stress their educational potential. Thus, for example, a reviewer notes of a cassette of the *Vishnu Sahasranam* mantra, "the learning and recitation of the most potent and beneficial among mantras has been made easy, by the attractive and melodious cassette movingly recorded by Kokila Vakani."[9]

However, the distinction between functional and recreational cassettes is far from airtight. Tapes of *artis* and *chalisas* may be played as background music, or sheerly for their entertainment or aesthetic value, while, on the other hand, devotees might employ virtually any appropriate *bhajan* cassette to accompany a domestic or temple *puja*. Further, the playing or mere owner-ship of any devotional-music tape can always be regarded as vaguely merito-rious, and functional in that sense.

Varieties of *bhakti git* may be grouped according to other parameters as well. The genre I have referred to as the mainstream *bhajan* is itself somewhat heterogeneous, although relatively cohesive in terms of style, audience, and production patterns. Mainstream *bhajans* may be grouped and marketed, for example, according to the author of the texts; thus, one finds cassettes of *bhajans* whose lyrics are attributed to Mira Bai (sixteenth century),[10] to Kabir (d. 1518), Nursi Mehta, and others, or which are derived from anthologies like the *Brahmanand*. Other cassettes contain or consist solely of *nirgun bha-jans*, which are more mystical and esoteric, or of songs promoting the Hindu revivalist Arya Samaj movement.

Much *bhakti git*, including mainstream *bhajans*, can also be classified ac-cording to the particular sect or deity to which it is addressed. The *bhent*, for instance, comprises an important category of songs addressed to the Mother Goddess, in her various manifestations (Kali Durga, Vaishno Devi, etc.). *Bhajans* in general may also be devoted to these or other popular deities, from Shiva to Santoshi Ma. Other devotional songs may be addressed to spiritual leaders. In North India, Sai Baba's following is particularly widespread, and cassettes of Sai *bhajans* occupy a significant niche in the devotional market. Other early-twentieth-century saints, like Swami Vivekanand, are also vener-ated on commercial cassettes, while the English-language discourses of Acharya "Osho" Rajneesh sell quite well in middle-class bazaars.

Many devotional cassettes are based on the epics—particularly the *Ra-mayan*, the *Mahabharat*, and the *Bhagavad Gita* (a short section of the *Ma-habharat*). We have mentioned Mukesh's rendering of Tulsidas' *Ramcharit-manas*. Other commercial cassettes present sections of the epics in their original Sanskrit, or in regional vernacular tongues. Both major epics, of course, are voluminous, and thus, together with other narratives such as the *Gita Govinda* and the *Bhagavat Purana*, provide a creative singer with virtu-ally inexhaustible sources for material.

Devotional musics may also be classified according to region and lan-guage. Such a taxonomy would contend, first of all, with the regional-language versions of pan-regional genres. Thus, for example, one encounters cassettes of Punjabi *bhents*, Gujerati translations of the *Bhagavad Gita*, and Marathi versions of Sai *bhajans*. Similarly, mainstream *bhajan* stars like Anup Jalota have recorded, with appropriate coaching if need be, in a few different languages; in doing so they can be seen as continuing the tradition set by playback stars like Lata Mangeshkar, who recorded in some eighteen languages, most of which she did not know.

Regional devotional musics also comprise several genres more or less unique to one area. Thus, for example, while Krishna is worshipped throughout India, the *rasiya* devotional songs celebrating his dalliance with Radha are actively cultivated only in the Braj area. Many devotional genres center around region-specific deities or cults; in these cases, a *bhakti git* classification based on region naturally conflates with one based on cult. Examples of regional cult genres abound. *Languria* songs, of the Braj region, are devoted to Kaila Devi, whose shrine stands southwest of Agra. An important category of Marathi devotional music is the *abhang,* a type of hymn dedicated to the Maharashtrian deity Viththala, with texts by saints such as Tukaram, Eknath, and Nandu; these and other Maharashtrian saints (e.g., Shravan Kumar, Gyaneshwar, Gajanan Maharaj) are also the subjects of numerous *kirtan* cassettes. Similarly, while several regions have traditions of sung *katha* (literally, "story"), in Rajasthan these tend to have a more explicitly religious content and are performed primarily in devotional settings like temple *jagrans*.[11] Cassettes of traditional and new *kathas* abound in Rajasthan. Other regional genres may have loose devotional affiliations. The popular Gujerati dance *ras* (also referred to as *dandia*), for example, acquires some devotional content by virtue of its association with the Navratri festival; Max Cassettes offers a tape of "disco *dandia* with *arti*."

Cassettes of devotional music in India are not, of course, limited to Hinduism. I shall consider Muslim *qawwali* below. Jain *bhajans* and Christian hymns are also marketed commercially, and Sikh devotional music enjoys a prodigious market in Punjab, Haryana, Delhi, and other areas where Sikh communities are found. Sikh music consists primarily of *shabd gurbani,* or settings of the writings of the Sikh gurus, and *shabd kirtan,* which may comprise newly written verse. Cassettes of these genres, and of explanatory *kath* discourses, abound, with some *ragis,* or singers (such as Bhai Harbans Singh) acquiring considerable renown. As with mainstream Hindu *bhajans, ragis* are expected to lead respectable and pious personal lives (Mansukhani 1982:129). The use of film tunes in *shabd kirtan,* as mentioned above, is explicitly discouraged by Sikh orthodoxy. On the whole, most Sikh music, even as marketed on commercial cassettes, has resisted the influence of film music and retains a more traditional aesthetic. Sikh *gurdwaras* (temples) often play cassettes from loudspeakers, occasionally to the dismay of non-Sikh neighbors. The widespread sale of cassettes enables Sikhs to hear *kirtan* and *shabd gurbani* at home, while the audience and pedagogical potential of *kaths* are expanded by domestic use. *Kirtans,* however, are intended to be sung congregationally, and there are those who regret the tendency of Sikhs to listen to cassettes at home rather than attend *gurdwaras* (Mansukhani 1982:76–77).

The preceding sketch should make it clear that although the cassette-based devotional music vogue was at first dominated by the mainstream Hindi *bhajan,* the subsequent decentralization of the cassette industry led to the marketing of a vast variety of more specialized forms of *bhakti git.* This diversification should well have laid to rest any fears that might have been voiced around 1980, to the effect that the allure of the pop *bhajan* might lead to a homogenization and decline of regional, sectarian devotional musics. Such trepidations, for example, have been voiced in regard to the phenomenal popularity of the television *Ramayan* of Ramanand Sagar, broadcast in 1987–88, which, it has been suggested, could serve to standardize and thus impoverish some of the rich, regional *Ramayan* folk drama and narrative renditions (Lutgendorf 1990:165–70). As it has turned out, the "democratic-participant" nature of cassette technology has enabled it to represent much of the prodigious richness and variety of India's devotional music. The primary distinction, of course, is that while televison in India is a capital-intensive state monopoly, cassette production is inexpensive and decentralized. Thus, for example, cassette stalls in a provincial Rajasthani town like Ajmer typically offer several tapes of film music, and of *bhajan* superstars like Anup Jalota and Narender Chanchal, alongside equally as many cassettes of Marwari *kathas,* sung by local vocalists, and produced mostly by small or medium-size companies like Yuki or Target which specialize in Rajasthani music. Indeed, in many cases the appearance of mainstream, potentially homogenizing genres has served to stimulate demand for specialized subgenres. The television version of the *Ramayan,* for example, sparked sales not only of audiocassettes of the soundtrack, but also of diverse regional-language counterparts. A Calcutta cassette producer relates:

> We had produced some *Ramayana* cassettes in the mid-1980s, but they weren't selling. But then when Ramanand Sagar's show [i.e., the TV *Ramayan*] started in 1987, they got a big boost. People were coming to us asking "Give us the *Ramayan* in Bengali!" Now those tapes, and others like them that we've made—they sell like hot cakes. People see it on the screen, and they want something like it on audio, in their own language.[12]

Similarly, the equally popular Durdarshan version of the *Mahabharat* appears to have served as a model for the revitalization of some regional epics. One singer of the *Dhola* epic (western Uttar Pradesh) compared the cassette of his own regional ballad to the television serial, proudly proclaiming to a visitor, "This is *our Mahabharat.*"[13] Thus, the extensive marketing of specialized, "Lesser Traditions" of *bhakti git* illustrates the way that, with media decentralization, such genres can coexist with pan-regional styles which would dominate more centralized forms of media.

Production and Marketing of Devotional Music

On the whole, the production processes and patterns of devotional cassettes resemble those of corresponding secular genres. Thus, a *bhajan* cassette of Anup Jalota may be conceived, recorded, and marketed more or less as would a *ghazal* tape by the same artist. More specialized genres, including recordings for smaller, regional audiences, are produced in roughly the same fashion as are other regional genres, aspects of whose production, outlined in chapter 4 above, are discussed in greater detail in chapters 8 and 9 below. A few observations may be made at this point, however.

I have noted above that the most popular Hindi *bhajan* singers—especially Jalota, Udhas, Sharan, and Narender Chanchal—record primarily for the largest companies. Of these companies, T-Series is the most active in recording regional and specialized genres. As with regional folk musics in general, hinterland performers like to record for T-Series because of its superior distribution network and prestige. Nevertheless, smaller and medium-sized companies continue to produce a significant portion, if not most, of the specialized regional *bhakti git*. The small companies, while lacking the resources, reputation, and breadth of T-Series and other large competitors, may be in closer touch with various aspects of local, sectarian demand and taste. Such is naturally the case with cassettes home-produced by performers or folklore enthusiasts such as Mohan Jhala and Chhanvarlal Gahlot of Jodhpur, who produce their own tapes and dub them singly for sale as masters to local vendors.

In many cases, producers are themselves ardent devotees of a particular sect or deity, and they take special interest in cassettes honoring the object of their faith. The most celebrated example of such devotion is T-Series' Gulshan Arora, who has built temples, distributed ample charitable donations, and produced several inexpensive cassettes in the name of Vaishno Devi, to whose beneficence he attributes his success. Managers of smaller businesses did not hesitate to tell me of their personal interest in producing cassettes about their patron deities or sects. Moreover, since devotional cassettes are regarded as enjoying longer sales life than secular musics, producers often expend more time, energy, and capital in producing them, and correspondingly, they take greater pride in them.

Devotional cassettes are not only produced by devotees, of course; it is quite common for Hindu-owned businesses to market Muslim *qawwali,* for example. It would be incorrect to regard such enterprises as illustrations of the greed and opportunism of producers willing to promote their adversaries for the sake of money; most cassette producers, indeed, like most Indians, are outwardly tolerant and respectful of other religions, and they see no fundamental contradiction in marketing a cosmopolitan range of products. A typical attitude was expressed by a Muslim cassette producer, who, when I asked how he felt about recording a tape of songs about Krishna, shrugged and said, "It's not an issue."[14] Naturally, performers themselves, such as *ragis, qawwals,* and *pandits,* may be more exclusively committed to one particular faith, and it would be unlikely that a militant Hindu chauvinist like Narender Chanchal would be inclined to lend his voice to a *qawwali* recording.

Some of the range of devotional product of a small regional producer may be illustrated by the remarks of V. K. Gari, a Calcutta-based entrepreneur:[15]

> I've produced a few cassettes about Ramakrishna, about his life, his relationship with his wife, his relationship with Swami Vivekananda. These I produced as *bhakti git* dramas, with dialogue and songs. I conceived and produced these personally, as I am to a great extent devoted that way. And they sell quite well, even abroad.
>
> This tape here is about Kali Tarapit, who is a very *jagra devi* [i.e., a very popular and currently potent goddess]; the tape tells of her temple in Rampura, here in Bengal—how she came in a dream to the man who built it, how he built it, the whole story. And this tape sells not just by the temple there, but all over. So these tapes are educational, but they are also entertainment, because we've put plenty of songs in.

Gari describes two different approaches to production:

> Here is a tape of *birha* [a popular Bhojpuri folk genre] on the *Ramayan,* using some film tunes. This sort of group comes to me, I hear their material, and if we like it we make them an offer, bring them to the studio and record, and then while editing I select the best parts. This sort of recording is done in one session; there's no need for rehearsals or overdubbing. The musicians know what to do, and anyway, they aren't used to multiple track recording; if you try to get them to lay a new track on, they just get confused and jumble everything up.
>
> Now this cassette here, about Kali Tarapit, is a different sort of thing. Here the whole tape is elaborately written and planned out. We have to write the script, record songs and background music, and get good professional actors to read the narration. So these are all very well-known people on this tape—film actors, radio announcers, etc. It's more work, and will cost 20–25,000 rupees to produce, but this one will sell forever.

Production procedures vary widely, especially on the folk levels. Some vocalists are simply hired as singers, and upon reaching the studio are given texts written by a lyricist. Alternately, many singers are themselves poets, or generate material in collaboration with a poet acquaintance. Mohan Jhala, a *katha* singer of Jodhpur, Rajasthan, relates:

I perform mostly at *jagrans,* perhaps once a month, and I've made lots of cassettes. When I record for Yuki [a Delhi label specializing in Rajasthani music], I go to them with my own material; they trust me and know that people will like what I sing. So I've done traditional songs, using old tunes, or ones that I made up; for *bhajan* texts, I use the *Brahmanand Bhajan Mala.* And I'm also a poet, so I've composed new songs and new *kathas.* Mostly on historical or religious subjects. I put jokes and comedy into the religious ones, especially so that young people will like them; there can be humorous dialogue, for example, between Vishnu and Nardua, Brahma's son. You can even put *masala* [spice] in religious *kathas,* like spicy jokes about Shiva and Parvati.

Muslim Devotional Music

Muslim devotional music has constituted a significant part of North Indian musical culture since the thirteenth century, if not earlier. Orthodox Islamic ambivalence toward music has never been particularly influential in India. While the Chishti and Naqshbandi Sufi orders embraced music as a means to attaining mystical annihilation, Indo-Muslim dynasts, with a very few exceptions, ardently patronized court music and dance. By the seventeenth century, the vast majority of professional musicians in the North were Muslims, whether descendents of Central Asian immigrants or, more often, progeny of low-caste Hindu hereditary performers who converted to Islam. Under the rule of the Mughals and, subsequently, the nawabs of Avadh, Indo-Muslim culture was an elite tradition cultivated by aristocratic Hindus as well as Muslims. Urdu culture, including *ghazal* and *qawwali,* continued to be patronized and enjoyed by Indians of all religions until the mid-twentieth century, when Indian Muslims slid further into socioeconomic decline and the Urdu language, as discussed above, was allowed to decay. While patronage of Muslim devotional musics is thus confined, more than ever, to Muslims alone, the Islamic community in India still constitutes some 90 million souls, or 11 percent of the population; thus, combined with Pakistan's 115 million people, Urdu-speaking South Asian Muslims constitute, among other things, quite a sizable market for commercial music.[16]

The most important genre of Muslim devotional music is *qawwali.* In its traditional form, *qawwali* is performed by one or two lead singers with accompanying chorus and instrumentalists. Harmonium and *dholak* barrel drum are the basic instruments, and rhythmic clapping is common. The lead singers indulge in improvised coloratura improvisation, which alternates with precomposed refrains. The texts, which are generally in Urdu, are most typically devotional, although many are secular and romantic (*'ashiqana*), and occasionally sociopolitical. The archetypical setting for *qawwali* is a shrine (*ma-*

zar) to a Muslim saint (never a mosque). A plurality of *qawwali* texts are in *ghazal* form, but as musical styles, *qawwali* and *ghazal* are quite distinct, as the latter is a serene, light-classical, solo form lacking the rhythmic intensity and devotional fervor of *qawwali*.

Like many contemporary North Indian music genres, *qawwali* is of considerable antiquity (dating back to the time of the fourteenth-century Amir Khusrau), but its modern form appears to be relatively recent. As Akmal Hyderabadi has documented, from the late nineteenth century the genre became increasingly professionalized as it spread beyond the *khanqah* (Sufi monastery) into Parsi theater, stage shows, and, with the advent of sound films in 1931, into cinema. The Colombo Gramophone Company marketed many *qawwali* records in the 1920s and 1930s until it was absorbed by HMV in 1938. *Qawwali* records continued to be influential and popular in subsequent decades, although connoisseurs deplored the commercial trend toward frivolous and trite lyrics. Meanwhile, All-India Radio marginalized *qawwali* into occasional religious slots, so that non-devotional songs received little or no air play (Hyderabadi 1982:99–104).

From the very inception of Indian sound cinema, *qawwali* was frequently incorporated into films. Film *qawwalis* generally employed more Western instruments, less improvisation, and were more often romantic than mystical. By the late 1940s, commercialized film and stage versions of *qawwali* had evolved, in association with top performers like Ismail Azad, and subsequently, Aziz Nazan, Yusuf Azad, Shankar-Shambhu, Habib Painter, and others. The modern *qawwali,* perhaps influenced by commercial film music, incorporates more melodic variety and sophistication than the old *khanqahi qawwali,* which had tended to use a limited number of stock tunes (Hyderabadi 1982:106–16).[17] While traditional-style *qawwali* persists in shrines, it also became a widespread form of entertainment at weddings and all manner of festivals, both for Hindus as well as Muslims. The genre seems to have reached a zenith of popularity in the 1950s and 1960s, after which the decline of Urdu and other factors began to attenuate its audience. My informants claim that *qawwali* is still regarded as essential, for example, in Hindu and Muslim weddings in Bihar, but that it has become too expensive for most engagements (at about three thousand rupees) and that many *qawwals* have had to turn to other part- or full-time professions.

Commercialization of *qawwali,* led by performers like Jani Babu, has had some of the same effects as in the case of *ghazal*. Most conspicuous are the increasingly larger accompanying ensembles, the greater reliance on the mass media rather than live performances, and the more secular, sybaritic *sharabi* (wine-oriented) lyrics. As I have noted in reference to *ghazal*, Urdu poetry, like Persian poetry, has traditionally celebrated drunkenness as a metaphor for mystical annihilation, and for antinomian hostility to religious orthodoxy. In the case of many contemporary *qawwalis* and *ghazals*, the text, and the bourgeois orientation of the performers and listeners tend to suggest a much more literal and openly epicurean interpretation of the eulogies to liquor. Regardless of the ambiguity or mystical metaphors that may be intended by some authors, I have noted that several of my acquaintances interpreted *ghazal*'s praise of inebriation in quite a literal fashion. However, sufficient ambiguity remains that the same text can be sung with mystical intent by devout Muslim *qawwal* Nusrat Fateh Ali Khan, and also be used in a commercial film to depict two lovers cavorting about in a drunken stupor ("Yeh jo halka halka surur hai . . ." [This subtle, light intoxication . . .]).[18]

The advent of cassettes has been contemporaneous with the marked decline of Urdu in India. Perhaps because *qawwali* still tends, unlike pop *ghazal*, to use a relatively pure Urdu, its audience has come to be increasingly restricted to urban Muslims. *Qawwali* and other Muslim devotional genres are the only Indian musics (aside from a few Sindhi cassettes produced in Bombay) whose cassette labels are written in the Urdu (Arabic/*nast'aliq*) script. Thus, *qawwali* has not enjoyed such a prodigious commercial cassette-based vogue as has *ghazal*. Nevertheless, cassettes have become by far the dominant medium for the genre, and their wide sales have compensated somewhat for the decline in live performances. The market category of Urdu "Muslim devotional" also comprises recordings of chanted or spoken speeches (*taqrir*), and *na't*, a long devotional poem sung to stock, relatively simple melodies, without instrumental accompaniment.

For several decades the leading *qawwals* have been Pakistanis, especially the Sabri brothers, Nusrat Fateh Ali Khan, and Aziz Mian. Given the indifference of the Indian police to violations of Pakistani copyrights, pirate cassettes of Pakistani *qawwali, na't,* and *taqrir* are widely sold in India. Indeed, I have noted that pirate cassette dealers in general tend to cluster around mosques and Muslim shrines, perhaps because such stores started out as retailers of Pakistani bootleg tapes and expanded into piracy of indigenous product. (Pakistani producers, for their part, freely issue pirate versions of Indian film hits, especially in Pasha Music Corporation's "Pyar ka Jhankar" series.)

In spite of such piracy, there are several legitimate producers of Muslim devotional tapes in India. A look at one small producer of *qawwali* and other assorted secular genres, the Calcutta-based Symphony Recordings India (SRI), may be taken as illustrative not only of typical *qawwali* producers, but of small devotional cassette producers as well. SRI's owner is a Hindu entrepreneur, although most aspects of its Urdu product are handled by enthusiast Siraj-ul Haq, for whom SRI constitutes a supplementary source of income. Haq relates (interview, December 1989):

> We did our first Urdu cassette in 1982, when I told the owner that it
> was my heart's desire to produce a life history of my *pir,* Huzur Muja-
> hid Millat Maulana Habib ul-Rahman, in the form of a monologue on

cassette. The text was written with my guidance by a local *'alim* (Islamic scholar), and we recorded it inexpensively. I marketed the cassettes at the *'urs* [death anniversary] of the *pir,* and the first night I sold several thousand tapes. After that I got more ambitious, and went on to do more cassettes of *qawwali, na't,* and religious speeches. Usually I am the one who thinks of the topics, for example, "Questions and Answers about the Quran." We hire local poets to write the *na't* texts, book a studio for 1000 Rs. for eight hours, and have a local singer recite it. Some of the singers or reciters can't adjust to the studio format, so we record them live, with an audience. Aside from selling cassettes in stores, we always attend the major *'urs* festivals, and typically sell 15,000 Rs. worth in two days.

Producing tapes of *qawwali* is a bit more expensive and time-consuming. We start by having a group sing for us, and we select the best songs. Alternately, we tell them what sort of topics we want, and they come up with the material. We don't just want to make money, we want to educate people as well. For instance, we commissioned this tape, *Jamai Babu,* about the evils of dowry. We called the poets and had them write lyrics, then our producer composed the tunes and showed them to the singers. In other cases the *qawwals* themselves compose the tunes. Next our producer composed the "music" [i.e., instrumental interludes], because the *qawwals* themselves just use harmonium and drum. For the recording the musicians get 400 Rs. each. The entire production might cost 10,000 Rs.; we sell wholesale to the retailers at 11.50 Rs. per tape.

As Haq notes, audience tastes vary, and a small producer like SRI must try to respond to current commercial trends.

We try to give people what they want. Some like film melodies, others don't. Devotional *qawwalis* sell well, although romantic ones do better nowadays. Usually we add Western instruments, because if a cassette just has harmonium and drum, it won't sell even two copies. Also, we've learned that there have to be several songs, with distinct melodies, on a cassette; if a tape just has one or two long songs, no one will buy it. So each song just uses a short *qata'* [fragment] as a text. People also like less singing nowadays, and more [instrumental] music. Each tape starts with our SRI announcement, then a short passage of *kalavat-e-Quran* [Quranic chant], although we know that most people just fast forward past that up to the song. People don't have time these days.

Haq explicitly sees cassettes as compensating for the decline of live performances.

Qawwali is dying in Calcutta these days, because no one can afford it. The factories and sweatshops used to hire *qawwals* for Biskarma Puja, but now they just rent a video. So people hear it mostly on cassettes like ours. People like to play these cassettes at home, especially to create a religious domestic atmosphere for their children.

Cassettes and Live Performance

As suggested in chapter 1, one of the most important aspects of the impact of the mass media is the extent to which mediated music, rather than nourishing and enriching a creative tradition, can impoverish it by replacing live performance, whether by professionals or amateurs. The rapidity and breadth of the spread of devotional-music cassettes may provide a case study for the effects of mediated music on performance traditions, although these effects remain in many respects difficult to assess.

There is no doubt that devotional cassettes have come to replace live performance in many contexts; the visibility of this process, indeed, has provoked criticism and commentary by journalists, musicians, and others in India. Scholars of Rajasthani culture have noted the replacement of live musicians with cassettes in Rajasthan's famed Bhattianji temple (Nazir Jairazbhoy, personal communication). We have also mentioned the concern voiced by a Sikh musicologist, that many Sikhs may prefer to listen at home to *shabd kirtan* and *kath* cassettes rather than attending temple functions. Similarly, the practice of playing cassettes of *vrats* and other ritual prayers has certainly replaced some domestic recitations and palpably cut into the livelihoods of Brahmin priests formerly invited to perform such ceremonies. Media theorist Usha Reddi bemoans this process at some length.

> The performing artist has also become a victim of the large-scale [cassette] industry, which by mass-producing cultural products has robbed him of independence and individual popularity through its distribution methods. Going beyond the musician, even the priests have been affected, as it is now possible to obtain recorded, and therefore uniform, versions of prayers and religious services to be performed during religious and cultural occasions. The priest who performed these services, as much as the artist who performed music during festivals, has become superfluous, replaced by the recorded music industry . . . Priests were an important part of the social gatherings, carrying out rituals, chanting prayers, giving instructions as to how the marriage would take place. This was the livelihood of the priest, as well as his social function. However, today, in homes and public places, it is possible to use a prerecorded cassette (generally audio but in some cases like Ganesh Pooja, a video-cassette) where precise instructions are given,

prayers are recorded and can be played through a public address system, thereby completely substituting for the live performance and the priest. These classes of people have, as a result, taken to other professions for their livelihood. (1989:407)

Similarly, one journalist notes that in Tamil Nadu, cassettes of Gayatri Japan tapes are particularly common in use for sacred thread ceremonies of Brahmin boys, conveniently obviating the presence of a priest (Shetty 1989). In general, there is no doubt that the cassette boom, in conjunction with other aspects of modernization, has clearly contributed to the decline of priesthood as a viable profession. There are, of course, positive as well as negative aspects to this development. On the one hand, as Reddi notes, cassettes may weaken once-vital performance traditions and promote a certain degree of standardization, since they can never duplicate the idiosyncratic stylistic and textual variations distinguishing individual Brahmin priests. A degree of dehumanization and impersonality is clearly injected in any ritual where a tape player is substituted for a human. On the other hand, the use of cassettes is a handy convenience for lay devotees, and there are many Hindus, especially among the poor, for whom the need to call a Brahmin for various sorts of functions (such as weddings and funerals) is a financial burden and, in effect, an onerous form of caste exploitation. Thus, one reviewer writes of a cassettes of *Satyanarayan katha*, "This cassette brings the ritual recitation of the *puja* within the reach of the common man." [19]

Most importantly, with devotional music, as with many other kinds of music to be discussed below, it is not clear in many cases whether usage of cassettes is actually replacing or merely supplementing live performance of one sort or another. [20] We have mentioned the practice of singing along with cassettes during household *pujas*. Similarly, while some temples do hire (in one manner or another) devotees to sing or chant prayers and *bhajans*, many temples have never offered such live performances, and the acquisition of a cassette player and speaker system does not constitute any creative atrophy (however annoying it may be for neighbors). Further, as has been suggested above, the decline of *qawwali* may be due to factors other than the spread of *qawwali* cassettes; as a product of inflation, film influence, and other developments, *qawwali's* decline is compensated for by cassettes, without which there might be little *qawwali* heard at all.

It is significant that some of the devotional genres most widely disseminated on cassette are currently flourishing as live performance traditions, perhaps, in fact, to unprecedented extents. The practice of hiring various sorts of musical bands to perform at urban *jagrans*, as mentioned above, is especially widespread, and temples appear to compete with each other for holding the noisiest, most frequent, and most garish extravaganzas. Similarly, whether despite or because of the vogue of Rajasthani *katha* tapes, live renditions of *kathas* by professional singers at Rajasthani temple *jagrans* seem to be held more often now than at any time in living memory (Komal Kothari, personal communication). On the whole, it seems clear that in the case of *kathas* and certain other genres, the current popularity encompasses both recorded and live performances, whose relationship may be mutually reinforcing rather than competitive.

Conclusions

The cassette-based devotional-music vogue constitutes a dramatic illustration of the oft-noted manner in which modern technology, rather than serving as a vehicle of secularization and "modernity," can be used to reinforce traditional religion. Just as the spread of roads and public transportation has greatly increased attendance at religious festivals throughout India, so have cassettes come to be widely used to disseminate religious messages, from urban, liberal, humanistic creeds to the most superstitious, quasi-animistic forms of rural folklore. Cassettes have become the first and in many cases the only mass medium to represent the extraordinary diversity and richness of India's myriad forms of local religious song and discourse. In the process, they have become valuable ethnological documents as well as sources of entertainment and enculturation.

At the same time, cassettes are not a neutral mass medium. Clearly, in some contexts the spread of tapes has been at the expense of live performance. Moreover, the use of cassettes in contexts previously free from media influence is undoubtedly introducing certain elements of standardization and depersonalization. Further, cassettes often serve to spread the influence of film-music aesthetics, which could either be regarded as an enrichment, or as a decadent commercialization, depending on one's viewpoint.

Cassettes have intensified the trend noted two decades ago by Singer, in which urbanization and the mass media promote a shift of attention and activity away from ritual and toward popular culture; accordingly, aesthetics and entertainment values gain importance in this process at the expense of values associated with religious merit (Singer 1972:162–63). In particular, sacred centers and occasions are further deemphasized, while, as Singer notes, "movie actors and concert artists compete with priests and pandits as performers." Such trends, as Singer observes, rather than illustrating a decline of religion, show how Hinduism and other Indian faiths have been incorporated in novel ways into an emerging popular culture (1972:187). In classical Hindu tradition, religion and knowledge are transmitted from what has been revealed (*sruti*) to seers, through that which has been retained (*smrti*) by pandits and storytellers. Singer notes that such a tradition "undergoes a transformation when it is transmitted impersonally over the mass media without the benefit of seers, gurus, or reciters" (1972:162). Most of the transformations that

Singer cites have been intensified by the advent of cassettes, while a few have been counteracted. Cassettes also reinvigorate the trend—extant since the eleventh century—toward *bhakti* devotion rather than ritual (*karmamarg*) or sacred knowledge (*jñanamarg*). At the same time, cassettes have now rendered outdated Singer's observation that as of 1972, the mass media were obliged by economies of scale to homogenize their product in order to appeal to a mass audience, and, further, that the media and its performers remained predominantly urban. As we have seen, cassettes have come to represent a great variety of rural and regional "Little Traditions," just as many cassette producers and performers are based in provincial towns and even villages.

In general, the vogue of devotional cassettes can be seen as playing an active role in the marked consumerism, commercialism, and media influence that have been pervading Indian religion in recent years. Other manifestations of this trend would include the lavish sums spent on public religious festivals, the increasingly garish and expensive private temples constructed in middle-class homes, and the phenomenal popularity of television religious serials (especially the *Mahabharat* and *Ramayan*). Thus, although the influences of cassettes upon the religious life in India are varied and often contradictory, they cohere with an overall trend toward commercialization, mass mediation, and in some ways, modernization of devotional discourse and practice.

7

The Politics of Parody:
Tune-Borrowing in Popular and Folk Music

Thus far we have examined two major musical genres—*ghazal* and devotional music—and the relation between their commercial ascendance and the advent of cassettes. In this chapter I shall depart somewhat from the genre-study approach in order to discuss a set of interrelated, overlapping musical phenomena, whose common feature—the use of borrowed melodies—is one of the most conspicuous and controversial characteristics of popular and folk music in India today. In Indian English, as well as in Western musicological discourse, this practice is referred to as *parody,* a term which in this sense has no pejorative or satirical connotations, but merely denotes the setting of a new text to a borrowed tune.

Of particular interest and relevance, for the purposes of this study, are the vogue of various kinds of recorded parodies marketed in cassette form, and, secondly, the widespread practice of parody in folk music (whether recorded or not) throughout India. The study of the latter phenomenon, particularly when it involves borrowing from the mass media, raises essential questions (outlined in chapter 1) regarding the reappropriation and reception of media content. A holistic look at this practice, however, obliges us to situate it in the context of a related set of phenomena in Indian musical life, some of which are only tangentially related to cassette culture, but which are nevertheless significant. Briefly, the phenomena in question are: the use of parody in traditional classical, light-classical, and folk music; the use of parody on commercial cassettes and in the realm of film music; and lastly, the current cassette-based vogue of outright cover versions (new renditions of previously recorded commercial songs).

These phenomena, in different ways, involve a set of interrelated themes: the simultaneous perpetuation and transformation of the time-honored Indian tradition of parody; the effects, upon parody, of cassette-based media democratization and extension of the media in general; the ideological and aesthetic implications of folk and cross-language parodies and reappropriation of tunes; and, lastly, the confluence of an Asian tradition of parody with Western-derived, bourgeois notions of legal copyright.

Parody in Hindustani Music

The emphasis on composition and individualism in Western bourgeois musical aesthetics has tended to marginalize the practice of parody not only in art music, but in most commercial popular music as well. It may be difficult for those raised in such a society to realize or remember that the use of stock and borrowed melodies has been basic to the musics of many, if not most precapitalist cultures. In India the practice of parody—in Hindi, *dhatu*—dates back at least to the thirteenth century, where it is mentioned as *kutti* in Sarngadev's treatise, the *Sangit Ratnakar*. Given the pervasive use of parody in contemporary classical music, there is little reason to doubt that the practice has been equally widespread for many centuries.

Song anthologies and a familiarity with contemporary practice enable one to document that the use of parodies and stock melodies has been fairly widespread in (vocal) classical *khyal* and semiclassical *thumri* for at least the last 150 years. A perusal of the compositions (*chiz, bandish*) in V. N. Bhatkhande's compilations (1954–59) reveals several instances of different texts being to set to identical tunes; in a few *rags* (e.g., Malkauns), such instances are so numerous that one can speak of a stock melody for compositions in medium-tempo *tintal*. The use of stock tunes is considerably more pronounced in the light-classical *thumri;* one nineteenth-century composer set twelve different texts to a single standard melody in rag Kafi (Manuel 1989:101).

In Hindustani music (both classical and semiclassical), melodic compositions are short melodies used only to punctuate improvisational passages. Thus, the emphasis is on improvisatory rather than compositional skill, and the use of borrowed tunes in instrumental music, and of parody in vocal music, is not necessarily regarded as reprehensible. One whose compositions all employ stock tunes, or who does not compose at all, will not necessarily be disparaged as a plagiarist or dullard if she or he excels in other realms. Conversely, a performer's skill at composing short *bandishes* may in itself be appreciated, but she or he will never attain renown unless also gifted at improvisation. Classical musicians feel free to borrow suitable folk melodies for use as refrains in light-classical pieces (especially *dadra*), generally announcing the origin of the tune before playing it. The one form of borrowing that is regarded as aesthetically unacceptable is the rendition, however stylized, of tunes derived from commercial film music. While some classical musicians enjoy film music and may perform film tunes informally among friends, it is safe to say that film music is scrupulously avoided in formal classical performances.[1]

Parody in Folk Music

If the usage of stock or borrowed tunes is familiar in light-classical music, it is virtually ubiquitous in most North Indian folk music. It may be stated, at the risk of overgeneralizing, that most Indian folk music places primary emphasis on the text, so that the quality or originality of the melody (*tarz, dhun*), and, in many cases, the competence of its rendition, are not the most important aesthetic criteria. In terms of the usage of stock tunes, one extreme set of examples would be the numerous narrative ballads (e.g., Bundelkhandi *Alha,* Braj *Dhola,* Punjabi *Hir, Sassi-Punnu, Sohni-Maiwal*) which are each sung strophically to a particular, distinctive, relatively simple melody. Innumerable other folk genres throughout North India are also sung to their own recognizable, discrete tunes, to which new or modified texts are freely set. In all these cases, the melodies are distinguishing features of the genres, such that they constitute stock tunes rather than parodies or borrowed tunes.

There are other genres that employ a variety of tunes, some of which can be borrowed from various sources. *Rasiya,* the subject of chapter 9, traditionally uses a finite set of characteristic melodies, some of which have been borrowed from other genres or regions. Bhojpuri *birha* traditionally employs a number of tunes of diverse origin, including those of *dhobi git* (washermen's song), *mallah git* (boatmen's song), *sohar* (birth songs), and other genres (Marcus 1989:99). Finally, there are innumerable other genres distinguished by their texts, in which new or borrowed melodies may be freely employed. One may note that traditionally such borrowings could occur horizontally, as it were, from neighboring regions, and/or vertically from the characteristic musics of different castes or classes in the social hierarchy. (Classical *bandishes* do not appear to be widely borrowed in folk music, although elements of classical music are standard in folk dramas like *nautanki* and *raslila.*)

With the spread of cinema, and especially since the 1970s, the usage of tunes borrowed from films has become increasingly common. I have mentioned in chapter 3 some of the many genres in which this practice is common. They include regional folk theater (*nautanki, jatra, ramlila*), seasonal songs (*garba, ras, malhar*), devotional genres (*bhajan, qawwali, shabd kirtan, na't*), life-cycle songs (*sohar, gali*), as well as entertainment genres such as *birha* and *rasiya*. Political and socioreligious movements, as discussed in chapter 10, also make liberal use of familiar film and folk melodies. Indeed, it is easier to enumerate genres (e.g., Vedic and Quranic chants) in which the use of film tunes is definitely *not* regarded as acceptable.

Inexpensive chapbooks containing song texts have been somewhat influential in this regard. Such books, which have become common since the 1960s, may be anthologies of familiar traditional song texts, or they may contain lyrics by contemporary poets. Customers may buy such books as souvenirs, or for idle reading on a bus, or for actual usage, whether in informal song sessions with friends, or, in the case of professionals, for use in folk theater or other contexts. Purchasers are generally expected to know the tunes of familiar song texts. If the lyrics are new, or unfamiliar, the book may indicate, beneath the title, that they should be sung to the tune of such-and-such a familiar song; this song may be a traditional folk tune, or it may be a film song.[2] Often, no indication is given, so that customers must use their own ingenuity in singing texts whose setting is not obvious. Young people often use film tunes for such purposes. Thus, a literate peasant teenager from Mainpuri district relates how she and her friends keep notebooks of favorite texts, setting them to popular film tunes they hear on the radio; in song sessions at weddings or other informal occasions, the elder women of her village will generally sit separately, preferring to sing traditional melodies.[3]

Parody and Cassettes

Insofar as parody has become common in the aforementioned folk genres, it is now well represented on commercial folk-music cassettes as well as in live performance. Thus, many cassettes of *nautanki, jatra, birha, rasiya, bhajan,* and other genres contain film tunes used as vehicles for new, regional-language texts. Because Indian cinema is created by a segment of the corporate elite, reflects largely conservative values, and is primarily urban in orientation, one might assume that the use of film melodies in regional-language tapes would be most popular among the middle and upper classes. In fact, the opposite seems to be the case. Most of the folk genres using film tunes are overwhelmingly lower-class in their audience orientation. (Naturally, one may generalize that most folk-music audiences are also lower class.) Moreover, in the realm of devotional music, middle-class listeners are more likely to disapprove of the mixture of film tunes, preferring singer-songwriters like Anup Jalota to country crooners who use film parodies. Similarly, low-budget recordings of folk music frequently employ snippets of film tunes played on whiny harmoniums in instrumental interludes between vocal verses; more sophisticated cassettes made by larger labels like T-Series, aimed at more "discriminating" listeners, will avoid such parodies and hire producers to compose original interludes using a variety of instruments. Paradoxically, then, in some genres, cassettes using film parodies, despite their obvious commercial influence, can be regarded as more "authentic" in their resemblance to actual folk practice, than can more elaborately orchestrated productions using only traditional or original melodies. Likewise, cassettes are in this respect more representative of actual practice than is folk music broadcast on All-India Radio, where use of film tunes by folk artists is generally prohibited.

Thus far we have been discussing the incorporation of film melodies in the context of specific folk genres. Another important category of commercially marketed parody comprises renditions of current hit songs which are not re-contextualized in any folk genre, but are marketed as regional-language cover versions of the originals (which are usually in Hindi). This fad has been intrin-sically tied to cassettes and to the diversification of music-industry ownership. Of course, as we have noted, Bombay film-music producers have often bor-rowed melodies from regional folk music and given them new or translated texts, generally in Hindi. But the advent of cassettes and the decentralization of the music scene have enabled this process to occur on an unprecedented scale, and in reverse. First of all, the new parody recordings are marketed independently of cinema, whether the borrowed hit melodies originated in film music or not. Secondly, the parody songs generally contain new texts in regional languages, rather than mainstream Hindi-Urdu; thus, they have been aimed at regional markets (Punjabi, Bengali, Marathi, etc.) and in that sense serve to promote linguistic diversity rather than Hindi-Urdu in pop culture.

For example, the three top hit songs of 1988–89, "Hawa hawa," "Tirchi topi-wale," and "Ek do tin," have all appeared in versions in various North Indian regional languages. Usually the regional parodies are marketed in the form of cassettes parodying several top songs. (Both for market purposes and in public conceptions, such tapes are classified separately from folk-music cassettes which occasionally use borrowed film tunes.) T-Series, Venus, and TIPS have been the most aggressive in tapping if not creating the lucrative market for regional-language parodies. Some current hit cassettes—both film and nonfilm—borrow Western tunes, such as Alisha Chinai's *Madonna* tape, consisting of Hindi-language versions of her idol's songs, with a cover depict-ing Alisha dressed, appropriately, in a gaudy brassiere and no shirt.[4] Interest-ingly, two of the most successful parody tapes (TIPS's 1989 *Follow Me* and especially *Love Me*, which sold over 300,000 copies)[5] have consisted of set-tings of current Hindi pop tunes, including those mentioned above, with English-language texts, thereby exploiting, and again, helping create an en-tirely new market for Anglophone, Indian-style pop music. Although English is not a "regional" Indian language, the vogue of such songs is another illus-tration of the ability of the cassette industry to target diverse, specialized mar-kets—in this case, a certain sector of educated, middle-class Indian pop mu-sic fans.

Aesthetic Implications of Folk Parody

In conversations with musicians and folklorists regarding the use of film tunes by folk and commercial musicians, my informants often pointed out that the practice of parody is many centuries old in India. When folk musicians bor-row tunes from other folk traditions, we may assume that the melodic diffusion is occurring as the result of firsthand exposure, whether between different regions, classes, groups, or individuals who have themselves played active roles in the creation or perpetuation of the melodies and musical traditions involved. The incorporation of film tunes into folk music, however, is in some respects a qualitatively different process from borrowing between folk musics. Commercial cinema is a unidirectional mass medium, produced by a corporate elite far removed, in socioeconomic, ideological, and often geographical terms from the folk communities which it influences. As such, the use of film tunes in folk music raises significant questions about the effect of commercial mass-mediated music on traditional folk styles.

As I have suggested, the ever-increasing popularity of film-music parodies is a subject of considerable controversy, not only to ethnomusicologists, but to many Indians as well. Such polemics apply to many genres, and are particularly strident when film tunes are used in devotional musics. One criticism mentioned above is that, on a very overt level, the borrowed melodies may remind listeners of the specific cinematic scenes in which they were picturized; such extramusical associations are particularly distracting and inappropriate in the case of devotional songs set to film melodies. On a more general level, the controversy has to do with the implications of folk performers incorporating commercial elements into otherwise "pure" traditions.

There are a number of distinct, if conflated aspects to this matter, some of which I have touched on in chapters 3 and 5. First is the question of the effect film parodies have on the size of folk-performance repertoire. An obvious danger is that film melodies may be replacing indigenous repertoire, resulting in homogenization and alienation, as once-creative communities throughout the country cease to produce their own art and become dependent upon a pan-regional, commercial entertainment industry for their repertoire. Local creativity would thus give way to commodity fetishism. There is little doubt that this process has indeed occurred in at least a few genres, such as the music of snake-charmers, which now appears to consist primarily of the theme from the film *Nagin*. Similarly, we have cited Kumar's statement that in Banaras, many *qawwali* singers direct their talents toward imitating film songs rather than drawing from their own distinctive musical heritages (1988:153).

On the whole, however, it is difficult to gauge the extent of this phenomenon, and to determine whether film tunes are replacing or rather supplementing locally produced melodies, and thereby enriching rather than depleting community traditions. It is significant that three of the genres whose adoption of film tunes is most conspicuous—*qawwali, rasiya,* and *birha*—have all, by historical accounts, become dramatically more musically sophisticated and complex in the twentieth century. The melodic repertoires of all three genres appear to have developed since 1900 from a few stock tunes to an unprecedentedly broad, diverse, and rich inventory of old and new melodies, constantly enriched by new accretions, whether borrowed or created by the performers themselves. It may be true that the overall popularity of these genres—relative to newer styles—has decreased because of competition from cinema. Nevertheless, it is difficult to say whether their increase in melodic variety and sophistication has been because or in spite of the contemporaneous adoption of film melodies. It is possible that film music, along with other aspects of modernization, has inspired greater creativity and repertoire expansion among performers of these and other genres. Indeed, it has often been noted that in many genres, from American cowboy music to the tango, the advent of commercialization has precipitated a marked demand for and production of new melodies, in contrast to the handful of stock tunes that sufficed in pre-media epochs. While assessment of these trends must await future research into individual genres, I shall make some preliminary observations about this process in reference to *rasiya* in chapter 9.

An even more complex and intangible, albeit significant question involves the ideological and aesthetic implications of film parodies. While Walter Benjamin speculated on the fate of the "aura" of a live performance when it becomes mass-mediated, here we are concerned with the reverse process, namely, the degree to which an entity borrowed from the mass media retains its commercial "aura" in live performance. As has been suggested, the use of film-derived melodies in folk music is regarded by some as the inappropriate and decadent introduction of cheap commercial aesthetics into an otherwise "pure" folk idiom. Film tunes, it could be argued, are not neutral entities, but, whether good or bad, are often inherently commercial in character, and are redolent, however subtly, of the entire meretricious entertainment industry from which they emanate. In this view, although perceived as harmless and attractive by their imitators, they serve as Trojan horses for the values of the hegemonic class and/or region. The new text settings and performance context only partially disguise the commercial aesthetic ideology which is encoded, however obliquely, in the melody, and whose incorporation corrupts and enervates the creativity, diversity, and integrity of folk culture.

It is not hard to find emic articulations of this viewpoint. As we have suggested above, many journalistic critics, folk purists, and scholars of various disciplines vocally deplore the use of film tunes in folk music, and especially in devotional music. Such attitudes are particularly typical of middle-class critics who, whether fond of film music or not, tend to regard its use in folk and devotional music with bemused condescension, if not contempt. The reaction of an urban, educated acquaintance of mine to a cassette of *rasiya* employing a film *tarz* was typical: although he did not recognize the melody, he recognized the style, and curling his upper lip, sneered, "This is totally *filmi*." India's leading film-music critic, Subhash Jha, is particularly outspoken in denouncing the practice, decrying one cassette of *bhajans* set to disco-style film tunes as "too ludicrous to be blasphemous" (Jha 1990a).

Many film songs, of course, are quite Westernized in their disco orientation and clear harmonic, rather than modal bases; others contain structural pauses in vocal lines, which are filled in by instrumental phrases. Even if such melodies are generally avoided by folk musicians, it is clear that some of the borrowed tunes do differ stylistically from traditional folk tunes. The implication, by extension, is that accordingly, even if folk-music traditions have always been syncretic and adaptive in their own milieu, the incorporation of features from a corporate, remote, commercial entertainment industry could represent a qualitatively different and potentially more alienating kind of influence.

Aside from noting that all folk musics are to some extent acculturated, syncretic, and thus "impure," a number of counterarguments to this perspective could be advanced. First, one could argue that such a homogenization process is welcome in a fragmented country like India. Another viewpoint would hold that such a process is not in fact occurring, because folk musicians tend to borrow melodies that do not clash excessively with the traditional folk styles in question. Further, most film songs, including a large number of those borrowed from folk traditions, do not closely reflect any regional origins, or else, as Anil Biswas has asserted, they are altered in such a way as to obscure their provinciality, becoming "generic" tunes conforming to a pan-regional mainstream aesthetic (personal communication). Thus, some folk musicians I interviewed tended to deny that the borrowed film tunes suggested inappropriate *filmi* aesthetics; said one *rasiya* producer of of a film melody he had used, "It's just a melody, nothing more."

Moreover, it could be noted that many film tunes, as the products of trained urban specialists, are more interesting and sophisticated than typical simple and unpretentious folk melodies; hence their adoption by amateur and professional folk musicians should be neither surprising nor reprehensible. As Usha Banerjee, an authority on Braj folk music, stated, "Of course they use film tunes. You can't expect them to go on singing the same old melodies forever" (personal communication, 1990).

One could also point out that the very ubiquity of parody in Indian musical culture makes it difficult to ascertain, in many cases, what sort of associations audiences in general may have with individual melodies. Thus, *rasiya* singer-composer and recording artist Sevaram Tanatan explained to me, "Yes, this *tarz* I've used here is from a film, but originally it came from a folk song of U. P. [Uttar Pradesh]; but most people don't know that." Similarly, many young people are first exposed to film-derived melodies upon hearing them in recycled versions by local folksingers; for such people, the primary associations of these tunes may be village life rather than cinema.

Some melodies undergo several diverse reincarnations. Prime examples are the two largest film-music hits of 1988 and 1989, respectively: "Ek do tin" and "Tirchi topi wale," whose peregrinations illustrate the variety of extramusical associations that a melody can acquire. "Ek do tin" (One two three) em-

ek do tin cār pāñc che sāth āth nau da - s gyā - rah te - rā cau - da

ploys an extremely (and unbearably, to some) catchy melody, whose refrain is roughly as shown above. The melody was popularized in the 1988 film *Tezaab,* with music by Laxmikant-Pyarelal, and subsequently acquired the familiarity and ubiquity of a national anthem. Blared from bazaar loudspeakers, sung by choruses of schoolchildren, copied in several subsequent films (e.g., by Bappi Lahiri in *Kanoon apna apna* and other films), and recycled by innumerable wedding brass bands and other folk ensembles, the song was virtually inescapable in North India for the next two years. Schoolteachers used it as a pedagogical device, since its text consists of the numbers one to thirteen. When the tune came to be commonly used in devotional music, particularly Hindu *bhajans,* some educated Indians disapproved, not only because of its evident commercial origin, but also because in *Tezaab* the song accompanied an erotic cabaret scene. Oddly enough, the tune originally came from a Maharashtrian Ganpati visarjan *bhajan.* While censors and sectors of the public have been known to object to the use of devotional tunes in erotic film scenes, in this case, not only did the censors pass the film, but in Maharashtra, "the mob who had grown up hearing the tune instantly recognized 'Ek do teen' as one of their own blood and lapped it up in ecstasy" (Ghosh 1989:89). There and elsewhere, audiences are reported to have danced in the theater aisles when the song commenced.

The song "Tirchi topi wale" underwent similar reincarnations. Composed by Kalyanji-Anandji and Viju Shah for the 1989 film *Tridev,* the song became phenomenally popular, partly for its tuneful melody, but especially for its conspicuous "breaks" in which a simple, somewhat primitive and exotic-sounding refrain is sung. This passage, the essential "hook" of the song, was itself plagiarized from a prior Latin rock hit by the Miami Sound Machine, entitled "The rhythm's gonna get you"; in this original version, the "oe-oe" phrase appears as a repeated interlude, intended to be reminiscent of Afro-Cuban cult music. In India, "Tirchi topi wale," and particularly the "oe-oe" riff went on to become national phenomena. As subsequent film music producers relentlessly recycled the riff, Subhash Jha (1990c) summed up the year's film crop, "The more melodious moments of the year . . . were in fact drowned out by the all-pervasive echoes of *Oye oye.*" In the 1989 elections, both the Congress Party and the opposition BJP used the riff in a political song disseminated on promotional cassettes. One journalist related:

MM=230   F min

(male:)o - e o-e   (female:) o - e o-e   (m:) o - e o - a (f:) o - e o - a (m:) o -

These days . . . when doctors inject, patients scream Oye-oye, when phones ring, friends greet with Oye-oye. The nation is red-hot with the oye-oye fever. The code words for every public sentiment, their sound can unify communities more effectively than all the national integration programmes on television. (Ghosh 1989:89)

In 1989 I noted that pedal rickshaw drivers lacking bells would routinely declaim "oe-oe" as they weaved through crowded streets. Yet the most widespread usage of the phrase was as an all-purpose heckle, whether for foreigners, otherwise laughable people, and, most provocatively, women. The delight young men throughout North India subsequently took in taunting women with "oe-oe" led to several fights, a murder (in Ahmedabad), and the subsequent banning of the song in several cities.[6]

Other similar examples abound, such as the Bengali folk song parodied in S. D. Burman's "Allah megh de," released in disco style by Runa Laila, which was subsequently plagiarized by Bappi Lahiri in "De de pyar de," and finally, by Benedict Subhash in "Baj ghanti baj gayi" (Jha 1990b). The peregrinations of such songs illustrate the variety of extramusical associations that a melody can acquire in its musical life. They show how both in live performance and in subsequent performances and recordings, a song can be effectively resignified. As we have seen, the "Ek do tin" melody variously came to be associated with Hindu devotion, a cinematic cabaret scene in *Tezaab,* other film scenes in which it was plagiarized, and the diverse folk genres in which it was employed. Similarly, "oe-oe" has been used in various contexts to connote Afro-Cuban cults, salsa, a rowdy scene in *Tridev,* the Congress Party, the Bharatiya Janta Party (BJP), and male harassment of women, to name a few. As Subhash Jha notes in reference to a tape of Punjabi versions of these and other hits, "The tunes have a life of their own, independent of their source of origin."[7]

While bourgeois critics may deplore the perceived introduction of commercial aesthetics into folk music, lower-class villagers themselves appear to be quite innocent of such inhibitions. As one folklorist observed, "Village folk don't worry about whether a parody is 'appropriate' or not; they do whatever they like."[8] Moreover, the widespread nature of the phenomenon itself clearly illustrates the pleasure that folk-music' patrons (primarily the lower classes) take in hearing popular tunes reappropriated into their own dialects and genres.

Indeed, folk parody may constitute just such a creative resignification process, rather than a capitulation to commercial dominant-class aesthetics and values. From this perspective, the use of parody illustrates how the proletarian and peasant bearers of folk culture, far from being passive, indiscriminate consumers, are able to absorb and claim dominant-class products (without compensation) as their own. Through parody, folk performers literally resignify tunes in such a way that they are incorporated seamlessly into the fabric of genres and performance contexts which affirm community values. Thus, when a *rasiya* group incorporates a film tune, its "alien" or "commercial" character may well be perceived as being subordinated to the local character of the performance, with its regional dialect, topical text content, simple instrumentation, and the idiosyncratic vocal styles of the singers. Further, in most genres in question, the text is considerably more important than the melody—and the texts remain original and community-based in origin.[9] Thus, audiences may feel that their performers are creatively empowering their community by turning a product of the commercial film industry into a vehicle for their own texts, sentiments, and values. For just as the intended, encoded meanings of the original product are socially given, so is it possible for them to be socially altered or reconstructed. As Marx observed, "Consumption produces production . . . because a product . . . unlike a mere natural object, proves itself to be, *becomes,* a product only through consumption."[10] The fact that a community is not itself the source for every component of an art form does not necessarily render that art alienating or inauthentic, for appropriated art can be authentic in its own manner. As a commentator on Afro-American culture noted, "It is not necessary for a people to originate or invent all or even most of the elements of their culture. It is necessary only that *these components become their own,* embedded in their traditions, expressive of their world view and life style" (Levine 1977:24). The fact that the song texts are invariably of local origin in folk-music parodies makes the borrowed nature of the melody even less inappropriate.

In most rock music, the secondary import of the lyrics may render the entire song, including its video realization, suitable for drastic resignification and appropriation. A particularly dramatic example was the usage of Bruce Springsteen's "Born in the USA" by both the Mondale and Reagan campaigns in 1980; while the text's indictment of the treatment of war veterans lent itself better to Democratic Party traditions, Springsteen's perceivedly redneck, macho posturing and the video's American flag cohered nicely with the jingoistic patriotism of the Reagan campaign. Indian film songs, of course, are presented in cinematic contexts with their own, relatively specific visually encoded meanings; but their tunes may be easily detached, divested of such associations, and resignified with new texts—especially since the text is the most important element in most Indian folk genres.

The conspicuous and deliberate appropriation of film tunes in Bhojpuri *birha* is particularly illustrative. *Birha,* as we have noted, consists of an extended narrative text sung to a pastiche of melodies freely borrowed from diverse sources. Typically, in introducing a new melody, the singer will interrupt his narrative, and say, "Here's the original *tarz*" (or words to that effect); he then proceeds to sing a few lines of the original source melody, with its original text, be it a wedding song or a film hit. Only after thus calling attention to the source, and giving the audience the pleasure of hearing the original setting, does he then proceed with the narrative, saying something like, "That was the original; but here, Ram says . . ." Thus, the use of film parody, far from being a source of embarrassment, is deliberately paraded as a reflection of modernity, and, perhaps, the creative expropriation from dominant commercial culture. The assessment of *birha* authority Scott Marcus is worth quoting at length:

> "Borrowed" melodies have always contributed a set of associations to the newly created song—associations which reflect the regional, caste, and textual identity of the melodies' earlier manifestations. The [use of the] latest Bombay film songs continues this tradition by giving the new songs an important aura of modernity, of being in sync with the latest trends and fashions . . . At the same time, the new songs are written by local poets and performed by local musicians, with the performances being produced and staged by neighborhood-based groups. Thus, the Bombay melodies serve as vehicles for the affirmation of regional identity. Musicians help mold the region's self-image as a dynamic North Indian subculture that is both modern and yet intimately linked to its traditional and ancestral roots. (Manuscript, 1991)[11]

It is clear that *birha* enthusiasts take great pleasure in hearing popular film songs resignified in local performances. If audiences merely wanted to hear the film songs rendered faithfully, with the original text and, ideally, the original instrumentation, then it seems likely that audiences would probably request *birha* performers to sing the film songs with their original texts, rather than substituting rustic Bhojpuri texts. Further, it is even doubtful whether such audiences would continue to patronize *birha* at all, when they could instead support ensembles which do straight renditions of film music. As it is, the pleasure that audiences find in film parodies, and the persistence of the parody tradition in folk music, do suggest that the process of parody offers distinctive sorts of aesthetic reward to listeners, which differ from the pleasures offered by either traditional folk music or pure film music. Parody seems to involve the affirmation of regional culture in appropriating tunes from the pan-regional "Great Tradition" of Hindi cinema, and fitting them with new texts in rustic local dialects. This sort of resignification offers a particular kind of creative expression, with its own potential for subtle social critique, affirmation of identity, and humor (e.g., juxtaposing the associations of the original glittery cinematic setting with the prosaic context of the humble folk performance).

Such resignifications are particularly obvious when the parodies are whimsical, as in a Haryanvi version of the film hit "Chandni," replacing the repeatedly sung heroine's name, "O my Chandni," (the heroine's name) with "O my jatani" (*jat* woman).[12] The implicit affectionate humor derives from the fact that women of the *jat* farming caste are generally more celebrated for their strength and feisty vigor, rather than the elegant delicacy portrayed by Sridevi in *Chandni.*

One could well argue that bourgeois disapproval of film parody reflects nothing more than elitist snobbery and a misplaced, Western-influenced fetish of originality, especially since most among the middle class take little or no interest even in "authentic" folk music, due to its perceived crudity and its plebeian origins.[13] Further, more than one folk musician, in response to my raising the issue, claimed that most film music derives originally from folk music, so that there should be no embarrassment about reclaiming it.[14] Certainly it is true not only that many film tunes are directly adopted from folk music, but also that aspects of mainstream film-music style derive to a large extent from folk music, especially in typical rhythms, modes, formal structures, and other parameters.

Accordingly, Marcus (1989:110) notes that while *birha* singers borrow freely from film music, they take particular pride in using local melodies, often making a point of informing audiences, "This is a Bhojpuri *tarz,* a completely traditional *tarz.*" Thus, Marcus continues, *birha* manages to affirm both the genre's rural and vernacular roots, as well as the cosmopolitan contemporaneity of urban popular culture.

While the resignification of film melodies in live folk performance may constitute a creative affirmation of syncretic regional identity, the implications of parody in elaborately produced regional-language cassettes are more ambiguous. As Yampolsky (1989) has noted in reference to Indonesian interlanguage parodies, such songs could be seen as revitalizing and empowering regional cultures, since hit songs are now available in various languages aside from the dominant one (Bhasa-Indonesia in that country, Hindi-Urdu in North India). However, much of the resignification that occurs in live folk performance is due to the context, the unpretentious instrumentation, the face-to-face contact with the performers, and the way that the borrowed tunes are generally woven into the fabric of an indigenous narrative song *text,* which remains the most important aspect of the performance. Such features are largely absent in the regional-language parodies produced by TIPS, T-Series, and other labels, where producers attempt to reproduce the style and instrumentation of the original hit; in such cases, the new lyrics are often of minimal importance, and, as critics observe, of minimal quality (Kanjila 1989). It may be more accurate to regard such songs as extending a hegemonic mainstream *style* into regional markets, as Yampolsky asserts is the case with Indonesian cover versions. In that sense, it could be argued that such slick regional parodies are better seen as reinforcing the dominant class/region/corporate aesthetic rather than constituting commercializations of the practice of tune-borrowing in regional "Little Traditions." If cassette-based regional-language versions are indeed promoting cultural homogeneity, we may again ask, as in chapter 1, what the implications of this trend are. Subhash Jha writes:

> One question nags the mind about all versions of Hindi songs in Punjabi, Marathi and Gujerati which have inundated the music market: Do they nurture national integration (some kind of extension of the "Mera Bharat Mahan" [My Great India] slogan) or do they encourage the opposite? Not that the recording companies care two figs either way! (Jha 1989a)

Parody in Film Music

The film-music industry is not the primary creative source of melodic material in India, upon which most other amateur and professional musicians are parasitically dependent. Innumerable film tunes have in fact been borrowed from various kinds of folk music, and in general, many features of the mainstream film-song style derive from traditional folk music and, to some extent, from light-classical music (e.g., *dadra*). Moreover, film-music composers have also found usable melodies in Western music, from nursery rhymes to Mozart's G-minor symphony. Finally, film composers often base new songs on prior Hindi film hits.

The amount of plagiarization within film music has greatly increased since the early 1980s, incurring repeated denunciations by critics like Subhash Jha, who see such parodies as reflecting the decadence of the genre. By far the leading offender, and the primary butt of criticism, has been film-music director Bappi Lahiri, who is regarded by some as largely responsible for the entire trend. Lahiri is a highly popular disco-oriented composer, who invites controversy and elitist disdain by boasting of the quantity of his output—scores for roughly 30 films a year, totaling over 360 films by January 1990, thereby earning mention in the *Guinness Book of World Records,* and the contempt of reviewers like the ever-quotable Jha:

> Off goes the composer, hunting for pop-rock tunes to pilfer from English, Swedish, African and Pakistani charts . . . This, then, is the tragedy of film music today. A tragedy engineered by Bappi Lahiri almost single-handedly. (Jha 1989b)

In response to such criticism, Lahiri has no difficulty in citing familiar cases of plagiarism by other directors.[15] Table 1 (pp. 297–98) below shows a few of the better-known parodies of recent years. While Lahiri's name is certainly prominent in this list (which is by no means exhaustive), the extent of the practice in recent years suggests a trend too broad to be "single-handedly engineered," and indeed, other factors may be seen as responsible. One factor contributing to plagiarization from Western pop is that much Indian film music has moved stylistically closer to Western rock since the mid-1970s. The aforementioned turn to action-oriented *masala* films has been one cause of this development. Another may be the inevitably increasing exposure of the Indian middle class to Western pop music, in conjunction with expansion of the bourgeoisie, of international communications, and of ties to NRI (non-resident Indian) communities in the West (including Trinidad). Thus, the increased introduction of rock style by R. D. Burman, Lahiri, and others is better seen as a response to the internationalization of Indian pop music rather than as a result of the predilections of individual composers.

Plagiarism from the West raises some of the same issues of appropriation and local creativity as does the use of parody in film music, albeit on a different scale. Some critics complain that film-music directors are forsaking Indian music in obsequious and opportunistic imitation of Western pop. One music director complains:

> As for lifting Western tunes, I think it is bad because rhythmically and melodically, we have such a deep musical culture. What makes the whole situation worse is that we're lifting the most superficial branches like disco and ABBA [Swedish rock group] when Western music is actually like a mighty tree.[16]

Meanwhile, defenders like Lahiri argue that they are Indianizing the elements they borrow in creative syntheses, and that, moreover, modern Indian culture in general borrows liberally from the West.[17] One could further add that, paradoxically, in plagiarizing Western pop tunes, Indian film-music composers are continuing the hoary and time-honored tradition of parody in Indian music, dating back to the *Sangit Ratnakar.*

"Versions": Recycling the Classics

It remains to consider one final related genre of commercially marketed recordings, consisting of cover versions of prior hits. Since these re-recordings employ the same text, in the same language as the original, they do not constitute parodies *per se,* and are referred to in India as "version" recordings. Nevertheless, their dramatic emergence and widespread current popularity are related to the other trends discussed in this chapter, and further, such recordings are classified by the music industry together with commercial regional-language parodies as "versions."

Commercial recordings of cover versions are neither new nor unique to Indian commercial music. In Western popular music, cover versions—for example, Peggy Lee singing Cole Porter standards—are generally intended to highlight the individual vocalist's idiosyncratic, distinctive interpretation of an extant composition.[18] In India, popular-music cover versions have emerged under different conditions, and for distinct reasons. As music critic and discographer V. A. K. Ranga Rao relates, until the advent of "playback" singers in the 1950s, film songs were generally recorded live—sung by the actor—during the filming of the movie, and then re-recorded in a studio for release as a record, or, one might say, as a "version" of the film rendition. Occasionally the studio rendition would be sung, with full ensemble backing, by a different, and presumably better vocalist than that seen and heard in the film; in at least one case, a different vocalist was used for the studio recording after a dispute over payment with the original singer. In the 1950s and 1960s, GCI (HMV) released a number of unsuccessful version records of classic film hits, sung by undiscovered "up-and-coming" vocalists, who, as Rao observed, remained obscure; these records sold as poorly as had Young India's versions of HMV hits in the 1930s (Ranga Rao 1986:26–27; Shah 1986:19). In the 1970s, when HMV's fledgling rival, Polydor, held rights to a few successful films, HMV reprised Polydor's hit songs in versions sung by the original vocalists (Ranga Rao 1986:29).

While such recordings illustrate that versions predated the advent of cassettes in India, the current popularity of commercial versions and parodies is quite unprecedented in India and, to my knowledge, unparalleled in any other country (with the possible exception of Indonesia, for which see Yampolsky 1989). The deluge of "version" recordings covering classic film hits now constitutes a separate market category that occupies a sizable niche in most urban cassette stores. (Every major hit song of recent years, regardless of its original language, has spawned several parody versions in regional languages.)

Rather than being a fortuitous fad, the boom of versions and parodies can be attributed to specific conditions obtaining in the Indian musical environment. The wide use of stock and borrowed tunes in Indian folk, light-classical, and even classical music constitutes an initial precedent. In the realm of popular music, a more immediate precondition has been the relatively lax Indian Copyright Act (of 1956–57, section 52), which allows any party to make a new recording of an existing work by filing a notice of intent and paying a nominal royalty; that is, permission of the original copyright holder is not required. Added to this legal tolerance is the unwillingness or inability of the government to prosecute the innumerable small cassette producers who release recordings, typically of folk or devotional music, which employ melodies borrowed from films or other pop music.

Beyond these factors, the primary impetus for the vogue of cover versions has been the inability of HMV to meet the demand for releases of its vast catalog of past film songs. HMV, by virtue of its longstanding virtual monopoly, held the rights to nearly all film songs recorded until the early 1970s. As mentioned above, while many of these were forgettable and forgotten, many others are still in demand, but have not been reissued, evidently due to HMV's failure to retain master copies, and a warehouse fire in 1983. The advent of cassettes and the subsequent emergence of competing producers provided, for the first time, a means of meeting this demand. T-Series founder Gulshan Arora was the first to capitalize upon this situation; since the original recordings were copyrighted by HMV, he set out to produce "versions" of the most popular classic film hits.[19] As the original vocalists were either prohibitively expensive (Lata), deceased (Kishore, Talat, Mukesh), or bound by contract obligations to HMV or other labels (Sapna), Arora scouted college talent shows for clone singers, coming up with a stable of inexpensive, undiscovered vocalists (especially Vandana Bajpai, Vipin Sachdeva, Babla Mehta, and Deepa Roy—the latter "discovered" singing in a hotel). He then released an ongoing series of "version" tapes entitled Yaaden (Memories), whose labels acknowledge, in small print, that the singers are not those of the original recordings. The versions are recorded in stereo, using modern technology, and thus offer considerably better fidelity than the originals. Arora went on to market re-recordings, with superior studio conditions, of crooners like Mahendra Kapoor singing versions of their own earlier hits. Other labels, such as Venus and Music India, followed suit, and the category of "version" recordings boomed. Most of these have been based on Hindu-Urdu film songs, but some labels have specialized in offering cover versions of songs in regional languages (such as Sargam's version series of past Marathi hits).[20] Some listeners evidently prefer the modernized orchestration and superior fidelity of such cover versions (Swamy 1991). A few version cassettes, however, appear to be aimed at purchasers who are unaware of what they are getting; an example is a recent release by Venus, consisting of Kishore Kumar hits, sung by Sudhesh Bhosle, whose name does not appear on the cover. Meanwhile, HMV belatedly began reissuing some of its back catalog, but its cassettes, as noted in chapter 3, remain considerably more expensive than those of other labels, including versions. At the same time, labels like TIPS have released versions of recordings whose originals are still available, such as Mohammad Yunus's renditions of Mehdi Hasan's *ghazals,* although the appeal and marketability of such tapes are dubious.

Critics and aficionados often complain that the version singers are inferior to their models. Nevertheless, the wide sales of these recordings suggest that the public, when given an alternative, is not as exclusively fixated on Lata, Kishore, and their sound-alikes as film producers have been. The vogue of versions also illustrates how cassettes can contribute to the decentralization of the music industry even where ownership of the repertoire remains monopolized.

Copyright

There are also legal aspects to these matters of parody and cover versions, involving the confluence of Indian practices, both traditional and modern, with essentially Western-derived concepts of music ownership.

Copyright law, with regard to music, has constituted, since its conception, a particularly problematic and controversial set of issues, providing livelihoods for the last century to many lawyers and advocates involved in interpretation. From one standpoint, music copyright can be seen as a natural extension of literary copyright. From another perspective, music copyright can be seen as a characteristically Western invention, conditioned by the social background of musical life in nineteenth-century Europe, and in particular, by such features as the capitalist disassociation of composers from the guilds and feudal patronage; the emphasis on composition (rather than improvisation) in Western classical music; the early commodification of music in the form of printed scores; and the celebration of the composer as an individual "genius" in Romantic ideology.

None of these conditions were characteristic of premodern Indian society. It is true, however, that in Hindustani music, compositions—short and relatively insignificant as they may be—have been prized and guarded as valuable possessions by their creators and those associated with them. Hence, one hears of *tabla* compositions being exchanged as dowries, and vocalists protecting their favorite *bandishes* from the ears of rivals or uninitiated students. As is well known, in the 1920s and 1930s V. N. Bhatkhande encountered considerable resistance from some singers in compiling his *Kramik Pustak Malika* anthologies of *bandishes,* which constituted the first such compilations with mass dissemination (1954–59).

On the whole, however, the concept of music ownership *per se* is a relatively insignificant and recent development in India. In Hindustani music, the emphasis on improvisation rather than composition largely negates the stigma of parody and plagiarism, while parody and usage of stock tunes is basic to many, if not most forms, of Indian folk music. *Rasiya* and *birha akharas* (clubs—to be discussed in chapter 9) guard their own song lyrics, but the melodic repertoire of stock tunes is regarded as a shared patrimony.

The advent of commodified music, in the form of commercial recordings, occasioned the application of some form of music copyright in India. Hence, British copyright law was introduced during the latter colonial period, and has continued, with some modifications, to provide the legal basis for modern Indian concepts of Indian music ownership. Those involved in implementing copyright law in India regard it as relatively undeveloped in their country. The British law, as inherited and amended, remains too outdated, porous, and vague, and has been the subject of much polemic and several lawsuits. As we have mentioned, since the extant law had been designed long before the cassette era, the rampant tape piracy of the late 1970s and early 1980s was essentially legal; only after vehement protests by musicians and producers (including full-page newspaper advertisements) was the law revised, in 1983, to prohibit piracy. That amendment required each cassette inlay card to display the name and address of the producer, and the date of production, and prescribed adequately rigorous punishments for infringement.

Indian copyright law remains singularly lax with regard to cover versions. Western copyright law permits cover versions only with permission of the original copyright holder. Indian law, by contrast, merely requires that the original copyright owner be notified of the production of a cover version, and that a nominal royalty (5 percent of retail) be paid if more than one-and-a-half minutes of a tune are employed.[21] If the melody alone is used (i.e., in parody), the rate is 2.5 percent. It is this loophole that has provided, for better or worse, the precondition for the vogue of commercial versions and parodies. As in the West, traditional folk melodies are not copyrighted.

Not surprisingly, the law as it stands is a subject of controversy and litigation. Enforcement is relatively lax, and smaller companies producing folk genres honor the law more in the breach than in the observance. The large companies, who own the copyrights to most film songs, generally do not bother prosecuting errant cottage cassette businesses, nor do they take the trouble and expense to strictly enforce exclusive recording contracts they hold with obscure folksingers. Most of them do, however, pay royalties to each other in accordance with the Copyright Act. Even then, disputes arise. Songs are supposed to be registered with a copyright office, but most companies do not bother to do so. An effective "open season" prevails with regard to foreign songs; the 1989 hit "Hawa Hawa," by Pakistani singer Hassan Jahangir, was parodied and "covered" by several Indian labels, with T-Series, Venus, and Western all claiming to be the copyright owners.[22] Euro-American pop hits are generally parodied and covered without compensation, although legitimate companies (notably, Magnasound) do secure permission before marketing the originals. Even sectors of the Indian government regard the Copyright Act somewhat casually, as the IPRS has filed a grievance against the state television agency for not paying royalties on music whose rights are held by IPRS members.[23] Furthermore, most Indians are cynical about their legal system, which is regarded as easily manipulated by the judicious application of *bakhshish,* the facile purchase of false witnesses, and other irregularities.

A former HMV executive related a representative copyright case to me. It seems that in the early 1980s, a Bhojpuri singer, one J. P., claimed that a song commercially marketed on an HMV cassette by singer A. N. was in fact J. P.'s composition. J. P. sent a few letters of threatening legalese to HMV, which, according to its custom, ignored them. Eventually J. P. initiated a court case. HMV, with some difficulty, then contacted the itinerant A. N. and asked him to verify the contract he had signed wherein he claimed to be the composer of all his songs. A. N., when pressed, admitted that he had plagiarized the opening lines of the song in question. HMV then attempted to settle the matter out of court by offering J. P. a sum equivalent to the royalties he would have received. J. P., however, demanded several hundred thousand rupees instead. The case subsequently went to trial. HMV then paid several Bhojpuri-area "peasants" to testify that the tune was traditional, and even had them sing a few "folk" variants of the song which HMV had composed for them in secret. The suit was thus dismissed on the grounds that the tune was evidently traditional and thereby exempt from copyright. As the executive in question noted, "In our system, it doesn't matter if you are right or wrong; all that matters is how much you can spend, and what sort of legal subterfuges you can come up with."

The legal loophole in the Copyright Act sanctioning versions, while legitimizing an ancient Indian tradition, is currently being challenged. HMV, the prime victim of the version boom, routinely returns uncashed the niggardly royalty checks it receives from the companies (mainly T-Series, Weston and Venus) that produce versions of its repertoire. When in 1989, Weston sent its royalty check instead to the IPRS in order to definitively legitimize its versions, HMV took Weston to court and managed to obtain a ruling prohibiting IPRS from accepting the royalties, and stopping Weston from releasing versions of HMV's material. In other respects, however, HMV does not appear to have evolved a policy on versions and parodies, as it too occasionally produces them (for example, Alisha's Hindi versions of Madonna songs).[24]

In January 1990 a judge in the Madras High Court sustained a suit by Echo Recording Company against the Nahata label prohibiting Nahata from marketing versions of Echo's songs. The judge in question argued that section 52(l)(j) of the Copyright Act violated the intentions of the Act itself and should be amended or reinterpreted. IPRS, meanwhile, has been energetically lobbying Parliament to have the Act revised to prohibit versions without more stringent requirements.[25] There is also considerable agitation within the music industry to allow composers and lyricists of film songs to receive royalties; at present, they are generally paid flat sums by the film producers, who then retain copyright to the music.

Conclusions

In this chapter we have examined a set of interrelated phenomena, all representing various aspects of the practice of melodic parody. The individual sorts of parody involved can be regarded as diverse perpetuations of the time-honored Indian tradition of tune-borrowing. At the same time, the forms that parody currently takes illustrate the way Indian musical traditions have adapted to modernity, and particularly, to the advent of cassettes. Firstly, we can see that the widespread practice of parody in folk music has continued, if not increased, with the advent of the mass media; while borrowing from other traditional musical sources continues, the mass media—and especially film music—have become important sources for melodies. Secondly, folk parodies, which were previously excluded from the mass media (cinema, state radio, and commercial recordings), are now well represented on cassettes of folk music. Folk parodies thus acquire a degree of legitimacy, enhanced dissemination, and, at the same time, notoriety due to their higher visibility among critics as well as those in favor of the practice. Similarly, the parody tradition has been perpetuated, in a distinctly modern fashion, by film-music composers, who borrow freely from folk music, Western pop, and each other. The vogue of cassette-based "versions," one could say, represents a natural extension of the parody tradition to embrace actual cover renditions of original songs. Like the devotional cassettes discussed in the preceding chapter, these phenomena together illustrate how aspects of modernity—specifically, modern technology like cassettes—can serve to reinforce and renew certain forms of tradition—in this case, the practice of parody.

In the first chapter I stressed the notion that a holistic study of any musical phenomenon must comprehend the forms of musical reception, rather than focusing solely on reified "sound objects" or recordings. Adorno and others have argued that commercial popular music is particularly conducive to "passive consumption," marked by physical immobility and more importantly, a vacuous, effortless, mindless sort of listening, for which lowest-common-denominator musical pablum is designed. There need be no doubt that such a form of musical reception may be as common in India as in any other society. However, as we have suggested, there are several other modes of reception of mediated music in India. While singing along and dancing to music are among the most obvious forms of consumption that are not entirely passive, the recycling of melodies by folk musicians is a particularly creative aspect of reception, illustrating that there are different modes of musical activity aside from composition, performance, and consumption. Folk parody involves aspects of all three of these activities, in the form of lyric composition, performance of a borrowed melody, and prior consumption of the tune employed.

Folk parody is thus an inherently complex and ambiguous practice, whose aesthetic implications are naturally controversial and contradictory. To some extent, Indian evaluations of the process are conditioned by class, with criticism coming mainly from bourgeois and Western-influenced sectors, while the lower classes remain cheerfully indifferent. For the latter, creativity continues to be situated primarily in the realm of song texts rather than melody. The appropriation of film tunes by folksingers may well represent the creative resignification of mediated material rather than alienated acquiescence to commercial values.

The advent of cassettes has in many ways blurred the formerly clear dichotomy between commercial music produced by a corporate entertainment industry and folk music. Cassette technology has created a broad continuum of forms of music-industry ownership—from corporate moguls to rural entrepreneurs—as well as forms of music itself, from slick, mass-produced disco aimed at a pan-regional, homogeneous audience, to regional folk music aimed at a specific, local set of listeners. Because of such diversity within the cassette industry, it is difficult to generalize about the effects and implications of phenomena like parody as promoted or represented therein. The parody performed by the obscure *birha* singer may have quite a different significance from the sophisticated, slick Punjabi "versions" produced in the TIPS studios, or the uninhibited plagiarizations of film-music composers. As we have suggested, folk parodies, as disseminated on cassettes of *birha, rasiya,* and other genres, can constitute an accurate representation of actual folk-music practice, affirming, in their own way, the creative synthesis of community values with freely appropriated and resignified elements of the dominant culture. However, this process, rather than representing pure resistance or community assertion, is inherently contradictory, as it involves commercialization, the spread of film music, and the placement of folk recordings on a cassette-based continuum that also includes the most manipulative and hegemonic forms of music. Folk parody, when marketed on cassettes, now finds itself commodified on a medium potentially subject to the strictures of Western-derived notions of copyright, however alien these may be to traditional Indian folk practice.

Thus, while promising above to explore the implications of parody and its role in music reception, I have concluded more by raising questions than providing answers. The most significant issues, involving the aesthetic ramifications of different types of parody, are at once the most subjective, and the most inherently contradictory. In their own way they serve to illustrate the hypothesis stated in chapter 1, that popular music is neither pure resistance nor manipulation, but rather a field upon which these forces are symbolically negotiated and contested. My evaluations of the relative merits of the conflicting tendencies—fragmentation/resistance vs. unification/hegemony—remains an ultimately unavoidable and intractable question, one which I shall confront below.

8

Regional Musics

In preceding chapters I have considered some of the major music genres—primarily *ghazal* and devotional musics—which evolved into cassette-based popular musics providing new alternatives to film music. Since the mid–1980s, by far the largest category of what in the Indian recording business is called "basic" (non-*filmi*) music, has been the vast and diverse panoply of regional folk and popular genres as disseminated on cassettes. I have briefly discussed some of the devotional regional musics in chapter 6, and must reiterate here the impossibility of dichotomizing sacred and secular song in many cases (such as Rajasthani *katha*). In this chapter, while not excluding devotional genres, I will explore in more detail the development and operation of the regional cassette-based music industry, with greater emphasis on musics which are more unambiguously secular.

Social Identity and Regional Syncretic Musics

It has become a cliche, however correct, to point out that syncretic popular musics often reflect, express, and mediate changing social identity in cultures undergoing socioeconomic transition. Most characteristically, musical taste constitutes a particularly overt and potent indicator of ideological orientation, with, for example, traditional-minded villagers and xenophilic urbanites patronizing quite distinct forms of music. In the pre-cassette era in India, this dichotomy was represented, in its most general level, by the distinct audiences and associations of folk music and, alternately, film music, with film music, as we have noted, being associated with modernity, Westernization, urban culture, and relative freedom from the confining traditions of caste, familial obligations, and the like.

In Indian economy, society, and musical aesthetics, the dialectic interactions of tradition and modernity are particularly complex and overt. Some 70 percent of the population remains rural, and feudal relations (*jajmani*) persist in some areas; caste and religion in general are alive and well, while some traditional practices, such as dowry, are intensifying rather than attenuating.

While urbanization has accelerated in recent years, studies have shown that village migrants to cities retain many aspects of rural life and values, clustering in slums segregated by region of origin, and continuing to endorse much of the fatalistic, superstitious, and generally traditional belief systems (Mishra 1970:53–58, 96). Hence rural folk genres are widely performed in cities, where performers of folk theater and music (for example, *nautanki* and *birha,* respectively) find concentrated audiences nostalgic for aspects of their village life.

At the same time, various forms of modernization, ineluctable throughout the twentieth century, have continued to intensify in recent decades. Nostalgia for village life notwithstanding, most migrants to cities evidently prefer urban life to the stifling tradition of the village (Mishra 1970:67–70). In the cities they come to enjoy greater access to the mass media, whose impact, on the whole, has tended to promote modern social values such as education and secular nationalism. As we have seen in chapter 3, films and film music, while in many ways contradictory and ambiguous in their orientation, have been associated, on the whole, with modernity, or, more properly, with a certain sort of modernity. Conversely, and not surprisingly, it becomes very clear through conversations with diverse Indians that folk music and folk culture in general are associated with tradition.

An excerpt of a conversation (in Hindi) I had with a teenager from rural Haryana was typical. The youth responded to my inquiry about his musical preferences, saying, "I like film music. Only old village folks and a handful of young people still like *sang* and *ragini* [traditional Haryanvi folk genres]." When I observed that traditional music appeared to remain popular among young people in neighboring Rajasthan, he opined, "Actually, the Rajasthanis are rather simple and backward people." (Conversely, some Rajasthanis take great pride in the vitality of their region's folk traditions.)

Similarly, one finds indigenous residents of cities like Banaras speaking condescendingly of villagers and rural migrants who congregate for *birha* performances. Even in the countryside, young people are drawn more than ever toward the glamor, the diversity, and above all, the social *freedom* associated with modernity in the form of film culture.

Film culture and film music tend to promote aesthetic and ideological homogeneity at the expense of the rich diversity of values and practices associated with individual communities based on region, religion, caste, gender, age, and occupation. Before cassettes, the public had a somewhat limited choice, consisting primarily of traditional folk musics and film music. Film music, on the whole, has constituted a meaningful and greatly enjoyed vehicle for the formation of a social identity synthesizing "modern," urban, and Western aesthetics with distinctly Indian features. At the same time, it has done so at the expense of regional and community values, which, while traditional in origin, were capable of being incorporated into new, syncretic, and more representative beliefs and art forms.

In recorded music, it was only with the advent of cassettes that Indians have been able, for the first time, to create and enjoy, on a mass scale, syncretic hybrid musics that are at once modern and affirmative of diverse community aesthetics and values. In accordance with the diversity of the public, the cassette-based regional musics that came to be marketed from the mid-1980s present a heterogeneous body of music, in terms of specific community aesthetics as well as the degree and nature of "modernity" represented. For the first time, syncretic popular musics could emerge which incorporate the full spectrum of extant traditional sources, and which are completely independent from film culture, with its attendant escapism, corporate control, and homogenizing tendencies.

The regional musics which have come to be disseminated on cassettes span a continuum from purely traditional styles to Indian-language disco, with a great variety of hybrid syntheses in between. In this chapter I shall explore some of the features of the development of these styles and the music industry which generates them. The following chapter will focus on a particular region—the Braj area—as a specific case study.

Cassettes and Diversification: Region, Language, and Genre

A considerable amount of regional music had been marketed before the advent of cassettes. Much of this output, particularly in Punjab and Gujerat, was associated with regional cinema, which accounted for roughly 30–40 percent of films in the postwar decades. In general, most regional-language film music tended to adhere to the stylistic norms of the mainstream Hindi film song, just as most regional films themselves have resembled low-budget versions of Hindi cinema (with the exception of social-realist Bengali films). Regional cinema was only active in the larger language areas, thereby generally excluding linguistic regions such as Braj, Garhwal, Chattisgarh, Bundelkhand, and Maithili-speaking Bihar. GCI and its subsidiaries and fledgling rivals did issue a large number and variety of non-*filmi* records in several regional languages and dialects, although, as we have seen, in quantity of sales they do not appear to have constituted more than 10 percent of the record market, with most of the remainder consisting of mainstream film music. Moreover, as we have noted, regional folk-music records consisted almost entirely of 78- and 45-RPM discs, so that the leisurely narrative ballads so typical of North Indian folk music were scarcely represented, if at all.

The spread of cassette technology decentralized and diversified the formerly oligopolized Indian recording industry by making the means of musical mass production, as well as playback technology, accessible to an unprecedentedly broad and heterogeneous public. While the initial impact of cassettes, aside from piracy, primarily involved lingua-franca *ghazals* and *bhajans*, the spread of cassettes to regional musics was an inevitable development. The years 1983–85 were the period of most dramatic expansion, when regional cottage cassette companies sprang up throughout the subcontinent, millions of rural consumers came to own indigenous or imported "two-in-ones," and all manner of regional genres and subgenres started appearing on cassette. By 1991 regional-music cassettes were estimated to account for 40 to 60 percent of the entire recording market in India.[1]

The decentralization of the music industry led to several forms of musical diversification, most notably within the parameters of region, language, genre, and performer. The increase in geographical and linguistic variety is perhaps the most visible of these. The pre-cassette recording industry had largely neglected many, if not most specific language areas of India. There appear to have existed no more than a handful of records representing the musics of Garhwal, Haryana, and Himachal Pradesh. Most records were in Hindi-Urdu, which, while understood throughout most of North India, is a primary native language only to middle-class Indians or residents of the Delhi-Meerut *khari-boli* region. That is, even in the so-called Hindi belt, villagers and lower-class town dwellers outside the *khari-boli* region generally speak dialects among themselves (Braj, Chattisgarhi, Maithili, Kannauji, Bundelkhandi, Bhojpuri, Avadhi, etc.) which may be mutually unintelligible, and are quite distinct from standard Hindi. Moreover, these regions and dialects have their own associated genres and repertoires of folk songs and ballads. The same may be said of other major language areas; for example, most Punjabis understand standard modern Punjabi, but in the villages the primary languages are distinct dialects of Punjabi such as Multani. The pre-cassette record and film industry, on the whole, made little attempt to represent these "Little Traditions," concentrating instead on lingua-franca genres.

Naturally, cassettes in lingua-franca tongues, especially Hindi, still abound, particularly as produced by the larger companies (T-Series, HMV, etc.). What is new is the flourishing of commercial tapes representing most of the larger regional dialects of North India. Hence, for example, Garhwali music cassettes have come to constitute a thriving industry, selling both in Garhwal itself and in North Indian cities (especially Delhi) where Garhwali migrant workers abound.

Similarly, even within regions and dialects that were represented by the record industry, cassettes have led to the dissemination and marketing of numerous specific genres that were deemed unsuitable or commercially unprofitable for the record industry. Particularly common among these, as mentioned above, are lengthy epic ballads (*Alha, Dhola* etc.) and *kathas*. Full renditions of these ballads may take many hours; ample segments, however, are presented on single cassettes or in the form of three-cassette packages, as produced, for instance, by Rathor Cassettes of Mainpuri district. Also marketed have been a wide variety of genres which were simply too limited in popularity for the record industry, but are adequate for the maintenance of local cassette producers.

Moreover, there is at least one instance of a cassette-based genre associated with a specific profession, namely, bawdy Punjabi songs for Punjabi truck drivers. While truck cabs generally seem to contain two or three riders, truck driving is not really a communal profession, and my informants concur that there was no song repertoire associated specifically with drivers until the advent of cassettes, which led to the emergence of this entirely new genre in terms of text.

Cassettes have also greatly diversified and increased the number of performing artists. As noted, the domination of film music by a tiny handful of vocalists, and a slightly larger clique of producers, constituted a degree of monopolization unparalleled in the international recording industry. In the early stages of the cassette era, the emergence of star vocalists like *ghazal* singers Mehdi Hasan and Anup Jalota, who were independent of cinema, was a relatively unprecedented event (Rahman 1987). While *ghazal* singers like Jalota and Pankaj Udhas went on to become involved in film music and other genres, the spread of cassettes, and especially of regional-language tapes, led to the recording of innumerable new artists. Some of these, such as Punjabi singer Gurdas Maan and Bhojpuri vocalist Sharda Sinha, have become renowned and wealthy singers; beneath them is a vast panoply of more obscure singers known only to their local constituencies.

As might be expected, the larger cassette companies—T-Series, MIL, Venus, and HMV—tend to take advantage of their extensive distribution networks by producing and marketing genres like *ghazal,* film music, and Hindi pop, which enjoy pan-regional popularity. Accordingly, while T-Series and some of its peer companies do target more specialized markets, they naturally tend to attract the most popular and renowned performers. To some extent, as with "majors" and "indies" in other recording industries, it remains the smaller companies that bear most of the burden of artist and repertoire research and development, discovering and promoting unknown talent and markets. As one small producer said of undiscovered local performers, "The crux of the problem was that the big companies were simply not willing to give these talented people a chance."[2] As artists and subgenres become better known, they then tend to be picked up by the large companies, who can offer better distribution, royalties, and prestige. Several smaller cassette producers expressed to me their resentment of large companies like T-Series, which would woo away performers who had been initially discovered and promoted by regional cottage cassette producers.[3]

Cassettes and Class Expression

Aside from diversifying repertoire in terms of region, dialect, genre, and artists, cassettes have also led to some fragmentation and specialization of the market in terms of socioeconomic class. Prior to the cassette era, interest in classical music was confined largely to the elite, but most film music was enjoyed by rich as well as poor. Urban audiences, and those affluent enough to afford radios, record players, and frequent movie tickets naturally had greater access to cinema, but both rural and urban lower classes did cultivate interest in film music insofar as they could gain exposure to it. However, if film-music audiences were diverse, the class background of the producers was not, but rather was limited to the corporate elite associated with the Bombay film world. The advent of cassettes dramatically changed the elite domination of the music industry.

The class background of the producers was significantly diversified. Setting up a cassette company does require a certain amount of capital, starting with around five thousand rupees (about three hundred dollars) for a duplicating machine. Most small producers find themselves obliged to invest considerably more. Nevertheless, many founders of cottage cassette companies, while not proletarian or peasants, are at most lower-middle-class, perhaps expanding into cassette production from owning a small electronics shop or recording studio. In this sense their class background is quite distinct from that of film and film-music producers, which is exclusively corporate elite. It has been noted that emergence of oppositional, proletarian mass-media content has often been inhibited by elite ownership of the media. Working-class expression can only be ideologically contradictory when that class does not own the relevant means of production—the mass media (Limón 1983). The extension of music-industry ownership in India to lower-middle classes could constitute a significant precondition for the emergence of more oppositional forms of music.

Certainly, cassettes have become vehicles for the dissemination of a wide variety of lower-class genres which are scorned by both rural and urban elites. Punjabi truck drivers' songs and bawdy Haryanvi *ragini* and Braj *rasiya* are obvious examples; beyond that, it may be stated that in the cities and towns, folk music in general, while formerly patronized by a broad social spectrum, has become increasingly identified with lower classes. As urban elites have gradually withdrawn patronage from and participation in various forms of folk theater (e.g., *nautanki*) and music (*birha, rasiya*), such genres may have acquired, in some cases, a certain sense of lower-class solidarity, reinforced by songs and dramatic scenes poking fun at Brahmins and elites.[4]

Members of the upper and middle classes tend to regard as vulgar the bawdiness of contemporary commercial *rasiya, popat, koli git, ragini,* Punjabi truck drivers' music, and Bhojpuri folk songs. Such elite scorn may only increase the appeal of such genres to the lower- and lower-middle-class men who purchase such cassettes, and in that sense, the uninhibited eroticism of these genres could be said to constitute a sort of oppositional quality implying lower-class solidarity. One could also argue that sexual discourse is an important aspect of sociopolitical life, and that a mass-mediated rejection of bourgeois conventions might not be without its progressive aspects. Another perspective, however, might regard such songs as reactionary, sexist, and hardly the stuff out of which socioeconomic revolutions are made. Further, many Indians attribute the lewdness of such contemporary genres not to folk precedents, but to the influence of film culture. Insofar as this assessment is correct, it becomes even harder to regard bawdy folk songs as expressions of lower-class identity, if the original inspiration for such erotica is the corporate film industry. Any identification of folk *masala* (which will be discussed in greater detail below) with subaltern solidarity is thus inherently problematic and contradictory.

Accordingly, the emergence of explicitly counter-hegemonic, mass-mediated song forms would be another matter. Songs promoting oppositional class solidarity are found among certain politicized groups of subalterns, such as the untouchable Mahars of Maharashtra (Junghare 1983). They are also promoted by leftist street theater groups associated, in North India, primarily with the CPM (Communist Party of India-Marxist) and IPTA (Indian People's Theatre Association). A few progressive folksingers—most notably, Balleshwar, of Bihar—have gained notoriety. Throughout most of the hinterland, however, progressive sociopolitical songs promoting lower-class mobilization do not appear to be widespread. Many individual castes, such as washermen (*dhobis*), have their own characteristic song forms. But in most villages, any potential sense of lower-class solidarity is weakened by caste and religious rivalries and factionalism. Political consciousness—of the sort that would unite the poor against the elite—is relatively low throughout most of India (Bengal and Kerala constituting the major exceptions). Thus, while cassettes may be providing lower classes with control of the means of music production, which could conceivably lead to the emergence of mass-mediated progressive song, on the whole, such song forms have not flourished, because they are not widespread to begin with on folk levels. Cassettes have in fact come to be widely used in political movements, as will be discussed in chapter 10. However, the most extensive use of political cassettes has not been identified with any particular class—except, perhaps, manipulative elites.

Gender

Much of Indian traditional music has been and remains gender-specific in terms of performers and/or audiences. In village North India, women's music comprises a large variety of amateur song types, related to work, weddings, son-births, seasons, and other occasions (see, e.g., Henry 1988:25–114). Other genres, such as bawdy *nautanki*-derived *rasiya* songs, and light-classical *thumri* and *ghazal* in the premodern period, have traditionally been performed primarily by professional women of low status, for male audiences. Conversely, music performed by men includes a variety of amateur genres, and to some extent a greater breadth of professional song types than those associated with professional female performers. As cassettes have so exponentially increased the quantity and diversity of mass-mediated musics, it might be natural to expect that some kind of women's music—music produced by and for women—might earn a substantial niche of its own on music-store shelves, and that cassettes could come to serve as vehicles of empowerment and solidarity among women.

It is true that one can now find cassettes of women's folk-song genres, such as wedding songs and Punjabi *giddha,* which may be played as background music during festivities, or used by women to learn new (or old) songs. Courtesan performers, especially in provincial towns, have recorded many cassettes of erotic *dadra, rasiya,* and other genres enjoyed primarily by men. But on the whole, cassette culture, like Indian public culture in general, is primarily male culture. From all accounts of informants, men constitute the vast majority of customers and thus naturally determine the gender orientation of most popular music. Further, my own impressions of consumption and usage patterns corroborate the observations made by Mills (1991:61–63) in regard to cassette usage in Herat, namely, that men, rather than women, generally own and manipulate cassette players, and that women are discouraged from using them even at home; as Mills observes, "The differential use of tape recorders is thus part of a larger, long-standing pattern of gender-based differences, which pertains even in the absence of . . . new, foreign gadgets." Finally, insofar as control of the means of production is a prerequisite to empowerment, it is noteworthy, although hardly surprising, that the cassette trade itself is completely in the hands of men, as far as I have been able to determine. I never encountered or heard of any female owner or manager of any cassette company (with the exception of a small feminist society in Delhi, to be discussed in chapter 10).

The representation of gender in Indian folk and popular music is an extremely complex subject. At this point it will suffice to point out that while cassettes have served as vehicles for the mass dissemination and even the evolution of a prodigious variety of musics in terms of region, ethnicity, language, and religion, most of these genres remain oriented primarily toward male consumers; a decentralized cassette industry may provide one essential prerequisite for the eventual emergence of a mass progressive women's song movement, but such a development, like the advent of a proletarian solidarity mobilization, will have to await a broader political consciousness among the Indian masses.

The Impact of Commodification

Thus far, this volume has tended to emphasize the ways in which the cassette-based music industry differs from the film-music industry in offering a much greater diversity of musics and styles, which more faithfully represent the variety of North Indian genres and aesthetics. Nevertheless, the effects of cassette technology are complex and contradictory, and in some respects reinforce, rather than counteract, tendencies manifest within the earlier, corporate-dominated Indian music industry. Cassettes, after all, are commercial commodities whose production is subject, in varying manners and degrees, to many of the same constraints and incentives of capitalist enterprises in general, such as goals of maximization of profit and economies of scale. Accordingly, if film music can be accused of manipulating consumers' aesthetics by superimposing values deriving from the inherent structure of the music industry, cassette-based musics can be seen to perpetuate some of the same tendencies.

In the introduction to this volume (as in other publications of mine), I have defined popular music, for my purposes, as music which is disseminated as a mass commodity, and whose style can be seen to have evolved through its association with the mass media. As suggested above, the variety of regional and devotional musics now marketed on cassettes spans a continuum, from folk (and classical) genres executed in purely traditional style, to others whose style has clearly been altered in the process of commercial production. In between these extremes lie a great number and diversity of recordings which defy facile classification into "folk" or "popular" categories, and whose precise categorization is not a goal of this volume. The study of regional cassette musics does require, however, some examination of the kinds of stylistic alterations that occur in the process of selecting, recording, and packaging musics for cassette dissemination. The influences of commodification via cassettes discussed below, then, are not unique to cassette production, but common to the recording industry in India (and elsewhere) in general. However, their visibility and palpability in the cassette industry allow us to witness the commercialization process in action.

An initial constraint is that commercial cassette producers, whether large or small, will only market genres whose audience is large enough to provide a profit. As noted above, a homemade recording of an obscure local singer may generate a profit with sales of only a hundred tapes. Most professional productions, however, require a larger investment and an accordingly larger market—even if it may still be incomparably smaller than that needed for a film score to be profitable. Thus, for example, there are relatively few cassettes of Avadhi (Lucknow-area) folk music, since there appears to be relatively little folk music that is distinct to that area, and, further, folk music is less vital and widespread there than in neighboring regions, such as the

Bhojpuri-speaking area.[5] Similarly, the Pahari regions of Himachal Pradesh, although relatively densely populated, are linguistically so fragmented that cassette producers have tended to market tapes only in the dialect of the Kangra valley (which, of course, was itself neglected by the pre-cassette record industry).[6] The Himachal hill regions differ in this respect from neighboring Garhwal (northwestern Uttar Pradesh), most of whose two million inhabitants understand lingua-franca Garhwali (while perhaps speaking slightly different dialects amongst each other). Garhwali music, accordingly, has come to constitute an extremely active and dynamic commercial market for cassettes. Further examples could be given, but the aforementioned should suffice to illustrate that while cassettes are able to offer incomparably greater regional and stylistic variety than film music, there are limits to the degree of diversity they represent. Thus, within a given region, cassettes may in fact serve to promote a degree of homogeneity and standardization—for example, disseminating standard Garhwali rather than peripheral dialects.

Aside from selection of genres and markets to be exploited, the cassette industry has tended to promote certain predictable stylistic changes and tendencies, some of which resemble and may be influenced by those features of film music or foreign popular musics. The most obvious of these tendencies— the preference for talented and professional-quality performers—is generally taken for granted, but is not insignificant. As anyone who has spent time in an Indian village can attest, ability to sing in tune is not a prerequisite to participation in amateur song sessions, and villagers generally do not appear to mind when collective songs acquire the texture of some kind of cacophonous parallel organum. As might be expected, professional cassette producers are more discriminating, and in selecting (or trying to select) only skilled vocalists, their product may be said to represent a certain kind of "ideal" rendition rather than an "authentic" one.[7] (It may nevertheless be mentioned that many, if not most folksingers represented on cassettes are not remotely as polished as film singers.)

A more overt sort of stylistic media-influenced alteration is the addition of nontraditional instrumental accompaniment. Of course, many cassettes employ purely traditional instrumentation, especially, for example, in cases where producers think their more traditional-minded listeners would disapprove. Cassettes of Rajasthani folk music generally feature sparse and plain instrumentation—typically, harmonium and barrel drum—as producers feel that Rajasthanis prefer unadorned, traditional textures.[8] In other cases, and particularly with smaller companies, producers eschew elaborate instrumentation because they are unable to pay for extra musicians, arrangers, and rehearsal time.

Individual producers also have different personal preferences. Most medium- and high-budget recordings, as produced by more ambitious entrepreneurs, do feature more elaborate accompaniment. This generally takes the

162

form of additional instruments and precomposed instrumental interludes. The added instruments typically include combinations of mandolin, "banjo" (a rectangular plucked stringed instrument with keys), sitar, *bansri* (bamboo flute), *shahnai* (oboe), and most commonly, either a Casio keyboard or else a synthesizer. In some cases only indigenous instruments are used, but they are combined in nontraditional ways (e.g., sitar with *shahnai*). In general, the concept of juxtaposing passages in contrasting instrumental timbres, although long since common in film music, is foreign to traditional Indian music.

Instrumental sections generally consist of opening and closing passages, and interludes in between verses. Such passages are referred to by the English term *music*.[9] Most Indian folk-song types, as well as *ghazal* and *bhajan*, are strophic. In many, if not most of these genres, vocal strophes would traditionally be separated by interludes featuring lively drum passages called *laggi*, during which the singer(s) may remain silent or reiterate the *mukhra* refrain. From the 1930s on, it became common in *filmi* as well as non-*filmi* recordings of folk and popular music to replace *laggi* passages with precomposed instrumental interludes ("music"). This trend has been intensified with the commodification and cassette dissemination of numerous other folk genres in recent years.

A look at a few contrasting, yet typical recording sessions may provide some sense of production procedures and the approaches used therein. As we have suggested, low-budget recordings of folk music for rural, lower-class audiences, as produced by small, cottage cassette companies, generally are the most straightforward and inelaborate in their instrumentation and recording procedures.

We may take as representative a session by folksinger Nemi Chand (witnessed in December 1990). Nemi Chand, a semiprofessional singer from Agra, has recorded several cassettes of Braj folk music, primarily *rasiya* and devotional songs. He and his brother are poets, composing lengthy retellings of episodes from devotional mythology. Trimurti Cassettes, a small-scale Agra-based producer of Braj folk music, has commissioned a cassette from Chand, paying also for the recording to be done in Delhi's Saraswati Studio. Saraswati, a medium-budget studio near Ansari Road, has eight-track recording, and is also home to Saraswati Recording, H. L Vir's sideline company producing regional music (primarily Garhwali).

Nemi Chand and his accompanists—who play harmonium and *dholak*—travel by train to Delhi, and are ready at the recording studio by 10:00 A.M. the following morning. Because they play together regularly, there is no need for rehearsals, or for a music producer. Saraswati's owner, H. L. Vir, directs the musicians in placement, installing the percussionists in a newly constructed, windowed booth. After cursory sound checks, the recording begins. Nemi Chand sings for about fifty minutes, reading the lyrics from a notebook. The genre is Govardhan Puja—a prayer about Govardhan, a Braj village renowned in Krishna lore, and in the *Puranas*. Specifically, Chand's verses are a leisurely, highly adorned retelling of a specific set of incidents in the *Puranas*. He sings them, in a somewhat high, but not unpleasant voice, to familiar *rasiya* tunes. He and his accompanists are all competent and familiar with recording procedure, so the session proceeds without problems. When Chand finishes, they listen to the entire recording and relax over tea served by Vir's lackey. Vir informs them that another seven minutes of music should be recorded to fill up a sixty-minute cassette. Chand flips through his notebook to find a segment of the appropriate length, and the recording is then completed. Vir makes one cassette copy from the reel-to-reel ("spool") master, whose fidelity they can compare with the marketed cassettes which Trimurti will produce. After more tea, Vir is paid for his time, and the musicians depart with the master and cassette dub. The entire process has taken less than three hours—a minimum, in some respects, but by no means inadequate or confining.

Another low-budget folk music recording session at Vir's Saraswati (witnessed in spring 1990) can serve in some respects as a contrasting example, in terms of efficiency of production. Rathor Cassettes, a small producer of Braj folk-music tapes in Kirauli, a market town near Mainpuri, has comissioned a local singer, Kamla Bai (pseudonym), to record a tape of *sohar*, folk songs celebrating the birth of a male child. Kamla Bai is the daughter of a courtesan (singer-prostitute) from Mainpuri. Like her mother, she gives occasional programs of Braj folk songs; she also sings some film tunes and occasionally records, when requested, for Rathor. Formerly wed to a drunken ne'er-do-well, she now struggles alone to provide for her two children. An occasional freelance producer, whom we shall call Shaukat Hussein, has been hired to run the recording, which, in this case, involves booking the studio (again, Saraswati), hiring the musicians (who play Casio keyboard, *dholak*, *naqqara*, harmonium, and *ghungru* bells), and overseeing the session. Hussein is given a flat fee to cover all these expenses, the remainder of which is his profit. He has thus hired acquaintances of his, after cajoling them into accepting rather minimal remunerations.

In this session, the musicians and singer have never performed together, so some rehearsal is needed. Hussein instructs the Casio player to provide some sort of "music" in between strophes. For these interludes, the "Casio-*wala*" (Casio-guy) draws from a repertoire of film-song ditties which accord with the mode of the song. The recording proceeds in an uneven fashion. During the semi-improvised "music" interludes, the Casio-*wala* and the harmonium-*wala* are getting in each other's way, and the concluding rhythmic cadences are not coming out smoothly. Several restarts are needed. During the music, Hussein, who is not himself a musician, waves his hands as if conducting, but fails to create order.[10] As a result of various problems, it takes five hours to record sixty minutes of *sohar*. Rathor, who is also present, decides that they should try to record an hour's worth of spicy *rasiya* songs in the remaining time. The performers are to try to simulate a *chap* (live program ambience) during which audience members come forth to give tips and have their largesse and names announced by the singer. Accordingly, in between strophes, Kamla Bai shouts "Eeeeey, woh aya!"—in this context, "Here he comes!" Rathor, reading from a list of retailers of his cassettes, then shouts into the microphone "Sushil Kumar of Kumar Electronics in Etawah has given fifty-one rupees" (or some similar announcement). Soon, however, he and Hussein stop the recording, as they have both decided that the ensemble should now include *naqqara*, a pair of kettle-drums used, among other contexts, in *nautanki* theater, and, since recent years, in *rasiya*. The *naqqara-wala*, who has been sitting idle all day, starts to play, but then announces that the humidity has loosened his drum skins so much that they are unplayable. There is little time left, and tempers are getting short as no one has eaten all day, so they conclude the session. Before leaving, however, they speak with a husband-wife team of *qalandars* (itinerant mendicant musicians) who have materialized looking for work. Hussein and Rathor know the wife, Tara, who sings well, and are interested; unfortunately, it emerges that she is unable to sing without playing *dholak* at the same time, and Vir claims that this format will be impossible to record presentably.

By way of contrast with both these low-budget sessions, we may have a look at a more sophisticated and expensive production. The lead performer in this case is Sharda Sinha, a Bihari woman of middle-class background, who has become the leading professional singer of Bhojpuri folk song since the advent of cassettes. She reportedly charges up to fifty thousand rupees for a recording, and her tapes sell throughout Bihar and eastern Uttar Pradesh. She is recording, in this case, for T-Series, who intends the performance to be a polished, high-quality production. Accordingly, T-Series has hired Jwala Prasad, who together with Charanjit Ahuja, is the leading music producer in Delhi. Prasad and Ahuja, like many Western music producers, are the real talent behind many successful recordings. They are not celebrities, and their names appear only in small print on cassettes, but they are well-paid and in constant demand. Prasad is from a prominent musician family of Jaipur, while Ahuja is from a nonprofessional Punjabi family. Both are largely self-taught in terms of arranging, composing, and familiarity with Western chordal harmony.

Prasad's main task in such sessions is to compose and arrange the "music." To do this, he, Sinha, and a few sidemen spend a day in the studio before recording. Sinha sings the first few strophes of each song, here consisting of new lyrics set to familiar tunes. Prasad then closes his eyes, hums and fiddles with a harmonium before him, and in the space of a few minutes composes an instrumental interlude, perhaps consisting of a short melody, which is harmonic in conception rather than purely modal, and is played on *shahnai*, with chordal accompaniment played on guitar and harmonium. A scribe of sorts jots down the melodies in Indian *sargam* (sol-fa), along with Prasad's instruction for instrumentation.

Prasad's skill is quite extraordinary. His interludes, composed on the spot, are highly tuneful and tasteful, and Sinha and the sidemen are all exclaiming and shaking their heads in approbation. (H. L. Vir told me, "He is remarkable; and if he brings in something that he has composed beforehand, it's never as good as when he makes it on the spot!") For their part, the sidemen are themselves remarkably competent. All the melodic soloists (here playing *bansri, shahnai,* and *sitar*) learn their parts after hearing Prasad hum them once, and all are able to provide impeccable improvised solos if requested to. They also know not to annoy their peers by doodling constantly during breaks. As in the West, the better producers tend to rely on a handful of such studio musicians, who are constantly busy.

The songs are recorded the following day. The new sidemen are quickly shown their parts before each song, and the "music" sections are rehearsed once or twice. Usually, each song itself can be recorded in one take. After each take, the performers listen to the recording, while sipping tea. The mood is relaxed and informal, and all appear to be enjoying the session, which proceeds without problems.

These sessions may be seen to represent two contrasting approaches to recording, which are in evidence in most commercial cassettes of folk music. In one style, common in low-budget folk music recordings, relatively minimal instrumentation is used (often only *dholak* and harmonium), and the rendition is essentially identical to what might be heard in a typical live performance by the same musicians. In the other approach, used by the larger and wealthier companies, a professional producer is hired to compose and arrange relatively elaborate, original accompaniment and instrumental interludes.

While the first approach is often occasioned by financial limitations, the two styles also represent distinct aesthetic approaches. For musicians like Prasad, as well as non-musicians who oversee production of the more elaborate recordings, the genuine artistry lies in the professional polish and sophistication of the arrangement. In order to achieve these, the producer's role may be quite active—unlike, for example, in the first session discussed above, in which there was no producer at all. Producers typically describe their role as "improving" or "decorating" (*sajana*) the song. Thus, for example, H. L. Vir says of his own productions of Garhwali music, "No, I am not in favor of the bare, aboriginal sound" (accompanied only by *dholak*). Vocalist Pamela Singh, when asked if her T-Series producers would allow her to record Punjabi songs with only *dholak* and harmonium accompaniment, replied,

> No, because it wouldn't sell. These days, commercial music has to be
> jazzy, with a lot of modern instruments, because it's been seen that

young people buy most of the cassettes, and they want to tap their feet to the music and maybe even dance, and just with *dholak* it wouldn't be successful. (Personal communication, October 1989)

Jagdish Arora, a freelance producer in Banaras, discusses his approach:

I try to beautify the song the way [film-music producer] Naushad used to do, that enhances rather than destroys its folk spirit. It shouldn't be filmi or pop, but it should be professional. So we add instruments to fill out the texture. Violin, sitar, clarinet, whatever, in the background, and harmonium, *dholak,* maybe *shahnai* in the foreground. I don't hesitate to Westernize the "music," but I don't violate the spirit of the song itself. (Interview, December 1989)

Arora despises the provincial, low-budget productions which record folk songs in one take, without any "improvement." "I will take six days to do one song," he boasts, "and those people are doing six songs in six hours. Productions like that are completely commercial, and they are ruining our music." Such an aesthetic may seem contradictory to some listeners, for the slick instrumental interludes and introductions naturally tend to make the product sound more like commercial, studio-produced film music than like folk music. In this context, one man's art is another's commercialism, and vice versa. Further, the positive or negative connotations of "commercialism" are themselves ambiguous in India; during the Sharda Sinha recording session described above, one sideman, while listening to the previous take, clapped his hands with pleasure and exclaimed, "Ek dam *commercial* hai!" (It's absolutely commercial!)—i.e. slick and professional, just like film music. For my own purposes, I might acknowledge that both types of recording could be regarded as commercial in their own ways; the "improved" kind is audibly "commercial" in its studio-made adornment, and brings its product, according to my criteria, closer to popular music than is "pure" folk music. At the same time, I do not intend to posit any value judgements about the aesthetic merit or demerit of either type of "commercialism," or its absence.

Producers may exercise varying degrees of involvement in the textual aspect of recordings as well. Of course, many producers are either poets themselves (such as the aforementioned Chhanvarlal Gahlot), or else (like Siraj ul-Haq) conceive of projects themselves and hire poets to write lyrics on the subject in question. Other folk-music producers, when not dealing with luminaries like Sinha, or poets such as Nemi Chand, may freely intervene in altering the song texts. Jagdish Arora, for example, routinely introduces changes in folk song texts. First, he may change obscure colloquialisms to more familiar terms, in order to broaden the potential audience. Second, he edits vulgarities, substituting, for example, Hindi equivalents of "sleeping" for "fucking" where possible. He observes,

We did several tapes of obscene *gali* [abuse] songs that women sing at weddings; we took out the four-letter words, left the other 95%, and kept the tunes intact. Now the forty songs I produced like that—I have heard people singing my cleaned-up versions in weddings.

Arora describes a third kind of intervention he undertakes:

Usually these folk songs are just short snippets, just a few lines, without much imagery.[11] So I have my poet try to imagine what the sentiment is, and then compose a longer text, to fit to the same tune. For example, we encountered a local folksinger named Surdas, who sang a beautiful *doha* [couplet] by Kabir for us, set to a very nice *tarz*. My brother [Harbans Jaiswal, mentioned above] and I liked it, so we asked Surdas to sing the rest, but he said "That's all there is." So we had our poet, Dhanshakan Mishra [?] compose some very nice *dohas* on the same theme, in the same style.

Arora goes on to describe a further intervention of his:

Surdas sang them, but then I realized that this was a women's song, and I don't think such things should be sung by men, and I told him so. He started to whimper, saying that he had been singing this *doha* all his life. So then we wrote some men's *dohas,* and made the song a duet, with Surdas and a woman singer. It was a big hit, and still sells.

Whatever one's judgment may be regarding the "authenticity" or aesthetic merit of such alterations, they do represent changes introduced in the commodification process, and reflect how a producer's inclination can condition the nature of the final product.

Another tendency of Indian popular musics which is being reinforced by cassettes is the promotion of short songs. While lengthy narrative song genres are widely marketed on cassette, other more flexible genres (e.g., *qawwali, rasiya, bhangra, ghazal,* and *bhajan*) tend to be compressed into four- to six-minute formats. Whether deriving from the influence of 78-RPM records, or from the desire to acquire several tunes in a single purchase (the favorites of which can always be replayed), the perpetuation of this custom on cassettes does reinforce the "sound bite" aesthetic in popular musics and extends it to genres previously uninfluenced by the mass media.

While reinforcing a degree of stylistic and formal standardization, cassettes have provided a remarkable stimulus for the creation of new texts and, in some cases, melodies. Many cassette companies (T-Series and several smaller producers interviewed) insist that their performers, regardless of genre, sing primarily new material, that is, material with new lyrics. In the case of regional folk genres such as *ragini,* a considerable amount of the familiar traditional repertoire may have been exhausted in the first few years of the cassette boom, so that the producers' demand for new material keeps several lyricists occupied (while generating much verse that aficionados find forgettable). Insofar as novelty is a virtue in itself, this aspect of cassette impact should not be regarded as unwelcome. The prodigious production of new texts also introduces a considerable potential for changes in the realm of subject matter; the most conspicuous of these, as we shall see below, has been the increase in ribald lyrics.

Song Texts in Regional Cassette-based Music

Most North Indian folk music is text-dominated, to a much greater extent, for example, than is Hindustani music. Indeed, the text orientation of genres like *rasiya, birha,* and *ragini* explains in part why singers with ordinary voices can become prominent, if they are skilled poets. At this point, it may be appropriate to point out a few distinctive aspects of song texts in regional folk music, primarily to contrast such genres with film music.

The most conspicuous contrast between regional folk musics and film songs is the wide variety of text topics in the former. The vast majority of film songs deal with sentimental love.[12] The same could be said of most Western commercial popular music, and Indian film songs are hardly unique among world popular musics in this respect. The subject of romantic love, of course, is inexhaustible, and is meaningful to practically every human above the age of six. Westerners, and others raised from birth on commercial popular music, may take it for granted that love is virtually the only topic of song texts; but anyone who is familiar with practically any kind of folk music, especially of precapitalist societies, cannot fail to notice how narrow love-oriented popular-song texts are in comparison to the rich variety of textual topics in folk music. The nearly exclusive dwelling on sentimental love in most popular musics may be a fundamental (although seldom acknowledged) aspect of bourgeois Western aesthetics, which in general seeks to obscure class antagonism, and to promote apoliticality, "art for art's sake," and essentially Romantic conceptions of expression. In a country such as India, the domination of sentimental love in film music is another instance of the homogenization and standardization needed in a genre which is designed to appeal to a vast and diverse audience; that is, sentimental love is perhaps the only concern that is shared by all listeners.

The exclusive emphasis on romance, particularly when it comes to be taken for granted, can be seen as a formidable impoverishment in comparison to the diversity of Indian folk-song topics, such as are well represented on the variety of regional musics now disseminated on cassettes. In some regional genres, such as Bengali *adhunik* (modern) song, sentimental love has become an increasingly popular text topic as the genre grows more commercialized via cassettes.[13] On the whole, however, many cassette-based regional musics present a broad spectrum of topical songs, dealing—like the folk genres from which they derive—with virtually all significant aspects of emotional life.

We may take as representative a cassette of Garhwali songs, which, while selected more or less at random, is quite typical of Garhwali cassettes and of much regional music in general. The tape consists of new and old songs, sung by Narender Singh Negi, who has established a reputation, via cassettes, as the most popular Garhwali singer. The song texts are paraphrased as follows:

(1) *Chali bhay motor chali.* A man from the Garhwal hills, after spending years working in the plains, is returning home. The truck in which he rides, dwarfed by the mountains, winds its way up the road, and its driver sounds its horn ("tarara ponpon," followed in the recording by the sound of a truck horn). The sound echoes throughout the hills, and the villagers rejoice, knowing that their relative is returning. He is bringing *gur* and *channa* (snacks) for them; although eager to be home, he tells the driver to slow down so he can get a better look at the comely lasses working in the rice terraces.

(2) *Na kata tau dalyun.* A boy admonishes a girl cutting firewood not to chop any more of the trees than she needs, for the trees are beautiful, and increasingly scarce in the denuded hillside.

(3) *Na baith chakhi ma.* "My wife is going to the fair. My brother works there, running the little Ferris wheel. I say to her, 'Keep your face covered in front of him, to show respect.'"

(4) *Basant dritu ma jai.* A young man urges his sweetheart to join him in celebrating the vernal *holi* festival, throwing flowers and water at each other.

(5) *Ghughuti ghurun lagi.* A girl laments the pain of separation from her parents; she asks a bird to fly to her maternal home and sing to them to remind them of her.

(6) *Dur pardesh chaun.* "Husband, you must go out of town [e.g., to Delhi] to earn money, there is no work here. . ."

(7) *Kanu larik bigri.* A girl's parents lament that her husband has brought her to live with him in the city, so that she can cook for him and their children can go to school; the parents think she has gotten spoilt, that she should be in the village with them, keeping the Garhwali traditions alive.

(8) *Bavan garhu ku desh.* "A district of 52 towns"—an old song of praise for the district, with its able-bodied young men ready to fight, etc.

(9) *Ganga jiki oun.* "It's hard to cross the Ganges, but anyone who can do it is blessed and will enjoy good karma . . . "

These texts, although in many ways unremarkable and typical, invite several observations. The most salient feature is that every text deals with a completely different topic, including commentary on religion, ecology, migrant labor, loneliness, social change, and other matters. Sentimental love, indeed, is conspicuously absent, although it is not an uncommon topic in Garhwali folk music. Equally significant is that the texts do not deal with an amorphous, idealized fantasy romance such as is generally portrayed in film songs, but rather portray specific situations which are each in their own way reflective of Garhwali life. The poverty which drives hundreds of thousands of Garhwali men to seek work in the plains (and especially in Delhi) has been one of the most basic features of Garhwali life for decades, and it is not surprising that three of these songs (1, 6, and 7) deal with different aspects of migrant labor. Similarly, deforestation in Garhwal, as in neighboring Nepal, has reached crisis proportions, causing erosion, landslides, and dire shortage of firewood; (2) above shows that concern about ecological destruction can be expressed not only by educated urban liberals, but by humble rural folk as well. Songs 4 and 5 reiterate traditional Garhwali concerns, while mentioning specific flora, fauna, and customs unique to Garhwal.

It should be obvious to the reader that all these song texts affirm aspects of Garwhali culture, not only in their use of Garwhali language, but in the specifically regional customs, concerns, objects, and beliefs referred to. Many such topics would never appear in Hindi film songs, since even if rendered in Hindi, they would be meaningless or insignificant to most non-Garhwalis. Yet it is clear that Garhwali culture and Garhwali sense of community are affirmed in these song texts (as well as in the use of traditional tunes, and the distinctively nasal, constricted timbre of Garhwali singing).

In regional folk and folk-pop musics disseminated on cassettes, one could easily find thousands of examples of such affirmations of local culture, however humble and indirect. A typical example is a kind of song found in several regions in North India, in which the wife asks her husband to bring a certain object from the market; the song proceeds strophically, with the names of different goods being inserted in the otherwise identical verses. Although the song form itself may be standard, the texts often, in their own way, affirm a sense of regional identity by citing nuts, spices, garments, ornaments, and the like, which are unique to the area in question. In terms of poetic merit and sophistication, such a song, which village women sing to pass time as they work, may be rather ordinary in comparison to many film songs, some of which are penned by highly talented and renowned poets such as Kaifi Azmi. But again, the difference between the film song's standardized content (as well as language and vocal style) and the rich variety of topical folk song is remarkable, and is one of the most distinctive contributions of cassette culture to the Indian mass media.

Cassettes and Lewd Regional Songs

The topical variety of the regional folk and folk-pop songs disseminated on cassettes renders further generalizations about text content somewhat difficult. Nevertheless, one may observe that two categories of textual subjects account for a large portion, and perhaps more than half, of regional cassette music. One of these topics (discussed in chapter 6) would be religion, whether in the form of narrative tales of the gods, expressions of devotional fervor, or praise of various deities or saints. The other category would comprise titillating erotic songs, ranging from the obliquely suggestive to the overtly obscene. The term *masala* (spice) is generally used to denote such erotica in music (while also implying fast-paced action in films). Such *masala* is characteristic of much traditional North Indian folk music; at the same time, informants seem to agree that the amount and degree of vulgarity in regional cassette music have come to surpass by far the proportion of spicy traditional songs. As such, the spread of lewd songs constitutes a significant feature of the cassette vogue, and one which merits discussion for its portrayal of gender relations as well.

Although some aspects of Indian sexual practice and attitudes might be regarded as repressed and conservative by Western standards, Indian folk and elite cultures have always reflected a healthy and uninhibited fondness for the erotic in art. In classical Hindu poetry, amatory and devotional sentiments mingled freely, while temple sculptures like those at Khajuraho portray the most varied and athletic forms of lovemaking. Explicitly erotic miniatures constitute a significant tradition in Indian painting, and until the mid-twentieth century, courtesans cultivated sensual dance styles accompanying spicy *thumris* and other songs (Manuel 1989:21–22). Erotica abounds in twentieth-century North Indian folk music, and there is no reason to doubt that such has been the case for centuries, if not millenia. Women's *gali* (abuse) songs directed at the groom's family are particularly renowned for their whimsical obscenity.

In elite culture, sensuality in art tends to take the form of expressions of longing, which can often be interpreted as mystical desire; Krishna's amorous exploits with the peasant girls of Brindavan constitute favorite topics for verse and painting, as do, to a lesser extent, the gamboling of Shiva and Parvati.

These same themes are common in folk culture, although a somewhat more typical subject is the titillating and often adulterous relationship between a married woman (here, *bhabhi, sali*) and her husband's younger brother (*devar, jija*). Historically, this relationship has precedents in tribal polyandry, the levirate by which the younger brother marries his elder brother's widow, and the classical aesthetic upholding adulterous love—or *parakiya* love—as more intense and passionate than marital relationships (Kakar 1989:9–20; Kakar and Ross 1986:93–94). By contrast, the latter are assumed to be too ridden with duty, responsibility, and formality to be passionate; the young wife, in oral and written literature, and often in reality, typically forms a more erotic and flirtatious bond with her *devar,* who may be closer to her in age, constitutes a natural ally against the domestic matriarchs, and is traditionally more playful and artistic than his dour elder brother.

Verse celebrating this sort of *masala* is extremely common in folk music throughout North India, and it is not surprising that it has become a popular theme in regional cassette-based music as well. In many cases, the titillation is only obliquely hinted at, as in (3) in the Garhwali excerpts above. More often, it is overtly presented. As a typical example (chosen from several thousand possible songs), we may take a Punjabi newly composed folk-pop song from a cassette by the singing duo of Sardul Sikander and Nuri. The first verses are roughly as follows:

SS: I've bought a new Maruti truck and built up its body at Khanna; O *bhabhi,* come and see it.

N: I can't come out open-faced; I'll look at it if your wife comes along.

SS: In the cabin I've put Nuri's picture, and I've got a new cassette by Surender [Shinda, presumably], come and hear it; everyone is looking jealously at my truck, why don't you?

N: If I get in your truck without a veil, what will people say?

SS: I've got the All-India permit, I'll visit all the *gurdwaras* [Sikh temples] and bring you earrings from Nepal . . .

This song's celebration of the titillating *dewar-bhabhi* relationship is quite typical, and there is no overt sensuality here. In other songs, the sensuality is superficially hidden, but intended to be understood by listeners. Thus, when a Haryanvi *ragini* describes a woman going out at night to pick a lemon in the field, an illicit lovers' union is assumed, especially since the lemon (*nimbu*) is a standard euphemism for the male organ.[14] Any reference to wetness is generally assumed to be erotic, in accordance with the romantic associations of the rainy season, as depicted in innumerable Indian miniatures (and in the obligatory wet-sari scenes in cinema). Thus, a Haryanvi song in which a woman relates, "It's monsoon season and my skirt is dripping wet," may elicit snickers and winks from male listeners. Similarly, a listening audience anticipating such euphemisms will have no difficulty interpreting another song on the same cassette, wherein the woman complains, "Your huge bull entered my field last night . . . "[15]

Even more explicit are the numerous cassettes of Punjabi truck drivers' songs, which feature titles like "Punjabi Hot Songs" and "Driveran di Mauj" (Drivers' Entertainment). This subgenre appears to be a product of the cassette vogue, and is unabashedly obscene. In one song, the *devar* urges his *bhabhi,* "You can ride with me in my truck, but it may not be so comfortable, as the road is rough and you'll get bumped again and again . . ." Other songs in this genre are even less subtle, for example, "Come grab my mangos and give me your banana . . ."[16]

Bhojpuri cassette-based songs are equally ribald, with lines such as, "My bed doesn't creak, only my earrings, as my lover undoes my bra" (Tiwari and Ahmed 1991:163). *Rasiya* songs sung in bawdy Braj-region *nautanki* theater, and now on cassettes, reach heights of ribaldry, as in the familiar "*Tapki jae jalebi ras ki*":

> My *jalebi* [an oily, deep-fried snack] drips with juice
> I got this craving from sleeping with a pillow between my legs
> I'm in heat now, my youth is buzzing like a bee hovering over a
>   flower
> My breasts are full of juice . . .
> However much you pump me I won't be satisfied
> The bachelor next door jokes with me and calls me *bhabhi*
> He wants to stick it to me, he's full of energy
> Your brother [her husband] has left me, when I was still stained with
>   turmeric [from wedding rituals],
> I'm only nine or ten years old

That this song, according to informants, derives from early- or mid-twentieth *nautanki,* illustrates that obscenity did not begin with cassettes. Nevertheless, folklorists, musicians, and other informants I interviewed generally tended to agree that the amount and degree of *masala* now disseminated on cassettes is unprecedented in popular or folk culture. Punjabi star vocalist Gurdas Maan asserts, for example,

> There was never this sort of vulgarity in our music before. There were joking songs sung by Asa Singh Mastana and Surinder Kaur, or Lalchand Varma, but it was the duet singers who came after them that made it vulgar. Mostly the villagers enjoy these cassettes, especially because there isn't much cinema in the countryside, so this is the only way they can get this entertainment. The cassettes have popularized this stuff. It's not just *masala,* but decadent *masala, masala* mixed with manure. (Interview, 1990)

Similarly, a two-page article in *India Today,* the nation's leading newsweekly, observes:

> The north Indian folk entertainment always had a zesty taste for the lewd but as it moves into the domain of private listening, thanks to eas-

ily available two-in-ones and cheap audio cassettes, the lyrics are getting bolder. (Tiwari and Ahmed 1991:166)

Some informants also complain that cassettes have taken *masala* songs formerly sung by women in private, and disseminated them as public commodities to lascivious young men. In the process, songs in which women freely express their condition—sexual longing, or ambivalent resentment against seductive neighbors or *devars*—become vehicles for their own embarrassment and objectification when marketed as public commodities.

Aside from the controversial nature of commercially marketing domestic or private forms of discourse, commodification of ribald folk songs can also be argued to have altered the portrayal of gender therein—even in the case of familiar traditional songs. It has often been noted that commercial popular culture in India and other traditional patriarchal societies tends to be predominantly male culture (Kumar 1988:9). Such has certainly been the case with Indian films, which, aside from devotionals, have always been attended primarily by young men, and whose increasing emphasis on action, violence, and obligatory rape scenes seems clearly designed for male audiences (Pratap 1990:69). As I have mentioned, the spread of video among the upper and middle classes has resulted in feature films being increasingly oriented toward lower-class male audiences, whom producers evidently assume to be even more fond of depictions of violence and rape. To some extent, mass-mediated popular musics like commercial Bhojpuri folk song may reflect or acquire aspects of the same male orientation. Producers and writers of regional commercial *masaledar* songs informed me that their products were aimed primarily at young men; many village women, I was assured, enjoyed such cassettes, but were less likely to buy them in the bazaars, which are frequented more by men.

The male orientation of such cassettes is particularly evident in their covers, which generally depict a scantily clad, seductively posed woman, archetypically offering herself to the male gaze. Such covers naturally suggest a certain interpretation to listeners.

Commercialization has masculinized folk music in other ways. While married rural women might enjoy singing spicy songs amongst each other in their homes and villages, they would never sing such songs in public, or on cassette. Instead, the lewd songs are sung either by male professionals or by "unrespectable" women—generally courtesans or women associated with *nautanki* theater. Lila Abu-Lughod has noted this phenomenon in reference to Bedouin popular song; while cassettes have revitalized Bedouin music, she observes,

. . . the new technology makes this discourse primarily masculine.
Cassette tapes, unlike recordings or personal singing, are truly public

and cannot be controlled. Modest women would never want their songs heard by strange men and would never enter a recording studio in town. So they are precluded by the new technology from actively contributing to the revival of Bedouin popular poetry with its radical force. (1989:10)

In fact, some middle-class women do record commercial cassettes, but only of devotional music or innocuous songs. Only courtesan women would record or professionally perform *masaledar* songs.

It is clear that the contemporary vogue of ribald cassettes is a complex phenomenon representing the intersection and rearticulation of a set of distinct traditions and influences. From one perspective, it constitutes a modernization and commercialization of traditional sensual Radha-Krishna portrayals, especially as conflated with stock titillating folk portrayals of *jija-sali* flirtation and spicy erotica in general. At the same time, it can be seen as reflecting the influence of the commercial corporate entertainment industry, and in particular, of contemporary *masala*-oriented films. In terms of class orientation, the erotic content of these films is in itself a contradictory phenomenon, as they are produced *by* a corporate elite, yet *for* an increasingly proletarian (as opposed to bourgeois) audience. Indirect Western influence, via cinema culture, is an additional factor. If the class content of *masala* cassettes is thus ambiguous and parodoxical, a gender interpretation of such music is even more contradictory and complex, as will be discussed in the following chapter in reference to Braj folk cassettes.

Cassettes and Live Performance

In chapter 6 I touched upon the effects of cassette dissemination on live performances of devotional music, noting the somewhat inconclusive and contradictory evidence regarding the oft-alleged tendency of the mass media to replace collective creation with passive consumption. Broadening the scope of the investigation to include regional musics in general provides more data but little more in the way of tangible conclusions.

As mentioned in the previous chapter, some evidence does suggest that in certain cases, cassettes have exacerbated the media's tendency to discourage live performance. Housewives may play tapes of *vrats* rather than reciting them or calling a *pandit* to do so. Similarly, several folklorists and journalists have claimed that cassettes have decreased the attendance at and frequency of live performance in diverse genres, such as Bengali *adhunik* song.[17] Some Punjabi and Rajasthani informants claim that the once inviolable tradition of women's singing at weddings is now quite often forsaken, as middle-class families simply play cassettes, whether of wedding songs or other kinds of music.[18] Ultimately, however, as with devotional music, it is difficult to state with certainty that live performance traditions of regional music are being weakened because of cassettes. Further, cassettes can generate their own sort of social intercourse, as family members listen intently and collectively to tapes, animatedly discuss them, and informally sing the songs they have learned.[19] It is also noteworthy that some genres which are now widely marketed on cassette, such as Rajasthani *katha* and Bhojpuri *birha,* today appear to be performed live more than ever before within memory.[20] Accordingly, it is clear that aside from studio accompanists, very few, if any, performers rely on recording fees for more than a small fraction of their livelihood; rather cassettes are seen as useful for publicity, and for the flat payment received, which is often no more than the standard fee for a live performance. Further, as pointed out before, most folk music cassettes are stylistically close enough to live performances that they represent mere recorded versions of standard performances rather than products of a studio-based genre like film music; in that sense, they can be seen as reinforcing the popularity of folk music rather than undermining it.

Performers have their own perspectives on the effects of cassettes. I encountered two respected singer-poets in the Braj region who claimed that they had refused offers to record out of fear that their audiences would subsequently listen to their tapes rather than book them for programs.[21] Most performers and producers, however, stated the opposite, arguing that cassettes provided renown which subsequently boosted an artist's demand and fees;[22] several examples were given of formerly obscure singers who had achieved fame via cassettes, and whose fees had risen exponentially.

Regional Cassette Musics

The Punjab

We have referred in passing to several of the diverse regional genres which have come to be disseminated on cassettes. At this point it may be appropriate briefly to survey the output of cassette producers in the major regions of North India, noting some of the parallels and distinctions between them. The Punjab hosts a particularly active and dynamic commercial-music scene.[23] Indian Punjab has been one of the country's wealthiest states, with its fertile soil, ample federal investment, and proverbially hardworking populace. Punjabis as a whole are celebrated for their indefatigable industriousness, and Punjabi migrants, who have settled since Partition throughout North India, have distinguished themselves as merchants and businessmen. (Several owners of regional cassette companies in various parts of North India are of Punjabi descent.)[24]

The Punjab is host to one of the subcontinent's richest regional cultures. Lahore was one of the centers of North Indian culture (and especially Urdu culture) in the two centuries preceding Partition. Yet it is perhaps in the realm of folk culture that Punjabi culture is most dynamic. Punjabi poetry is particularly outstanding, with the works of writers like Waris Shah, Bhalle Shah, Baba Farid, and, more recently, Shiv Kumar Batalvi (d. 1973) constituting a lyric devotional patrimony shared and cherished by wealthy and poor Punjabi Hindus, Sikhs, and Muslims alike, whether transmitted by books or by folk-singers. Noteworthy among Punjabi folk-music genres are narrative ballads (*Hir, Mirza Sahiban, Sohini-Maiwal, Sassi-Punnu,* etc.), women's genres like *giddha,* and *bhangra,* which accompanies a vigorous male dance performed at the vernal Baisakh festival (in April) and at weddings and other occasions. All these genres are especially associated with the *jat* cultivator caste, which comprises some three-quarters of the Punjabi population (of all religions).

While North Indian jokes often lampoon Punjabis as provincial and rustic, in fact, aspects of Punjabi culture—and particularly music—in the twentieth century, far from being isolated, have had prodigious impact beyond the Punjab's borders, and have been especially receptive to creative syncretism with Western culture. The Punjab has generated an unusually large number of NRIs (non-resident Indians, i.e., emigrants)—especially in Great Britain and Canada; many of these emigrants maintain contact with relatives in their homeland, and introduce Western commodities, customs, and culture in visits there. Punjabi folk music has been particularly influential on Hindi film music, especially through the work of Punjabi film composers like Ghulam Haider. Quite a few Hindi film melodies derive from Punjabi folk music.[25] The Punjab itself has sustained one of the most active regional film traditions, with distinctively Punjabi music, even if such films did not gain the international renown of Bengali cinema. In the postwar decades, Punjabi non-*filmi* popular music emerged as a dynamic regional tradition. The various duet and solo songs recorded by Asa Singh Mastana and Surinder Kaur were particularly appreciated for their tuneful melodies and soulful, often philosophical lyrics. Other singers, such as Jamla Jat, Prakash Kaur, Madan Bala Sindu, Kuldip Maanak, and Mohammad Siddiq popularized similar newly composed songs using characteristic Punjabi modes, melodies, and rhythms; in doing so they promoted a modernized, slick kind of music which was at once distinctively Punjabi, and yet sophisticated and professional enough for middle-class urbanites to enjoy (Pushpa Hans, interview, January 1990).

Punjabi pop music underwent a dramatic surge in creativity and popularity in the early 1980s, concurrent with the spread of cassettes. In musical terms the primary development was the emergence of pop or "disco" versions of so-called *bhangra,* consisting of characteristically Punjabi vocal melodies set to *bhangra*'s lively eight-beat *kaherva* meter, with various disco-derived percussion effects in the background. Aside from the rhythm and the accompanying dance style, the new Punjabi pop songs (properly called *git*—generic "song"—by knowledgeable Punjabis) bore only a loose relation to traditional

bhangra, which is primarily instrumental, having only occasional shouted vocal stanzas (*bolis*). Nevertheless, the faddish up-tempo dance music came to
be called disco *bhangra,* and Punjabi pop music entered an unprecedentedly
active and vital phase.

Modern Punjabi popular music emerged more or less simultaneously in
India and Great Britain, with developments in each country reinforcing the
other. The social significance of pop *bhangra*'s rise in Great Britain was conditioned by the immigrant experience, and, as Banerji and Bauman (1990)
explain, the coalescence of a hybrid music genre served to express a syncretic
social identity that has been at once Punjabi and modern. The emergence of
pop *bhangra* in Great Britain is dated specifically to 1984, when Alaap, a
Punjabi immigrant folk-music band, released an LP *Tere chunni de sitare,*
which, like the torrent of imitative subsequent releases, "was as genuinely
Indian as it was recognizably disco" (Banerji and Bauman 1990:142). *Bhangra* groups subsequently proliferated throughout Punjabi immigrant communities, performing at nightclubs and at "daytimer" concerts. Animated social
dancing enlivened performances, to the surprise of Britons who had regarded
Indians as hopelessly shy and repressed. In spite of the fact that none of the
groups were able to support themselves by music alone, the *bhangra* musical
scene became quite active, with its own recording labels, radio programs,
concert venues, and even curious attention from the mainstream pop media.
As the recording industry remained disorganized and plagued by piracy, South
Asian grocery-store chains ended up purchasing distribution rights to many
hit records, so that the musicians themselves profited relatively little. Groups
like Heera and Holle Holle, nevertheless, enjoyed star status among Punjabi
immigrants, and the music grew in sophistication, building on "imaginative
use of sampling techniques and high-tech synthesizers" (Banerji and Bauman
1990:146).[26]

Punjabi pop music in India developed in a manner parallel to, although
distinct from its British counterpart. As in Great Britain, the new music
emerged as a syncretic hybrid, synthesizing disco rhythms and instrumentation with characteristically Punjabi modes, melodies, and *bhangra* meter.
Similarly, it can be said to have evolved as a symbolic expression of social
identity for Punjabis (and especially the young) who were exposed to and
interested in modern Western culture, but who wished to retain some sense of
Punjabi identity. For such people, pure rural folk music was too old-
fashioned, plain, and backward, and Western pop music, although attractive,
did not in any way affirm Punjabi identity; thus, like many syncretic popular
musics, the new Punjabi pop developed as a felicitous creative fusion of old
and new, rural and urban, and Western and indigenous.

Beyond this level, the Indian efflorescence of Punjabi music differed somewhat from its British-based sibling. Although pirate cassettes of Heera, Alap,
and a few other British groups are found in Delhi markets, these bands are not

well known in the Punjab proper, especially since they concertize little, if at all, in India. Some of the leading Indian performers, such as Surender Shinda and Sardool Sikander, remain much closer to rural Punjabi culture in their text topics, stage attire, and audience orientation; a few performers, such as Sikander, are from the *mirasi* caste, which traditionally provides music at rural weddings. Most importantly, Punjabi pop music does not accompany the same amount and kind of social dance that has developed in Britain. There is no tradition of social couple dance in Punjab (nor elsewhere in India). Typically, at Punjabi weddings a few men may dance excitedly around the drummers, and occasionally a woman will dance a few steps, to applause and cheers from those standing by, before returning, giggling, to her *sahelis* (female friends). In stage shows by top performers, men often start dancing in the aisles or even on stage with the band, to the distress of ushers. But there are no nightclubs in India where couples can dance to Punjabi music (or any music, except Western pop, in discotheques located in urban five-star hotels). Rather, pop music is heard on cassettes, and at weddings and other festivities where professional groups perform.[27]

Accordingly, lyrics are much more important in Indian-based Punjabi pop than in its British-based counterpart, whose texts are generally short and insignificant, of the "Hey let's dance" variety. The Indian songs, although fast and rhythmic, are meant primarily for listening, not dancing; in their emphasis on texts, they are thus much closer to the songs of Asa Singh Mastana, or, for that matter, to most of Punjabi traditional music, which, with the exception of *bhangra,* tends to be text-oriented. (Stylistically, the modern pop songs, in their intense, virile vocal delivery, bear little resemblance to Mastana's rather effeminate crooning style.) As such, the texts of Indian Punjabi pop songs are much richer, longer, and generally more interesting than those of the British groups; singers occasionally use lyrics of renowned writers like Shiv Kumar Batalvi, Amrit Preetam, and Prakash Sathi. Many songs, as mentioned above, are more or less ribald doggerel about *jija-sali* relationships. Others, even those sung by urban performers, are in one way or another evocative of rural life, which remains the perceived hearth of Punjabi identity. Most songs are in some way suggestive of *jat* attitudes and values—hard work, hard play, humor, machismo, and a distinctive combination of earthiness and wistful philosophy. Quite a few songs deal with the inexhaustible topic of the interface of traditional and Western culture; a typical example is Dilshad Akhtar's "Desi bandri vilayati cheehan" (Native girl, foreign style)[28] describing the familiar figure of the village girl returning from Great Britain who speaks an unintelligible mixture of Punjabi, Hindi, and English, and who is chased by the local men, revered by her girlfriends, and utterly exasperated by life in India.

The dominant figure in the modern Indian Punjabi pop music scene has been singer, poet, and actor Gurdas Maan. Maan was the seminal figure in the inception of the style in 1980–81, and remains the most creative, popular, and dynamic composer and performer. Photogenic, intelligent, and gifted with a fine voice and a charming stage personality, Maan offers something to everybody. Musically, his cassettes (generally produced by Charanjit Ahuja) contain the same slick, professional, harmonious fusion of Western pop and Punjabi ethos as do those of other leading performers like Surender Shinda. In some cases, his evocation of traditional culture is distinctively self-conscious, and deliberately intended to expose young Punjabis—via modernized pop music—to the richness of their traditional culture. A fine example is the commencement of his "Mela char din ka" (A festival of four days), where he sings a few poignant couplets of Waris Shah[29] to the traditional melody of *Hir*, over a disco-type rhythmic accompaniment. Such expressive combinations of old and new, of Punjabi and Western, endear Maan to Punjabis of all generations and backgrounds, and, via cassette dissemination, have won him an audience vastly larger than that of Mastana or any other Punjabi performer.

Maan is particularly celebrated for his lyrics, which, in the best folk tradition, deal with a wide variety of topics. Maan is explicit in his intent to comment on a a broad spectrum of issues and sentiments, saying, "I try to present reality in my songs, not just love. How long can you go on presenting a man praising his sweetheart? So I look for new things" (interview, January 1990). His best-known songs have dealt with such subjects as the tragedies of Partition ("Chulla"), the hypocrisy of back-biting and gossip ("Chugliyan"), the conflicting values of urban youth and the older generations ("Mamla garbar hai"), and, perhaps above all, the meaning of *jat* identity in a changing world, typically presented with an affectionate humor. A typical example is "Thora thora hansna," describing a husband slinking drunk into his house, and being set upon by his wife wielding a rolling pin: "He ducks as she strikes, and she smashes the television. He shouts 'You've broken it!' and she screams 'It was your fault for ducking!' If the Americans and Russians want to fight, they should use our Punjabi women . . . "

Gurdas Maan's rise to fame has occured at a difficult time, when the Punjab has been wracked with the most bloody and uncontrollable violence, in an unending cycle of separatist terrorism, heavy-handed police repression, and central-government obduracy. Maan is well aware that being any sort of public figure in the Punjab today carries significant risks. Amar Singh Chamkilla, the most popular Punjabi singer after Maan, was murdered by terrorists in 1988, for reasons which remain unknown. Although evening programs have been impossible in the state for several years, Maan still occasionally performs there, and continues to call for peace and moderation. At the same time, with the continuing crisis in the Punjab, and Maan's ever-growing national renown, it has been a natural career move for him to broaden his audience beyond Punjabi speakers. Hence, like several other Punjabi pop singers, he often deliberately uses a simple Punjabi that is largely intelligible to many

Hindi speakers, and he also increasingly sings in Urdu. In a memorable television feature in 1989,[30] he presented a series of songs in Urdu and Punjabi, artfully juxtaposing peasant topics, attire, and stage settings with slick urban backdrops and disco-oriented numbers. Naturally, as Maan broadens his audience, he loses some of his admirers, particularly older Punjabis who are fonder of Waris Shah than disco. Nevertheless, he also manages to ride the crest of a current vogue of Punjabi music among non-Punjabis, represented most visibly in the success of Malkit Singh's "Tutuk tutuk," a recycled version of a Punjabi-Pushto ditty, which sold over half a million cassettes throughout North India. (The vogue of this recording also illustrates how "re-discovered" folk songs can enjoy the ephemeral mass popularity of commercial hits.)[31]

I have dwelt on Gurdas Maan at some length here because I feel his music represents a particularly dynamic kind of creative, self-consciously syncretic fusion of disparate cultural elements that enable it to reflect and articulate the social identity of a people in transition. Maan's music, like that of other leading Punjabi pop performers, at once entertains an audience involved in socio-economic transition, affirms and popularizes aspects of traditional culture, and enhances social awareness, without making crippling concessions to commercial pressures.[32] Such music illustrates that there can in fact be alternatives to both traditional folk music and homogenizing, standardized pop mass-produced by an unrepresentative and remote corporate elite. Unlike film-music texts, Maan's lyrics do not restrict their subject matter to the common denominator of sentimental love, but seek to constitute an all-embracing syncretic folklore. Moreover, Punjabi pop is not a studio art disseminated solely by a corporate entertainment industry, but a stage art rooted in live performance, nourished by dozens of professional groups and, obliquely, by deep-rooted traditions of folk dance. This aspect of the contrast between Punjabi pop and mainstream film music is particularly evident in stage performances. In their occasional live concerts, film singers generally render their songs exactly as recorded, standing poker-faced and immobile, face hidden behind a notebook of song texts. Maan, by contrast, dances about animatedly while singing, interacts in the most spontaneous and endearing way with his audience (such as dancing with a child who runs onstage), and freely inserts new lines of text in his songs. It was not surprising that in a January 1990 stage show, where Maan was preceded by film singer Anuradha Paudwal, audience members chatted, ate snacks, and wandered in and out during Paudwal's lifeless renditions of her hits, but came to life during Maan's performance, dancing in the aisles and creating general pandemonium. Other Punjabi performers cultivate similarly animated stage personae.

Although rooted in live performances, Punjabi pop music could never have achieved such popularity without the mass media, and specifically, cassettes. The audience of earlier performers like Mastana was limited not only by the music's style, but by the paucity of phonographs. Maan himself, of course, has acted in a few Punjabi, Hindi, and Haryanvi films, but, as we have seen, his music differs in fundamental ways from mainstream film music; as a result, it is disseminated primarily via cassette, and constitutes, in effect, one of many regional folk-pop genres that have emerged in inextricable association with the the advent of cassette technology.

Rajasthan

Rajasthan, although adjacent to the Punjab, presents quite a contrasting sort of musical culture, with one of the few similarities being the prominent role of cassettes since the early 1980s. Unlike the Punjab, Rajasthan is a poor and underdeveloped state, with arid land, irregular rainfall, negligible industry, isolated villages, and inadequate communications and transportation infrastructures. Many indigent Rajasthanis migrate to Delhi and elsewhere in search of work, and Marwari business families are found throughout India; nevertheless, Rajasthani culture remains somewhat provincial and unacculturated, reflecting little Westernization, and, in comparison with the rest of India, relatively little influence of film culture. Such isolation and material poverty are compensated, in some senses, by the extraordinary richness of Rajasthani folk culture, from textiles and jewelry to folklore and music, which have provided a gold mine for ethnologists (and tourists).

Rajasthani folk music is particularly rich, and remains considerably more popular, even among the young, than do traditional musics in most other parts of the subcontinent. In the postwar decades, a few dozen 78- and 45-RPM records of folk music (especially ribald songs) became familiar in the towns, while a handful of films in Rajasthani dialects popularized songs in more-or-less standard Hindi film style. For most Rajasthanis, however, music continued to be apprehended through traditional media, such as professional and amateur performances at weddings and other events, and by a variety of itinerant professional music, puppetry, and theater groups. By 1980, cassettes were beginning to have some impact. Local entrepreneurs, like Jodhpur's Chhanvarlal Gahlot and Nandu Records, began recording local performers and selling individual tapes (for around fifty rupees) to shopkeepers who could duplicate copies for customers. By 1985 an active regional cassette industry had emerged, consisting primarily of small provincial producers. Thus, six or seven companies currently operate in Jaipur, marketing music in the local dialect. Their products are not to be found in neighboring Marwar (Jodhpur area), whose residents purchase Marwari-language tapes, produced primarily by the Delhi-based Yuki and Target labels, specializing in diverse kinds of Rajasthani music. Mewar (Udaipur area) and Jaisalmer-Barmer districts constitute other distinct linguistic and musical regions. Slick

T-Series cassettes of Marwari and Jaipur-dialect songs are bought primarily by upper-class Rajasthanis, with rural customers purchasing most of the regional product.[33]

Bhajans and various kinds of secular folk songs are well represented on Rajasthani cassettes, but by far the largest category of Rajasthani tapes are of *katha* (story), an extended narrative tale sung to one or more stock melodies. Rajasthani folklore includes a vast number of such tales, which can be said to make up the predominant genre of Rajasthani folk music in general. Most *kathas* come from a repertoire of traditional stories, such as distinct local variants of episodes from the *Ramayan, Mahabharat,* or *Puranas,* tales of regional deities like Baba Ramdevji, historical legends like *Raja Harishchandra, Amar Singh Rathor,* and *Dhola-Maru,* and tragic romances like *Nagchi.* In the absence of canonic texts of these stories in regional Rajasthani languages, a poet or poet-singer may write his own version of a *katha* retelling a familiar episode, with some new and original elements (spicy humor, inventive rhymes, etc.). *Kathas* may also be written on current or recent events, such as the *sati* (widow-burning) that occurred in Rajasthan in 1987, or incidents in the struggle for Independence.

The performance of a *katha* is generally associated with some sort of religious occasion. In some villages, hundreds of residents may collectively recite some *katha* more or less unique to that locality in a night-long ceremony, generally to beseech the gods to solve some problem such as a cattle epidemic. Domestically, housewives may gather to recite *kathas* from memory. In recent decades, cheap printed chapbooks of *kathas* have come to be widely sold in markets, enabling literate housewives to sanctify weekly fast (*vrat*) days by reading a *katha,* such as that of *Satyanarayan* or *Santoshi Ma.* Alternately, a *jagran (rati jagah),* or night-wake ceremony, can be held, for which a *pandit* could be called to recite a *katha,* whether for a son's first haircut (*mundan*), a *vrat,* the blessing of a new house, or a new job, the amelioration of an extended illness, or some other such auspicious or unfortunate situation. Large and small temples will also hold open-air *jagrans* in the warm months, for which a professional singer will be called to perform a *katha.* Hence, in a town like Jodhpur, on virtually any summer night one can hear the sound of at least one amplified *katha* wafting across rooftops.

Evidence suggests that traditionally, an entire *katha* would generally be recited to a single, simple, stock tune. In recent decades, however, professional rendering of *katha* has become considerably more sophisticated, with singers introducing different melodies from diverse Rajasthani genres. Professionals cultivate individualistic styles and repertoires, compete for jobs, and may be paid several hundred rupees for a performance.[34]

Riding the crest of this increase in professionalization and sophistication has been the vogue of cassette *kathas,* which have proliferated since 1985. By

1990, Yuki's catalog alone included some 140 *kathas,* rendered by various performers. The *katha* cassettes reflect the trend toward increased melodic variety and sophistication, as well as higher standards of intonation and delivery. There is little evident trend toward commercialization, for example, in the form of film tunes, or expanded, nontraditional instrumental ensembles. Rather, most producers assert that their Rajasthani customers prefer their music to be traditional in style, accompanied only by harmonium and *dholak.* In this sense, the Rajasthani cassette-based music scene differs markedly from that of the neighboring Punjab, where syncretism with Western pop music is evident in most cassettes.

Katha cassettes may be used for idle domestic listening. Alternately, as mentioned above, during a *vrat* a woman might play a *katha* tape while doing her domestic chores. Folklorist Komal Kothari opines, however, that if a serious boon is sought, housewives would not regard playing a tape as equivalent in merit to recitation or, even better, commissioning a public professional performance. Nevertheless, *katha* tapes abound, and each month brings new releases. Singer-poets like Mohan Jhala of Jodhpur and Bhagwan Sahai Sen of Jaipur generally compose their own lyrics; lesser-known vocalists are hired by poets like Chhanvarlal Gahlot to record.

Komal Kothari has been one of several folklorists concerned that the spread of the mass media may homogenize and thereby impoverish the present rich diversity of regional folklore traditions. A Rajasthani Bhil version of the *Mahabharat* epic, for example, stresses the experience of Draupadi, and commences where the "Great Tradition" epic ends. Some South Indian versions of the *Ramayan* invert the tale's morality, making Rama the villain and Ravana the hero. As suggested in chapter 4, it may be inevitable, for example, that the phenomenal popularity of the Durdarshan *Ramayan* and *Mahabharat* epics, with their audience exponentially larger than any prior versions, may to some extent weaken local variant traditions. Similarly, critics of the current BJP-VHP (Vishwa Hindu Parishad) Hindu chauvinist movement argue that it seems to be intent not only on intimidating Muslims, but in standardizing and codifying a single "Great Tradition" of Hinduism. Again, the role of cassettes in such a development may be significant. On a micro-regional level, cassettes may naturally promote some standardization, as it is unlikely that every rural folkloric variant will be recorded and marketed. On the other hand, cassettes have already come to document an extraordinary and unprecedented variety of *kathas,* representing local regional variants as well as idiosyncratic renditions by individual artists. As with many other regional musics, the flourishing of *katha* and the spread of cassettes are reinforcing and invigorating each other in a remarkable burst of creativity. As producers and artists observe, cassettes are serving to spread Rajasthani music and folklore to migrants throught the country, who would otherwise be losing touch with their traditions. Cassettes are educating young and old about their own culture, and in the process, documenting musical traditions more extensively and professionally than any team of ethnomusicologists could hope to do.[35]

Bengal

Greater Bengal, comprising Bangladesh and India's West Bengal, constitutes one of the subcontinent's largest language areas, with some 170 million people sharing a common language and, to a large extent, a common musical culture, despite religious diversity and political partition. Bengal has supported a fairly large indigenous recording industry since the 1930s. Throughout this period, commercially marketed musics have included various kinds of folk music (e.g., Baul music, *jatra* theater music, *polli git*), devotional *bhajans, qawwali* by local singers like Nabina Qawwal, and above all, a considerable body of newly composed topical songs constituting the category referred to as *adhunik Bangla gan* (modern Bengali song). *Adhunik* song emerged in the early twentieth century, drawing stylistically from ribald theater songs, *tappa,* devotional Ramprasadji songs, and other sources. Its text topics ranged from social commentary to love, and were considerably more varied than those of film music. *Adhunik gan* evolved in close connection with the record industry, which became influential in Bengal from the 1930s; as such, *adhunik* song should be regarded as a commercial popular-music genre rather than a light-classical or folk music (Ray 1973:6–7, 218–19). *Adhunik* song enjoyed great popularity among all urban classes for several decades, enriched by contributions of vocalists like Hemant Mukhopadhyay (Kumar), Sandhya Mukherjee, Suptri Ghosh, Sudhir Lal Chakravarty, and composers like S. D. Burman, R. C. Boral, Pankaj Mullick, Salil Choudhury, Rajanikanta, Kazi Nazrul Islam, and the extraordinarily fecund Atulprasad (who would often compose twelve songs a day in the late 1930s—Ray 1973:13). Rabindranath Tagore's compositions came to be regarded as a somewhat distinct category of *adhunik* songs, meriting their own designation as *Rabindra sangit.*[36]

With the advent of cassettes, recorded output of *adhunik* song and other types of Bengali music has increased, and Calcutta has emerged as a center for production of Orissi and Bhojpuri music as well (especially since Calcutta itself hosts an immense community of Bhojpuri migrant workers). Fledgling *adhunik* singers have been known to subsidize their own cassettes as vanity productions. However, most critics, journalists, and informed commentators do not see the present as a particularly vital period for Bengali music. *Adhunik* song has been in a state of decline since the 1970s, with less topical variety, less lyrical depth, and above all, less interest on the part of the young. Cassettes have served to popularize Hindi film music as much as Bengali music, and much *adhunik* song has come to imitate mainstream film music, thereby losing its Bengali character (Barin Mazumdar, interview, December 1989).[37] Bengali music and cinema are both regarded as being on the defensive against mainstream Hindi forms (Mitra 1986). Further, the spread of cassettes is alleged by some critics to have exacerbated the declining interest in live performances of *adhunik* song. Interest in *Rabindra sangit* is also waning; cassettes of this genre are still produced, although they must all be approved by the board of Vishwabharti, which holds Tagore's copyrights and dictatorially attempts to prohibit any recordings which do not meet the committee's standards of taste and fidelity to the original.

If any form of indigenous Bengali performance art is thriving, it would be *jatra* folk music-drama, which, while incorporating various sorts of garish cinematic effects, is undergoing a remarkable revival (Das Gupta 1987). Cassette producers find that popular plays subsequently enjoy considerable demand as audiocassettes; producers typically edit the lengthy dramas down to one hour, so that they can be marketed on cassette. Naturally, vinyl records were quite unsuited for reproduction of *jatra,* and the genre's current mass-media dissemination via cassettes is a new and auspicious phenomenon, documenting and spreading the plethora of new and old dramas currently in vogue, with very little use of studio effects, nontraditional instrumentation, and the like.[38] At the same time, however, cassettes have come to replace live music in many *jatra* productions (Das Gupta 1987:109).

Maharashtra

In Maharashtra, HMV had been recording and marketing various kinds of Marathi music since the early decades of the century. Aside from film songs in mainstream style, most of these recordings were of relatively sophisticated theater songs, topical *bhav git,* which can be seen as a Marathi counterpart to Bengali *adhunik gan,* and *lavni,* a secular Marathi song form which is perhaps the most characteristic and popular non-*filmi* genre of the region. The commercial Marathi record market, dominated by these genres, was thus aimed largely at middle-class urbanites who could afford turntables. In Anil Chopra's words, "Then the cassette came along and a total revolution took place" (1988b:27). The advent of cassettes, aside from increasing the amount and proportion of local music disseminated, has had the effect of proletarianizing the mass media, leading to the proliferation of commercial versions of folk or neofolk genres, aimed largely at the working classes, and marginalizing older light-classical forms.

A large portion of cassette output consists of *lavni.* While *lavni* exists in several forms, from rustic folk *dholakchi lavni,* to semi-classical *baithakchi lavni,* and film-style *lavni,* the latter form is by far the most popular in cities and towns, and it is that style that is most represented on commercial cassettes. Although resembling film music in style, *filmi lavni,* unlike film music proper, is commonly performed live in the context of urban stage shows and music drama. Its text topics are more varied than those of film music, and in some cases extend to social commentary, as in the humanistic, anticaste songs of Madhu Kada.

Cassettes have also served to further popularize two relative newcomers to the mass media, *koli git* and *popat*. *Kolis* are fishermen, whose distinctive music, or stylized versions thereof, has enjoyed considerable popularity in the Bombay area for several decades, as disseminated primarily via cinema and radio. Cassettes labeled *koli git* have now become the primary vehicle for the genre, even if their only resemblance to the original song form is the use of the characteristic fast 6/8 meter, and the text content portraying light romance and nostalgia among the fishermen's community (as imagined by urban audiences).

Popat consists of bawdy songs oriented, like other *masaledar* regional musics, primarily at working-class men. The genre arose in the mid-1980s, deriving loosely from Marathi theater, but evolving primarily as a cassette-based form (especially since it is seldom heard on radio or in films). In this sense it can be seen as a Maharashtrian counterpart to other ribald genres laden with double entendres, such as Punjabi truck drivers' songs, which have developed in direct connection with the cassette industry.[39] *Popat*'s lack of pretention is evident in the humble tribal ethnicity of its two most renowned recording artists, Anand and Milind Shinde, who have become pop idols among working-class teenagers.

Also widely marketed on Marathi cassettes are the various devotional *abhangs* and *bhajans* mentioned in chapter 6, children's music, and *powadas*, consisting of sung narratives of the martial exploits of Shivaji and other Maharasthrian warrior-heroes.

The Marathi cassette trade reaches a peak in the Ganpati season, when, as in Bengal's Durga Puja, the public goes on gift-buying sprees.

Other Regions

The vast Bhojpuri-speaking areas of Bihar and eastern Uttar Pradesh make up one of North India's larger linguistic areas. Although fertile and intensely cultivated, the Bhojpuri region could be said to resemble Rajasthan in that its rural people are relatively poor and isolated, and, correspondingly, retain a strong interest in traditional regional culture, including folk music. As a result, Bhojpuri music constitutes an active market for cassettes, though limited by piracy and the poverty of its audience. Some thirty companies are estimated to be involved in production of Bhojpuri music; oddly, none of these are based in Banaras, the urban center of Bhojpuri culture. Partially as a result, piracy and bootleg tapes of live concerts abound. Aside from various devotional and topical songs recorded by singers like Sharda Sinha and Hemkunt Jha, the most popular genre is *birha,* a twentieth-century product which has evolved into a narrative tale set to a suite of melodies borrowed from other folk genres, or, commonly, from films. *Birha* is omnivorous in its use of parody, and also in its selection of subject matter, which can range from mythological tales to current political events. (Within a few months of Rajiv Gandhi's assassination in 1991, a commercial cassette of a *birha* on the subject was being marketed.) As a live-performance genre, *birha* is thriving as never before, and *birha* cassettes have proliferated accordingly. As Scott Marcus observes, the majority of these are bootleg recordings of live concerts, which present, as it were, a more "authentic" aesthetic than do the studio-produced *birhas,* which are generally carefully edited and "improved" with added instruments (personal communication).

In Gujerat, the most popular contemporary music genres are modernized versions of *garba* and *ras—disco garba* and *disco dandia.* These commercialized stylizations became popular in the mid-1970s, as an extraordinary fondness for folk-style dancing spread among college clubs, and subsequently middle-class urban neighborhoods. Centered around the autumnal Navratri festival, garish extravaganzas featuring live music, sound systems, and hundreds of dancers in competing groups have come to enliven urban Gujerat and Gujerati communities elsewhere every year. In the wake of the fad, cassettes of *disco dandia* have attained great popularity, creating their own superstar recording artists (especially the duo Babla and Kanchan).

As mentioned previously, cassettes have led to the emergence of an active recording market in Garhwal, where none previously existed. Several small companies based in Delhi now specialize in Garhwali music, producing primarily topical folk songs using distinctively Garhwali melodies and vocal style. One journalist, estimating that one out of four families in rural Garhwal owns a cassette player, asserts that cassettes have greatly revitalized and popularized local music and folklore, making old and new songs and epics available to the most isolated and illiterate hill-dwellers (Abhinav 1989). Accordingly, Garhwali music producer H. L. Vir of Saraswati Records has noted that in towns where he and other producers have marketed Garhwali cassettes, sales of film-music tapes have dropped markedly, again illustrating what should by now be obvious—that when Indians are presented with a mass-mediated alternative to common-denominator film music, many will forsake the latter.

Haryana has also come to constitute an active market for regional cassettes. Haryana, by Indian standards, is relatively affluent and developed, and Hindi film music appears to be the most popular music genre. Nevertheless, Delhi-based cassette producers have found lower-class rural Haryanvis to be avid purchasers of local music like *ragini* and other genres, consisting primarily of lewd double-entendre songs, similar to those popularized in Haryanvi films. Tapes of Haryanvi narrative stories (*kissa*), such as *Mor Dhaj,* are also marketed on cassette.

A considerably smaller, but lively market for cassettes is that based in Goa, generating a variety of stylized Konkani folk musics, as well as Portuguese-derived *mando, dulpod,* and other genres. In the pre-cassette period, only four or five records of Goan music were available. In 1976, when cassettes had barely begun to penetrate India, bandleader Alfred Rose produced a cassette of Konkani music; after a subsequent tape of Oslando D'Souza's *mandos* and *dekhnis* sold ten thousand copies, cassette production of Goan music surged. By 1986 competing companies were producing five or six releases every month, including twenty-one cassettes of Alfred Rose alone. While the market was eventually saturated by such excess production, cassettes have served to promote a significant revitalization of Goan music, even though the vogue consists primarily of light, sentimental, and whimsical songs rather than high-brow Portuguese and Konkani traditional music.[40]

Hindi Pop

Hindi, the lingua franca of the North, and one of the two official national languages, has also become the vehicle for an essentially new category of non-*filmi* popular music, the so-called Hindi pop. While Hindi is not precisely a regional language, Hindi pop and English-language pop constitute specialized, if pan-regional, genres worthy of consideration here. Standard Hindi, although for several decades a first language to many North Indians, has few direct roots in folk culture per se, unlike its regional dialects. As such, the Hindi pop emerging in tandem with the cassette boom does not tend to draw from folk music, but from Western pop music and Western-influenced mainstream film music. Stylistically, then, much of it resembles modern film music; what distinguishes it is that its leading performers have arisen independently of cinema. Accordingly, unlike invisible playback singers, they must be photogenic, and they tend to cultivate distinctive pop images. The most prominent Hindi pop star, the aforementioned Alisha Chinai, has adopted and abandoned various images, particularly "baby doll," which was followed by a period of Madonna imitation. While scholars of popular culture generate esoteric articles deconstructing Madonna's image in the West, it might be quite another subject to try to interpret the sociological meaning of an Indian Madonna clone. Hindi pop, like modern Punjabi popular music, emerged more or less simultaneously in India and Great Britain, where singers like Nazia Hasan and Babla were successfully marketing their own Hindi-language rock to local NRIs. Much of Hindi pop is among the most Westernized of Indian contemporary music, even encompassing explorations into rap.[41]

For several decades, Hindi films and film music have enjoyed considerable popularity throughout much of the world, from Vietnam to Bulgaria. Indian films and film music do not seem to have been created with international audiences in mind. With the cassette-based diversification of the music industry, however, a few performers have emerged who consciously orient their musics toward NRI communities. Most prominent among these musicians are the duo of Babla and Kanchan. The most successful of Babla and Kanchan's cassettes have been Bhojpuri- or Hindi-language songs synthesizing film-song style with modern calypso/soca. Such songs are aimed primarily at Caribbean Indian communities living in the Antilles or in Great Britain. Particularly popular was Kanchan's mid-1980s hit, "Kaisi bani," written by Trinidad Indian calypsonian Sunder Popo. As Meyers notes (1991:239), Kanchan Indianized this and other contemporary soca hits by singing them in Hindi, with her Lata-like girlish voice, and by using characteristic studio techniques typical of Hindi film songs (e.g., echoic soundfield, and "ping-ponging," or double-tracking of the vocal line with a right-left bounce). Other songs of theirs are evidently oriented toward East Africans of Indian descent, whether living in Africa or in Great Britain; an example is the song "Mzuri Sana," which uses mixed Hindi and Swahili.[42] The popularity of Babla and Kanchan, and of the British-based Punjabi groups outside India, reflects a new stage in the internationalization of Indian music, wherein performers, labels, and styles emerge that are oriented more toward NRI communities than consumers in India; tapes of these performers are not widely sold within India itself, and thus they are largely outside the purview of this study.[43]

Anglophone Pop

It remains to mention in passing one final new linguistic market for popular music, namely, the category of English-language pop. English, of course, is not a "regional" language of India, but does serve as a lingua franca for the educated middle class (and is one of the two official national languages). Aside from a few whimsical film songs or passages therein, English had never been used as a medium for any Indian popular music before the mid-1980s. At that point, a small but highly visible category of Anglophone pop came into vogue. The widest-selling cassettes consisted of English cover versions, with rather vapid and inconsequential lyrics, of contemporary Hindi-Urdu hits ("Ek do tin," "Hawa Hawa," etc.), released on the TIPS label.

A few Anglophone rock groups also emerged as appendages to the Indian music scene. Of greatest interest to critics and educated members of the younger generation has been the *sui generis* music of Remo Fernandes. Fernandes, born into an affluent, Westernized Goan family, started recording and producing cassettes of his own idiosyncratic music in his homemade studio. Soon after, he was contracted by CBS and has gone on to establish himself as a fanzine pop idol to some, and a thoughtful, intelligent, and quite unique composer and performer to others. Remo self-consciously promotes his Goan heritage by including local folk songs, in Konkani and Portuguese, in most of his concerts, and featuring them in his cassette *Old Goan Gold*. His own music, however, is totally Western in style. For our purposes, his songs are noteworthy especially for their topical variety. Remo, unlike film composer's, does not restrict himself to the subject of sentimental love, but addresses a wide variety of topical subjects in his music. His songs have commented on such matters as the exasperating Goan telephone system, drug abuse, alleged state neglect of Goa, and Bombay yuppie culture. Far from avoiding controversy in fear of alienating potential fans, Fernandes has eloquently condemned India's current wave of communal violence in his song "SOS India":

> Religious madness catching hold of the nation
> Politicians' gladness, their manipulation, children's sadness
> They cannot understand why mother hates, why father kills,
> Killing in the name of love, killing in the name of God
> Killing in the name of a language,
> Killing in the name of a temple, killing in the name of a mosque
> Killing in the name of a gurdwara, killing in the name of a church
> Killing in the name of Krishna, killing in the name of Allah
> Killing in the name of the Saint, killing in the name of Christ
> O stop, in the name of man, in the name of man, stop.

It would be difficult indeed to find such eloquent commentary on such a controversial subject in commercial film lyrics, designed, as they are, to accompany the most escapist and sentimental melodramas. The presence of such topical, potentially controversial material on the mass media, like the emergence of Anglophone pop itself, has been dependent on the cassette-based diversification of the music industry.

Conclusions

Cassettes have served as vehicles for the recording and marketing of an extraordinary diversity of Indian folk musics, representing and documenting an incomparably broader stylistic spectrum than was ever presented by film music or the pre-cassette record industry. In the process, cassettes have provided an archetypical illustration of the ability of modern technology to reinforce tradition. Just as modern transportation has enabled religious pilgrimage to achieve exponentially larger dimensions in India than ever before, so has the advent of cassettes led to an unprecedented degree of mass-media representation and, in many cases, genuine revival of many traditional folk-music genres.

It is not the case, of course, that any form of modern technology, alone and unaided, can reinforce tradition. Cassettes can revitalize tradition and regional, community values because they are conducive to decentralized, grass-roots control, and it is that form of control that is the crucial factor in such a sociomusical revolution, rather than the mere existence of a given technology. Thus, it is only when technology and mode of production are seen as cultural phenomena, with specific *social* dimensions, that their diverse possible effects can be explained.

Aside from disseminating traditional musics, much cassette output has consisted of various sorts of modernized, "improved," commercialized styles syncretizing traditional genres with Western or otherwise modern elements. Insofar as they embody and respond to the changing social identities of Indian communities in transition, the resultant musical hybrids have their own sort of "authenticity" which makes them more expressive and resonant to their partic-ular audiences than traditional folk music.

The ramifications of the cassette-based diversification and expansion of the music industry, far from being esoterica perceptible only by scholars, are plainly apparent to many Indian observers, musicians, and especially cassette-industry personnel. Concord Records founder Biswanath Chatterjee states:

> I was convinced that it was humanly impossible for a few large compa-
> nies to do real justice to all the artistes and all the repertoire available
> in our country, and that the future of the recorded music industry in
> India called for smaller recording companies which would operate with
> a higher degree of efficiency, in different regions and with a repertoire
> different from that of the larger companies.[44]

Harbans Jaiswal, the founder of a small cassette company (Mamshar) in Luck-now, elaborated:

> My friend, an agriculturalist, points out that a different fertilizer may
> be needed for every hundred yards of land, because here there is a po-
> tassium shortage, there a nitrate shortage. But the big fertilizer compa-
> nies just make a general product, and the crops suffer. It's the same
> with folk music. Lata Mangeshkar's songs will sell, because they're
> melodious, well-produced, and extensively promoted, but the special
> heart and soul of a region—only a local can convey that. Especially for
> the little guy, who's illiterate, who only knows his own little dialect—
> if he hears his own dialect sung on the media, by a local who knows
> the soul of the region, he is so happy. With regional music, even people
> who sing out of tune can make hits, because they have soul.

Industry personnel see cassettes as helping to preserve, revitalize, and spread traditional musics. Jaiswal continues:

> People forget their songs and customs when they move to the cities,
> and cassettes educate migrants as to how their regional songs go. Every

region should keep its music alive, and for that, cassettes are a great thing. (Interview, September 1989)

Similarly, Sailesh Mathur, director of Yuki Cassettes, which specializes in Rajasthani folk repertoire, states:

We are certainly trying to preserve the old traditions by marketing the folk music which has been totally dying out in this country. Big companies can't do that with all types of music, because they're busy with films, *ghazals, bhajans*—so we are promoting a lot of talent, giving work to a lot of singers. (Interview, 1989)

A small-scale producer of Marwari music in Jodhpur asserts:

Before there were cassettes, so many Marwaris didn't even know what *Mand, Jhumar, Birani* were. It was difficult to attend live programs when transportation was so poor. Now, with cassettes, Rajasthani music has spread throughout the country—especially among the Marwari communities that are everywhere from Bombay to Calcutta. Yuki alone has several hundred cassettes which are in demand. (Chhanvarlal Gahlot, interview, 1990)

Finally, *India Today* journalists comment on the preference of many rural Indians for cassette-based folk music:

Not for the villagers then, the mellifluous sentimentality of film music, pop philosophy of modern ghazals, or the synthetic brilliance of Indian pop. Increasingly they are rejecting the technical finesse in favour of the homegrown and the intelligible. (Tiwari and Ahmed 1991:166)

Cassettes, as we have seen, have led to decentralized grassroots control of a significant sector of the mass media; they have stimulated the revitalization and creative syncretization of a wide variety of traditional musics; they have created opportunities for innumerable singers and artists to be represented on the mass media, in a manner inconceivable in the context of the film music industry; finally, they have facilitated the dissemination of a far greater diversity of topical themes than were present in film music, thus contributing to the ability of diverse Indian communities to affirm, in language, style, and text content, their own social identities on the mass media in an unprecedented manner.

It would be grossly inaccurate, however, to present only the positive aspects of the cassette revolution. In chapter 10 I will consider some of the unfortunate political ramifications of the cassette boom. At this point we may note that on aesthetic terms, there are many Indians who regard the advent of cassettes as a mixed blessing. In several conversations with folklorists, musicians, aficionados, industry personnel, and the like, I found that again and again, informants, while acknowledging the benefits mentioned above, would opine that the vast majority of secular material currently disseminated on cassettes is of inferior quality, when judged by traditional standards. Such critics, obviously, represent one emic point of view, which although clearly not representative of the purchasers of the tapes in question, is so common and widespread that it must be noted here. The primary criticism is generally that much of the cassette-based folk-pop music is vulgar, cheap, and trivial. This complaint was aimed especially at the regional ribald songs oriented toward lower-class consumers, whether in Haryana, the Punjab, Gujerat, Maharashtra, or the Braj and Bhojpuri regions. To some extent, then, this criticism may reflect a certain class bias, rooted in Victorian-influenced bourgeois disapproval of lower-class earthiness. At the same time, however, I encountered such views from most of the older musicians I interviewed, few of whom were not of humble backgrounds. Women also tended to disparage such cassettes on the same grounds, sensing, whether intuitively or quite explicitly, that they were objectified by such erotica and effectively excluded from contributing to its evolution. Thus, the ambivalence toward such musics reflects not only a class-based perspective, but dimensions of gender, age, and taste culture as well.

The mixed blessings of cassette culture become more evident when a given genre is examined closely, in its traditional and cassette-based incarnations. The following chapter is presented as such a case study.

9

Rasiya: A Case Study in Commercialization

Lajpatrai Market, on Chandni Chowk across from Shah Jahan's Red Fort, is the retail center of Delhi's electronics industry, and to some extent, that of North India as well. Inside its maze of crowded walkways and bustling shops are several hundred consumer electronics stores, repair stalls, wholesale outlets for cassette producers, and cassette retailers. Six days a week the narrow lanes are packed with commotion as industry personnel, customers, distributors with boxes of tapes on their heads, construction workers laden with building materials, and the occasional placid yet thoroughly disruptive cow crowd past each other. From Lajpatrai Market, a dozen or so cassette producers send workers laden with cassettes to distributors throughout North India; upstairs, in dark, tiny workshops, laborers crouching over dilapidated machinery assemble cassettes, duplicate them, print labels, and seal the finished products.

In fall 1989, at the commencement of my research into the Indian music industry, I found myself wandering through the market. It was a typical busy day. In front of one cassette shop, a group of *hijra* eunuchs were dancing, to celebrate, as I discovered, the store's opening. *Hijras* have an uncanny ability to learn where and when such openings or other auspicious occasions are taking place, such that they can materialize uninvited, as in this case, singing, dancing, and ultimately demanding *bakhshish,* without which they threaten to create an uproar by exposing themselves.

I discovered a small retail stall advertising all manner of cassettes of regional folk music from Haryana, Garhwal, Bhojpur, Rajasthan, the Punjab, and the Braj area, produced by Delhi-based companies. Chatting with the salesman, I asked what cassette was particularly "hot" these days. Despite the vagueness of the question, the clerk, without any hesitation, produced a copy of "Meri chhatri ke niche a jao" (Come join me under my umbrella), the current runaway bestselling cassette of the *rasiya* genre.

Returning home with several other blind purchases, I found the title song of "Meri chhatri" to be quite a catchy tune, essentially identical to that of a current film song; the singer, one Ram Avtar Sharma, had a certain sensual sauciness quite appropriate to the suggestive text, portraying a Delhi bachelor

196

urging a comely woman drenched by a downpour to join him under his umbrella. Like most Indians outside of the Braj region, I had never heard of *rasiya* as a musical genre, although I was familiar with the word as connoting a libertine epicure, and, by extension, the seductive and playful Krishna. *Rasiya,* as I learned in subsequent months, was the single most prominent folk-music genre of the Braj region, and one which had in recent years become widely disseminated as a cassette-based commercial popular music. Like many Indian folk genres, it is familiar to a few million casual participants within its home region, largely unknown elsewhere, and passionately cultivated as a poetic and musical genre by several practitioners. Its traditional form was also the subject, I eventually discovered, of a thorough doctoral dissertation by an Indian woman (Usha Banerjee 1986), which, for better or worse, did not deal with the field of my particular interest, the impact of cassettes and commercialization. In the following year and a half I intermittently pursued the study of *rasiya,* finding it to be a vast subject whose horizons receded endlessly before me the more I progressed. Increasingly aware of and discouraged by the limits of my knowledge, I recognized nevertheless that the genre could constitute an exemplary case study of continuity and change under the influence of the cassette industry; eventually I felt marginally prepared, despite my limited understanding of many aspects of the traditional forms of *rasiya,* to assess the nature of the commodified versions of the genre, and their relation to the traditional styles which continue to flourish. This chapter, then, is presented as a case study, which will explore many of the themes introduced previously—for example, the commercialization of *bhakti,* the portrayal of gender, the implications of parody, the relation of live and prerecorded performance—but in reference to one genre within a particular region.

Braj Culture and *Rasiya*

The Braj region comprises the area in which the Braj Bhasha dialect of Hindi is spoken; its nucleus is Mathura, with the towns of Bharatpur, Agra, Aligarh, Mainpuri, and, roughly, Banchari, marking its borders, which are linguistic and cultural rather than geopolitical. In many respects, the Braj area can be seen as a typical region of the North Indian plains; physically, its essentially unremarkable fields and towns resemble those of neighboring regions, and, like other linguistic zones, it has its own repertoire of local songs, dances, and folk tales, most of which can be seen as counterparts to those in other regional cultures. Around 75 percent of its thirteen million inhabitants[1] live in villages, which tend to be less isolated than those of Rajasthan or Bihar, but perhaps not as cosmopolitan as many Punjabi towns.

In other respects, the Braj area is somewhat special. Since antiquity it has been the center of the Krishna cult, and the area has been revered throughout

India since the sixteenth century as a focal *bhakti* pilgrimage site and the former homeland of Krishna himself. The region is dotted with various sites associated with particular exploits of Krishna's, however fanciful or apocryphal. Each year brings many thousands of Hindu pilgrims from throughout India, who tour such sites, visit local ashrams, bathe in the Yamuna where Krishna sported with the peasant girls (*gopis*), and immerse themselves, as much as possible, in the local culture, most of which remains suffused with Krishna imagery and worship.

Because of the centrality of the region to the Krishna cult, and, to a lesser extent, because of the Mughal courts in nearby Agra and Delhi, by the sixteenth century a refined form of Braj Bhasha had developed into the primary literary Hindi dialect of North India, used as a vehicle especially for devotional poetry and songs (including the major genres of Hindustani classical and light-classical music). This pan-regional, cultivated form of Braj Bhasha exerted its own reinforcing influence on aspects of Braj culture in its homeland, while *Braj-basis* (Braj-dwellers) have continued to practice Krishna-*bhakti* to an extent that justifies the region's renown as a cradle of modern devotional Hinduism.

Aside from its sacred sites, its innumerable temples, and its profusion of mendicants, *saddhus,* pilgrims and ashrams, the Braj region is also known for its colorful *raslila* folk theater, portraying the amorous and mischievous exploits of the youthful Krishna in Brindavan. Somewhat less familiar elsewhere, although deeply cherished by *Braj-basis,* are other forms of folk song and lore. Particularly noteworthy are the local variants of the *Dhola* epic, seasonal songs (*holi, malhar/savan, barahmasi*), women's songs (*sohar,* wedding songs, etc.), *nautanki* theater (also called *swang, sang, sangit*), a form of *dhrupad* sung in temples, and, most popular among folk-song genres, *rasiya.*

Rasiya is cursorily described in various Indian publications as a song form performed during the vernal Holi festival, whose texts portray events in the life of Krishna. While the archetypical *rasiya* does correspond to this definition, the genre exists in a wide variety of forms, which are in fact performed, in various contexts and styles, throughout the year, and in reference to all manner of topical themes. Rasiya texts can be grouped into devotional (*dharmik*) and secular categories. Most, but by no means all of the former have to do with Krishna, depicting his amorous dalliance with Radha and the *gopis,* and generally adhering to the traditional *lilas* or stock incidents and themes depicted, archetypically, in *raslila* drama (Hein 1972:163–78). The secular *rasiyas* are more varied in subject matter. These, in fact, can be about anything, from vasectomy to politics. Most, however, are *masaledar* (spicy) erotica, dealing in one way or another with sex and intimate gender relations. As we shall see, such songs are often quite lewd and explicit.

Rasiya's performance contexts are as varied as its text topics. The genre is often sung collectively by amateurs, be they women undertaking a local pilgrimage, villagers gathered around a fire during a cold evening, or passengers on a bus. *Rasiya* is also commonly performed in temples, sung responsorially by a leader and assorted devotees, generally at the end of a session of *samaj* singing otherwise devoted to group renditions of *dhrupad* compositions. Devotional *rasiyas* may also be incorporated into *raslila* drama, and may be performed in ashrams and temples by hired professional singers. Ribald versions of the genre appear in *nautanki* theater. Quite distinct forms of *rasiya* are cultivated by all-male music clubs called *akharas,* which perform individually or, more often, in a competitive match (*dangal*) with a rival *akhara*. Finally, since the mid-1980s a form of *rasiya* has come to be widely disseminated on commercial cassettes—but in order to appreciate this development it is necessary to contextualize the genre in wider synchronic and diachronic perspectives.

Protean as *rasiya* has been, various distinct and documented incarnations of it have appeared and coexisted during the last 120 years; the emergence of these variant forms can be seen to reflect and correspond to specific fundamental situational developments in Indian culture as a whole, in which the current information and media revolution, including the cassette boom, figure significantly.

Song Texts in Secular Folk *Rasiya*

Song texts in traditional *rasiya,* and especially in the *akhara* style, deal with an extremely broad range of topics, from esoteric mythology to political movements. Commercial cassettes, on the whole, do not represent this topical spectrum, but instead consist mostly of erotic *masala,* having certain affinities with the lewd Punjabi and Haryanvi texts cited in the preceding chapter. Most commercial *rasiya* tapes thus draw only from one traditional theme of the genre. In doing so, *rasiya* cassettes illustrate some of the transformations that a traditional genre can undergo in the process of commodification. In this case, the changes are most apparent in the field of erotica and the representation of gender relations. In order to appreciate these developments better, however, it is necessary to consider the traditional portrayal of these subjects in greater depth.

Most familiar *rasiyas* sung by ordinary villagers are either devotional songs portraying Radha and Krishna, or else they are secular, lightly erotic songs depicting heterosexual relationships. Both categories of song can be seen as representations of gender relations, as Krishna and Radha constitute implicit archetypes for many of the couples in ostensibly secular songs as well. For purposes of comparing and contrasting traditional and commercial song texts, however, it will be most fruitful to focus on the secular, *masaledar rasiya* songs in both performance contexts. Although in many respects traditional, *rasiya* texts are in most ways quite contemporary, not only in their themes, but also in their language and imagery,[2] and indeed they constitute remarkably frank expressions of modern attitudes toward heterosexual relationships.

Insofar as *rasiya* texts appear so uninhibited in their portrayal of gender relations, and because of their wide popularity among both men and women, *rasiyas* may be taken as sites for the dramatization, negotiation, and symbolic mediation of many aspects of gender relations and sexuality, especially conflicts and frustrations. Certain stock themes and topics recur in erotic *rasiyas*. A village woman whose husband is away complains to her friend that the *radua* (bachelor) next door is making eyes at her, or offering her money. Or she asks her husband not to press himself on her when they visit her maternal home. Alternately, she speaks amorously to her husband or lover. In other songs, the woman tells a friend (*sakhi*) or sister-in-law about a sexual escapade with her *devar* (husband's younger brother), whether a secret, passionate tryst, or a furtive, forceful violation at night. Some *rasiyas* portray the woman telling her *sakhi* of her sexual longing and frustration, whether for her husband who is out of town, for a bachelor, her brother-in-law, or some other person. In others, she asks her husband to bring her gifts from the market, such as a radio, an electric fan, etc.

Texts of two of the most familiar *rasiyas,* such as are commonly sung by village women (as well as men), are given here:

(1) Kau din uth jay mero hath, balam toi aiso marungi
Someday, husband, I'll raise my hand and give you such a beating
you provoke me so much, you aren't afraid of anyone
I'll tell your mother and sister about you
I'm not kidding, I won't feed you *roti* all day
You can starve, I won't feed you unless you beg
You don't give me a moment's peace, you only say what you want
Every day, how long will I bear this?
Believe me, I'll go back to my parents' house, and I won't return
I'll take the marital vows with someone else

(2) Meri eri bahut khojae, mohe najar lagi kau radua kin
My heel itches, some bachelor must be staring at me
One day I met the brahman, and my feet gave in, I can't sit or
    stand still
One day I met the *maina,* and my eye make-up got all disheveled
I weep and weep [that I ever met him]
One day I met the *gujar,* and the color in my headdress got all
    messed up

200

A familiar sub-style of *rasiya* is *languria,* which is connected, whether explicitly or implicity, with the local goddess Kaila Devi. *Langurias* are either devotional, or, like these examples, they may be essentially secular; in either case, mention is made of the *languria,* which may be, ambiguously, a child, a companion, a potential lover, a devotee of Kaila Devi, or a junior male divinity accompanying her.[3]

> *(3) Do-do jogini ke bic akelou languria*
> Between two *jogins* [*jogi* women] there is a sole *languria*
> the elder says to him go buy me some *tikau* [?]
> the younger says get me some *halva*
> the elder says go buy me a watch
> the younger says give me a waist-band
> the elder says go buy me a sari
> the younger says bring me a scarf
> the elder says get me a hair-piece
> the younger says spread my hair part for me

In the song above, flirtation is hinted at in the final line, where the younger *jogin* makes a request that would only be made of a lover.[4] The next *languria,* like many *rasiya* songs, reflects its modernity in the use of the English word *fashion:*

> *(4) Nai-nai fashion ki jogini ne ye bigari languria*
> These modern-fashion girls have ruined our *langurias*
> I go to fetch water, and he [implicitly, her husband] follows behind me
> I'd like to push him into the well;
> When I collect cow-dung and pat it in into cakes, he's behind me
> I'd like to cake him up with dung;
> When I go into the hot kitchen he trails me
> I feel like whacking him with the rolling-pin
> When I clean up our bed, there he comes
> I want to shove him off it.

Many *rasiyas* are titillatingly erotic without being vulgar or overtly lewd. As such, they are sung not only by men, but occasionally by women; the latter, however, would only sing such suggestive lyrics either when gathered beyond earshot of men—for example, at an informal song session in a courtyard when the men are in the fields—or at a distinct occasion, especially, during a wedding, after the groom departs from his family in the *barat* procession. The following song is typical:

> *(5) Moku das-das ke dikhave bahna not, ye radua bairi bajmar*
> He shows me ten-rupee notes, that cursed—may lightning strike
>   him—bachelor

Sister, whenever I go out he stares lasciviously and ensnares me with
   his eyes
Like that he wounds me deliberately in my breasts
It makes me gasp when I go out and hear him cough at me
He's getting high sitting around doing nothing [lit., eating *rotis* for
   free]
My husband is out of town and these murderers are trailing me
O sister, I fear that the wall of my own lust may be broken

This song, like many *rasiyas,* is more unambiguously in the realm of titillating *masala.* Still, as one informant explained, the erotica in traditional *rasiya* (including contemporary noncommercial *rasiya*) often consists more of a *ras*—an aesthetic mode—than a crass delight in obscenity for its own sake (Braj Vallabh Mishra, personal communication). In many instances, sex in traditional *rasiya* is referred to, if at all, by means of distinctive euphemisms and double entendres (*do-mani, do-arth*). For example, a familiar traditional *rasiya* contains the line, "The *devar* [husband's younger brother] went to bed, and his *batasha* [a sugar-ball used for prayer rituals] was distributed," implying that the *devar* and his *bhabhi* made love.[5] Similarly, in the familiar song below, the first line is taken as a euphemism for coitus:

(6) Utar bicchu jhanjhro main mari sharm ki mari
I so ashamed when my anklets are removed
but I like when my *devar* does it
I've gotten to this point
Put the buttons on slowly

Another familiar euphemism for coitus encountered in *rasiya* is the phrase "Bharatpur was pillaged" (*Bharatpur lut gaya*) referring superficially to the fortress city west of Mathura, whose martial *jat* population resisted the British colonial army for several decades. Thus, a popular *rasiya* of Jangaliya Davedar (fl. 1940s and 1950s) relates:

(7) Akeli dar lage rat mori amma
I'm afraid at night, mother;
When the soldier opened my *choli* [chest garment]
Both my breasts came out
And when he grabbed my skirt
Bharatpur was looted, mother

Listeners familiar with such euphemisms have no difficulty understanding lyrics such as, "You've given me a bad name, *launda* [boy, or penis]; the sugarcane crusher is petite, but the piece of cane is thick . . ."[6] In other cases, the implicit sexuality would be introduced for humorous effect. A prominent Hathras-style singer relates:

So I would sing, "The mendicant woman squealed, 'It's rammed inside me, it hurts, take it out,' " and someone would be sure to protest, "What vulgarity is this?!" Then we say, "Wait, listen to the whole verse," and we'd sing, "A thorn has come into my foot, please take it out."[7]

There are familiar traditional *rasiyas,* however, which, while dealing with familiar stock themes, are considerably more explicit and obscene. Such songs are not likely to be sung by village women, but either by men or, most characteristically, by "unrespectable" women in the context of *nautanki* theater. One such song is given above on page 174 ("tapki jae . . . " [My *jalebi* is dripping with desire . . .]). Such songs often differ from domestic *rasiyas* not only in the degree of obscenity, but also in the unambiguity with which female desire is presented. Two further examples are given below:

(8) Kaise katun sakhi javani
How will I pass my youth, O friend?
My parents have forcefully married me to a seven-year-old boy
I flatter him and call him lovingly to the cot
Then he pees and spoils my skirt

(9) Jeth maupe mange de dau ka jithani
My *jeth* [husband's elder brother] is importuning me, o *jithani* [*jeth*'s wife]
I've brought white-white cheeks from my parents' house
He wants to bite me, shall I let him?
I've brought white-white balls from my parents' house
He wants to put his stiff thing in me, shall I let him?
When I came here my cunt was like a frail pipal leaf
If he asks me to be broken by him shall I let him?
When I came I brought my stomach from my parents' house
O *jithani,* he wants to do it to me, shall I let him?

According to informants, while such songs are familiar, village women would be unlikely to sing them, and many women—particularly Muslims, Brahmins, and middle-class women in general—would be embarrassed even to hear them, especially in the company of men. Nevertheless, as we shall see, such ribald songs are the staple of the cassette *rasiya* repertoire.

Gender Representation in *Rasiya*

The emergence of a commercialized, cassette-based form of *rasiya* has elicited mixed reactions from *Braj-basis.* Much of the ambivalence, as we shall discuss below, relates to the representations of gender and sex therein, and the public dissemination of what was previously a repertoire performed only in controlled situations. The portrayal of gender in *rasiya* (as in much North

Indian verse) is complex and contradictory, and requires somewhat expansive discussion.

Those familiar with North Indian folk and popular culture may note that songs portraying the solicitous, pestering male are hardly unique to *rasiya*. To some extent they can be seen as secular counterparts to the portrayals of Radha and Krishna, with Krishna as the insatiable seducer—teasing, vexatious and yet charming. Krishna is, of course, the original and archetypical *rasiya*, or seductive epicure. The adulterous nature of his escapades with Radha and the *gopis* is echoed in contemporary secular *rasiyas*, which more often than not depict some sort of extramarital relationship. As Sudhir Kakar has pointed out, the teasing, persistent, narcissistic Krishna-type lover—and the desirous yet annoyed and apprehensive Radha-type woman—are also stock figures in commercial Indian cinema (1989:36–37).

On a general level, the depiction of gender relations in *rasiya* suggests a social context where sex is seldom accompanied by warmth and tenderness, but is rather a physical craving which, whether felt by the man or the woman, is feared by the woman as potentially disruptive to social order. If more refined forms of Braj poetry tend to dwell on the inchoate, frustrated *yearning* for tenderness and intimacy with an ideal lover, *rasiya* texts are much more closely rooted in immediate daily life, depicting frustrations, fears, conflicts, and occasional furtive, passionate moments of union.

Many secular *rasiya* texts appear to be explicitly male, if not sexist in their implicit gender portrayal. Folklorists and musicians assert that most *rasiya* texts are composed by men, and in particular, by known twentieth-century poet-composers, who might be *rasdharis*, *akhara-bazis*, *nautanki* musicians, or individual poetasters.[8] Moreover, *rasiyas* are often sung in male-oriented contexts—particularly night-long *dangals*, all-male parties with a courtesan singer, or informal sessions within the *akharas*. Hence it should not be surprising that many texts can be interpreted as confirming or reiterating sexist stereotypes men may have of women. Insofar as the songs can be interpreted as portraying women as fundamentally libidinous and potentially unfaithful, many of them can serve to reinforce an ideological complex justifying misogyny, harassment, heckling, and rape: "women all want sex, though they pretend not to." Accordingly, cassette covers of secular *rasiyas*, with their seductive maidens in lascivious poses, seem archetypically designed for the objectifying, voyeuristic male gaze.

An essential aspect of Braj aesthetics is the adoption of the female persona by the male, be he a poet, dancer, or religious devotee. The overt rationale for the gender inversion indulged in by Braj men is that they are all *bhaktas* (female devotees) of Krishna, regarding the human soul as feminine and taking Radha's devotion to Krishna as paradigmatic (Entwistle 1987:91–95). Hence, even when the role of Krishna himself is enacted in dance or narrated, mimetic song, as often as not the scene will consist of one of the many *lilas* in which

Krishna disguises himself as a woman.[9] As Kakar and Ross note, "Bhakti is pre-eminently feminine in its orientation, and the erotic love for Krishna (or Shiva as the case may be) is envisioned entirely from the woman's viewpoint, or at least from her position as imagined by the man" (1986:88).

Such role inversion permeates secular *rasiya* as well as *bhakti* devotion, and significantly complicates their interpretation. The male dancing and mimetic gestures that often accompany *rasiya* (especially, of course, when performed by a transvestite at a *dangal*) imitate women's folk dance and the graceful *gopis*, while, as we have seen, male poets usually assume the female perspective in secular as well as devotional *rasiyas*. Commercial *rasiya* lyricist and producer M. H. Zaidi observes,

> When I write texts I try to represent, for example, a sexy woman who
> is being whistled at; she is obliged to act indifferent or angry, but inside
> she is flattered; it's that sentiment I try to portray.

Accordingly, as one Braj woman told me, "No, women are not allowed in the *akharas*, but in the *akharas* the men all become women."[10]

In spite of this male orientation and assumed authorship, many secular *rasiya* texts seem quite convincing in their portrayal of the female perspective, and may well constitute genuine expressions of women's sentiments. Women in *rasiya* texts complain of sexual harassment (5 above); they rail against their selfish husbands and domineering in-laws (1, 4); they beg to be allowed to visit their own family, or to attend a fair; they ask their husbands to bring them gifts from the bazaar; and they describe their anxiety and fears over giving in to the importunate *devar* or bachelor (2, 5, and 9).

Two factors may contribute to the ability of Braj women to interpret *rasiyas* in ways affirming their identity. First of all, the all-female performance contexts, in which men are necessarily absent, allow women to express sentiments—such as sexual desire (as in 2, 5, and 8)—which might otherwise be used to their disadvantage by men. As has often been noted, even in traditional cultures lacking formal oppositional women's movements, women often make music together in ways which enhance female bonding, bypass social restrictions on female performance, and affirm gender identity. With men absent from such gatherings, women are free to express their own sentiments and dramatize their gender perspective in musical and lyric form (Koskoff 1987:9). The informal song sessions of Braj women would appear to be instances of such occasions which, in the absence of men, strongly suggest that the songs they sing—including the slightly ribald *rasiyas* which men snicker at—are genuinely expressive of their condition. *Rasiya* texts may also affirm female identity in that most of them are narrated from the persona of a woman addressing a sister, sister-in-law, or friend (*sakhi*), depicting an implicit support group. When women perform such songs among themselves, this effect may naturally be enhanced.

Secondly, the most popular *rasiya* songs are ambiguous enough to accommodate multiple and divergent readings. Due to such ambiguities, the same songs which women find expressive of their condition may reinforce sexist stereotypes men entertain, and may be enjoyed by men for the voyeuristic titillation they afford. Accordingly, feminist criticism has argued that the concept of the male gaze, although essential and basic to gender analysis, must not be applied in an exclusive and simplistic fashion. Thus, Mulvey's assertion that Hollywood films present *only* or primarily the male gaze has been challenged on the grounds that women may interpret cinema from their own perspective, whether corresponding to that intuitively intended by the producers or not (Gamman and Marshment 1989:5). Accordingly, a central tenet of hermeneutics and contemporary literary theory is the notion of multiple readings of given texts, and that great art forms in complex societies must embody contradictions. While *rasiya* may not be an illustrious high-art genre of the elite, it lends itself to polysemic interpretation by its audience of several million North Indians. Moreover, it deals with gender conflicts and controversies in an open and frank manner, while retaining its popularity as a shared tradition amongst both men and women. I would argue that much of appeal of some of the most popular and familiar *rasiyas* rests on their carefully balanced ambiguities which accommodate divergent interpretations.

The most conspicuous ambiguity in erotic *rasiya* texts is the attitude of the woman toward her husband, her would-be seductress, or toward sex in general. The male image of a sex-hungry woman can serve to legitimize various forms of oppression, from forced seclusion (*pardah*) to abuse and rape. Kakar notes the pervasiveness of the "mother-whore complex" in Indian culture, and the horror and scorn which are heaped upon woman when seen as a sexual being (1989:17). Insofar as *rasiya* texts promote such an image of women, they may thus reinforce sexism.

While as we have seen, several *rasiyas* do portray the woman as libidinous, more common are songs wherein the attitude of the woman is unclear or ambivalent. In fact, the female persona and predicament as portrayed in most songs are relatively rich and complex, while the man is perceived as a one-dimensional, libidinous lech. While in some cases the woman overtly resents the advances of her seducers, in others she is torn between a hinted desire and a keen awareness of the social penalties of sexual transgression.[11] Thus, in (2) above, the protagonist is driven to weeping and distraction due to the solicitations of men, and her own ambivalence. In (5), she curses the *radua* (bachelor) who trails her and offers her money, while fearing that she may not be able to control her own desires indefinitely. In (9), she confers, more noncommittally, with her sister-in-law as to whether she should give in to her brother-in-law's advances. In (3), the younger woman's desire is suggested quite subtly, first by the request for a *tagri,* and, only slightly more explicitly, in the final line where she asks him to part her hair.

Such subtleties and ambivalences as are inherent in *rasiya* texts make their interpretation by outsiders all the more difficult, however, and I should stress that my own analyses here are tentative, based as they are on a handful of interviews and conversations with Braj women. For obvious reasons, it was not feasible for me to interrogate village women regarding their attitudes toward sex and ribaldry, and a definitive analysis of gender representation in traditional *rasiya* will have to await further research, ideally by a local Indian woman.

While *rasiya* songs may be interpreted by women as affirming their own gender identity and articulating their complaints and frustrations, it would be a mistake to construe such songs as oppositional "protest music." First, as I have argued, many songs are ambiguous enough to be interpreted quite differently by men, or even other women. Secondly, they do not overtly advocate or portray actual challenges to male dominance, but merely dramatize women's predicaments and, frequently, helplessness.[12] As I shall suggest, this ambiguity is exploited in commercial cassettes, which are oriented less equivocally toward the male gaze. Before discussing the impact of cassettes on *rasiya*, however, it would be appropriate to situate the genre in the context of its development and interaction with the mass media in the twentieth century.

Rasiya and Socioeconomic Modernization

Little is known about the historical evolution of *rasiya* in its most characteristic form, as a folk genre sung informally by rural villagers. While it is clear that much of the current melodic and textual repertoire is of twentieth-century origin, the genre itself could be centuries old, and, according to Usha Banerjee (1986:24), appears to date in some form at least as far back as the sixteenth century, when Braj poets like Chandrasakhi penned Krishnaite verse labeled *rasiya*. Nevertheless, it is in a somewhat distinct form that the genre emerges into relative historical daylight in the late nineteenth century. *Akhara* genealogies, which are consistent and specific enough to be trustworthy, indicate that in the 1870s, two pairs of brothers from Hathras visited Bharatpur during a festival, and were inspired by folk songs they heard there to cultivate a new form of *rasiya* in Hathras. These brothers founded two music *akharas*, which became the models for several other *akharas* which flourished in Hathras and a few other nearby towns. A distinctive Hathrasi style of *rasiya* subsequently evolved, as cultivated by learned poets and skilled singers, and avidly patronized by the local elite. Competitive open-air *dangals* between rival *akharas* came to be focal events in local cultural life, typically attended by one or two thousand spectators. The Hathrasi *rasiya* style emerged contemporaneously with the development of *nautanki* theater (*swang*) in Hathras (Hansen 1989:65), from which *rasiya* singers borrowed certain prosodic and melodic elements.

The Hathrasi *rasiya,* which continues to flourish, though on a lesser scale, employs as a melodic core a distinct set of stock melodies. Typically, a solo vocalist, in a high-pitched, shouting voice, renders a few lines of verse, and then is joined by a chorus of *akhara* members who reiterate a line to a stock refrain tune. The melodic repertoire appears to derive from a number of different sources, including tunes borrowed from neighboring regions. The emphasis in Hathrasi *rasiya,* however, is on the lyrics. *Dangal* competitions are judged primarily by the cleverness, erudition, and poetic merit of the verses which the rival *akharas* demonstrate in responding to each other's insults, political arguments, or mythological riddles. A formidable variety of prosodic structural verse forms (essentially unique to *rasiya*) are used, mastery of which is acquired through years of study with a prominent poet.[13]

For the purposes of this study, what is most significant about the Hathrasi *rasiya* is how its emergence appears to have been conditioned by a primary, fundamental stage in the socioeconomic modernization of India, which preceded and eventually culminated in the mass-media dissemination of the genre. The emergence of *rasiya akharas* in the late nineteenth century was contemporary with the rise of other *akharas* devoted to music, theater, and physical culture throughout North India. The Hathrasi *rasiya akharas,* like their counterparts in wrestling, *birha,* and theater, were voluntary, nonsectarian, intercaste, discipular organizations which convened for competitive *dangals,* which constituted focal events in community cultural life. As Freitag has suggested in reference to Banaras (1989:29–31, 119–21), such *akharas* reflected the decentralization of artistic patronage after the decline of Mughal authority, and the formation of voluntary, intercaste and intercommunal associations in a transitional period of urbanization, patronage change, and emergence of new mercantile elites. *Akharas* also contributed to the detachment of women's popular culture from the realm of public culture, as *akhara* performances of music and drama have tended to be all-night affairs with minimal attendance by women (Freitag 1989:119). As such, the emergence of *rasiya akharas* can be understood as conditioned by the initial stages of modernization of Indian society, introducing a new dimension of urban-elite patronage, artistic cultivation, semiprofessionalism, and male orientation in an otherwise rural, relatively ingenuous folk genre.

Rasiya and Mass Culture

The Hathrasi *akharas* enjoyed great vitality and popularity until the 1960s and 1970s, when their number, degree of activity, elite support, and ability to entertain the public appear to have declined. The days of the *akharas* are by no means over, as six or seven remain active in Hathras alone, and *dangals* still occur frequently in the Braj area, although not as often as before. But audiences have to some extent dwindled to a core of aficionados who cultivate interest, with others remaining indifferent or bewildered. The decline of elite patronage, and subsequent proletarianization of the genre, may well be one factor, as educated middle classes take less interest in rustic, lower-class events like *rasiya;* to the extent that such is the case, the attenuating elite interest, and the correspondingly lower-class orientation of the genre, would appear to parallel similar developments in urban popular culture, as in Banarsi *birha,* temple renewal festivals, and *nautanki* (see Freitag 1989:31–2, 121; Hansen 1989:73; Kumar 1988:7). Informants generally cite two factors as precipitating the decline. The first of these, the increased expense of live performances, is somewhat dubious, as the exponential inflation occuring during these decades has applied, to some extent, to public disposable income as well as musicians' fees. Indeed, the increased, or perceivedly increased expense is most likely a symptom rather than a cause of the decline of live performances.

The second cause cited by informants—the advent of cinema—appears considerably more substantial. The decline of Hathrasi *akharas* was roughly contemporaneous with the spread of mass culture, and especially cinema culture in the Braj region. Of course, cinema had been in India since the turn of the century, and sound films had been popular in cities virtually since their introduction in 1931. Still, most older informants assert that cinema had little impact in the Braj area until the 1950s, during which period films and film music became more accessible, popular, and influential on cultural attitudes and tastes.[14] The advent of cinema appears to have taken its toll on public interest in *rasiya,* along with many other traditional genres.

The spread of cinema may be regarded as representing an emergence of mass culture in general, insofar as it was accompanied by the expansion of radio broadcasting and accessibility, and, to a lesser but not inconsiderable extent, phonographs and television. All these media could conceivably be, and were in fact used to some extent to reinforce local regional culture, including Braj culture. HMV produced a few records of local courtesan singers such as Gulab Bai (d. 1990) and Kamlesh Arya (long since married and "respectable"). A radio station founded in Mathura broadcast much local music. From the 1960s, publishers in Braj towns began issuing cheap, pamphlet-like chapbooks of local songs, including some two hundred books of old and new *rasiyas;* as such pamphlets proliferated, they introduced elements of literacy into an otherwise predominantly oral tradition. A few film directors, especially Ravinder Jain of Aligarh, incorporated tunes from *rasiya* and other Braj music into commercial movies, notably *Dayaavan, Bobby, Jyoti bane jwala,* and above all, *Jamuna Kinare* (1971). The latter movie, produced by a Braj folklore enthusiast,[15] has been one of only two feature films made in the Braj dialect; partly due to its lack of access to the mainstream Hindi market, the film flopped.

On the whole, however, the mass media in this period tended to promote mainstream commercial culture, and especially Hindi film culture, rather than regional community values. The intensification of cinema exposure inaugurated a new epoch of film-culture hegemony, which may be regarded as a period of mass culture dating roughly from the late 1950s to the early 1980s.

Film Parodies and Hathrasi *Rasiya*

The impact of mass film culture on *rasiya* has been evident, first of all, in the aforementioned decline of live performances by the *akharas*. Secondly, it has led to the widespread incorporation of film melodies into performances of Hathrasi *rasiya*, starting from the 1950s. Typically, a film melody will be introduced in the latter part of an *akhara*'s turn in a *dangal*, after a set of long songs (*chhand, rasiya* proper, etc.); ideally, in large towns the rendition of film parodies will coincide with the conclusion of cinema shows, for example, at 9:00 P.M. and 11:00 P.M., so that film buffs leaving the theater may be drawn to the *dangal* happening nearby (Vijender Sharma, interview, January 1991). Technically, *akhara* members do not regard the use of film parody as *rasiya* proper, which has its own discrete repertoire of melodies, but refer to it as *chiz* (thing, melody); still, film tunes have come to be a standard feature of *akhara* performances, and by extension, of Hathrasi *rasiya* in general, since the 1950s.

In chapter 7 I have discussed some of the uses and implications of film parody. The incorporation of film *tarz* into Hathrasi *rasiya* constitutes in many ways a representative instance of this phenomenon, inspiring similar controversies and having similar implications. Musicians themselves are explicit about the impact of cinema and the need to compete by incorporating film tunes. Vijender Sharma, the most renowned contemporary *rasiya* performer of Hathras (and *ustad* of the hoary Kali Paltan *akhara*), states:

> We use a fair amount of film tunes nowadays. People request them, and
> on a single popular film *tarz*, so many *rasiyas* can be sung. You can
> mix them into *chhand*, after segments of *chhand* introducing Hathrasi
> *bahr*, then maybe *rasiya* [proper], then a film tune. The public likes it
> . . . There are fewer *rasiya* programs now, because for three rupees
> you can go to a film and see everything. That's why we use film tunes.
> Because of films, people are less interested in traditional music,
> whether *rasiya, sang,* or *khyal-bazi*. And we definitely have to mix in
> film tunes with other things, to keep people happy, so that they'll stay
> all night. It didn't used to be this way, even after films had been around
> for a while. (interview, January 1991)[16]

Not surprisingly, older aficionados and musicians tend to deplore the use of film parody, arguing that it impoverishes and cheapens local traditions and leads to the loss of traditional melodies.[17] Meanwhile, of course, the public immensely enjoys the use of film parody, such that it has become one of the main attractions of Hathrasi *rasiya* performances. Some musicians and commentators also regard the practice with indulgence. *Rasiya* scholar Usha Banerjee notes, "Of course it may represent a loss. But how long can people go on listening to the same old tunes? Naturally they like film tunes" (interview, 1990). Musicians note that film tunes have in their own way enriched the repertoire of available melodies, and they observe that they tend to choose film melodies that are compatible with the *rasiya* style and aesthetic.[18] One *rasiya* producer belittled the importance of whatever cinematic associations film melodies might introduce into *rasiya,* claiming, "It's just a melody, nothing more." While acknowledging that use of film tunes in devotional music was controversial, he said, "*Masaledar rasiya* is one thing; worshiping God is another" (M. H. Zaidi, personal communication). Similarly, *rasiya* musicians, like those mentioned in chapter 7, point out that many film tunes originally derive from folk songs.

In many cases, as we have noted above, melodies are recycled in so many different contexts that different listeners may associate them with various contexts. I was given several opinions regarding the origin of the tune of the aforementioned current cassette hit, "Meri chhatri ke niche." Some attributed it to the film song "Yeh jo halka halka suroor hai" in *Soten ki beti;* others claimed it came from an older film. Another informant, having heard the tune used in a *rasiya dangal,* assumed that version of the song to be the original. Older folklorists and musicians, however, verified to my satisfaction that the tune was an old *rasiya* melody, which had been forgotten, and subsequently became a hit when rediscovered by Ram Avtar.[19]

We have suggested in our prior discussion of parody that the phenomenon may be better regarded as the creative appropriation and resignification of borrowed melodies rather than an indication of creative atrophy. Such may well be the case with the use of film *tarz* in Hathrasi *rasiya*. Informants described the eagerness with which audiences attend *dangals* partly in order to hear what new film song was going to be used in what novel manner. If it were the case that such songs were popular only as film songs per se, then we can assume that audiences would not bother to attend *rasiya* performances, but would rather simply listen to the actual film songs, or patronize ensembles which did cover versions of their favorite songs. Similarly, we might expect *rasiya* performers to sing the original texts, rather than creating new ones; why should audiences put up with hearing a new text, if they really wanted the original song approximated as closely as possible? As it is, the interest and delight that audiences find in film parodies, and the persistence of the parody tradition in decades of *rasiya* and other genres, strongly suggests that audiences enjoy the process of parody itself. They appreciate the affirmation of regional culture implicit in appropriating the Bombay corporate-derived tune and fitting it with a new text in their own local dialect; further, the act of resignification is itself a particular kind of creative expression, with its own potential for subtle social critique, affirmation of identity, and humor.

The practice of parody, indeed, is basic to *rasiya;* most of the melodies used therein are stock tunes, and many of these have been borrowed from other genres.[20] Audiences take particular pleasure in hearing the clever reinterpretation of familiar tunes and texts in Hathrasi *rasiya.* A fine example is that mentioned above in passing, involving the hit "Meri chhatri": in a *dangal,* the competing *akharas* were engaged in a political polemic, one group representing the Congress Party, and the other taking the side of the Janta Dal.[21] The former at one point addressed themselves to Kamla Bahuguna, wife of former Uttar Pradesh chief minister H. N. Bahuguna, who had defected from the Congress Party. They then broke into a rendition of the hit song "Meri chhatri" (in which the coveted woman is named Kamla), recontextualizing it as an invitation to rejoin the safety of the Congress Party: "Come join me under my umbrella, why are you standing there all drenched, Kamla?"[22] The audience roared with appreciation and laughter.

In discussing the use of film tunes in *rasiya,* I have concentrated on the Hathrasi style, where parody is particularly conspicuous, and explicitly controversial. Villagers also make their own use of film tunes in their renditions of *rasiya* and other genres, setting texts published in chapbooks to current film hits heard on the radio. Finally, film parodies are also used in *rasiya* as disseminated on commercial cassettes.

The Advent of Cassettes

As noted in the preceding chapter, the regional cassette industry bloomed throughout North India in the period 1982–86. The Braj region was no exception, and indeed has proven to be a particularly active market for cassettes, which provided, for the first time, significant quantities of commercial recordings of local genres in Braj Bhasha. The larger producers emerging during this period were medium-sized Delhi-based companies like Max, Rama, Sonotone, and Parco, which also produce tapes in other nearby regional languages (Haryanvi, Punjabi, Bhojpuri, Garhwali). Several smaller producers of *rasiya* and other Braj genres also materialized within or near the Braj region itself, generally producing lower-budget recordings, but offering greater variety in terms of genres and performers.[23] The market has tended to fluctuate. After an initial surge, it was buoyed again by the prodigious success of "Meri chhatri" in 1989; a slump ensued in summer 1990, due to some oversaturation, and, more importantly, disruption of all manner of commerce due to persistent riots over the Mandal Commission affirmative-action plan, and the Ram Janmbhoomi-Babri Masjid controversy (discussed in the next chapter). By winter 1990–91 the market had revived considerably.

Cassettes and the "Little Tradition" of *Rasiya Bhakti*

Rasiya, in its archetypical traditional form, is a Krishnaite devotional genre, and as such it represents a regional "Little Tradition" of Krishna *bhakti* which, while compatible with mainstream Hinduism, constitutes a particular local form of expression. *Languria* is more specialized and region-specific, and is little known outside the Braj area. *Languria* songs are associated with Kaila Devi, a goddess whose shrine stands several miles southwest of Agra. Both *rasiya* and *languria* are the sorts of local devotional genres which have come to be widely disseminated on the media, for the first time, with the advent of cassettes.

Devotional *rasiya* tapes are sold primarily in stalls around Krishnaite temple sites, where they are purchased as souvenirs by visiting devotees. In Brindavan, Krishna's home town, they outnumber secular and lewd *rasiya* tapes, which are found only in certain stores. For some reason, piracy seems to be particularly endemic among devotional Braj tapes.

As is the case with cassettes of other devotional genres, religious *rasiya* tapes contain both old standards as well as new compositions. The tapes of familiar songs are more popular among tourists and pilgrims than among locals, who hear and sing them enough that they feel little need to purchase recordings of them. As with other devotional genres, producers naturally select competent vocalists rather than trying to represent the "authentic" cacophony of amateur village or temple song sessions. Nontraditional instrumentation is occasionally added, although most recordings are made on limited budgets which do not allow for elaborate ensembles. In most (but not all) cases, songs are kept to a maximum of five minutes, unlike in informal amateur sessions, where they may go on for twenty minutes or more.[24]

Local professional singers sometimes produce cassettes at their own expense in order to boost their renown and performance bookings; thus, for example, Brindavan's Banvari Lal Sharma, a talented singer and composer of Krishnaite *rasiya* and *bhajan,* produced two cassettes and a chapbook of his compositions in order to promote his already active performing career, which carries him throughout North India.[25] A few local middle-class women, like Mathura's Madhur Sharma, have also recorded cassettes of devotional *rasiya.*

Nevertheless, while devotional *rasiya* tapes constitute a significant part of the Braj commercial-cassette market, they account for only a minority of all commercial *rasiya* tapes (perhaps 15–20 percent), the remainder of which are tapes of secular music, and especially ribald *masaledar* songs.

Secular *Rasiya* Cassettes

The emergence of the *rasiya* cassette market in the space of two or three years was quite a remarkable phenomenon, although in many ways typical of the burgeoning regional cassette industry. In a set of genres previously represented by less than ten 45-RPM records, a few hundred commercial cassettes soon became available, representing a considerable range of local singers and grassroots poetic talent, and effectively responding to a demand for local music which had lain dormant and unsated before cassettes.

At the same time, cassettes, like other mass media, have not constituted neutral, passive vehicles for the dissemination of folk or syncretic genres, but have tended to condition their content and consumption patterns in ways which, although predictable, are not insignificant. Most of the effects of commodification on secular *rasiya* as represented on cassettes correspond to the various commercial trends I have discussed in reference to devotional *rasiya* and regional musics in general. Producers prefer short songs to lengthy narratives. Vocalists need not sing so loudly as they may be accustomed to doing in live programs, where amplification is not always present. Producers naturally prefer competent singers to incompetent ones, although for various reasons, the best singers sometimes go unrecorded.[26] Synthesizer or Casio keyboard may be added to provide "music" in the interludes between verses. Another more orthogenetic change is the standard adoption, since around 1986, of the *naqqara* drum-pair in virtually all *rasiya* recordings. The practice, occasionally encountered in professional folk performances, of prefacing songs with spoken introductions (in lingua-franca Hindi, not Braj Bhasha) has also become standard on cassettes.

Most significant, perhaps, is the selectivity of the cassette producers, who do not record indiscriminately, but tend to follow established trends in terms of style and subgenre. Singers performing in peripheral dialects are generally not recorded, and thus, for example, there are no commercial recordings of Mevati *rasiya,* a distinctive subgenre sung by the Mev ethnic group living to the north of the Braj heartland.[27] More importantly, of the several varieties and styles of *rasiya* singing, at least 85 percent of *rasiya* cassettes represent only one style, featuring a solo singer, accompanied by harmonium, *dholak,* and *naqqara.* Thus, the collective temple style is not recorded at all, and the antiphonal Hathrasi style, although the most sophisticated and cultivated of *rasiya* substyles, is found, as of 1991, on less than six obscure cassettes.[28] Thus, while commercial cassettes have disseminated an incomparably greater variety of regional musics than did the record and film industries, there are limits to the diversity of styles and genres they represent; like the unidirectional "old" media, cassettes do serve as "gatekeepers," selecting and streamlining the product passed on to consumers, although to a far lesser extent than did cinema and records.

Song Texts in Commercial *Rasiya*

While traditional *rasiya* encompassed devotional texts and a wide variety of topical themes, the vast majority of commercial *rasiya* recordings are of the *masaledar* variety. The abundance of titillating *masala* in traditional *rasiya,* indeed, has undoubtedly constituted a significant factor in its emergence as a cassette-based pop genre. Just as cassettes are said to have proletarianized genres like Marathi *koli git,* so have they promoted the emergence of a mass-mediated derivative subgenre of *rasiya* oriented primarily toward lower-class males. Secular *masaledar rasiyas* are denoted on cassette covers as "Braj ke tapakte rasiya" (the dripping *rasiya* of Braj), or "chulbule rasiya" (playful *rasiya*), "chatpate rasiya" (spicy), "tapkile" (snazzy-colored), "katile" (thorny)—all intended to connote lewdness, as opposed to devotional *rasiyas,* which on cassettes are subtitled simply "Braj ke rasiya." As *rasiya* singer-poet and recording artist Sevaram Tanatan says, "Only ten percent of the audience likes devotional *rasiyas* nowadays, and they are mostly older people."

In the first wave of *rasiya* cassettes, most of the familiar, traditional erotic songs (including 1–9 above) were recorded and re-recorded, by various singers for different labels. As with other similar genres, producers subsequently came to prefer to market new *rasiyas*—new song texts set to the stock *rasiya* melodies. This policy has led to a burst of new song texts, representing a certain sort of vitality in the genre. Aficionados, however, regard much of the contemporary output as somewhat ordinary, if not cheap in quality. The great majority of new texts adhere to familiar themes of traditional ribald *rasiyas,* such as *jija-sali/devar-bhabhi* flirtation, the predicament of a woman being courted while her husband is away, her longing for her husband, or her requests for gifts, visits to the fair, and so forth. Erotic double entendres remain common. A *bahu* (young wife) who has been ignored by her husband complains to him, "I've got a wasp in my bra, it's bitten me, I'll call the doctor and get an injection from him." Or she writes her husband, who has been gone working for months, "Take a vacation, the lemon in your garden is ripe, come and eat the oranges . . ."[29] Some cassettes insert snippets of spicy dialogue. One typical tape, *Gone wali rat* (Wedding-consummation night), commences with an old woman addressing a young man:

Woman: I don't feel good, I'm all befuzzled [*paserani* for *pareshani*]. I'm old, but when I was young I used to pee a lot, in such a way that it would come out in a spiral. I used to have sex with two men at once. Now my teeth are falling out, my mouth is empty, what can I say? When my late husband used to come home from the army, he would give me a wonderful bath, rubbing me all over. He'd give me *gulla* [*sic—rasgulla*], *langur* [*sic* (monkey)—*angur* (grape)].

Man: Monkey?
Woman: My tongue is dead meat, it doesn't move anymore . . . [30]

In many cases the treatment of traditional themes is freely modernized. In a variation on the stock song theme in which the wife requests gifts from her husband, several cassettes now feature songs in which she implores him to bring the latest cassette from a particular label, for example, "We don't have any good *rasiya* tapes, bring me the latest Max cassette, with X on harmonium, and Y on dholak" (i.e., the personnel in the recording); or, similarly, "O my little *devar,* bring me the latest Rathor folk music cassette, with sound recording done by A. S. Rathor, and music by . . ." Even more explicit advertisements appear: "O *devar,* bring me a tape of Hari Singh Premi, from Brij Cassettes, at Charra Adda in Aligarh"; the same singer promotes other skills of his as well, portraying a husband telling his wife, "Go get an injection from Hari Singh . . ." In other songs, the wife now requests a television, so that she can watch the Sunday-morning *Ramayan* and *Mahabharat* series; she continues, "I've been going to the neighbors to watch it, but they insult me and tease me . . ." The traditional portrayal of the *bahu* requesting her husband to take her to the fair now takes the form, "Get a motor car, I'll sit in it and you take me to the fair" (or to see the movies, etc.). Such songs may even be regarded as loosely devotional when the wife is requesting to be taken in a Maruti (car), for example, to pay her respects to Kaila Devi. The husband boasts of his new tractor, the wife proclaims "My husband got a B.A." A traditional *rasiya* in which a woman relates how she offers herself to the moneylender in lieu of debt repayment ("Main to baniya yar bana lungi" [I'll befriend the baniya]) is modernized predictably, "I tell the truck driver, 'Take me to see Chandni Chowk,' and if he asks me for money, I'll pull away my veil . . ." A few songs refer to previous modern hits, such as Nand Kishore's "Listen to me, you with the umbrella," which portrays a woman's response to the aforementioned hit "Meri chhatri . . ." (Come under my umbrella); in the rebuttal, which uses the same tune, she warns "I've got a sharp nail on my shoe" (to kick with). Other songs comment on social changes, especially the alleged dissipation of the young (their drinking, gambling, bad breath, etc.).[31]

The following song is in most respects quite typical and unremarkable; yet while from one perspective it merely contains more cheap *masala,* it can also be viewed as engaging the endless subject of the modernization of traditional attitudes:

It's not the fault of unmarried girls, it's just today's fashion
Having two braids, and buttons on the back [instead of wearing
    traditional modest garb],

Wrapping your two *sitarams* [here, breasts] in the front
It drives the bachelors crazy
It's the cinema fashion
Wearing those tight shirts, squeezing your breasts . . . [32]

Vasectomy (*nasbandi*) is also a popular topic in modern *rasiya;* of course, it may qualify as *masala,* but it is also a contemporary issue of considerable interest and import, given the conflict between state promotional campaigns, male superstitions, and traditional desires for big families with many sons. *Rasiyas* represent various points of view. In this excerpt, the man urges his wife to have her tubes tied:

Your mouth is dry, your teeth have fallen out,
your skin has turned dark, your womb is empty for once
We've got too many kids already
but that won't happen again, why are you sulking?
You aren't happy unless you're pregnant,
but you should do this operation
your last child is but an infant, and now you want another
we're poor, we can't afford more,
our pajamas are torn, your son is crying . . . [33]

Such examples should suffice to illustrate that cassette-based *rasiya* is not an artificially preserved, frozen folkloric genre, but a living tradition which is modernizing in a spontaneous and natural fashion, while maintaining thematic, melodic, and stylistic continuity with its older forms.

Disparaging Perspectives

Despite its evident vitality and modernity, commercial *rasiya,* like other regional cassette-based genres, is not without its detractors. Aside from educated middle-class urbanites with no interest in folk music, commercial *rasiya*'s critics include many elders, folklorists, folk musicians and poets, and a variety of other individuals whose temperaments are offended or bored by the genre. A primary criticism is that the quality of the lyrics is often indifferent and ordinary, and that their mediocrity is only made more conspicuous by mass-media dissemination. Many folk *rasiyas* also have rather unremarkable texts, but they enjoy a degree of venerability due to their (presumed) age, and their adherence to established thematic and stylistic norms.

An even more common criticism is that the commercial *rasiya* cassettes are vulgar and cheap, dwelling, as they do, almost exclusively on titillating *masala.* Given the responsiveness of the cassette industry to grassroots demand, producers are clearly responding to customers' tastes in concentrating on such material. The young men who enjoy such cassettes presumably constitute a more significant consumer group than the assorted women, elders, musicians, and folklorists who deplore such texts. Nevertheless, most of my own informants tended to disparage the excess and quality of *masala* in *rasiya* cassettes—perhaps, of course, because so many of the informants I tended to seek out were aficionados, musicians, and folklorists rather than typical consumers. Their opinions are thus significant as one rather disparaging emic perspective.

One criticism is that there is too little variety in commercial cassettes, and that they do not represent the topical diversity and richness extant in *rasiya* as a genre. "*Masala* is nice every now and then," one *akhara-bazi* told me, "but one doesn't want to be subjected to it constantly." Another criticism I frequently encountered (related to the first one mentioned above) was that the *masala* of commercial cassettes was lacking in the artful subtlety and cleverness found in traditional, and especially Hathrasi, *rasiya*.[34] The quality of erotica in cassettes, by contrast, is regarded as cheap, commercially oriented, and artless, designed to appeal primarily to young men reared in a sexually inhibited atmosphere and delighting in wanton vulgarity.

A third argument against the obscenity of *rasiya* cassettes is that the ribald *rasiyas* extant in folk music were intended to be sung in familiar and controlled domestic contexts, such as sexually segregated song sessions, and that their mass dissemination is inherently inappropriate. *Rasiya* authority Usha Banerjee explains:

It's really only rural folk—like Ahirs, and Gujars—whose women sing
such songs, never Brahmins or Muslims; and even then, they would
just sing one or two *masaledar* songs and then move on to other kinds.
But we don't like these racy cassette covers, and the fact that these
songs are being presented to the outside via cassettes. These things are
for the home, like *gali* [abuse songs] in a wedding, after the kids have
gone to sleep. (personal communication)

Similarly, one may note that cassettes typically combine lewd *nautanki*-derived *rasiyas* with more chaste and subtle village *rasiyas;* such packaging, together with the sexy cassette covers, tends to vulgarize the entire recorded genre in the eyes of some. In effect, cassettes have reconstituted the boundaries between private and public musical life.

It may be noted here that differences of opinion on *rasiya,* as with many other genres, often take generational forms. Thus, for example, while chatting with the owner of an electronics-repair shop in a market town near Mainpuri, I met a young man who was bringing his cracked cassette player in for service; it emerged that his father, irate upon hearing the smutty *rasiya* tapes that his son was playing, had hurled the cassette player against the wall—for the second time. I was impressed with the need for earphones, which have yet to be manufactured or imported in India. Until they are available, one cannot make the categorical observation that cassette technology has privatized cultural consumption. In crowded living conditions, watching television and listening to cassettes at home may often become a collective affair with the participation, whether intentional or not, of several members of the joint family, as well as neighbors.

Aside from the controversial nature of commercially marketing domestic or private forms of discourse, commodification of *rasiya* can also be argued to have altered the portrayal of gender therein—even in the case of familiar traditional songs. We have noted above that commercial popular culture in India and other traditional patriarchal societies tends to be predominantly male culture. To some extent, mass-mediated popular musics such as commercial *rasiya* may reflect or acquire aspects of the same male orientation. Producers and writers of commercial rasiyas informed me that their products were aimed primarily at young men; village women, I was assured, enjoyed *rasiya* cassettes, but were less likely to buy them in the bazaars, which are frequented more by men.

The male orientation of *rasiya* cassettes is particularly evident in their covers, which almost invariably depict a scantily clad, seductively posed woman offering herself to the male gaze. Such covers naturally suggest a certain interpretation to listeners. In some cases they may obliquely distort the meaning of a traditional song. For example, in the well-known *rasiya,* "Mauko das-das ke not" (5, above), as we have seen, the woman, pestered by the ardent and lewd bachelor next door, longs for her husband's return, curses her pursuer, and feels guilty and tormented by the desire that she does acknowledge. The cassette cover (shown below), however, portrays none of this ambivalence, instead showing the woman smiling mischievously at the beckoning bachelor. Similarly, in the familiar song "Moy pihar men mati chher," the wife asks her husband not to press himself on her when they are in her parents' home; the cover of the popular cassette version of this song, however, shows the woman gladly accepting the husband's caresses.

Commercialization has masculinized rasiya in other ways. While married rural women might enjoy singing erotic rasiyas amongst each other in their homes and villages, they would never sing such songs in public, or on cassette. Instead, the *masaledar* rasiyas are sung either by male professionals or by "unrespectable" women—generally courtesans or women associated with *nautanki* theater. As with other erotic regional songs, women (aside from courtesans) are thus effectively prevented from contributing directly to the development of commercial *rasiya,* even though they have been (and continue to be) active carriers and re-creators of traditional, amateur *rasiya.*

Unfortunately, an understanding of gender politics is at least as problematic in commercial *rasiya* as in traditional forms of the genre; thus it would be audacious for a Western male to attempt to "read off" gender representations from cassette texts, or, more usefully, to attempt to portray Indian women's interpretations of such texts. "Can the subaltern speak?" asks Gayatri Spivak (1988), in an essay stressing the discursive limitations facing the sympathetic Westerner who seeks to decode and represent oppressed neocolonial subjects, especially women. The inherent ambiguities in *rasiya* gender portrayals, and in Western attempts to interpret them, are further confounded by the possibility that in one context, lower-class women may in fact be speaking for themselves, while their own words, in commercial contexts, may be appropriated by and transformed into male discourse.

To some extent, the portrayal of gender in commercial *rasiya* (as in many other cassette-based folk genres) can be thrown into sharper relief if compared and contrasted with that of other Indian commercial popular-music genres. Heterosexual relations as depicted in *rasiya,* like those of commercial cinema, film music, and the Urdu *ghazal,* involve stock character types rather than the nuanced individual personalities of bourgeois narrative. The lusty bachelor next door, the ambivalent young wife, and the flirtatious *devar* and *bhabhi* are comparable in aesthetic function to film culture's stereotypical young lovers thwarted by parental opposition, or the *ghazal*'s lachrymose and ardent Majnun. At the same time, *rasiya*'s stock figures are ordinary village folk rather than commercial cinema's glamorous, rich, blow-dried stars, or the *ghazal*'s ill-fated lovers, who are generally portrayed in such a way as to lack any concrete social background. Further, commercial *rasiya* is significantly lacking in the pervasive and saccharine *sentimentality* of film song and film discourse in general, which clearly reflects a marked degree of bourgeois aesthetic influence in film culture. Nor does *rasiya,* either in form or content, display the hyperrefined, somewhat self-indulgent elegance of the *ghazal.*

I have suggested above that the nature of the sensuality in erotic cassette-based folk-song genres (such as *rasiya*) can be seen as a rearticulation of a set of intersecting traditions, including rustic folk humor, traditional *devar-bhabhi* and Radha-Krishna erotica, and the licentiousness of film culture and, indirectly, Western culture. While these discursive traditions may differ in their origins, patronage patterns, audiences, and other features, their contemporary commercial forms have clearly been conditioned by the nature of the disseminating mass medium involved. As I have argued, the capital-intensivity, mass audience, and oligopolistic corporate control of Indian cinema have played crucial formative roles in the aesthetic conventions employed therein. The Urdu *ghazal*'s protean versatility and flexibility have facilitated its highly successful transition from refined Indo-Muslim culture to the cassette market, while accommodating marked changes in musical style and audience interpretation. Similarly, commercial *rasiya*'s particular syncretic rearticulation of discrete aesthetic traditions can be attributed, in large part, to the nature of its media dissemination. The pervasiveness, low expense, and accessibility of cassettes, their orientation toward male consumers, and their easy incorporation of folk and film artistic conventions have all conditioned the particular form and consumption patterns of commercial *rasiya,* as of other cassette-based folk musics. It is in this sense that we can regard commercial *rasiya* as part of a distinctive cassette culture, whose discursive norms are rearticulated under the conditioning influence of the idiosyncracies of cassette technology.

M. H. Zaidi, *Rasiya* Producer

Thus far we have been talking about commercial *rasiya* in rather general terms, thereby to some extent obscuring the fact that the genre is produced by a finite set of individuals, with distinct roles, interests, temperaments, and talents. It may be useful, then, to look a bit more closely at a few individuals involved in different aspects of *rasiya* cassette production. M. H. Zaidi, whom I had the good fortune to befriend in the course of my research, is in some respects a representative and typical figure fulfilling one set of functions in the various stages of cassette production.

Zaidi was born into an artistic family of Aligarh, as his father, under the stage name Master Surkhi, led a *nautanki* theater troupe. The business had been profitable for forty-some years, but by the mid-1980s, cinema had taken its toll on audience interest, and Surkhi retired, with his extended family, to a working-class suburb in New Delhi. Although Zaidi had assisted in managing the *nautanki* shows, and had an interest in the field, his father encouraged him to pursue a more promising and reputable profession. By 1985 in Delhi, Zaidi had taken note of the burgeoning regional cassette industry, and realized that he could play a role in it by virtue of his personal familiarity with underemployed *nautanki* singers, and with the *rasiyas* so commonly performed in *nautanki* theater. That year, Zaidi proposed a series of *rasiya* cassettes to the owner of the then-fledgling Max Cassettes in Delhi, and his offer was accepted. For his first cassette (Max 835), he hired a *nautanki* singer for eight hundred rupees and had her record ten traditional *rasiyas,* including the pornographic "Tapki jae jalebi ras ki" (see p. 174 above); for text sources, he employed common chapbooks sold in bazaars. The tape, which was one of the first *rasiya* cassettes, did quite well, and Zaidi claims it was one of the initiators of the *rasiya* cassette boom. Max then commissioned a dozen more recordings from him, four or five of which were released. Zaidi continued to draw primarily from the traditional text repertoire, but, in accordance with producers' demands, he took to composing his own lyrics, which he would then set to stock tunes or, in a few cases, to film tunes.

Zaidi is in some ways a representative commercial *rasiya* poet; his verses adhere to the stock ribald themes, with the obligatory light eroticism. He does not speak of his poetry with any particular enthusiasm or pride; typically, he will write on demand, after first having a few drinks to stimulate his muse. I translate here a *rasiya* text of Zaidi's, which may be taken not as an example of extraordinary literature, but rather as a very typical and representative specimen of the sort of *rasiya* lyrics now found on commercial cassette:

> A wasp is biting me, what shall I do, friend?
> First it came into my eye and buzzed about; what shall I do?
> Now it has landed on my cheek and scratched me; what shall I do?
> Now it has sat on my lips and kissed me; what shall I do?
> Now it has landed on my breast and pressed me; what shall I do?
> Now it's on my waist, taking my measurements; what shall I do?
> Now it has pushed into my skirt, and it's biting me; what shall I do?
> Now it's doing its heart's desire, what shall I do?[35]

This song is a typical *rasiya* in several ways, aside from being set to a traditional *rasiya* tune. Each line ends with a refrain, which, in performance, leads to an instrumental *laggi*/"music" interlude, where the *naqqara* and *dholak* animatedly accompany a repeated ostinato rendered on the rectangular Indian banjo. Like many folk songs (e.g., nos. 2, 3, 4, and 9 above), it proceeds by means of sequential textual variations on a given line. The double-entendre role of the wasp as male lover is standard in *rasiya* (while the rhyming of wasp and sting—*tataiya, daiya*—is common in Braj children's limericks). Also typical is the ambivalence and essential passivity of the woman.

When I met Zaidi in 1989, he had produced a dozen or so successful cassettes, and, although supporting his entire extended family (including seven children), he had a motorcycle to show for his efforts. The year 1990, unfortunately, proved to be disastrous for cassettes as well as other businesses, due to persistent riots over the Mandal Commission affirmative-action plan, and the Ram Janmbhumi/Babri Masjid controversy (discussed in the next chapter). Cassette production, even for large producers like T-Series, was at a standstill, except for devotional tapes, whose market is more reliable. By December, Zaidi had been obliged to sell his motorcycle and take up tailoring to pay bills. Zaidi's ambition throughout was to start his own recording company, but this required a capital outlay of at least five thousand rupees for a duplicating machine, and in the current slump, even daily subsistence was proving difficult.

Nevertheless, Zaidi had managed to obtain a few contracts; one was a booking of veteran *nautanki* songstress Gulab Bai, for the prestigious T-Series label. The others were for a fledgling cassette company, which was commissioning a few tapes from him. For one cassette, he was to receive two thousand rupees to cover the musicians' fees, with the remainder constituting his profit. The two of us set off one day for Sahibabad, some twenty miles east of Delhi, to try to contract *rasiya* singer Ram Avtar Sharma. En route, we stopped at a wretched shanty slum populated by jugglers, puppeteers, singers, and other street performers, primarily from the Bhojpuri region. These migrants eked out a subsistence living performing in and around Delhi. Zaidi finalized an agreement with one shabbily dressed Bhojpuri singer to record for eight hundred rupees. I had never heard of the singer, whose cassette audience was primarily in eastern Uttar Pradesh, but as we passed a tea-stall near another migrant-worker slum, Zaidi pointed out that the rustic-sounding tape blaring from the stall was of the same singer.

After another hour of searching, we managed to track down Sharma, in his home on the edge of a farming village. Sharma had earned a reputation as the most popular singer of *rasiya* on cassettes. His "Meri chhatri ke niche" had become a runaway hit in 1989, and he had since recorded another fifteen or so cassettes. Although making no attempt to compose lyrics, Sharma was a competent singer, with a sure voice, and a somehow saucy and indulgent style, well suited to the rendering of ribald *rasiyas* intended to be "dripping" with *ras* (juice). I was surprised to find him to be a slight fellow of some twenty-three years. Chatting over tea at a nearby stall, I learned that he had taken up singing as a hobby in his youth in Aligarh. Although lacking any musical training, he had grown familiar with the traditional *rasiya* repertoire from hearing women sing it around the house. His ancestry was in fact Haryanvi, not of Braj, and he also had recorded a few tapes of Haryanvi music. His family owned some land and animals, and had a *pukka* (concrete) house, and thus singing remained more a hobby than a profession for him. As such, he rarely performed live, due to the rowdy and occasionally drunken behavior of audiences at *rasiya* programs. He also was reputed to record for as little as a thousand rupees, which I found surprisingly low in comparison to other regional music stars.

Zaidi and Sharma began talking business; Sharma made it clear that Zaidi's offer of one thousand rupees was far too low, while Zaidi reiterated that business was stagnant due to the riots, and that the fledgling company could not afford more. After further fruitless negotiation, Zaidi arose resignedly, and we said our farewells. As we walked out the door, Zaidi turned again to Sharma and said, "So you'll come to the studio on Tuesday?"

Sharma looked vacantly off in the distance, and replied, "OK."

"So he agreed after all?" I asked Zaidi as we walked out of earshot.

"I tell you, that's my forte," he replied, grinning. "I can get these people cheaper than anyone else can."

Two hours later we had returned, by public buses, to Zaidi's neighborhood, taking some eight hours to accomplish what would have taken ten minutes but for the lack of telephones. Zaidi went off to buy some rum and to find a reasonably quiet place in which to drink and compose some doggerel for the upcoming session.

As it turned out, the recording was indefinitely postponed due to problems with the producers. To make matters worse, Gulab Bai had passed away. In the next few months Zaidi's financial condition deteriorated further and he had to rely on tailoring, which is an unremunerative calling even in the best of times. Fortunately, by summer 1991 the cassette market had revived, and Zaidi, with a bit of help from a foreign friend, had started his own little recording company, and was actively recording singers like Maina Rani who had somehow remained undiscovered by the cassette industry. It remains to be seen whether the market can accommodate another small producer with no hoard of capital to draw from.

Singer-Poet Sevaram "Tanatan" Sharma

We may turn now to a *rasiya* artist who is too distinguished to be taken as "typical," but who nevertheless is representative in his own way. Sevaram Sharma was born (ca. 1952) into a landowning Brahmin *pandit* family of Agra, and ran a small pharmacy. From adolescence he had cultivated an interest in singing and folk poetry, adopting the pen-name "Tanatan" (literally, "twanging," but colloquially, "the greatest"). Like several other amateur Braj poets, he had published a few cheap chapbooks of his verse, and gave occasional radio programs and live performances. Tanatan made his first recordings in 1982 for Gupta Cassettes, a small local producer of Braj folk music. He claims that he was the first to commercially record *rasiya,* and also the first to give spoken introductions to his songs on recordings, a practice (derived from folk procedure) which has since become standard on cassettes. He subsequently purchased an Indian-made duplicating machine and started his own label, also called Tanatan. By 1989 he had made several recordings for the Delhi-based Max label, which enjoyed more extensive distribution than he could acquire on his own. By this time he had given up publishing chapbooks, since cassettes were a far superior mode of dissemination. While he maintained his other sources of subsistence, cassettes became his passion.

Tanatan occasionally composes melodies, but more often, like most Braj musicians, he draws from a set of traditional and film tunes. A few of his cassettes use only film tunes, such as *Rajiya phans gai,* whose melodies all derive from the film *Nagin.* He points out that some of the film tunes he uses originally come from folk music, whether audiences realize that or not. Most of his cassettes are recorded with harmonium (played by himself), *dholak,* and perhaps a Casio keyboard; one of his tapes, *Disco languria,* features a raucous-sounding electric guitarist. Yet Tanatan stresses that he uses colloquial rural Braj Bhasha, and that he deliberately avoids *filmi*-type orchestration which his audiences, he claims, would regard as inappropriate to Braj music.

While Tanatan takes pride in his singing, arrangements, and choice of melodies, his main interest is in composing lyrics, in accordance with the primary emphasis on texts in *rasiya* and other Braj folk music. He regards most traditional *rasiyas,* as well as the professionals who sing them, as boring and stupid, and he takes no interest in the trivial erotica found on commercial cassettes. While many middle-class urbanites might share his view, Tanatan deplores bourgeois genres like pop *ghazal* even more, especially for their exclusive emphasis on sentimental love.

> What is this *ghazal* nonsense? People talking as if there's nothing in the world but love and romance, while poor people toil all their lives for this country and go unsung. I side with the slaves, I sing from their perspective.

What interests Tanatan is satire (*vyang*) and light, witty social commentary, written in colloquial language, and developing traditional rural themes in a fresh and original manner. "I am a third kind of poet," he asserts, distinguishing himself from pop poetasters and ingenuous folksingers. "My audience is mostly Braj townspeople, not uneducated rural hicks. The old songs found in books are for dull-witted fools who don't understand anything, they just like the rhythm and say *vah-vah* [bravo]." Tanatan contrasts the vigor and topical contemporaneity of his songs with classical music and pop *ghazal* in a poem appearing on one of his tapes:

> *Thumri* is like a cough, *ghazals* are like a cold
> *dhrupad* and *malhar* have gone to sleep
> Because they are all feminine [nouns], they remain like slaves
> *Rasiya* is everyone's man, and that's what Sevaram sings.

A certain gender perspective typical of much *rasiya* is also suggested in this verse. Tanatan could be classified with some of the amateur authors of *rasiya* chapbooks, whose lyrics are often superior to most of those found on commercial cassettes; as a cassette artist, he invites comparison with Rajpal Singh Tailor, another singer-poet with several recordings to his credit. In other ways, however, Tanatan and his music are *sui generis,* and not without merit and interest. One of his cassettes (Max 1268) starts with a song representing another personal manifesto of sorts:

> Hear Sevaram's songs full of satire
> Men and women are standing dumbfounded
> The tune they have been waiting for has come
> The sound of the *bin* [snake-charmer's pipe] fills the Max cassette
> The braying and raucous cacophony of disco and film music
> This useless clatter that gives one a headache
> That music is foreign-sounding, neither melodious nor sweet
> Now listen to Max Cassette's folk beat [*desi tarana*]

Tanatan loosely refers to most of his music as *rasiya,* although his criteria are somewhat different and broader than those employed by most. What distinguishes his art as *rasiya,* he says, is the use of Braj Bhasha, the general presence of a narrative story (however short), and the rural themes.[36] Thus, his cassette *Rasiya 440 volt* uses no *rasiya* melodies; his *Chatpate languria* mixes new melodies with the traditional *languria* tunes, while all but one of the tunes on *Disco languria* are new. A few of his cassettes have no connection with *rasiya,* but use stock rural subjects and dialect. *Rakhi kahe pukar ke* is a tape of *malhar,* rainy-season songs in which the young wife thinks longingly of her parents; here, Tanatan has set new verses of his to suitable film melodies. His *Galiyon ka pauchar* (Torrent of abuse) contains free adaptations of women's wedding songs, including *gali* songs in which the women of the bride's family ritually insult the groom and his relatives. Rendering the songs sequentially and narrating the stages of the wedding, he reaches the *gali:*

> The relatives and onlookers are dancing and enjoying themselves
> And Sevaram is singing *gali*
> The sourfruit and berries are ripening,
> Birds pick them, eat them, and shit all over the courtyard . . .
> The groom's mother is serving food
> She looks like a *gujri* [bumpkin] selling curd
> Food has been served to the *thakur* [groom's father]
> And curd is smeared all over his moustache
> Mice have eaten away part of his beard where he left food before . . .
> Our bride is so beautiful and fair
> The pathetic widowers in her in-laws' village will faint when they see
>   her . . .

Tanatan's *rasiyas* portray various rural vignettes. In "Nek dastkhat," an educated woman tells her peasant husband, "If you learn to sign your name I can have you made director subinspector of police; now study, you bespectacled fool." In the eight songs in *Sali salon ka warrant,* he lampoons the custom of complaining about about one's in-laws ("while I was snoring peacefully, they stole my Bata shoes . . ."). Another song reworks the traditional complaint (for example, 8 above) of the wife forcefully married to a young boy.

> My father has bought me a toy and I have to play with him
> I'm twenty-five and they have found me a husband who is twelve
> He still remembers his mother's milk, and wets his bed
> I call him "sweetheart" and he calls me "auntie"
> My fate is ruined as he wanders about the house with his shorts
>   open . . . [37]

In another song, Tanatan presents a modernized version of the wife's traditional complaints about her husband:

I got a fool for a husband
In trying to get a job he gave the refrigerator away as a bribe
He opened a shop and lost all my money
He has a B.A. but can't get work
He sits in the house all day like a girl . . .
I arranged an interview for him
And then he gave away our sugar and kerosene as a bribe . . .

Tanatan's *languria* cassettes are similarly original.

Languria is about Devi Maiyya [Kaila Devi], and a *jogini* goes to the
mela [Kirauli festival in March], and a man who goes is called a *languria*. But there's nothing special in that, and the *languria* songs all
have to do with the same four or five things. "Do do jogini ke bich
men," and so on. So I've introduced satire and social commentary into
languria, and I was the first to do that. The rest just copy me. Like this
one here, "Automatic languria." It still has to do with Devi Ma, and the
jogins, and the theme of three women talking about their husbands is a
cliche in Braj poetry. But here I've modernized it. The one woman says
she wants a job for her husband, the second wants . . . and the third
says she wants an "automatic *languria*." Then here, on this cassette,
"Disco languria," the tunes are all original, or else from films.[38]

While disparaging the uninspired vulgarity of many *rasiya* cassettes, Tanatan
is not above devoting several songs to vignettes which *Braj-basis* would interpret as sexual euphemisms:

The truck driver lured me with his smiles
He took me to Bombay for free . . .
As I sat in the cab he pushed on his horn . . .

Similarly, the following song text would appear to be an utterly traditional-
style complaint directed at Yasoda, the mother of the mischievous Krishna.
An Agra student familiar with contemporary *rasiya*, however, assured me that
the first lines were to be interpreted sexually:

O *maiya*, your Kanhaiya is grabby
He sticks his finger in [the milk pot] and licks it with relish
This is not just today, but everyday
He pushes us and knocks us down, grabbing like an eagle
He breaks the mud pot of one of us, and pulls on the dress of another
He throws stones and makes our skulls soft
He lifts our veils and stares at us
Please explain to him, otherwise I will throw him down and beat him
    someday[39]

Whether or not Tanatan intended this poem to be interpreted as erotic, the fact that a typical listener would understand it thusly suggests the conditioned expectations and assumptions now applied to commercial *rasiya* cassettes.

Tanatan provides an example of how a self-conscious innovator in a "folk" genre like *rasiya* can use the mass media—first, chapbooks, and subsequently, cassettes—to disseminate and popularize his own songs and lyrics. In the the past there have clearly been many such educated poet-singers who have contributed to the vitality of folk genres like *rasiya,* whose names are subsequently lost, or perhaps survive in the form of obscure sobriquets in old song texts. With the advent of cassettes, dissemination becomes incomparably faster and broader, while musicians' names, identities, and output are more likely to be preserved and recognized, even if the popularity of many cassettes is ephemeral. Tanatan's ability to promote his own art, through his own cottage cassette company, and subsequently, contracts with larger producers, also illustrates a degree of control that a poet-musician can have over his own art, which has little parallel in the film industry, where songs must be tailored to fit the demands of scripts.

Conclusions

In this chapter I have examined the impact of cassette technology on Braj folk music as a case study in the cassette-based commercialization of regional folk music in India. While in many respects typical, the emergence of commercial *rasiya* tapes is not in every sense representative of all major North Indian folk-pop music traditions, as these vary so greatly from region to region. Thus, for example, commercial cassettes of Braj music do not exhibit the Westernization, and especially the disco influence, evident in Punjabi pop music; accordingly, there are relatively few *Braj-basi* NRIs, and Braj culture as a whole remains much more provincial than modern Punjabi culture, with its strong demographic and financial ties to Delhi, Canada, Great Britain, and elsewhere. The *masala* orientation of modern *rasiya,* although resembling that of counterparts in Bhojpuri and Punjabi music, is far from universal in India; in Rajasthan, as mentioned, most of the commercial cassette output consists of *kathas* which are explicitly or implicitly devotional; similarly, vulgar erotica does not appear to be extremely widespread in Garhwali cassette musics. The disparate forms that commercialization has taken in these regions presumably derive from broader sociocultural conditions.

In other respects, however, the cassette-based commercialization of *rasiya* may be taken as typical of North Indian regional musics. In the most general sense, of course, the emergence of pop *rasiya* demonstrates how the decentralization of the means of media production makes possible the emergence of mass-mediated forms of regional lower-class genres like *rasiya*. Although disseminated on the mass media, and typically occupying shelf space adjacent to film-music cassettes, commercial *rasiya* differs in significant ways from film music, which previously dominated the popular-music scene in the Braj region as elsewhere. Unlike film music, commercial *rasiya* has no ties to a corporate film industry, nor to the values of consumerism, Westernized glamor, and fantasy promoted by popular cinema. *Rasiya* performers and composers are not cogs in a vast corporate production system, but are independent creative agents, however finite their audiences may be; thus, even if the notion of artistic freedom is a bourgeois Western concept, there remain qualitative and quantitative differences between the constraints (and possibilities) facing a film musician, and a humble folk cassette artist like Tanatan. *Rasiya*'s texts, while tending to adhere to traditional, stereotypical topics, are not constrained to avoid controversy or to limit themselves to sentimental love; thus, creative poets and poet-singers like Tanatan are free to compose *rasiyas* dealing with a wide variety of contemporary topics, including pointed social commentary. Invariably, *rasiya* texts deal with ordinary people in relatively ordinary situations, unlike most commercial films, with their voyeuristic and alienating focus on the Westernized elite and a fantasy world of cabarets, mansions, and gardens. Cassette-based *rasiya* is much closer to folk music than to commercial popular music; none of its performers rely solely or even primarily on recordings for their livelihood[40]; the genre's style has not changed dramatically since the advent of cassettes; and if anything, cassettes have strengthened the oral nature of *rasiya*'s dissemination at the expense of written modes, insofar as poets like Tanatan switch from publishing chapbooks to producing cassettes; finally, it is difficult to verify, at this point, that recordings have had any marked effect on live performances, whether in terms of frequency, style, or function.

At the same time, cassette-based *rasiya* has emerged as a somewhat distinct subgenre of traditional *rasiya,* now exhibiting *some,* although not all, of the developments and changes typically associated with commercial popular music. While still constituting an oral tradition, the nature of memory and tradition have changed somewhat with the advent of the mass media; for one thing, innovations, such as the incorporation of *naqqara,* and spoken introductions, spread much faster than they would otherwise (Middleton 1990:134). Imitation of idiosyncratic styles, and appropriation of other poets' lyrics are facilitated by cassettes, and have even occurred in the realm of commercial recordings.[41] *Rasiya* cassettes, rather than representing a cross-section of traditional styles, consist mostly of a solo, professional style with accompaniment. Moreover, most recorded texts (as well as cassette covers) are of the erotic *masaledar* variety, oriented primarily toward young male customers; the "male gaze" implicit in such an orientation effectively prevents the participation of "respectable" women (non-prostitutes) in the evolution of the subgenre.

It would be tempting to conclude that the preference for secular erotica over *bhakti* devotion in commercial *rasiya* cassettes represents a secularization process, concomitant with the spread of market relations, grassroots media control, and commercialization in general. I suspect, however, that such an interpretation would be difficult to substantiate. It is more verifiable that the *masala* of *rasiya* cassettes, like that of contemporary commercial cinema, reflects an orientation toward lower-class consumers, who are uninhibited by Victorian prudishness and liberal egalitarian attitudes toward women. Further, while such a development seems to reflect an earthy, rustic provinciality, some of my informants implicitly associated it with the allegedly corrupting and crass influence of film culture in general. Such interpretations suggest that a class-based reading of commercial *rasiya* is complex, contradictory, and inseparable from equally contradictory issues of gender, age, and the role of popular culture in general.

Secular *rasiya* cassettes: (upper left) *Come join me under my umbrella*; (upper right) *He's flashing ten-rupee notes at me*; (lower left) *Don't press yourself on me at my parents' house*; (lower right) *Spicy languria*, of Sevaram Tanatan.

(upper left) Punjabi star singer Gurdas Maan; (upper right) Punjabi truckdrivers'
songs; (lower left) Michael Jackson clone; (lower right) Alisha Chinai: "Madonna."

Bawdy Bhojpuri folk-music tapes: (upper left) *Bastard banana*; (upper right) *Nine-inch banana*; (lower left) *Bhojpuri eggplant*; (upper right) *Bhojpuri rasiya*.

Which is the genuine *Aafreen*? None. All are pirate copies.

Religious genres: (upper left) devotional *rasiya*; (upper right) *bhajans*; (lower left) *Build the temple* (militant Hindu speeches and songs); (lower right) *qawwali* tape, denouncing bride-burning.

10

Cassettes and Sociopolitical Movements

In previous chapters I have attempted to relate musical developments with technological ones, treating both as social phenomena encompassing aspects of cultural superstructure as well as material base. The sociopolitical ramifications of these developments are naturally most visible in the realm of cassettes explicitly linked to partisan causes. Nevertheless, in devoting this chapter to the overtly sociopolitical uses of cassettes and cassette-based music, I do not intend to reify the realm of the political, which is in fact inherent to any manifestation of popular culture. Sociopolitical stances, however general or ambiguous, are implicit, if not explicit, in any artistic production, including the various music genres discussed in this volume.

The very choice of language for song texts ultimately can be seen to have political implications, especially in a country where linguistic policies—such as the role of Hindi in the south, or the official status of Urdu in Uttar Pradesh education—have been the subjects of demonstrations and riots. The mass media dissemination of regional musics celebrating local culture via the use of autochthonous dialect, style, and genres bears obvious implications in a nation whose unity is as fragile as India's.

Moreover, when we acknowledge gender relationships to constitute an important dimension of sociopolitical terrain, we can recognize that even the most ostensibly trivial or light *jija-sali* doggerel portrays, and generally can be seen either to endorse or oppose a particular representation of gender and sexual politics. Much of traditional folklore, for example, glorifies *sati* (widow-burning), and the mass dissemination of such material via cassettes cannot be viewed as a neutral phenomenon, especially since the evidently coerced immolation of Rup Kanwar in 1987 and the groundswell of Rajasthani public opinion glorifying the deed.

Similarly, devotional music in general cannot be regarded as apolitical; in India, where religious conflicts take explicitly political forms, and religious and caste communities are treated as vote blocs, any usage of the mass media—whether commercial or state-run—to propagate sacred themes or narratives is potentially contentious. Durdarshan's epic serials have certainly been no exception, with secularists denouncing the state patronage of the *Ramayan* and *Mahabharat* productions as promoting Hinduism, and Hindu radicals condemning the compensatory *Tipu Sultan* series as glorification of an alleged bigot.[1] Further, some of the devotional-music cassettes produced in the last decade—such as Symphony Recording's aforementioned tape of anti-dowry *qawwalis*—overtly confront contemporary social controversies. What distinguishes the cassette types discussed in this chapter, then, is not the presence of a sociopolitical message, which can be found in any work of art, but the deliberate use of cassettes by an organized movement to mobilize popular opinion.

In twentieth-century India, music has often been linked to sociopolitical movements. The text orientation of most North Indian folk music, the weakness of print-based media, and the extensive if decentralized network of traditional folk media (theater, itinerant performers, etc.) have made music a natural vehicle for the expression of sociopolitical causes. Anticolonial *rasiyas* and patriotic *birhas* constitute obvious examples, while, as we have seen, competing groups in *rasiya dangals* will assume the platforms of opposing political parties for sport. The Arya Samaj employed *bhajan* sessions to spread its messages of Hindu revival, family planning, opposition to untouchability, and other related causes (Vatuk 1979). Leftist organizations have made extensive use of music to educate, encourage, and mobilize the North Indian poor. In particular, the Bengal wing of the CPM (Communist Party of India-Marxist) has long made effective and imaginative use of folk media—song, *jatra* theater, and graffiti—to gain electoral success, while the Indian People's Theatre Association (IPTA) has employed newly composed political folksongs and street-theater dramas for a variety of causes, from anticolonialism in the 1940s to communal harmony at present; in doing so, IPTA has attracted the support and collaboration of some of India's leading musicians, including the young Ravi Shankar. Even Hindustani classical music was enlisted, in its own way, into the anticolonial struggle, in performances arranged by V. D. Paluskar, which would invariably terminate with the patriotic hymn "Bande Mataram."

Since Independence the central government has also made concerted efforts to propagandize through folk music and theater. The most extensive use of folk media has been in the promotion of family planning. Since at least as early as the mid-1970s, folk ensembles have been commissioned to compose and perform songs and dramas on the radio and on tours hailing sterilization. While it is difficult to measure the success of such programs (especially in the wake of the counterproductive excesses of the 1975–77 Emergency), they have certainly made sterilization a familiar concept throughout the country, whose merits and alleged demerits are the subjects of many spontaneous songs and dramas. Indeed, in the relative absence of a Western bourgeois aesthetic of "art for art's sake," music committed to a sociopolitical cause is not regarded in India as tainted or corrupted, as it often is, for example, in the bourgeois West.

Before the advent of cassettes, the mass media played only marginal roles in disseminating overtly sociopolitical music. The supposedly nonpartisan state-run broadcast media have been enjoined to keep party politics out of folk-music programs, while the political parties themselves have enjoyed minimal access to radio or television. The print media have been uninhibited by such factors, but their impact has continued to be limited by low literacy rates throughout the country. Most importantly, the recording industry was dominated by film music designed for sentimental interludes in escapist cinematic fantasies. In this respect Indian popular music differed markedly from mass-mediated syncretic genres like Nigerian *apala* and *juju,* which had long abounded with topical proverbs, praise for political candidates, and some sociopolitical commentary (Waterman 1989:20–22, 67–68, 104–7, and elsewhere).

In such conditions, cassettes have turned out to be ideal vehicles for sociopolitical mobilization, both by institutional and grassroots organizations. Cassettes are not monopolized by the state, or by any corporate oligopoly; they are resistant to censorship, and inexpensive enough to be produced as well as consumed by lower-class as well as affluent activists. Illiteracy is no impediment to access or appreciation of tapes, and, finally, cassettes can rely on a vast, if unorganized duplication and dissemination network comprising both pirate and legitimate retailers and producers. Cassettes, as I have suggested, can be seen to constitute an ideal example of the "new media" which, as envisioned by Enzensberger and others, could form the vehicles for grassroots lower-class empowerment, opposition, and mobilization, in a way which the expensive, state- or corporate-dominated "old" media could not function. As we have seen, control of the means of cassette production is not dominated by any religious, caste, class, or ethnic community, but is distributed among a wide variety of large and small producers heterogeneous in every significant parameter except gender. Not surprisingly, cassettes, containing both song and spoken monologues, have been discovered to be remarkably effective media for propaganda, and are now regarded as indispensable for every major sociopolitical campaign.

I have mentioned the systematic and highly efficient use of audiocassettes to disseminate Ayatollah Khomeini's speeches during the Iranian Revolution. This strategy has been imitated, in idiosyncratic ways, in several Indian sociopolitical campaigns, with results, in some cases, that have been in their own way equally drastic. Unfortunately, as we shall discuss, if Marxists and progressives would regard the Iranian Revolution with ambivalence, some of the causes for which cassettes have been most extensively used in India are even less like the leftist mobilization and subaltern empowerment envisioned by Enzensberger.

Jagori: Cassettes and Women's Liberation

Indian women today, as in the past, remain victims of a range of abuses, including wife-beating, mistreatment of new brides, female infanticide, persecution of widows (whose presence is regarded as inauspicious), and rape by policemen, rural landlords, and other authority figures. Some forms of abuse—notably, dowry extortion and dowry murders—rather than declining with modernization and Westernization, have become endemic in recent decades, evidently under the influence of capitalist consumerism. Legal measures such as the prohibition of dowry have proven utterly ineffective, while many courts continue to treat women as second-class citizens. In the absence of a totalitarian government enforcing aspects of women's empowerment (as in Cuba, Libya, or Iraq), enhancement of women's status will have to be led by grassroots civil organizations.

Some of the preconditions for the spread of such movements do exist in India. Although proportionately small, there is an infrastructure of several million educated, progressive-minded women in various positions of influence and employment. In educated circles, a sophisticated discourse of women's empowerment has emerged, encompassing a growing body of feminist scholarly literature, and a highbrow monthly news and culture magazine (*Manushi*). Around two hundred grassroots women's organizations have also sprouted throughout the country (Bumiller 1990:132). Although formed primarily by educated upper- or middle-class progressives, some such organizations make concerted and, within their limited spheres, effective attempts to reach lower- and lower-middle-class women, whose exploitation is the most severe.

One such organization is Jagori, which, from its office in New Delhi, conducts a variety of activities, including providing shelter and counseling for abused wives, organizing women's workshops, and promoting educational programs. Jagori has made wide use of audiocassettes to disseminate songs promoting women's causes. As of 1990, three cassettes of songs[2] had been produced, containing pieces both by educated feminists like Kamla Bhasin as well as songs composed by lower-class activists and participants in workshops. Most of the songs, with texts in colloquial Hindi-Urdu, are set to familiar tunes—generally folk songs, film songs, and *qawwalis*. An inexpensive chapbook containing the song texts is also available, although oral dissemination via cassettes, workshops, and informal song sessions remains most effective.

As we have noted in the preceding chapters, there is a large variety of women's folk-song genres which present, in one form or another, female perspectives on life. Other genres, from *rasiya* to the light-classical *thumri*, whether sung by men or women, are presented from the female persona, depicting what may in many cases be taken as genuine women's complaints and

239

concerns; as we have seen in *rasiya,* these may portray domestic abuse, longing for intimacy, yearning to visit parents, ambivalence toward seductive
neighbors, and demands to be allowed out of the confining "four walls" of
home to visit a nearby fair (*mela*). While many such songs may be taken as
authentic and tradition-honored expressions of women's frustrations, they do
not constitute "protest songs" which directly challenge sexist practices and
promote activist, reformist solidarity. The songs generated by Jagori, by contrast, illustrate the form a committed women's music can take. The strident
and aggressive tone of the song below (sung to the tune of a Rajasthani folk
song) is typical:

> Hear how together with other women we can gain our rights
> Brother got freedom, we got the four walls
> Why don't we smash these walls?
> First we'll demand our rights at home, and then outside as well . . .

The following song, set to a lively *qawwali* tune, emerged from a workshop:

> What have you gained by sitting and suffering silently?
> Nothing will change that way
> Only by opening your mouth and speaking
> Will the times change.

> These centuries-old traditions handed down to us
> Where have they come from, and why?
> Think about them, understand
> Why have you made them your own?

> How did this *parda* [seclusion of women] befall you?
> Is it part of religion?
> What religion, what *parda*?
> This is all the work of men . . .

Other songs address broader issues, expressing, for example, women's perspectives on the contemporary communal conflicts waged by men:

> God has become divided in temples, mosques, and churches . . .
> The Hindu says the temple is his abode
> the Muslim says Allah is his faith
> Both fight, and in fighting die
> What oppression and violence they wreak over one another!
> Whose goal is this, whose scheme? . . .

Other texts indict war, illiteracy, religious obscurantism, drug and alcohol
abuse, and the sexism ingrained in religions created by and for men to the
detriment of women. (Interestingly, another song indicts family planning as a
Malthusian harassment of the poor.)[3] The songs are performed on the cassettes

by a women's chorus to the accompaniment of *dholak*, without elaborate instrumental backing, just as they are intended to be rendered by ordinary women; in this sense they invite comparison with, for example, the leftist folk music promoted in the United States by singers like Pete Seeger. Thus, in shunning the snappy and slick orchestration of film music, they sacrifice a degree of market appeal, but can be produced on a minimal budget and can function as performance models which can be imitated by any amateurs. A narrator encourages women to compose their own texts, or to change those on the cassette, using whatever familiar tunes they know and like. The cassettes are thus designed ideally to serve as an inspiration to amateur performance, and to further creativity and self-expression on the part of women who are not trained musicians, but who retain strong traditions of informal collective singing. Similarly, the chapbook encourages women to use the songs as they like, and to freely alter the texts and/or melodies.

The use of familiar folk and film melodies in these cassettes should provide another illustration of the convenience and efficiency of the practice of parody, which allows amateur performers to appropriate, resignify, and revitalize familiar tunes in the service of progressive community values. Singers may exercise musical creativity in selecting suitable favorite tunes, and, more importantly, they may compose their own lyrics, thereby giving new life to melodies whose original familiar texts may long since have lost their interest and appeal.

Jagori also distributes a cassette *Khilti kaliyan* (Blossoming buds) made by IPTA activist and dramatist Safdar Hashmi, who was murdered by Congress Party thugs in 1989. *Khilti kaliyan* narrates various vignettes of village life, as seen by a female health advisor, in which women energetically confront various sorts of adversity—caste oppression, dowry extortion, illiteracy, unemployment, and the like. Songs set to familiar tunes articulate the women's problems and reactions; as the inlay card notes observe, unlike the passive lamentations of traditional women's folk songs, "There is no self-pity in these songs, no despair, but rather the hope that women will triumph, and that joining together they'll call others to swell their ranks." Above all, the narrative and song texts stress the importance of acquiring literacy:

Only by learning to read and write will women change their fate
Only with literacy will women acquire the gait of men
An educated woman won't remain subjugated
She won't put up with social oppression

The Jagori cassettes represent precisely the kind of oppositional, grassroots use of the new media that Enzensberger and other progressives have envisioned. Free from state and corporate patronage and guidelines, resistant to official or market censorship, and oriented toward amateur consumption and reproduction rather than commercial success, the Jagori tapes could ideally be duplicated informally throughout North India, inspiring other low-budget cassettes and strengthening the foundations for a national women's movement. Cassettes have provided an ideal technological infrastructure for the mass dissemination of an Indian feminist discourse; it is only the subjective social conditions that inhibit the spread of such a message.

Regional Movements in Eastern Bihar

The politics of language have been overt issues of contention in many cases since Independence. In 1969, the attempted imposition of Hindi in education and government discourse sparked violent riots in Tamil Nadu, while one of the vehement demands of the contemporary Hindu militant movement has been the repeal of Uttar Pradesh's recent recognition of Urdu as a second official language. Language is often an explicit nexus of conflicts relating to class, regional identity, and center-periphery interactions. In this sense, the proliferation of regional-language cassettes constitutes in itself an inherent empowerment of vernacular cultures at the expense of mainstream Hindi discourse, whether the latter is associated with state broadcast media or the commercial film industry.

In a few cases, cassettes of music in local dialects have been explicitly associated with organized regional culture movements. Carol Babiracki, in her research in the Ranchi area in 1983–84, discovered that two such movements were flourishing in eastern Bihar, in association with the Nagpuri and Panchpargania revivals (personal communication, November 1991). These two languages have traditionally been regarded as regional dialects of Bhojpuri and Bengali, respectively; however, both have recently been granted official recognition as bona fide languages in their own right. Like most regional languages, they are intimately associated with local folklore, songs, oral literature, and the like, and thus connote distinct subregional ethnic cultures as well as dialects. The Nagpuri and Panchpargania languages have recently become the vehicles for organized movements devoted to the promotion of local culture. To some extent, these mobilizations have been motivated by hostility toward outsiders (Bengalis, Uttar Pradesh Hindi-speakers, etc.), who are resented as opportunistic landlords and industrial bosses. While tapping grassroots sentiment, these movements are led by a number of formal sanskritic ("traditional") organizations which promote local literary culture, folk dance, and local music. Aside from folkloric performing troupes, commercial audiocassettes play significant roles in the dissemination and popularization of Nagpuri and Panchpargania music. Produced locally in *ad hoc* studios, such cassettes offer a range of music, including traditional folk songs, newly composed songs in folk style, and such syncretic hybrids as "Nagpuri *filmi*," "Nagpuri disco," and "Nagpuri *qawwali*." As might be expected, such distinct genres have their own adherents and critics, just as the various representative organizations are to some extent in competition with each other; all, however, are devoted, in their own way, to promoting local culture and music rather than Hindi film culture. (To date no feature films in either dialect have been produced.)

A similar movement has emerged contemporaneously in connection with the demand on the part of Adivasis (tribals) and local Indo-Aryans (non-tribals) for regional autonomy in the Jharkand region comprising parts of Madhya Pradesh, western Bengal, and southern Bihar. Babiracki notes that local entrepreneurs and cultural organizations have produced commercial re-cordings of local folk music in association with the Jharkand movement. Such recordings, like regional-dialect cassettes in general, promote local culture and identity, generally at the expense of vertical class and caste divisions and mainstream Hindi pop culture.

Cassettes and the 1989 Elections

The 1989 general elections marked something of a watershed in Indian poli-tics. For the first time since Independence, the Congress Party, which had hitherto dominated the central government (with the brief and aberrant excep-tion of the Janta coalition period of 1977–80), suffered a decisive defeat re-flecting a fundamental and irreversible structural decline. Secondly, the 1989 elections can be said to have been the first in which the mass media—and especially audio- and videocassettes—played a significant partisan role.

Throughout the three decades after Independence, the Congress Party had largely monopolized the central as well as most state governments, drawing on its venerable anticolonial legacy, its association with Nehru and Mahatma Gandhi, and its successful maintenance of a set of coalitions of regional, caste, class, and religious voting blocs. While limiting the amount of genuine electoral competition, Congress dominance provided sociopolitical stability and marginalized radical parties of left and right. From the mid-1970s, how-ever, Congress's comfortable hegemony began to unravel. Indira Gandhi's personalistic, authoritarian rule encouraged party sycophancy at the expense of genuine collaboration and coalition; Congress's thinly disguised support of radical extremist groups—from Sikh separatist J. S. Bhindranwale to Bengali Maoist Naxalites—tarnished its image and ultimately strengthened regional parties. More voters were alienated by the imposition of martial law during the 1975–77 Emergency, and the rise of a neofascist Youth Congress wing led by Indira's son Sanjay. While Indira regained power after the collapse of the fragile Janta coalition in 1980, her assassination in 1984—at the hands of Sikh separatists whom she had once supported in order to split the Punjabi opposition—further weakened the Congress Party structure. Her son Rajiv, initially supported by the party machinery and by a sympathetic electorate, soon proved to be an opportunistic and ineffective prime minister who, despite his political inexperience, adopted with dismaying rapidity the corrupt, un-scrupulous, and divisive tactics of his mother; his evident involvement in the Bofors kickback scandal made him an easy target for opponents. As a result, by 1989 the Congress Party had lost such prestige and popularity that, for the first time, a genuine competitive electoral competition was occuring in the national political scene. The national contest soon devolved into a three-way struggle between the remnants of Congress-I (I for Indira), the Hindu chau-vinist Bharatiya Janta Party (BJP, formerly the Jan Sangh), and the Janta Dal coalition led by V. P. Singh with the support of the left-of-center CPI (Com-munist Party of India) and CPM.

The role of the mass media in the 1989 elections was unprecedented. In the United States, it has been taken for granted for several decades that effective television coverage is one of the most essential ingredients for electoral suc-cess; skillful if scurrilous manipulation of television by the Republican Party in the Reagan-Bush era has been particularly influential. In India, the mass media have been far less significant in national elections, until recently. The state-controlled broadcast media, obliged to maintain ostensible impartiality, do not play fundamentally persuasive roles in political contests. The print media are not committed to impartiality, but their influence remains limited among a largely illiterate electorate. Oddly, the most influential mass me-dium, in its own indirect way, had been commercial mythological cinema, in which M. G. Ramachandran (MGR, of the Dravida Munnetra Kazhagam [DMK]) and N. T. Rama Rao (NTR, of the Telegu Desam) had both estab-lished images as beneficent deities; both politicians capitalized overtly on their celluloid personae in order to lead regional parties to electoral success in Tamil Nadu and Andhra Pradesh, respectively. Earlier DMK leaders (Anna-durai and Karunanidhi) had succeeded by virtue of similar cinematic reputa-tions, as did MGR's mistress and eventual successor, Jayalalitha.[4] NTR, the pioneer in political use of commercial cinema, had released a Telegu film, *Vira Brahmendra Swami Charita,* on the eve of the 1985 elections, in which a sage predicted the replacement of a widow ruler (i.e., Indira Gandhi) by an actor. NTR's opponents subsequently used similar tactics against him, lam-pooning his governership in commercial movies. In 1989 Janta Dal supporter Raj Babbar produced a film, *Mr. Clean,* constituting a thinly veiled attack on Rajiv Gandhi.[5]

The potential of videocassettes to win votes was first exploited in India in the 1983 Andhra Pradesh state elections; subsequently, for the 1985 parlia-mentary elections, Rajiv Gandhi's Congress-I Party distributed some five thousand prints of a twenty-minute film of Indira Gandhi's speeches (Agrawal 1986). In 1989, conditions were ripe for an unprecedentedly massive and sophisticated usage of the new media—specifically, audio- and videocas-settes—by the competing parties.

Video technology played a prominent role in the opposition parties' 1989 campaign, and particularly in that of the BJP. J. K. Jain, a member of the Hindu fascist Rashtriya Swayamsevak Sangam (RSS) party and founder of New Delhi's Jain Studios, rented out assorted video equipment, and especially seventy-five specially constructed "video *raths*" (chariots)—vans fitted with three-hundred-inch video screens—to opposition parties. The BJP made most extensive use of this equipment, renting twenty-five vans apiece in Madhya Pradesh, Maharashtra, and elsewhere, touring towns and villages to show promotional documentaries made by Jain Studios, focusing on themes of inflation, unemployment, rural poverty, and Congress corruption. One thousand copies of one BJP video were distributed in Maharashtra alone, to be disseminated by the local party wings in collaboration with the Shiv Sena (a right-wing organization devoted, among other things, to the expulsion of all non-Maharashtrians from Bombay).[6]

The "video *raths*" (chariots) attracted considerable attention, and have since become standard features in Indian campaigns. In the 1991 elections, Jain Studios expanded its arsenal to 108 *raths,* while over a dozen other competing studios emerged in Delhi alone. As Jain noted, "This kind of campaign doesn't exist anywhere else in the democratic world; here access to all the legitimate media is blocked" (Crossette 1991). The video boom has also included the emergence of video newsweeklies like "Newstrack" (produced by *India Today*) and "Observer News Channel," which cover current events with greater imagination and freedom than the lackluster state television.[7]

With the broadcast media inaccessible to campaign promoters, only audiocassettes came to rival video as a propaganda mass medium. In the 1989 elections, all three of the competing parties compiled promotional audiocassettes which were distributed to party activists. The cassettes were then widely duplicated on India's extant legal and pirate dubbing infrastructure. They were played through sound systems at rallies, in front of party offices, from cars fitted with rooftop speakers (otherwise used to advertise films), and in tea-stalls and other streetside venues throughout North India. Most of the cassettes relied primarily on parodies using familiar film songs—a technique which had been used on grassroots levels for decades beore the advent of cassettes.[8]

A BJP cassette distributed in North India combined patriotic film songs with monologue, spoken in Sanskritized Hindi, offering familiar, and rather implausible campaign promises ("there will be work for everyone, pensions for the elderly . . . "); the speaker indicted Rajiv's foreign education, diet, manners, and wife, and concluded with a poem with the refrain "You may be the bridegroom of Italy, but not of India" (referring to Rajiv's Italian wife). The most effective and widespread of the audiocassettes appear to have been two tapes disseminated by the Janta Dal, both of which merit brief description. One of these was produced by film star and JD supporter Raj Babbar, who enjoyed access to Bombay studios, musicians, and music producers.

Babbar's tape was the most slick and professional of the various cassettes, and soon came to constitute a collectors' item of sorts. It featured repeated versions of a tuneful, up-tempo theme song, with the refrain "Support Janta Dal, put your stamp on the wheel" (the party logo).[9] Subsequent verses vowed to end broadcast-media bias and establish peace with India's neighbors, while offering the familiar promises of curbing inflation, peasant indebtedness, government corruption, foreign debt, and unemployment. The bulk of the tape consisted of parodies of familiar songs. The first used the tune and refrain of a popular *qawwali* ("Jhum dara ab jhum, o saqi"); its verses blamed the series of grisly communal riots in North India on Congress Party machinations, and went on to accuse Rajiv of embezzling national wealth for his in-laws. The next song, based on a film hit, reiterated similar themes, advocating communal harmony and respect and support for regional cultures and languages— in contrast to the BJP and, increasingly, Congress, who sought to appeal to Hindu voters by scapegoating Muslims. The final song was based on a film song from *Naya Daur,* which commenced "Yeh desh hai vir javanon ka . . ." (This is the country of brave young men . . .). Babbar's tape retained the melody and the rhyme, yet changed the text to deride the Congress hand logo: "Yeh hath nishan hai choron ka . . . " (This hand is the symbol of thieves, of corrupt thugs; don't vote for it, teach it a lesson . . .).[10]

Another Janta Dal tape was produced by political scientist Mohan Guruswamy, who served on the party's executive committee. Guruswamy's tape, although no less trenchant, was a more homemade affair, relying on pastiche rather than parody. In between passages of sardonic monologue were interspersed various popular political songs which suited the party's campaign themes. A few were drawn from older films (*Andhi, Upkar, Roti Kapra aur Makan*), for which lyricists like Kaifi Azmi and Utpal Dutt had written populist texts indicting inflation, corruption, and government inaction. The song from *Roti, Kapra aur Makan* (Bread, clothing, and shelter), a lament about inflation, contained a fortuitous reference to a hike in the price of sugar, which in fact had recently risen during Rajiv's tenure. Another song sarcastically honored the campaigning Congress politicians: "Here come the great men to buy our votes again, with their hands folded; let us welcome them . . ." A *qawwali* by the Sabri Brothers, "Gore log kala danda" (White people, black stick), cohered conveniently with the opposition mudslinging against Rajiv's foreign education and Italian wife. Particularly effective was a recent anti-Rajiv song, "Sale jhut bolela, kali Dilli ka chora jhut bolela" (The bastard from disgraced Delhi is lying), from a commercial cassette by leftist Bhojpuri folksinger Balleshvar. Guruswamy edited out a few particularly scurrilous lines (such as one ridiculing Gandhi as a *hijra* transvestite) while leaving intact the rest of the song (which continues "He's a middleman for foreigners and amasses black money . . . "). A love song from *Madhumati,* in which the lover describes his ardently beating heart, was juxtaposed with sarcastic commentary to lampoon Rajiv's slogan "My heart beats for India," so as to imply that Gandhi's palpitations were due to his anxiety over having to face a hostile and disillusioned electorate. Guruswamy, having produced the recording essentially for free, distributed 3000 copies to local constituencies (20 to each candidate), from which he estimates that another 15,000–20,000 copies were informally duplicated throughout the north (Guruswamy, interview, 1990).[11] In fact, campaign managers were so impressed by the spread of the cassettes that they abandoned press advertisements, which were especially expensive. The Janta Dal cassettes were synchronized with an ongoing poster war waged with Congress, and they served as examples to several other JD candidates, such as Mulayam Singh Yadav, who had their own promotional cassettes produced. As Guruswamy observed,

> With the air waves denied to you, one has to use other means to express oneself. Cassettes are a small man's medium. They take advantage of the pirate and informal duplication facilities already in place throughout the country. And the person who duplicates, who is presumably a party enthusiast, takes some pride in it, and feels that he is contributing something; and so the cassettes spread like chain letters, even if the quality gets pretty awful by the end.

As copies of the Janta Dal cassette multiplied, Congress Party spokesman Anand Sharma denounced the tape's "abusive, filthy, and vulgar" language in a press release, calling the Balleshvar song's reference to "disgraced Delhi" "an insult to the glorious Indian heritage and culture."[12] It was harder to denounce the film songs, which were long since part of the patrimony of North Indian pop culture. Political film songs were also used in promotional cassettes by other parties, eventually including Congress, which had been mocked by journalists for playing apolitical and irrelevant film songs at its rallies while cassette-disseminated opposition parodies were being sung on the streets.[13] Interestingly, in Tamil Nadu, both Congress and the DMK made use of songs from MGR's films. The DMK used the hits because of their association with MGR and their mention of the rising sun, the DMK's party symbol; for its part, Congress made use of a few of MGR songs which referred to "the hand," which was recontextualized to refer to Congress's party logo.[14] Meanwhile, both the BJP and Congress parties produced audiocassettes using, among other tunes, the "Tirchi Topi Wale" theme, with its famous "oe-oe" catch phrase. So ubiquitous had this tune become, and so numerous and diverse were its reincarnations and resignifications, that its original cinematic associations were clearly of little importance.[15] Similarly, if the practice of parody outfits popular melodies with new meanings, the use of pastiche by Guruswamy and others illustrates the potential for a different sort of resignification of extant popular music—similarly demonstrating how commercial popular music may be creatively reproduced and reinvigorated rather than simply passively consumed.

Regional and Sectarian Movements

Since 1980, and especially since 1989, India's sociopolitical stability has been challenged as never before by a set of violent dissident movements which have posed seemingly insoluble threats to the country's unity. The emergence and electoral success of the DMK in the late 1960s, along with simmering separatist rebellions by Nagas and Mizos, had long constituted irritants to the country's political unity, but these have been overshadowed by far more radical developments in the recent past. Most prominent among these have been separatist movements by Sikhs, Kashmiri Muslims, and Assamese, and, most perniciously, the rise of Hindu fundamentalist militancy. The intensification of these dissident movements since the late 1980s has shaken as never before the fabric of post-Partition Indian society and political integrity.

It is tempting to try to relate these developments to similar fissiparous tendencies painfully visible in the former Soviet bloc, and in countries such as Sri Lanka, and to hypothesize some general decline of the concept of the nation-state in the late-twentieth century. The internationalization of capital and of information technology has undoubtedly contributed in a general sense to such disruptions. Yet even within India, the disparate conflicts, while sharing certain conditioning factors, differ in their origins, motivations, and underlying causes. Two shared factors may be noted. The first is the decline of the Congress Party, which constitutes a cause as well as an effect of the emergence of dissident movements. Whatever the faults of the party and of its decades of hegemony, its prestige and initial policies of accommodation and consensus provided an extended epoch of relative sociopolitical stability in India. The eclipse of the party, and of the fragile coalition of voting blocs it incorporated, has created a power vacuum in which chaos and violence run rampant.

A second unifying feature of the contemporary dissident movements is the role of the mass media, and particularly the new media like cassettes and video, which are free from central government censorship and conducive to local and often subversive control. In previous chapters we have emphasized the positive aspects of diversification of the music industry, noting how cassette technology has provided a medium for the affirmation and revitalization of various musical traditions associated with disparate ethnic, religious, regional, linguistic, and class/caste communities. The negative side to such centrifugal effects is the tendency of media decentralization to fragment the nation into irreconcilable and antagonistic interest groups. Of course, we should not assume that the existence of Kashmiri music tapes is inherently linked to political separatism, or that any consumer of Hindu devotional cassettes is necessarily in any way supportive of militant fundamentalism. Nevertheless, cassettes are part of an Indian information revolution which has greatly enhanced mass-media promotion of North Indian cultural diversity at the expense of Hindi mass culture. Regional-language and sectarian-music cassettes can be seen to exist on a continuum shared with explicitly extremist tapes which, in some cases, have played significant sociopolitical roles. The rise of cassettes has also occurred at a time when a consensus is emerging that federal control of the broadcast media should be reduced in favor of greater regional autonomy. How this independence is to be achieved without further fragmenting the country's structural integrity remains to be seen.

The ongoing crisis in the Punjab illustrates the current inability of the central government to control regional and ethnic conflicts. While there is no need here to dwell on the causes of the persistent anarchy and terrorism, contributing factors worthy of mention have been the growing economic clout of Sikhs, the related increased power of the Sikh religious establishment, the aforementioned decline of the Congress Party and its ongoing cynical and opportunistic machinations—which include supporting the militant separatist Bhindranwale in the early 1980s, and reneging on the Rajiv-Longowal accord of July 1985. While the majority of Punjabi Sikhs seem to want compromise and peace, the situation has deteriorated to where a few hundred militants have been able to terrorize the state. Analysts have cited the spread of cassette recordings of militant speeches as another factor contributing to the violence (Kohli 1990:359).

Given the atmosphere of terror and intimidation, heightened by the murder of star vocalist Chamkilla, most Punjabi popular music cassettes strive to avoid controversy and remain studiously apolitical. Gurdas Maan could be taking a risk even by daring to sing, in the most general sense, about the merits of reconciliation and peace. The dramatic cassette-based flourishing of Punjabi popular music could be said to enhance a sense of cultural independence from India, but such music is enjoyed, patronized, and performed equally by Punjabi Sikhs and Hindus, not to mention Pakistani Muslim performers like Mohammad Siddiq. Cassettes, however, have played a significant role in the growth of Sikh separatism, particularly by being used to spread the speeches of militant preachers like Bhindranwale. Whether consciously inspired by the Iranian Revolution or not, Sikh separatists have, by numerous accounts, made effective use of cassettes since the early 1980s. Informants relate that tapes of songs celebrating the Khalistan struggle and praising Bhindranwale and Beant Singh (an assassin of Indira Gandhi) are disseminated throughout the Punjab. Although openly seditious, the tapes circulate beyond censorship of the state, whose repressive apparatus is incapable of enforcing minimal law and order, not to mention regulating the cassette industry. (One may note the contrast with Indonesia, where decades of military rule have created a police-state atmosphere in which any criticism of the government on cassettes is effectively prohibited.)

Meanwhile, in Kashmir, since the mid-1980s, the Muslim majority (65 percent of the state population) has grown increasingly alienated from the Indian government, which annexed the state by force in 1947. While the leadership of the popular moderates Sheikh Abdullah and his son Farooq mollified Kashmiri separatism for decades, the independence movement intensified in the eighties and has been exacerbated by Congress Party's transparent rigging of the 1987 state elections, as well as by the rise of Hindu chauvinism in the Indian hinterland. With Pakistan supplying arms and logistical support to separatist guerrillas, law and order, along with the tourist-based economy, have completely broken down since the late 1980s, and reconciliation of Kashmiri Muslims to Indian rule seems less likely than ever. Although Kashmir may not host a particularly dynamic regional cassette industry, tapes of separatist songs circulate widely, mixing calls for Islamic *jihad* with appeals to Kashmiri nationalism. Such tapes are evidently produced both in Pakistani Kashmir as well as in India. A visitor to POK (Pakistani "Azad Kashmir") in spring 1990 reported that the most popular cassette in the region was entitled *The call comes from Kashmir,* commencing "Allah is great! O warrior of Islam, warrior of God, pick up your sword and come to the battlefield." [16]

Cassettes and the Contemporary Hindu-Muslim Conflict

The final sectarian conflict to be considered here is at once the most bloody, the most pernicious, and that in which cassettes have played the most disturbingly incendiary role. Since early 1989, a wave of chauvinist Hindu militancy has swept across North India, fomenting riots and pogroms in which over a thousand lives—predominantly Muslim—have been lost. The movement has been led by the BJP, which, while professing at its highest levels to be secular and moderate, has orchestrated blatantly communal and inflammatory sentiments at the grassroots level, in collaboration with its allies, the openly chauvinist Vishwa Hindu Parishad (VHP), the RSS, and the Bajrang Dal. The ostensible primary issue of the agitation is the Hindu demand to destroy (or "relocate") an otherwise insignificant mosque in Ayodhya (near Lucknow), which was built by the Mughal emperor Babur, according to Hindu activists, on the site of a Rama temple which he had destroyed. Movement leaders have targeted over three hundred other Muslim edifices for subsequent destruction as well. Aside from this Babri Masjid/Ram Janmbhoomi (birthplace) issue are a host of other complaints to the effect that the largely impoverished Muslim minority in India (11 percent of the population) continues to harbor imperial designs, and has been coddled and appeased by a Western-oriented, anti-Hindu government courting the Muslim vote bloc.

It is not entirely clear why this persecution of Muslims is occurring now.

Since the 1970s, every year or two has brought some grisly massacre of Muslims somewhere in North India, but the level of present violence is unprecedented since Partition. The issue of the Babri Masjid itself has only achieved national prominence since the late 1980s. One obvious factor, as in other contemporary conflicts, has been the eclipse of the Congress Party, which had prevously repressed overt Hindu chauvinism and maintained a fragile coalition of Muslims and assorted Hindu blocs. Prosperity among some Muslim communities due to remittances from migrant workers in Gulf states has also fueled Hindu resentment. Another factor has been V. P. Singh's championing, during his prime ministership (1989–90), of an affirmative-action policy reserving a large share of civil-service jobs for lower castes and untouchables; while Muslims are not included in the favored groups, they provide a handy scapegoat for Hindu dominant castes, which want at all costs to divert attention from caste oppression and to prevent an alliance of Muslims with poor Hindus. Thus the current agitation is to some extent an elite manipulation of volatile Hindu masses.[17] It is possible that another contributing factor may be the anxieties, insecurities, and resentments caused by the liberalization of the Indian economy, with its attendant growing income inequalities, consumerism, and socioeconomic dislocations. For their part, many Muslims, losing faith in Indian secular democracy, have turned in desperation to fundamentalist and occasionally militant strains of Islam.

Whatever its social motivations, the grassroots mobilization led by the BJP/VHP/RSS coalition is archetypically fascist in the way it exploits the repressed anger and anxieties of the masses, turning them against ostracized scapegoats, and transforming their irrational feelings into mechanisms for sectarian violence, which weakens the oppressed masses by dividing them. Since 1989 the coalition has instigated riots and massacres in dozens of towns throughout North India, with particularly destructive carnage occuring in Bhagalpur, Ahmedabad, and Jaipur. In Aligarh, Muslim passengers were pulled off train cars and butchered in scenes reminiscent of Partition. Riots have occured in towns like Badayun and Agra, whose Hindu and Muslim communities had coexisted peacefully for centuries. In several instances, the police, rather than attempting to curb the violence, have actively participated in and even instigated massacres.[18]

Inflammatory speeches by firebrand Hindu chauvinists like Uma Bharati have helped foment violence. Rumor-mongering and flagrant distortions by Hindi newspapers have also contributed to the conflagrations. Yet journalists agree that, with the neutrality of broadcast-media reporting,[19] audiocassettes and, to a lesser extent, videocassettes have played fundamental roles in instigating riots. One commentator noted, "The wave of communal frenzy has been spread deliberately by a device fortunately unknown until recently: the video-cassette and the audio-cassette" (Bhattacharjea 1990:34). In the aftermath of an assault on the Babri Masjid by Hindu militants on October 30,

1989, J. K. Jain produced an inflammatory video focusing on police retaliation against the angry, stone-throwing mob, portraying the latter as peaceful and hapless victims of police brutality. The video was eventually banned, though no action was taken against Jain, who claims to have distributed 100,000 copies of the cassette throughout the country.[20]

Audiocassettes containing inflammatory songs and speeches appear to have had even wider distribution, in accordance with the greater proliferation and accessibility of cassette players throughout the country. The basic arguments recurring in these cassettes are the same as can now be heard, depressingly but not coincidentally, from Hindus throughout North India. The Muslims came to India as looting, marauding invaders. Not content with regaining Pakistan after Partition, they now want Kashmir and the rest of India as well. Muslims shun birth control in order to increase their numbers. They are assisted by other Muslim countries, while Hinduism struggles to survive in India alone. Muslims kill cows, so it is a small matter for them to kill people as well. Their *Quran* preaches holy war against infidels. They were the ones responsible for the massacres during Partition. The prime minister, appeasing fundamentalist Muslims, overturned the Supreme Court decision in the Shah Bano case (which declared Muslim divorce laws to be the same as those of Hindus)—so why should Hindus abide by any ruling of the courts against the Ram Janmbhoomi project? And so on.

There should be little need here to refute these arguments and accusations, or to rebut the entire rationale for the Ram Janmbhoomi project, which is based on mythology rather than historical fact.[21] Unfortunately, some Muslim leaders (especially Syed Shahabuddin and Imam Bukhari) have provided ammunition for Hindu chauvinists by promoting Muslim militance and confrontation.

Four instigatory Hindi-language cassettes were produced in summer and fall of 1990. They consist primarily of recordings of incendiary speeches by various militant leaders. One tape, entitled *Mandir ka nirman karo* (Build the temple), is a professionally produced recording, with a recurring up-tempo theme song, in which the vocalist sings:

> The time has come, wake up, young people, and go to Lucknow,
> you must vow to build Ram's temple
> The conches sound, Ram's forces are standing ready for battle.[22]
> Gandiv [Arjuna's bow] is twanging, his conch calls
> Whoever joins with the wicked, smash their dreams
> Turn the political dice and blast their policies
> Advance in the battlefield of politics and hit hard
> To compare Ram with the wicked is beyond disrespect
> Destroying his temple is the limit of madness

Don't play their farcical game of acting in a courtroom
Liberate the *janmbhoomi* of the jewel of the house of Raghukul
If they don't heed your words, whip out your swords . . .
Face our enemies with courage, now isn't the time for contemplation

The speakers on the cassette[23] continue with such arguments as:

Some say we're trying to make this into a Hindu nation. I say it already
is a Hindu nation. In 1947, when Partition happened, it was settled,
that Pakistan would be Muslim, and India would be Hindu . . . If they
want to be Rahim or Raskhan [a poet-devotee of Krishna], then we'll
welcome them, but if they want to be Babur or Aurangzeb, then Hindu
youths are ready to be Rana Pratap and Shivaji . . . [Uttar Pradesh
Chief Minister] Mulayam Singh has tried to extinguish the flame of
Hinduism, but it still burns, it can't be snuffed out . . . Now Muslims
with swords in their hands are driving the Hindus out of Kashmir;
would this be tolerated in any country? . . . The temple will be built,
there's no further need for discussion. That decision has been made.
We will build it, whether with love or by force . . .

In another cassette, entitled *Jai Shri Ram* (Hail Ram), BJP member of Parliament Uma Bharati rants:

Chandra Shekhar says we should build the temple, but change the loca-
tion. I ask him would you change your father? . . . We've wasted 44
years while these elitists court the Muslim vote bank. We need people
like [Sardar] Patel and Subhash [Chandra Bose] who are willing to sacrifice their lives for the motherland, who can wipe away her tears and
gun down the traitors . . . You Muslims link yourselves to [bigoted
Mughal emperor] Aurangzeb, not to India. We sang songs of Hindu-
Muslim amity, we were ready for brotherhood, but it didn't happen.
Your *Quran* preaches holy war, while our tradition calls for peace and
accommodation even if we're being ground underfoot . . . So we tried
to have peace, but now we want our temple . . . You'll see on October
30th. When ten Bajrang Dal members sit on the chest of an Ali, then
we'll see whether the place will be called Ram Janmbhoomi or Babri
Masjid . . . We'll see if this country will be Hindu or Muslim . . .
Hindus, wake up—they've looted you and you stayed silent; they
sacked your temples and raped your mothers and daughters, and you
kept quiet. What reward did you get for your equanamity? . . .

She continues with a poem also reproduced on the inlay card:

May our race not be blamed, and may our mothers not say that
    when we were needed, we weren't ready

If there must be a bloodbath then let's get it over with
Because of our fear of a bloodbath before
Our country was divided [i.e., in Partition]
Since their arrival until today, they have killed so many Hindus
We tried to appease them, but there was bloodshed after all
Instead of having it simmer slowly, it's better to have it burst with a
    big flame
If they don't understand our words, then we'll make them
    understand with kicks;
If there must be a bloodbath, then let it happen!

A third cassette, *Ayodhya kand* (The Ayodhya Chapter) (i.e., in the *Ramayan*, when Ram returns triumphantly to his home), was produced after the October 30 assault. Graphically bewailing its failure, a series of speakers berate V. P. Singh and Mulayam Singh Yadav. VHP leader Ashok Singhal continues,

They call us militants, but if that were true, there wouldn't be a single
Muslim alive in this country . . . Who was here first—Babur or Ram?
. . . See how they're killing our devotees in order to save the mosque.
Well, we're going to liberate not just three temples, but three thousand
. . .

The most incendiary of the cassettes contained a speech by self-styled *sanyasin* (religious mendicant) Sadhvi Ritambhara, whose language is so abusive and vulgar as to cause embarrassment even to some BJP members. "Why should I not use foul language against those who have been oppressing us all these years?" she asked a reporter.[24]

The four Ram Janmbhoomi cassettes have been estimated by some journalists to have been among the hottest-selling tapes of 1990. They were officially banned by the government within weeks of their appearance in 1990. Nevertheless, I had little difficulty purchasing three of them in Delhi's Lajpatrai Market in December 1990, and saw them being sold openly in Mathura.

After the seeds of hatred and mistrust had been spread by these cassettes, and, in some cases, by rallies featuring militant speakers, it remained to actually incite the violence. The standard technique, employed in Agra, Jaipur, Bhagalpur, and elsewhere, has been for a heavily-armed Hindu procession to march through a Muslim neighborhood chanting communal slogans; sooner or later a scuffle breaks out, or is provoked, and then the rampage begins. In other cases, cassette recordings of blood-curdling screams, gunfire, and other sound effects have been used to foment riots. One might find it difficult to imagine more inflammatory cassettes than those described above, but those seized by Agra police, and used to devastating effect elsewhere, reach new heights of malevolence. *The Times of India* describes their use in Agra in November 1989:

> The riot at Agra which left 22 dead and shattered the communally in-
> terdependent shoe and tourism industries was apart from anything else,
> electronically engineered. The police seized some audio cassettes,
> which screamed slogans inciting both communities, it was reliably
> learnt. The cassettes started off with "Allah-ho-Akbar" then "Jai Shri
> Ram", followed by *bachao-bachao* [Help, help!] and *maaro-maaro*
> [Kill, kill]. These were played by Maruti car stereos at full volume in
> the dead of the night. The unidentified cars would zip off into the dark-
> ness, leaving behind two panic stricken and suspicious communities,
> who would then begin screaming and pelting stones at each other.

The instigation of the riots, between Agra communities who had never before fought, was attributed to VHP provocation (Mishra 1990).[25] Similar cassettes were used to start a riot between the previously amicable Hindu and Muslim communities in Ghaziabad in the same period.[26] (In December 1992, Hindu militants destroyed the Babri Masjid, sparking riots and police firings throughout India in which over one thousand people were killed.)

I have discussed these tapes and reproduced some of their vitriolic dema-goguery at length here in order to illustrate the kind of poison that a "people's medium" is capable of disseminating. Such uses of new technologies like cas-settes illustrate that democratic, grassroots control of the mass media is hardly a guarantee of progressive, humanistic expression. The Ram Janmbhoomi campaign, although encouraged by upper-caste Hindus, is in fact to a large extent a genuine populist movement, with Westernized, secular-humanist lib-erals in government envisioned as the elitist adversaries.[27] But grassroots mo-bilization is not by definition progressive, nor a manifestation of enlightened self-interest. Indigent Hindus suffering from class and caste exploitation will profit little from violence directed against a lower-class scapegoat. Thus, a grassroots, "people's" medium will be no more enlightened than its patrons and producers, and if the "people" in question are fascist bigots—or capable of being provoked to act in such a way—then their media are quite likely to reflect it. Further, while open to much greater diversity, the new media are just as susceptible to hegemonic discourse as were the "old" media; the CIA can make cassettes as easily as any fledgling leftist group.

The use of cassettes to provoke religious hatred and violence in India illus-trates how the idealistic dream of a grassroots-controlled mass medium can turn into a nightmare of venomous abuse, cynical manipulation, and blood-shed. Not without reason did the journalist cited above consider it "fortunate" that cassettes have only become available recently. For the abuses of grass-roots media in India and elsewhere may well make some on the left as well as the right wish for some curbs on freedom of speech in the name of social responsibility. But for better or worse, the new media resist censorship and control—there is no turning back the clock. As we enter the 1990s, the possibility of an Orwellian 1984 becomes ever more remote. Advocates of radical media messages rising from the revolutionary masses must acknowledge, as never before, how far "the people" may be from such a consciousness, and how their media may reflect their worst sentiments as well as their best.

11

Conclusions: A Micro-Medium in Macro-Perspective

In 1987 media theorist Dennis McQuail asserted, "The new media, in their most interactive forms, are as yet not very widely diffused and have not acquired a clear definition as alternatives to the dominant media still in use" (1987b:158). While McQuail's statement may still be accurate in reference to integrated systems of digital networks (ISDN) and other high-tech innovations, the spread of cassette technology in India illustrates how some new media have in fact already displaced old media (here, records), engendered new forms of media content, and revolutionized patterns of control, consumption, and dissemination of the relevant media—here, the music industry. In exploring such developments in this text, I have attempted to relate them to questions of community identity, aesthetic diversity and freedom, and the merits and dangers of centripetal or, alternately, centrifugal tendencies promoted by popular music and popular culture in general; above all, the emergence of new media such as cassette technology obliges us to reexamine the relationship between two notions which have hitherto seemed self-explanatory: *monopoly* and *pluralism*. The forms that these polarities take in India are conditioned, above all, by the nature of control of the means of cultural production, the subsequent media content, and, finally, the reception and possible resignification of popular music by consumers.

As we have seen, the rise of the modern pop *ghazal* represented a transitional development in the emergence of cassette culture, constituting the first efflorescence of a mass popular-music genre independent of cinema. Oriented toward an affluent bourgeoisie acquiring an unprecedentedly clear sense of class identity, the pop *ghazal* represented, in Hall's terms, a rearticulation of elements drawn from its semiclassical predecessor in a form which was accessible to those unfamiliar with art music or high Urdu. Regarded as kitsch by purists, and as pretentious and dull by lower-class audiences, the *ghazal* nevertheless found a vast market among educated, urban middle-class South Asians who identified with the music as being more genteel and elite in ethos than was the increasingly proletarian-oriented film music.

In the wake of the still-flourishing *ghazal* emerged a new form of Hindu *bhajan,* drawing stylistically from *ghazal,* but lacking its sensuous, epicurean ambience. Before this mainstream *bhajan* could exert its own pop "Sanskritizing" or homogenizing effect, the spread of cassette technology beyond the Hindi-speaking middle class precipitated the cassette-based dissemination of all manner of diverse regional and sectarian devotional musics. If cassettes have served as a vehicle of hybridization and modernization for the pop *ghazal* and *bhajan,* the subsequent mass marketing of diverse devotional musics has represented an archetypical example of the oft-noted phenomenon of modern technology reinforcing and revitalizing tradition.

A primary effect of cassette technology has been to facilitate the emergence of new stylized folk-pop genres whose financing, styles, origins, and often language are independent from those of cinema culture. Indian films serve their own functions, providing entertainment, relaxation, and escapist diversion, which may constitute significant aids to psychic survival in the adversities of Indian life. When for most people, reality means toil, poverty, harsh climate, and rigid socioreligious restrictions, cinema may be valued precisely because it provides an alternative. At the same time, the profoundly asymmetrical power relationship between the producers and consumers of commercial cinema privileges the ideology and aesthetic of the former, who have a vested interest in the maintenance of the status quo. Thus, Indian intellectuals routinely charge that commercial films, while entertaining and distracting audiences, manipulate and alienate them, obscuring class consciousness and the mechanisms of domination.

The production of film music, and its original encoded meanings, are embedded in the context of commercial cinema and corporate capital. While detaching film music from its original cinematic contexts, cassettes serve as a vehicle for the spread of film songs, especially in rural areas previously having little access to the mass media. At the same time, cassettes make available an extremely wide variety of alternative popular and folk musics, as produced by an economically, socially, and ethnically heterogeneous set of entrepreneurs. The subsequent emergence of new forms of media culture, with their own distinct attendant social relations, has itself engendered new syncretic forms of popular music which have altered the Indian musical soundscape. These styles have naturally been influenced, in varying degrees and manners, by film music, which has promoted an openness to musical syncretism and in its own way, constituted a set of stylistic expressions of the new social identities arising from urbanization, the spread of the mass media, and modernization in general. Meanwhile, however, the new regional hybrids have been able to affirm, revitalize, and fashion a sense of *communitas* among diverse subgroups; in this respect their relationship to mass film culture has been competitive rather than symbiotic.

Many of the regional musics now disseminated on cassette are traditional genres marketed in more-or-less traditional styles, with relatively little audible influence of commercialization or mass consumer culture. Cassette dissemination of the more traditional of these genres, aside from constituting handy study materials for folklorists, has ensured a place in consumer culture for archaic yet still expressive genres which might otherwise be increasingly vulnerable to obliteration by a homogenizing mass culture. From one perspective, what makes some of these genres particularly "authentic" is the manner in which they can be seen to evolve and change as they adapt to the new media and social contexts. Such phenomena as the accretion of new melodies in *Dhola,* and the contemporaneity of diction and subject matter in modern *rasiya* and Punjabi pop music illustrate how these cassette-based genres, far from being frozen, artificially preserved museum pieces, are living entities syncretizing tradition and modernity in text content as well as style. In many such cases, even where influence of film music is evident, the borrowed elements have been woven into the fabric of an art form which, however commercial, lewd, or ingenuous, in its own way affirms a sense of community identity, whose preservation and adaptability is especially crucial in the case of societies in transition. Arjun Appadurai has noted:

> These newly emergent hybrid forms, and the middle-class, cosmopolitan cultural world to which they belong, do not necessarily constitute a degenerate and kitschy commercial world, to be sharply contrasted with a folk world we have forever lost. In fact, it may be the idea of a folk world in need of conservation that must be rejected, so that there can be a vigorous engagement with the hybrid forms of the world we live in now. (1991:474)

One might qualify this insight with the observation that new media like cassettes have extended control of and access to the emergent, hybrid world of public culture to lower classes as well as the middle class. In general, the range of hybrid musics now marketed on cassette, whether emergent, residual, elite, or proletarian in orientation, can be seen, in Hall's terms, as "contested terrain" where dialectics of class, gender, ethnicity, age, religion, and other aspects of social identity are symbolically negotiated and dramatized.

The spread of cassettes creates new possibilities of musical and even sociopolitical discourse, by extending media control and access to an unprecedented variety of groups; idealists like Enzensberger would see in such developments a potential for progressive mobilization and democratic cultural aesthetics. In such a rigidly hierarchic society as India, with class and gender stratification sanctioned by traditional religion and culture, social polarities are in many cases inherently antagonistic. At the same time, competing groups are often bound to each other by such complex and reciprocal ties that their forms of self-expression are profoundly contradictory and ambiguous. For example, the Indian lower classes, like counterparts elsewhere, are at once exploited by and dependent upon capitalism and the dominant classes.

Their own sense of class consciousness may often be so colored by caste, religious obscurantism, and other factors as to render inchoate, ambivalent, or even reactionary any expression of subaltern identity. Similar contradictions and ambiguities mark the representation of gender in Indian song; an archetypical example is folk *rasiya,* wherein one finds the bewildering phenomenon of women singing lyrics composed by men who, in writing, assume the female persona, but in a style largely created by and for men.

Such contradictions are basic in the realm of popular culture, which functions as a primary site for establishing and negotiating social identity in modernizing societies, especially in countries such as India where the mass media have proliferated in advance of socioeconomic modernization. The expression of community identity can depend on the nature of control of the mass media, the ability and propensity of distinct groups to resignify received media content, and, of course, the degree of community self-consciousness. The advent of cassettes in India has provided one essential precondition for the emergence of such a liberated discourse, by freeing the means of popular-music production from the monopoly of a film-based mass culture. With the proliferation of a vast panoply of folk, popular, and syncretic cassette-based musics produced by and for all manner of Indian minorities and subgroups, we may ask with renewed interest whether such developments could, now or in the future, correspond to Enzensberger's vision of a progressive, oppositional discourse animated by decentralized, democratic control of the means of production.

As discussed in chapter 7, the ubiquity of a homogenizing, mass-produced film music embedded in an escapist and alienating entertainment industry does not in itself guarantee the stupefaction of the public. Adorno, in effectively equating media content with effect, neglected the extent to which the ascription of meaning to popular music is itself a site of struggle and contest, and the manner in which musical meaning is co-generated by audiences as well as producers. Far from being inert, passive consumers, Indians have exhibited a remarkable fondness for appropriating and resignifying elements of commercial music—most typically by setting new texts to film melodies. The importance of the text in Indian folk and popular music enables amateurs and professionals to weave borrowed tunes into the fabrics of their own musical and dramatic discourse, and, in the case of film songs, to free such melodies from the cinematic contexts which so specifically defined their extramusical significance. In effect, the protean polysemy of melody, and its subservience to text in Indian folk song, enables groups and individuals to use mass culture as a source of raw materials, divested of dominant, encoded meanings, in the assertion of local community aesthetics and values. Of course, the reverse process can and does also occur, as when a folk tune is incorporated into a film, or used to promote a predominantly bourgeois political party.

The advent of cassettes has made the process of parody at once more visible, and more multidirectional, popularizing new melodic sources and new stylized genres with voracious appetites for borrowed tunes. In the process, cassettes have further blurred the already oversimplistic distinction between producers and consumers of music, highlighting the existence of various intermediate agents, who imitate, recycle, recreate, and freely appropriate elements of mass culture. As Middleton observes (1990:139–40), there is no sharp dichotomy between activity and passivity, but rather a continuum stretching from original production, at one end, to a hypothetical "Pavlovian automaticity of response" at the other. Associated with cassettes are a range of musics situated on this spectrum, including, for example, new production, recombination and variation, cover versions, parodies, participatory listening (singing along, dancing), attentive listening, and the use of music as background noise. The proliferation of cover versions and parodies on cassette-based musics illustrates how consumption and recycling of popular-music artifacts can be creative social practices which may in their own oblique way constitute oppositional critiques.

More overtly oppositional art forms, of course, are to be found in the production and marketing of original hybrid musics, many of which now assert and celebrate regional and sectarian identity at the expense of pan-regional mass culture. Unfortunately, as we have seen, the development of the cassette industry in India illustrates that the new forms of media content are ridden with ideological and aesthetic contradictions, and that they are easily manipulated by dominant, or even neofascist forces as well as dominated groups. Further, the very assertion of regional and sectarian difference, as embodied in grassroots cassette production, brings its own dangers of social fragmentation and internecine feuding, as India's contemporary regional and communal conflicts illustrate so depressingly. Cassettes are contributing in their own way to the contemporary power vacuum in India, and to the related intensification of regional and sectarian identity at the expense of nationalism. The spread of cassette technology is also contemporaneous with a popular and parliamentary mobilization to decentralize and demonopolize the state-run broadcast media in the interests of democratization. Such agitations, as well as the prominent role cassettes have played both in reasserting regional identity and fueling political mobilizations, have posed with particular urgency a set of questions regarding the nature of media pluralism. Such questions have been articulated by Mattelart and Piemme (1982:414):

What are the possible material conditions in which an effective pluralism can function, one which resolutely turns its back on the search for consensus as well as the religious certitudes of dogmatism? Does such a pluralism imply that anyone can say anything? If not, where can the line of demarcation be drawn between what is allowed and what is not? Who decides this line and who monitors it? How can we reconcile the existence of pluralism with the fact that opinions are never present with equal strength in the communication field? Are there certain cases of urgency or where priorities have been established in which it is better to tone-down pluralism?

On a global level, the advent of new media—resistant to centralized control and easily permeating national boundaries—is accompanying the internationalization of capital, the decline of Leninist communism, and the notion of the nation-state in general, which, whatever their contradictions and inequities, provided a degree of sociopolitical stability in a world of antagonisms and inequalities. Not long ago the world was divided into two superpower camps, with the third world sharply distinct from the developed nations; at the same time, the news and entertainment media were effectively (if ever more tenuously) dominated—and often censored—by state or corporate bureacracies. The international information revolution—including the advent of inexpensive micromedia—has in its own way contributed to the disintegration of one superpower bloc, and to the impending redrawing of national boundaries throughout much of the world. With increasing numbers in the victorious military superpower now living in conditions formerly associated with the third world, a new sort of power vacuum and instability have come to characterize international relations as well as the Indian situation. The advent of democratic-participatory media such as cassettes will clearly play a significant role in the restructuring of cultural identities, national and subnational ideologies and aesthetics, and power relations in the transitional period. Media decentralization has no inherent progressive virtue in itself; "small" does not necessarily equal "beautiful" from the perspective of opposing unequal socioeconomic orders. It could well be argued that ultimately grassroots control of micromedia, affirming the identity of the "small" and "local," is of genuine value only insofar as these media manage to convey a sense of the dialectic relationships between the immediate and the abstract, the regional and the international, the individual and the collective. The internationalization of capital and information technology themselves increase the degree to which populations throughout the world are inherently interconnected; the progressive potential of the new media lies only in their ability to link the "local" with its remote socioeconomic and objective causes. To a considerable exent, such potential, in the case of India, remains largely theoretical, except for the peripheral, although not entirely insignificant, efforts of groups like Jagori, discussed in the previous chapter. From this perspective, one must appreciate how limited the effects of an "information revolution" and emergent "cassette culture" are upon fundamental socioeconomic relations and modes of production in the traditional sense of the term.

> The production of a communication alternative is more than ever linked
> to the production of new social relations . . . New social relations are
> not the means for a new communication. And a new form of communi-

cation will not be the means for new social relations. One and the other undergo, in parallel, the same long, slow effort in the construction of a popular culture. Neither populist, not anti-science, nor anti-intellect— these all being characteristics of mass culture in the traditional sense— this popular culture will be forged from the contributions of multiple groups in struggle, in which economic resistance, the questioning of individual and collective forms of power, artistic practices and every- day activites all intersect. (Mattelart and Piemme 1982:418)

If the impact of cassette technology in India illustrates some of the possible negative as well as positive consequences of media pluralism, the attendant instability and the potential for new forms of political as well as mass media democracy justify more than ever a proverbial attitude of "pessimism of the intellect, and optimism of the will."

Notes

Preface

1. Note that, by extension, I am using the terms *popular music* and *popular culture* to refer to more restricted, specifically mass-mediated entities, in contrast to two recent and important Indological books, which are referred to repeatedly in this text, and which use the term *popular* in simple contradistinction to *elite;* I am referring to Freitag's *Culture and Power in Banaras* (1989) and Kumar's *The Artisans of Banaras: Popular Culture and Identity, 1880–1986* (1988).

Chapter One

1. See related criticisms of Geertz and homology theories in Thompson (1990:131–35) and Middleton (1990:147–54, 159–66).

2. Noteworthy examples are Coplan (1985), Peña (1985), Waterman (1989), and Limón (1983).

3. See, for example, Sutton (1985), el-Shawan (1987), Wong (1989–90), and Manuel and Baier (1986). Racy's thesis (1977) on the Egyptian record industry is the only book-length study of its sort by an ethnomusicologist.

4. For a general discussion of these issues in relation to non-Western popular music, see Manuel (1988b, ch. 1).

5. In my opinion, Kakar's dismissal of the manipulative effects of the film industry leads him to ignore the role the industry has played in actively shaping its products, and weakens his analysis of Indian cinema as authentic representations of popular fantasies. This criticism, however, should not be taken as a characterization of Kakar's work as a whole, which I consider highly insightful and provocative.

Chapter Two

1. Roberts (personal communication) notes that until the mid–1970s, the Kenyan urban middle classes regarded Swahili-based music as crude, instead preferring Congolese music sung in Lingala. For further data on the recording industry in Africa, see Graham (1988), and Collins (1985).

2. Roughly four million out of Lima's seven million inhabitants are from the

mountain highlands. Data on the Andean recording industry are derived from interviews in April 1991 with John Cohen and Thomas Turino, to whom I am grateful.

3. For example, Cuban journalist, musicologist, and state television employee Leonardo Acosta claims this to be the case in his country (personal communication, June 1991).

4. "The industry, as producers, wear same lens [*sic*]," in *Weekly Spectator* (Accra), 20 May 1989 (courtesy of A. Kaye).

5. "Trafic de cassettes," *Jeune Afrique* (Paris) 56 (February 1989).

6. "L'industrie musicala africaine n'est encore qu'a l'état embryonnaire," *La revue du mondo noir* (Paris) (June 1988): 44 (courtesy of A. Kaye).

7. Personal communications with Andrew Kaye and Chris Waterman, 1991. See also Stapleton and May (1987:272–73).

8. Andean data are again derived from John Cohen and Thomas Turino.

9. David Edwards, cited in Appadurai, Korom, and Mills (1991:18).

Chapter Three

1. The main subsidiaries included Megaphone-Hindustan and Senola in Calcutta, Hutchinson in Madras, Jai-Bharat and Hind in Bombay, Jienophone and Gulshan Frontier in the Punjab, Marwari Record Company in Rajasthan (Gopal 1987), Twin, Zonophone, Columbia, and Odeon. See Kinnear (1990) and Gopal (1987), which, together with correspondence from Kinnear, constitute the sources for the information presented on the early recording industry in India.

2. Hindi and Urdu employ the same grammar and basic vocabulary, and, on levels of simple speech, are roughly identical. In complex speech and literary discourse, the languages differ enough to become mutually unintelligible: Urdu employs Perso-Arabic diction and is written in the Arabic *nasta'liq* script, while Hindi uses Sanskritized vocabulary and the *Dev-nagari* script.

3. Interview with Lucknow folklorist Smt. Vidhya Bindu Singh, in 1989.

4. Mythologicals constituted roughly 10 percent of films from the 1930s to the 1960s, and less than 2 percent in the 1980s (Rao 1989: 446).

5. Hindi film producer Raj Khosla asserts, "Hindi cinema has done a tremendous job, a tremendously patriotic job in unifying the country by popularizing Hindi." He also notes that as a producer, "our motive is to reach as many people as possible in all parts of the country" (Pfleiderer and Lutze 1985: 38).

6. One lower-class youth from a Braj village told me, "Ninety percent of the people I know want everything they see in films; only ten percent will say 'It's not my fate to have such things, so I'll just be content with what I have, and with our own folk music.'"

7. For similar emic indictments of commercial cinema's alleged reactionary obscurantism, by Indian commentators, see Utpal Banerjee (1985), Roberge (1985:34–35), Bhattacharya (1989–90), Abbas (1977:71), Rangoonwala (1975:117ff, 132ff), Krishen (1981), and the state-commissioned reports of the Rangachari and Khosla Committees (in Purohit 1988:2:1001–2, 1020, respectively). The assessment of influential Bengali intellectual Nirad Chaudhuri, which may be taken as representative of a certain class of intellectual opinion, is worth quoting:

To anyone who has any respect for life, or any feeling for the extraordinary filigree of sensibility which men and women as children of love and life have woven around the sex act, any reverence for it as the fountain of life, this contemporary discharge of low, cheap, and unceasing smut and rut is agony. Yet there is no escape from it . . . This degradation, which is regarded as smartness by those who are wallowing in it, should not be called an abyss. That would be to give it an undeserved verbal dignity. It is gutter . . . (1966:265).

8. For example, lyricist Kidar Sharma states, "To begin with a good lyric must be easily understood" (interviewed in *Cinema in India* January–March 1990, 22).

9. Lahiri scored thirty-three films in 1986; in February 1985 he composed and recorded thirty-two songs.

10. Lata is often claimed (e.g., by the *Guinness Book of World Records*) to have recorded over 30,000 songs, but this figure—which I have erroneously replicated (in Manuel 1988b:179)—now appears to be grossly exaggerated. According to film-music discographer and savant Har Mandir Singh, Lata recorded 4,405 Hindi songs between 1931 and 1980 (as compared to Asha's 5,454); Singh estimates her current total oeuvre at well under 6,000 recordings (as reported in an interview with Anil Biswas; see also *India Today* 30 April 1991, 50).

11. Snake-charmers I interviewed in 1991 claimed that their repertoire included some two dozen traditional melodies, while acknowledging that they generally played the *Nagin* theme.

12. Film tunes are scrupulously avoided in classical music. See chapter 7, n.1.

Chapter Four

1. Philip Yampolsky (personal communication) hypothesizes that the advent of the cassette industry in India may have been delayed by the relative extensiveness of the phonograph market, which made cassettes less essential than in a country like Indonesia, where there were very few record players even as late as the 1960s.

2. As of 1991, debt servicing consumes 30 percent of India's export earnings, reaching levels comparable to those of such crippled debtors as Nigeria and Brazil. Per capita calorie consumption declined in the 1980s, with non-union rural workers suffering the worst privations (Brahmananda 1989; Coll 1990).

3. It is commonly noted that some seventy million Indians enjoy a higher standard of living than the average Australian.

4. "Rural consumerism," *India Today* 15 March 1990, 109.

5. The music industry, however, has continued to be subject to various customs taxes, although not as onerous as previous levels. Around 1989 the state raised the customs duty on imported polyester film, the basic raw material of tapes, from 40 percent to 145 percent, causing a marked rise in retail prices of cassettes, most of which still use imported film.

6. "Large Investments in Tape Coating Plants," *Playback and Fast Forward*, July–August 1990, 8, 82. The Onida-JVC collaboration was reportedly cancelled due to JVC's dissatisfaction with the quality of Onida's manufacturing.

7. In 1982 a 26 percent excise tax was imposed on audiotapes, but was removed within two years (Mohideen 1989: 8). The 1990 budget again imposed a heavy excise

tax on cassettes, which was rescinded after protests and lobbying from the music industry. See "Music Industry Escapes Excise Noose," and "All Music Companies Raise Prices," in *Playback*, July–August 1990, 4, 80; and 12, 85, respectively. In 1989, the import duty on loop-bin duplication systems was raised from 65 percent to 210 percent (see *Playback*, April 1989).

8. See also Vijay Lazarus interview in *Playback*, June 1986, 30.

9. See also *Playback*, July–August 1990, 35, and November–December 1991, 7.

10. As estimated by a market survey commissioned in 1991 by the IPI (in *Playback*, November–December 1991, 7).

11. "Boom time for audio cassettes," *The Hindu*, 12 May 1989.

12. One cassette producer, for example, told me that his one-to-four duplicators were obtained from an unlicensed and since-disappeared Indian manufacturer. Other companies may prefer to use cassettes containing some smuggled components.

13. See *Playback*, November–December 1990, 11.

14. *Playback*, August 1986, 16.

15. *Playback*, May 1986, 23.

16. Bhargava (1991:59), and *Playback*, July 1987, 6, and July–August 1990, 4.

17. *Playback*, November–December 1990, 7, 11, and Bhargava (1991:91).

18. For example, AJit Kohli, interviewed in 1990. Legitimate producers I met, while admiring Arora's skill, have little praise for his scruples. As one disgruntled producer told me, "If Vaishno Devi has helped this robbery, then she is not a *devi* (goddess) but a devil!"

19. See interview with Vijay Lazarus in *Playback*, June 1986, 30–35.

20. See Mohideen (1989:8), and "Magnasound is No. 2," in *Playback*, November–December 1989, 9.

21. *Playback*, May–June 1991, 14.

22. Interview with producer-lyricist M. H. Zaidi, March 1990. Import duties and restrictions on quarter- and half-inch tape (used for masters) oblige many producers to acquire tapes from smugglers. See *Playback*, April 1989, 4–5.

23. Interview with T-Series' Ajit Kohli, December 1990.

24. Interview with producer Siraj-ul Haq, January 1990.

25. Biswanath Chatterjee, interviewed in *Playback*, August 1986, 37.

26. Folklorist Komal Kothari managed to extricate him from this situation (personal communication).

27. Harbans Jaiswal, founder of a fledging cassette company (Mamshar) in Lucknow, makes this point, and continues, "I can't afford big artists, so I give new ones a chance. So my costs will be low, and my sales will be low, but even if I only get one hit out of five cassettes, I'll make a profit" (interviewed in September 1989).

28. "The World of Goan Music," *Playback*, December 1986, 86–87.

29. Saraswati's H. L. Vir, interviewed in January 1991.

30. See Bhargava (1991:91), and *Playback*, November–December 1989, 7. *Tridev's* sales were based on the song "Tirchi Topi-wale," whose success derived from its "Oe-oe" hook borrowed from the Miami Sound Machine's "The Rhythm's Gonna Get You."

31. According to CD producer Lyle Wachovsky (personal communication).

32. Interview with Anil Chopra, April 1990; Chopra (1986); "Export of audio cassettes hit," *Playback*, May 1986, and Nair (1986).

33. "Mixers off OGL import list," *Playback,* November–December 1990, 16.

34. Interview with Anil Chopra in March 1990. Chopra explains, "Anyone can do it. You just buy some heads and micromotors, have the PCB ready, you put the spiders in, solder it, and put the cabinet on top."

35. Interview with Anil Chopra, March 1990, and Bhargava (1991:93).

36. "North Music Spends Rs. 17.24 m On Radio Publicity," *Playback,* January–March 1990, 16, 74.

37. *Playback,* May 1987, 22.

38. *Playback,* November–December 1990, 16.

39. See also "Hotels Pay Royalty to IPRS," in *Playback,* January–March 1990, 14.

40. *Playback,* November–December 1991, 24. Copyright law is discussed in further detail in chapter 7.

41. Marcus himself, who was recording dozens of performances with professional equipment and consent of the artists, was obliquely approached by a supposedly legitimate music producer who wished to market bootlegs of these recordings.

42. *Playback,* February 1989, 10.

43. See interview with Vijay Lazarus, *Playback,* June 1986, 31.

44. Ibid.

45. *Playback,* April 1989, 7.

46. "The World of Goan Music," in *Playback,* December 1986, 86.

47. The 1991 IPI survey was conducted by Market and Research Group Pvt. Ltd., reported in *Playback* November–December 1991, 7. Pradip Chanda, president of HMV and of the IPI, also earlier estimated 1991 piracy at 40 percent of the market (in Bhargava 1991:60), as did another informed estimate (Swamy 1991). An IFPI report estimated 1988 piracy as constituting 52 percent of the Indian market, with sales worth some $150 million (*Playback,* May–June 1991, 35). These latter figures strike me as inflated.

48. See the letter from a frustrated Singapore-based distributor, *Playback,* December 1987, 2.

49. "MPK" on 23 labels!" *Playback,* November–December 1990, 19.

50. Magnasound is licensed to market Warner-Electric-Atlantic recordings, while Bremen carries Bertelsmann product.

51. "The World of Goan," *Playback,* December 1986, 86. Ethnomusicologist Charles Keil has called for an abolition of copyright, arguing that the notion of ownership of music is alienating and absurd, and that if the music industry collapses due to subsequent piracy, then so much the better, since recorded music in general promotes passive listening and discourages communal creation of music.

52. See "Royalty from piracy!!," in *Playback,* July 1990, 16. HMV, for its part, vigorously denies any collaboration with pirates (*Playback,* May–June 1991, 14).

53. "Tips and Venus cary [*sic*] out Piracy raids," *Playback,* May–June 1991, 8.

54. *Playback,* May–June 1991, 5, and November–December 1991, 6.

55. "Asmara for CDs in US," *Playback,* July–August 1990, 21.

Chapter Five

1. "Begum" is an honorific for a married Muslim woman.

2. Innovative and eclectic singer-producers Babla and Kanchan, known for their

fusions of Indian pop with calypso/soca, have released one recording of "disco *ghazals*." From 1989 to 1991, the most popular films (*Qayamat se Qayamat tak, Mainne Pyar Kiya, Chandni, Ashiqi*) were sentimental melodramas with melody-oriented, rather than disco-style music, suggesting a trend back to earlier film music styles (Swamy 1991).

3. The fondness of Indians for distorted sounds has been commented on by a number of observers. In recording a leading *tabla* player, I found that he preferred a distorted timbre generated by setting the recording level too high; Helen Myers, in a 1990 presentation on Braj wedding music, noted that the village women she observed liked to sing through a grossly overloaded speaker system, inviting comparison with Curt Sachs's hypothesis regarding the appeal of the "masked voice." The quite unnecessary presence of audio distortion on records produced on generally presentable equipment also supports the hypothesis that distortion is enjoyed by many Indians. Sutton (in press) has also commented on this aesthetic in relation to popular music in Indonesia.

4. The *santur* is a zither struck with light hammers; *surmandal* is another zither, strummed for glissando effects rather than played melodically.

5. Interviewed in *Playback*, June 1986, 31.

6. Thus, for example, *The Patriot* (23 April 1985) excoriates a contemporary singer for "stooping so low" as to sing a *ghazal* based on the tune of an old film song of Mohammad Rafi. Similarly, critic Subhash Jha derides the current *ghazal* star Bhupinder for using film melodies in the instrumental interludes between verses (*Hindustan Times Magazine,* 30 September 1989, 4).

7. I have argued elsewhere that the introduction of concepts of aesthetic balance, closure, and symmetry—as opposed to open-ended, non-teleological improvisation—in the commercial *ghazal* is a characteristic of bourgeois aesthetics (Manuel 1985).

8. *The Patriot,* 23 April 1985.

9. Most contemporary poetry is better than the couplet recorded by Bhupinder, which one reviewer described as "hitting an all-time low": "Mainne *fon* karke unko bulaya, unki mummy ne ake uthaya" (I tried to call her on the phone, [but] her mother answered!).

10. See also ur-Rahman (1982:122).

11. Urdu scholar Frances Pritchett (personal communication) has been one of several scholars to note such mistakes in Jagjit Singh's cassette *Ghalib.* Such complaints, of course, are not entirely a recent phenomenon; compare criticisms made by vocalist Hafiz Ahmad Khan (Durry 1972:23).

12. An HMV executive informed me that a professional *ghazal* singer told him, in response to his own query, that he did not understand the first words in a once-famous couplet of Ghalib's he had just sung ("Ibn-e-Mariam [son of Mary, i.e., Christ] hua kare koi . . .")

13. Regarding pop Pashtu *ghazal,* see Heston (1991:310).

14. Kippen, for example, notes how *tabla* pedagogy in music schools has become oriented toward the study of obscure *tals* (meters) with Hindu-oriented names like Brahma tal, Vishnu tal, Lakshmi tal, etc., rather than toward the study of performance practice, which has been dominated, until recently, by Muslim musicians (1988:138).

15. See, e.g., Subhash Jha, in "Tune In" (*Hindustan Times Magazine,* 30 September 1989, 4), and the opinions of highbrow Pakistani singers Abida Parveen and Ghu-

lam Ali, cited in "There is music in me," *Times of India*, 1 May 1988. It is unfortunate that most Urdu *ghazal* criticism, like studies of Western literature, has tended to focus almost exclusively on the reified texts of the most distinguished poets, largely neglecting the great mass of ordinary verse, and the essential aspects of reception study—what Urdu verse *means* to different sorts of audiences in different times. Therefore, while it may be true that modern audiences interpret traditional imagery in different ways than did earlier readers, the major Urdu literary studies (e.g., Sadiq 1984) shed little light on this question.

16. The invocation of inebriation could scarcely be more unequivocal than in the verse of Mir (d. 1810):

Unfold this useless prayer-mat for drunkards to sit on
Venerate the wine and show reverence to the glass . . .

I am sorry if I cannot walk straight
But do not be angry with me, for I am drunk

17. Sources are, respectively: Madhumanti Maitra, "Recreating past melodies," *Telegraph,* 26 August 1989; Essjay (Subhash Jha), "They're ghazals—believe it or not!" *Times of India,* 13 September 1989; *Times of India,* 9 November 1988 (no author cited); Amit Agarwal, *Times of India,* 29 March 1989; and Raghava Menon, "Ghazals sung with precision," *Times of India,* 4 June 1988. I have assessed the modern *ghazal* in a similarly negative vein (Manuel 1992).

18. Hyder continues: "These serials are creating the impression that the ghazal is a product of tawaif [courtesan] culture, which most emphatically it is not . . . For our media even a modern Muslim middle class does not exist. The heroine is always an overdressed, bejewelled, beveiled praying mantis. The lecherous nawab, the paan-chewing bigamous hero, the siren dancing girl, the doleful poet, are the stock characters of our cinema and television . . . " ("A Tradition Betrayed," *Times of India,* 19 May 1989).

Chapter Six

1. See Slawek (1986) for a more expansive discussion of *bhakti* music in India. Slawek also discusses the various colloquial and often contradictory distinctions between Hindi-language *bhajan* and *kirtan,* with which we need not concern ourselves here. Commercial cassettes of Hindu devotional music use the term *bhajan* rather than *kirtan.*

2. Vinay Kumar Gari, of Sound Recording, Calcutta, interviewed December 1989.

3. Interviews with T-Series' Ajit Kohli, and H. L. Vir of Saraswati Records, December 1990.

4. Interviewed by Anil Chopra in *Playback,* August 1986, 31.

5. For example, reviews in *Playback,* January 1990, 48, advertising that *bhajan* recordings on hit film tunes "should interest both filmi and bhajan buffs," while another such cassette should be "particularly delightful to those familiar with the [film music] originals."

6. This point was stressed by folklorist Komal Kothari in a 1989 interview.

7. Vinay Kumar Gari, of Sound Recording, interviewed in December 1989.

8. The stories themselves, as marketed in cheap chapbooks, are each about twenty-five hundred words long. The Satyanarayan *katha* concerns a family who failed to worship Satyanarayan and subsequently experienced misfortune; the Santoshi Ma *katha* relates the tribulations of three women in their devotion to their patron goddess.

9. In *Playback,* March 1987, 67.

10. The authenticity of any of the verse attributed to Mira Bai is highly dubious.

11. In contrast, the Punjabi narrative ballads (*Hir, Sohni Maiwal, Sassi Punno,* etc.) are essentially secular. They are seldom encountered on cassette.

12. Sound Recording's Vinay Kumar Gari, interviewed in December 1989.

13. The visitor was anthropologist Susan Wadley (personal communicaton).

14. M. H. Zaidi, a producer and lyricist of Braj folk music. Note that Bade Ghulam Ali Khan, a Muslim, evidently saw no personal contradiction in composing and popularizing the aforementioned Hindu *bhajan* "Hari Om Tatsat."

15. A Calcutta resident of Punjabi origin, he is the founder of Sound Recording.

16. Urdu is the native language to only some 15 percent of Pakistanis. It is, however, the official language of that country and is widely understood and used as a lingua franca there.

17. *Qawwali* specialist Regula Qureshi (personal communication) notes that her elderly informants corroborate this assertion. The term *qawwali* (or its Hindi variant *kawwali*) is loosely applied in rural North India to a variety of songs that are neither devotional nor in Urdu. In eastern Doab cities such as Banaras, *qawwals* also perform Hindu devotional songs, in Hindi, which they term *qawwali.*

18. In the film *Soten ki beti;* Nusrat Fateh Ali Khan uses the text in EMI TC-CEMP–5103, A:2.

19. *Playback,* February 1987, 67.

20. A case in point was the installation of a closed-circuit video monitor outside guru Siddhivinayak's Bombay temple in summer 1991, so that the throngs of devotees could get his *darshan* (viewing) even though the temple itself was closed for reconstruction ("Video to the rescue of Siddhivinayak," *Times of India,* 16 August 1991, 5).

Chapter Seven

1. I base this claim on some twenty years of involvement with Hindustani music, and discussions with knowledgeable informants, such as sarodiya Kalyan Mukherjea. Karnatak music connoisseur and discographer V. A. K. Ranga Rao informs me (personal communication) that vina player Emani Shankara Shastri used to perform the song "Dhire se ajare" from the film *Albela* as a light piece, and that Balamurali Krishna used to sing the film version (from *Andala Ramudu*) of "Palluke Bangara Mayena," making a point of announcing its source and defying anyone to deny its beauty. Generally, classical musicians perform compositions associated with their own pedagogical lineage, and will avoid borrowing from rival traditions out of pride.

2. The chapbooks are printed on such crude, yellowed, and worm-eaten paper that they look like collector's items even when fresh from the press. More than once, while perusing such pamphlets in bazaars, I have eagerly grabbed one which appeared to be

a genuine antique, only to discover that it recommends singing its texts to new film songs like "Ek do tin."

3. A daughter of Umesh Pandey, interviewed by Scott Marcus.

4. Not all such tapes are so well received. One commercial flop was a T-Series cassette of Hindi versions of Michael Jackson hits, by Mithun Chakravarty, entitled *Mithun: The Indian Jackson.* Subhash Jha derided the cassette in a review entitled "The Indian Jackson is Bad"; his article concluded, "Beat it, Indian Jackson!"

5. " 'Love Me' Sets a Trend," *Playback,* November 1989, 10.

6. "Pop goes the East" in *Sunday Mail,* January 28–February 3 1990, 8.

7. Jha, 1989, in "Tune In" (a review column in the *Times of India,* which I came across in the form of a fragment without the date shown).

8. *Rasiya* scholar Usha Banerjee, personal communication in 1990.

9. One may note that the converse process—setting film texts to folk melodies—does not appear to be widespread among folk musicians.

10. *Grundrisse,* cited in Middleton (1991:92–93).

11. John Chernoff describes how Indian film songs have become sources for creative reinterpretation and appropriation in faraway northern Ghana:

> In recent years, popular movies from India . . . have caused a sensation.
> People remember the songs and set their own words to them. Along with the
> singing, the melodies provide inspiration for long improvisations on plastic
> flutes. To fit the music, a young man called Ali Bela, after the swashbuckling
> hero of some of the films, created a whole style of drumming . . . The music is
> beautiful, and I was impressed by the notion of walking in the streets of Tamale
> and coming across a musical group with a name like Bombay, gathered to sing
> Dagomba homilies fitted to Indian movie tunes . . . (Chernoff 1979:129–30)

12. Max 2216.

13. Similarly, as Lutgendorf (1990:142) has noted, the condescension with which many bourgeois Indians regard the television *Ramayan* and *Mahabharat* may be due less to the perceived commercial nature of these serials than to their affinities with folk theater (overacting, didactic digressions, interminable length, etc.).

14. Such responses were elicited from *rasiya* singer-composers Sevaram Tanatan and Pradip "Pappu" Sharma, among others. *Playback* editor Anil Chopra (personal communication, 1990), echoed these sentiments, saying, "Film music is mostly folk music anyway—one tune is based on a Punjabi song, another from somewhere else, which everyone can relate to."

15. "Why pick on me?" *Sunday Mail,* 3 February 1990, 5–7, and an interview with Lahiri in *Playback,* January 1987.

16. Jerry Amaldev, interviewed in *Playback,* December 1986, 30–31.

17. See interview in *Playback,* January 1987, 27.

18. In rock music, the emphasis on individual or band creativity has limited the amount of commercially marketed cover versions, with the odd instances, such as Springsteen's rehash of "War," standing out as conspicuous exceptions.

19. Indian copyright only applies to songs and soundtracks less than fifty years old.

20. Such hits consist primarily of film songs, *bhav git, koli git,* and devotional *abhangs.* See "Marathi Versions Booming," and "Marathi Versions are Evergreen," in

Playback, January–March 1990, 11, and July–August 1990, 14, respectively.

21. The relevant passage is in the 1957 Copyright Act, section 52(j), which reads:

The following acts shall not constitute an infringement of copyright, namely
. . . (j) the making of records in respect of any literary, dramatic or musical
work, if (i) records recording that work have previously been made by, or with
the license or consent of the owner of the copyright in the work, and (ii) the
person making the records has given the prescribed notice of his intention to
make the records, and has paid in the prescribed manner to the owner of the
copyright in the work royalties in respect of all such records to be made by
him, at the rate fixed by the Copyright Board in this behalf . . .

22. "'Oye oye' sells over a million tapes," *Playback,* November–December
1989, 7.

23. "Govt. breaking the law?" *Playback,* November–December 1990, 23.

24. "IPRS Grouse on Versions," *Playback,* January–March 1990, 8.

25. "Echo wins version case," *Playback,* July–August 1990, 4, and "IPRS Presents
Memorandum to MPs," *Playback,* July–August 1990, 23.

Chapter Eight

1. According to a survey commissioned by the IPI (*Playback,* November–December 1991, 7).

2. Paramjit Singh, founder of the fledgling Golden melodies label, *Playback,* January 1987, 80.

3. Such sentiments were voiced by Chhanvarlal Gahlot (Jodhpur), Jagdish Arora (Banaras), and others.

4. Such is clearly the case, for example, with folk theater such as *nautanki.* See Hansen (1989:73).

5. Folklorists and musicologists I interviewed (Vidya Bindu Singh, Mudra Rakshasa, and Harbans Jaiswal) attributed the weakness of indigenous Avadhi folk music to such factors as: (1) the relatively developed, semi-urbanized economy of the region (as opposed to neighboring Bihar, for example), which has facilitated a greater penetration of film culture, and (2) the lack of an urban culture reinforcing and promoting local dialect and folklore—many Banarsis take pride in cultivating Bhojpuri language and culture, but Avadh's cities of Lucknow and Faizabad are traditional centers of Urdu culture, not rustic Avadhi.

6. Interview with percussionist Olvin Brown, whose wife has recorded over a dozen cassettes of Kangra-Pahari folk music for the Sonotone label.

7. Banarsi producer Jagdish Arora asserted, "If you record the villagers themselves, you'll find that they all sing *besur* [out of tune] and *betal* [out of rhythm]. You have to be very selective" (interview, December 1989).

8. Personal communication with Sailesh Mathur of Yuki Cassettes in 1990.

9. For example, "X ne iska tarz banaya, aur Y ne iska *music compose* kiya" (X composed the melody [of the song], and Y composed the 'music' [instrumental interludes]).

10. Meanwhile, the visiting ethnomusicologist is growing increasingly disturbed by (1) the harmonium-*wala*'s curious habit of playing parallel major first-inversion

chords indiscriminately beneath every melody note, (2) the recording level, which strikes him as too high, and (3) the *ghungru-wala,* a teenager who has no sense of time and plays consistently out of tempo. Eventually, forsaking ethnographic detachment, I point out the errant *ghungru* to Hussein, who reprimands the player (to no effect).

11. While Arora is clearly speaking in reference to his own experience, it must be pointed out that many folk songs—especially narrative ballads—are long, if not interminable, and are quite rich in imagery.

12. Hindi speakers can verify this by perusing anthologies of film-song texts sold in bazaars.

13. Bengali music critic and journalist Barin Mazumdar, interviewed in December 1989.

14. For example, Max's *Meri nind uchtagi,* B:3. The lemon serves as a similar symbol in traditional ribald *thumris,* for which see Manuel (1989:21–22).

15. Max's *Tu meri sali,* B:1 and A:4, respectively.

16. "Far mere amb mainu kela dede . . . " Zail Singh, as chief minister of the Punjab, reportedly attempted to ban such songs, but to no avail (Pushpa Hans, personal communication).

17. For example, Bengali music critic Barin Mazumdar, interviewed in December 1989.

18. For example, Punjabi singer and musicologist Subhash Goyel, A. S. Jaswal, and Maya Kothari; Punjabi vocalist Pushpa Hans vigorously denied this assertion (personal communications).

19. Abu-Lughod (1989:8–10) also reports this phenomenon in Bedouin families.

20. Personal communications with Komal Kothari and Scott Marcus, respectively.

21. *Dhola* singer Ram Swaroop, and *rasiya* performer Vijender Sharma, interviewed in 1989 and 1990 respectively. Although Sharma is the most popular and sought-after performer of Hathrasi *rasiya,* a rival of his scoffed at this assertion, saying that the cassette producers and AIR committees both shun him because of his faulty intonation (he is in fact celebrated more for his stage presence and lyrics than for his singing). Both Swaroop and Sharma cited the case of one Adhar Chaitanya, who had recorded several popular cassettes of *katha* for Rathor Cassettes, allegedly saturating his market to the extent that his concert bookings plummeted. I was unable to verify this claim.

22. I was assured this by producers Harbans Jaiswal, Chhanvarlal Gahlot, performers Pamela Singh, Olvin Brown, and several others.

23. As a linguistic and cultural region, the Punjab straddles India and Pakistan; since the mass migrations during Partition, Pakistani Punjab is almost entirely Muslim, while Indian Punjab is populated by roughly equal proportions of Hindus and Sikhs. Much of Haryana's population is also Punjabi.

24. For example, Sailesh Mathur (Yuki Cassettes, Delhi), Harbans Jaiswal (Mamshar, Lucknow), Jagdish Arora (independent producer, Banaras), V. K. Gari (Sound Recording, Calcutta), and Vyas Kumar (Max, Delhi).

25. Particularly well-known examples are the hits "Reshmi shalwar kurta," derived from the Punjabi tune "Wite pani parindie," and "Husn Paharon ki" in the film *Ram teri Ganga maili hai.*

26. The intriguing article by Banerji and Bauman (1990) is the main source for data here on British pop *bhangra.* Note, however, that it quotes me out of context (on p.

149) to imply that piracy bankrupted most legitimate recording companies in India; my statement was in reference to Banaras rather than the entire country.

27. Thus, for example, in Delhi there are around half a dozen professional groups who perform at weddings and various other occasions. As with rock groups, the best of these perform original material, while the others do covers of contemporary hits. Various folkloric groups and youth clubs also perform folk *bhangra*.

28. T-Series SPNC 01/21.

29. The couplets are particularly relevant for the strife-torn Punjab today: "Waris Shah says our lives are in the hands of God and cruel time, like a goat in the hands of a butcher. We all are doomed to die; no one, whether rich or poor, is immortal. We are here for but four days, why should we fight? Repent on your sins."

30. "Pop Time," a Sunday-evening showcase of pop performers, which has become one of the most widely watched shows on Indian television.

31. Folk songs in the West, like "La Bamba," can also acquire "hit" status.

32. Maan related how his producers wanted him to cut a section of his early hit "Dil da mamla"; he doggedly refused, arguing that it was integral to the song. After the song became a hit, his producers have deferred to him on all artistic decisions (interview, January 1990).

33. Interviews with C. Gahlot, Mohan Jhala, and Yuki's K. K. Wadwa.

34. All data on traditional *katha* derive from personal communications with folklorist Komal Kothari, in January 1990.

35. The Archive and Research Centre for Ethnomusicology in Defence Colony, New Delhi, is providing a valuable service by collecting many such folk cassettes from all over India. Such recordings await research.

36. Sarodiya Dr. Kalyan Mukherjea, personal communication, September 1989.

37. Such sentiments are also found in reviews by other critics, for example, Pepe Gomes in the *Telegraph,* 3 June 1989.

38. V. K. Gari, of Sound Recording, interviewed in December 1989.

39. Data on Maharashtra derive primarily from interviews with Ashok Ranade and Anil Chopra, and short visits to Bombay in 1986 and 1990. *Popat* means "parrot," and by extension, the male organ.

40. "The world of Goan music," *Playback,* December 1986, 86–87.

41. *Playback,* November–December 1991, 19.

42. This song was pointed out to me by Shubha Chaudhuri. "Mzuri sana" is Swahili for "Hello, how are you?"

43. Indipop is a representative British-based label. Meyers (1991:240) implies that "Kaisi Bani" was a significant hit in India around 1986; while I cannot verify this claim, I rarely came across Babla and Kanchan's tapes in 1989–91 in India.

44. Interviewed by Anil Chopra in *Playback,* July 1986, 34.

Chapter Nine

1. This figure is an estimate, representing the total populations of Mathura, Etah, Mainpuri, Agra, and Aligarh districts.

2. Many *rasiyas* refer to the woman wearing a sari, rather than the skirt (*lahnga*) traditional to rural Braj; one also encounters references to cars, radios, and phrases such as *chakke gaye mere chut,* a slang expression derived from cricket, loosely mean-

ing "they scored six runs, I [the pitcher] lost control altogether," but colloquially used to mean "I freaked out" (e.g., in the familiar song "Gajab bhaiyo daiya").

3. See Entwistle (1983) for further discussion of devotional *languria.* The genre is also distinguished by its predominant use of two stock melodies.

4. The lines to this song may often appear in different order; this variant, however, is particularly common, and is reproduced in a popular chapbook.

5. "Rat batashe bait gae somat rah gaya lahoro devariya."

6. Opening lines of the familiar song "Launda badnam hua nasiban tere liye."

7. From Vidha Babu of Aligarh. "Jogin ne ek taras vicharo, bitar ghus geo nikaro—kanto ka dare, chalte men kaske beri, bhaiyyo ar pare, piya . . . " Recorded on Parco 622, B:3. Note that this sort of teasing is so familiar in Indian songs as to be a cliche. In a cassette of Punjabi truck drivers' songs, the woman sings, "I tell you mine is very tight, put your hand there and see . . . yes, that's how tight my silk shirt is" (on *Punjabi Hot Songs,* TMC–1013)

8. This assertion is based on several interviews with musicians, composers, folklorists, and ordinary Braj men and women. Several typical popular *rasiyas* mention the author's name in the final lines; in most such cases, the named authors are known twentieth-century individuals. A few courtesans, such as Gulab Bai (d. 1990), are believed to have composed a few *rasiyas.* It remains possible that many *rasiyas* have been composed or recomposed by anonymous women, but there is no hard evidence for this supposition.

9. Of the 106 *lilas* summarized by Hein (1972:163–78), 17 involve Krishna disguising himself as a woman (numbers 22, 26, 33–35, 43, 45, 50, 57, 62, 63, 79, 80, 82, 85, 90, and 100).

10. The gender-crossing practiced by Braj men in devotion and the arts has inspired various interpretations. Kakar and Ross, writing from a rather orthodox Freudian perspective, interpret the cultivated ambisexuality as a search for bisexual wholeness rooted in the male's Oedipal longing for union with the mother (1986:99–100); Carstairs regards Braj androgyny as thinly veiled homosexual desire, while a Tantric explanation sees men as seeking the *shakti* (power) of women (in Entwistle 1987:92). A feminist perspective may see male androgyny as chauvinistic co-optation of femininity. Thus, for example, Kaplan (1987:93ff.) opines that the studied androgyny of heavy-metal rock stars reflects a desire to render feared and intimidating women irrelevant and superfluous through narcissistically adopting feminine characteristics. At this point it may be difficult to say whether men enjoy such songs as "Kau din uth gayo hath" (no. 1) out of Oedipal identification, superficial titillation, or genuine empathy for the female condition.

11. Such songs can also be seen, again, as secular counterparts to the dilemma of Radha, who is often annoyed by Krishna and obliged to resist him in public, but who secretly desires intimacy at the same time. A typical example is the *Dan lila,* wherein Radha and the *gopis* protest Krishna's exaction of a road-tax from them. Similarly, in Jayadev's *Gita Govinda,* (Miller 1982:20) Radha laments:

My heart values his vulgar ways, refuses to admit my rage,
feels strangely elated, and keeps denying his guilt . . .

Such ambiguity may also be found in other Braj-Bhasha genres, such as texts in the light-classical vocal forms *thumri* and *dadra.* A particularly familiar case in point may the well-known *thumri* "Ja main tose nahin bolun, garva laga lun" (Go, I won't speak to you, I'll embrace you). Different musicians have interpreted the apparent non sequitur of these lines in different ways for me. One instrumentalist opined that the lines are simply fragments carelessly put together and then accepted indiscriminately by singers. *Thumri* aficionado (and film composer) Anil Biswas suggested that the proper rendering should be "I *won't* embrace you," while a third artist, the venerable singer and pedagogue D. C. Vedi, argued, most convincingly, that the artistry of the vocalist's rendition lies in singing the first line in such a way as to suggest that the protagonist does not really want her lover to go.

12. Similarly, in the Indian folk tales analyzed by Kakar, "the woman's choice in love . . . is limited to appeasement and masochistic surrender" (1989:52).

13. The *akhara*-based *rasiya* is not entirely an oral tradition, as poets and students maintain notebooks of their lyrics.

14. For example, Vidha Babu of Aligarh (Lala Lachhi *akhara*), interviewed in February 1990.

15. Laxmi Narayan Garg, son of renowned author Kaka Hathrasi, and owner of Hathras's distinguished Sangit Karyalaya press.

16. *Sang* is a local term for *nautanki* theater; *khyal* refers to a local solo song form, also known as *lavni* (having no connection to its Maharashtrian namesake).

17. Such sentiments were expressed, for example, by folklorists Mohan Swarup Bhatia and Ram Narayan Agarwala of Mathura, and elderly *rasiya* singer and *rasdhari* Swami Kalyan Prasad of Brindavan (interviewed in spring 1990).

18. Kalyan Prasad: "I've used this tune "Chor Babul ka ghar" from an old film, because I like it, and it's like a Braj tune . . . Of course there are many more tunes in use now, including film ones."

19. Ram Narayan Agarwal and Swami Kalyan Prasad both sang old versions of the tune for me; it also appears in Bhojpuri *birha*, for example, on a pirate cassette of Ramdev entitled *Git Govind—Truck Driver.*

20. For example, the tune of *malhar* is often introduced in *chhand*. Venerated Hathrasi *rasiya* poet Hoti Lal Sharma states that the basic tune of *chhand* itself derives from *jhulna* (a folk genre) as sung in Aligarh district (personal communication). The names of two other common tunes used in the Hathrasi style, *Kasganji bahr* and *Rohtaki bahr,* indicate their regional origins. One of the most common stock *rasiya* tunes derives from the repertoire associated with the *alghoza* flute.

21. The *akharas* are not, however, associated with particular parties, but may adopt stances in a given context; if the first *akhara* takes the Congress side, the answering *akhara* will take that of an opposition party.

22. "Meri chhatri ke niche a jao, kyon bhige Kamla ho khari khari? . . . "

23. These producers include Rathor (Kiravli, Mainpuri district), Rahul (Bulandshahr), Gupta/Kumar, Tanatan, Brij, Trimurti (Agra), Shishodia (Ghaziabad), another "Brij" (Aligarh), and Jhankar (Farukhabad). T-Series has also produced a few *rasiya* cassettes.

24. An exception would be a cassette such as that described on p. 163, where the vocalist, Nemi Chand, recorded a leisurely narrative song lasting fifty minutes.

25. Accordingly, I sought out Sharma after coming across his cassettes and chapbooks.

26. Agra-based *nautanki* songstress Maina Rani is, in my opinion and that of sev-

eral aficionados, the finest solo *rasiya* singer. Oddly "undiscovered" by producers, as of 1991 she had yet to record, although my acquaintance, producer M. H. Zaidi, was currently negotiating with her.

27. Anthropologist Susan Wadley tried to interest a Braj music producer in *Dhola* performances by a Mainpuri singer, Ram Swarup, but the producer claimed that the vocalist's dialect was too tinged with Kannauji (the adjacent language area on the east side) to appeal to a broad enough market.

28. I found that enthusiasts of this style in Hathras itself did not seem disturbed by being ignored by the commercial cassette industry, as they greatly preferred to hear *rasiya* in live *dangals*, which still occur with some frequency. As Vipra *akhara* vocalist Chandu Lala, the owner of a milk shop, told me, "When you have a milk shop you don't need to buy a glass of someone else's milk."

29. The last two songs are found on Rama 613-RAS and Shishodia 133.

30. From *Gone wali rat*, Max.

31. Songs referred to in this paragraph are, in order, on Max 1344; Rathor *Sadaba-har languria*, B:4; Brij, *Rasiyon ka rasgulla*, A:5; Max 1278, A:2; Parco 653, 622; SCI *Braj ke languria git*, A:2; Tanatan *Nand Kishore*, A:2; Max 1257, B:2; Rathor *Jangaliya*, B:2; Parco 801, A:5; Rajpal Singh Tailor, *Muskurate Rasiya*.

32. From "Phasan [fashion] kare kamal," Max 1338.

33. From *Braj ke tapakte rasiya*, vol. 6, Max 1344. A common superstitious perspective on sterilization, which is more commonly performed on men, is presented in a *rasiya* by one Kishansingh Mahashay, printed in a chapbook (*Rasiya ka Bomb*): "How can I play Holi, I don't have it in me any more . . . My *pichkari* [syringe for squirting colored water] has been punctured, I'm out of juice, my youth is passed, there's no fun in Holi . . . "

34. It took me several interviews before I came to understand this point. Typically, when I would ask an informant his or her opinion of the commercial cassettes, (s)he would complain of their vulgarity. I would then ask if such erotica was a recent development, at which point (s)he would invariably answer, "Oh no, listen to this one . . ."

35. "Kat gaiyo re tataiya," Max 1182, B:3. Zaidi heard the title refrain of this cassette—"Kinne le nai angiya" (Who took my bra?) in a village women's song, and he subsequently wrote new verses for it.

36. Nemi Chand, in the lengthy narrative recording described on pp. 163 uses *rasiya* melodies exclusively, but claims that the performance is *puja* (prayer) rather than *rasiya*, since the latter does not narrate a tale. Tanatan was interviewed (in Hindi) in October 1989 and January 1990.

37. *Rasiyon ka sartaj*, Max 1006, A:3; "Nek dastkhat" is A:2 on the same tape, and the subsequent song cited ("I got a fool . . . ") is B:2. *Sali salon . . .* is on Max 1274.

38. Entwistle (1983:91) observes: "Since there is no scriptural tradition giving Lamguriya a fixed identity, the popular imagination has been free to make up songs about him more or less at whim. The result is that the songs provide no consistent picture of Lamguriya but reflect the attitudes, ethos and predilections of the singers rather than any established mythology or dogma."

39. These two excerpts are from *Rasiyon ka sartaj*, Max 1003, A:1; B:4.

40. Thus, for example, Ram Avtar Sharma and Sevaram Tanatan record frequently and perform rarely, but their livelihoods derive from other, nonmusical sources.

41. Tanatan notes that an entire cassette of Ram Avtar Sharma's derives from an earlier cassette of Tanatan's; his *languria* "Devi maiya ko prasad" (on *Nashedar Languria,* Max 1003, B:4) was recorded by Kusum Lata on Rathor Cassettes' *Katile Languria.*

Chapter Ten

1. Tipu Sultan was an eighteenth-century potentate who fought valiantly against the British; fundamentalist Hindus have argued, with little historical rigor, that he persecuted Hindus and thus should not be celebrated by the state-run media.

2. The cassettes are entitled *Toro bandhan* (Break the shackles), *Buland irade* (High intentions), and *Mil-jul gayen* (Meeting together). Jagori's office is at B–5 South Extension, Part 1, New Delhi 110049. Bumiller (1990:141–42) describes how the Ahmedabad-based organization SEWA uses video technology to teach women how to organize cooperatives, access small business loans, speak in court, make better mud stoves, and accomplish other tasks.

3. Songs quoted are "Tu khud ko badal," "Mat banto insan ko," and "Family Planning."

4. NTR's conflation of cinematic and political roles was particularly deliberate and explicit, as during campaigns he would tour clad in saffron robes, riding a convertible transformed to resemble a chariot. Hindi film idol Amitabh Bachchan easily won a parliamentary seat also, although he subsequently abandoned politics.

5. "Cinema in poll war," *Hindustan Times,* 8 October 1989.

6. "Opposition's gonna get you," *Sunday,* 12–18 Nov., 1989, 38–39; "Electioneering in 'video raths,'" *Times of India,* 14 February 1990. A similar film made for Haryana's chief minister consisted mostly of renditions of folk songs.

7. As of late 1991, "Newstrack" appears to be the only financially viable video newsweekly.

8. Socioreligious as well as political movements have made liberal use of film parodies. Bumiller (1990:73) relates how supporters of Rup Kanwar's 1987 *sati* sang songs set to Hindi film tunes.

9. For the benefit of illiterate voters, all parties employ symbols: a hand, for Congress; a lotus for the BJP; hammer-and-sickle for CPI; a wheel for Janta Dal.

10. The song goes on to lambast individual Congress leaders, "This hand is the symbol of Balram, whose house is full of contraband . . . This hand is the symbol of [H. K. L.] Bhagat and the butchers of Delhi . . . " (Bhagat was allegedly one of the instigators of the 1984 post-assassination riots in which over a thousand Sikhs were slaughtered in Delhi).

11. Guruswamy also produced a disco-oriented tape aimed at college students, which was less successful.

12. "Cong criticises JD cassette," *Times of India,* 11 November 1989. The tapes were also featured in "Songs that go bump in Cong camp," ibid.

13. *Mainstream,* 25 November 1989, 32.

14. "The magic spell of 'MGR' still works," *Times of India,* 19 November 1989.

15. The Congress tape, which also parodied the current hit from *My name is Lakhan,* replaced the original "Tirchi Topi Wale" lyrics with Hindi verses proclaiming, "Everyone loves Rajiv, the saviour of the poor; he must win, or else people will regret

it." The Congress Party tapes seemed to this author to be uninspired and drab, reflecting the prevailing demoralization of the party.

16. "POK: The 'other' Kashmir," *India Today,* 31 March 1990, 24.

17. For an expansive articulation of this view, see Bilgrami 1991.

18. In summer 1989, over one hundred Muslims, constituting the entire population of a village near Bhagalpur, sought refuge from a Hindu mob in a police station; by the next day, all had been massacred, by the mob and/or the police, who subsequently assisted in burying the corpses. In Meerut, in May 1987, a police massacre left over two hundred Muslims dead. In the December 1990 turmoil in Agra, PAC (Provincial Armed Constabulary) members ascended rooftops in the Muslim quarter and shot to death at least eight Muslims who were doing daily chores in their courtyards below. One hundred three persons were killed in Ahmedabad riots (November 1990), and seventy-five in Aligarh (December 1990). Police were also responsible for earlier massacres, such as that of Moradabad in 1980.

19. Descriptions of the riots on radio, television, and in English-language newspapers generally report the numbers killed, but not their religions; while this policy is intended to prevent retributions, it allows other media and publications—such as Hindi newspapers—to falsify descriptions of events by claiming, for example, that only Hindus were killed. English-language newspapers and newsweeklies, while more balanced than Hindi-language papers, have, on the whole, excoriated V. P. Singh for his affirmative-action and anticommunal policies.

20. *Akhbar-e-nau* (Delhi), 14–20 December 1990 (translated in *India Speaks,* 3(52), 25 December 1990, 23).

21. The spurious nature of the entire Ram Janmbhoomi mythology is ably demonstrated in a document prepared by Romila Thapar and other leading historians for the Centre for Historical Studies, Jawaharlal Nehru University, excerpted in the *Times of India,* 6 November 1989. The document notes that Rama was not even popularly identified with present-day Ayodhya (formerly Saket) until the eighteenth century, and that the myth regarding the alleged destruction of a famous Rama temple there originated in the colonial period. The Muslim nawabs of Avadh in fact patronized and supported Hindu temples and worship in Ayodhya.

22. This is a standard line ("Shanka-nad ho raha, javano, Ram dal teyyar khara . . . ") describing the commencement of the central battle in the *Mahabharat.* Here it has been altered to apply to Ram, rather than the Pandavas.

23. Uma Bharati, Rajmata Vijay Raje Scindia, Ashok Singhal, Dau Dayaji Khanna, and Purjaswami Pramanandi Maharaj.

24. *Sunday Observer,* 16 December 1990.

25. Other groups and individuals often have vested interest in starting riots. A political party—such as the Congress Party, in Hyderabad in 1989—may wish to provoke civil unrest in an opposition-governed state in order to embarrass that party. Other individuals may wish to foment riots in order to loot, settle old scores, or eliminate enemies or business rivals, personally or via hired thugs, in the ensuing chaos. Muslim militants have also provoked some clashes, although the outnumbered Muslim communities are usually worsted.

26. "A voice in the dark set Ghaziabad aflame," *Times of India,* 31 January 1991, p. 9. Also see "How a simmering cauldron was ignited," *Times of India,* 16 December 1990, p. 13.

27. The 1987 *sati* (widow-burning) of Rup Kanwar in Rajasthan polarized activists in a similar fashion, pitting Hindu fundamentalists (with upper-class Rajput instigation) and regional-language newspapers against the educated, Westernized, and perceivedly irreligious elite, represented by English-language newspapers (Bumiller 1990:71–73).

Glossary of Indian-Language Terms

Words are transliterated here according to the system of Platts (1968). All terms are Hindi-Urdu unless otherwise noted in parentheses. Note that the unaspirated and aspirated palatals rendered, respectively, as *ch* and *chh* in the text proper are here transliterated as *ć* and *ćh*.

abhang. (Marathi:) A kind of Maharashtrian hymn.

ādhunik. Modern; hence, *ādhunik gān:* a genre of Bengali light music.

akhāra. A men's club, for wrestling, music, or other activities.

ārtī. Chanted hymn concluding a Hindu prayer ritual.

'āshiqāna. Romantic (as opposed to devotional, e.g., in reference to Urdu poetry).

baḥr. In Urdu poetry: meter; in Braj music: melody-type.

baiṭhakći lāvni. (Marathi:) *Lāvni* sung in semi-classical style, i.e., as if in a *baiṭhak* (formal sitting).

bakhshīsh. Alms, tip, bribe.

bandish. In Hindustani music, a musical composition.

banjo. A rectangular plucked zither with keys (Japanese tesho koto).

bāṅsri. Bamboo flute.

bārahmāsi. Folksong genre of western Uttar Pradesh, with topical text, sung to a particular distinctive melody (lit., "twelve month").

bhābhī. Elder brother's wife.

bhajan. Hindu devotional song (Cf. *kirtan*).

bhaktā. A female (or metaphorically female) devotee of a Hindu deity.

bhaktī. Hindu devotion, religion, faith.

bhangra. (Punjabi:) A lively dance and song genre of the Punjab.

bhāv gīt. Maharashtrian devotional song.

bheṅṭ. Gift; a kind of North Indian devotional song to the Mother Goddess.

birhā. Separation; a Bhojpuri folksong genre.

bol banāo. In Hindustani semi-classical music, the process of ornamenting, interpreting, and dramatizing a text by singing it with melodic variations.

braj-bāsī. A dweller of the Braj region.

ćatpaṭā. Spicy.

ćhāp. Stamp; in folk music, the donation of a tip.

ćīz. Thing; in Hindustani music, a composition.

ćulbulā. Playful.

dādra. In Hindustani music: a light-classical genre; a folk-derived *tāl* of six beats.

ḍaiya. Sting, e.g., by a wasp.

ḍanḍia. A folk Gujerati dance, wherein dancers strike wooden sticks together (also called *rās*).

ḍangal. A competitive event.

devar. A husband's younger brother (syn. *jījā*).

dev-nāgari. The alphabet used for Sanskrit and certain North Indian languages, including Hindi.

dharmik. Religious (e.g., as opposed to secular or romantic, in music or verse).

dhāṭū. In music, the setting of a text to a pre-existing melody.

dholak. A barrel-drum used in folk music.

dhrūpad. Archaic genre of Hindustani music.

dhun. Melody, tune (syn., *ṭarz*).

dohā. Couplet.

filmī. Film-style (adj.).

gālī. Abuse; a folksong genre typically sung by women at weddings, directed at the groom and his family.

garbā. Gujerati folk dance.

gazal. The primary genre of Urdu poetry; the musical rendition of such poetry.

ghazal. See *gazal.*

giddha. Punjabi women's song sung at weddings.

gīt. Song; generic term for any pre-composed song.

gopī. Cowgirl; Braj peasant girl, e.g., with whom Krishna sported.

gurdwāra. Sikh temple.

ḥalwā. A kind of sweet.

hijra. A caste of transvestite castrati, who often sing and dance semi-professionally.

Hir-Ranjha. A Punjabi folk ballad, narrating the fate of the ill- starred lovers Ranjha (a shepherd boy) and Hir (his beloved).

holī (horī). Hindu springtime festival; a genre of folk and/or light-classical music sung during that festival.

jajmānī. The Hindu feudal system.

jāgran. Waking; a night-long festival at a Hindu temple.

jalebī. A kind of deep-fried snack.

janmbhūmī. Birthplace.

jat, jāt. A caste of cultivators in north-central India and Pakistan.

jātra. A kind of Bengali folk drama.

jaymāl gīt. A kind of folksong of Uttar Pradesh.

jeṭh. Husband's elder brother.

jhūlnā. To swing; a swing; a kind of folksong associated with swinging.

jījā. Husband's younger brother.

jiṭhānī. Husband's elder brother's wife

jogī. A kind of religious mendicant.

kaharva. A quadratic *tāl* used in folk, popular, and Hindustani light classical music (having eight beats in the latter).

kaherva. See *kaharva.*

kajlī (kajrī). A kind of Bhojpuri folk or light-classical song sung during monsoon season.

kāṇḍ. Section or chapter of a book (e.g., of the *Ramayan*).

kāṭh. Sikh discourse.

kathā. Story; a sung version of a narrative tale.

kaṭhin. Difficult.

khānqah (khānaqah). A Sufi monastery.

khari birha. "Plain *birha*"; a kind of field holler sung by Bhojpuri peasants.

khari boli. The *lingua franca* dialect of Hindi, native to the Delhi-Meerut area.

khyāl. Thought, idea; the primary genre of Hindustani music; in western Uttar Pradesh, a solo song form, also called *lāvni* (having no particular connection with Maharasthrian *lāvni*).

kirtan. Devotional Hindu song.

kissa (qiṣṣa). Narrative story (Cf. *kathā*).

koli. Caste of Maharashtrian fishermen; hence, *koli gīt:* folksong associated with that caste.

laggī. Percussion interlude between verses of a folk or light-classical song.

lāṅgūriā. A junior male divinity accompanying Kaila Devi; a kind of Braj folksong mentioning that divinity.

lāvni. A folksong genre of western Uttar Pradesh (also called *khyāl*); a (wholly distinct) Maharashtrian folk, popular, and light- classical music genre.

līlā. Play, sport, game, esp., that of Krishna and the Braj cowgirls.

Māhābhārat. Hindu epic narrating the war between the Kauravas and Pandavas.

mahfil (mehfil). A sitting, or semi-formal party, perhaps with music, dance, or Urdu poetry.

malhār. A folksong genre of Uttar Pradesh sung during rainy season; a rainy-season *rāg* of Hindustani music.

manganhār. A caste of Rajasthani professional musicians.

masālā. Spice; in arts and entertainment: action, lewdness.

masāledār. Spicy, lewd.

mīrāsi. A caste of Muslim professional musicians in North India and Pakistan.

mukhra. Face; the pre-composed "catch" phrase of a light-classical song; in Hindustani music, the part of the composition's first line leading to the first beat of the *tāl*.

musha'ira (mush'ara). Urdu poetry session.

naqlī. Fake, imitation; e.g., of a cassette: pirated.

naqqāra. A stick-played drum-pair used in North Indian folk and archaic ceremonial music.

nasbandī. Sterilization, esp. vasectomy.

na't. Sub-genre of Muslim *qawwālī* praising Mohammad.

nauṭankī. A folk theater genre of North India, also called *swāng, sāng, sāngīt* (not *sangīt*).

pān. A snack made of betel nut, lime juice, a leaf, and other ingredients.

paṇḍit. A learned Brahmin, especially one who performs prayers and rituals professionally.

parda. A curtain; the Indo-Muslim custom of secluding women.

pīr. A Muslim holy man or teacher.

pollī gīt. Bengali folksong.

popaṭ. (Marathi:) parrot; (slang:) penis; a genre of lewd urban folksong.

285

powāda. (Marathi:) sung narratives of martial exploits of Shivaji and other Maharashtrian warrior-heroes.

pūjā. Hindu prayer ritual.

qāfiya. The final rhyme in line of a *gazal* (the penultimate rhyme being the *radīf*).

qawwālī. Muslim song genre, most characteristically devotional.

Rabindra sangīt. Genre of Bengali light music consisting of compositions of Rabindranath Tagore.

radīf. The penultimate rhyme in a line of a *gazal* (preceding the *qāfiya*).

raḍua. (Braj-bhasha:) a bachelor.

rāg. A melodic mode in classical Hindustani or Karnatak music.

rāgi. A professional singer of Sikh devotional music.

rāginī. A genre of Haryanvi folksong; in archaic Hindustani modal taxonomies, a subordinate *rāg.*

Rāmāyan. Hindu epic, focusing on the exploits of Rama in regaining his wife and throne.

Rāmlīlā. North Indian folk theater performed during Dussera (Dasahra) based on the *Ramayan.*

ras. Juice; aesthetic sentiment.

rās. A Gujerati folk dance.

rās-dhārī. A professional performer of *rās-līlā* theater.

rasiya. Juicy, tasty, full of *ras;* a libertine, rake; Krishna; a genre of Braj folksong.

rāslīlā. North Indian folk theater performed during *holī*, portraying the life of Krishna.

rath. Chariot.

śabd-gurbāni. Musical settings of the writings of the Sikh gurus.

śabd-kirtan. Sikh devotional songs, with old or newly composed texts.

sajānā. To decorate, embellish, dress up.

sālī. Elder brother's wife (syn., *bhābhī*).

samāj. Society; song session in Hindu temples (e.g., in the Braj region) where *dhrūpad* compositions are sung by the congregation.

sampradāya. Sect.

sāng (swāng, sāngīt). Western Uttar Pradesh and Haryanvi term for *nauṭankī* folk theater.

sāngīt. Syn. for *sāng.*

sangīt. Music.

sāntūr. A struck zither used in Persian and Hindustani music.

sāraṅgī. A bowed instrument used in Hindustani music.

sarod. A plucked lute used in Hindustani music.

satī. Virtuous, faithful; a widow who is immolated on her husband's funeral pyre; the act of such immolation.

sāvan. The fourth Hindu month, corresponding to the monsoon season; a genre of North Indian folksong sung during rainy season.

shahnāi. Double-reed aerophone used in Hindustani and North Indian folk music.

sharāb. Wine, liquor.

sohar. North Indian folksong genre sung by women at the birth of a son.

surmaṇḍal. Trapezoidal zither strummed by Hindustani vocalist.

swāng. Syn. for *sāng, sāngīt, nauṭankī.*

tabla. Drum pair used in Hindustani classical and light-classical music; the right-hand drum of this pair.

tagrī. An ornamented thread or chain worn around the waist.

tāl. Rhythmic meter in Hindustani music.

tānpūra. Chordophone used as drone instrument in Hindustani and Karnatak music.

tappā. Archaic genre of Hindustani music; a genre of Punjabi folksong.

taqrīr. Speech, oration; term used for Muslim semi-melodic religious discourse.

tarannum. A form of reciting Urdu poetry (especially *gazal*) using simple melodies.

tarz. Melody, tune.

tataiya. (Braj-bhasha:) Wasp.

thumri. Semi-classical genre of Hindustani music.

'urs. Marriage; religious commemoration of the death-anniversary of a saint, celebrating the saint's union (metaphorical wedding) with the divine.

vrat. A ritual fast performed by Hindus, often accompanied by recitation of a narrative didactic story, concluding with a prayer.

Bibliography

Abbas, K. A. 1977. *Mad, Mad, Mad World of Indian Films.* Delhi: Hind Pocket Books.

Abhinav, Kalura. 1989. Lokgiton ke saye men panpati sanskrit. *Hindustan Times (Dainik),* 10 October.

Abu-Lughod, Lila. 1989. Bedouins, cassettes and technologies of public culture. *Middle East Report* 159 (July–August): 7–11, 47.

Agrawal, Binod. 1986. Cultural response to communication revolution: Many modes of video use in India. *Gazette* 38:29–41.

Appadurai, Arjun. 1991. "Afterword." In *Gender, Genre, and Power,* 467–76. *See* Appadurai, Korom, and Mills 1991.

Appadurai, Arjun, Frank Korom, and Margaret Mills, eds. 1991. *Gender, Genre, and Power in South Asian Expressive Traditions.* Philadelphia: Univ. of Penn. Press.

Arnold, Alison. 1988. Popular film song in India—a case of mass market musical eclecticism. *Popular Music* 7, no. 2 (May):177–88.

Awasthi, Dilip. 1987. Cine closure: Protest against tax rates. *India Today,* 30 November, 14–15.

Awasthi, Suresh. 1977. Nautanki: An operatic theatre. *National Centre for the Performing Arts Quarterly Journal,* 4 June, 23–36.

Badhwar, Inderjit. 1987. A supersuccess story. *India Today,* 30 April, 110–12.

Bagdikian, Ben. 1983. *The Media Monopoly.* Boston: Beacon.

———. 1985. The United States media: Supermarket or assembly line? *Journal of Communication* 35(3):97–109.

Banerjee, Sumanta. 1976. Bad days for the ghazal. *Times of India,* 26 December, 13.

———. 1985. The U.S. media: Supermarket or assembly line? *Journal of Communication* 35(3):97–109.

Banerjee, Usha Rani. 1986. Braj ke rasiyon ka adhyayan. Ph.D. diss., Banaras Hindu Univ.

Banerjee, Utpal. 1985 "Indian cinema: Myths, archetypes, and cult figures." In *Indian Films Today: An Anthology of Articles on Indian Cinema.* New Delhi (unpaginated).

Banerji, Sabita, and Gerd Baumann. 1990. "Bhangra 1984–8: Fusion and professionalization in a genre of South Asian dance music." In *Black Music in Britain: Essays on the Afro-Asian Contribution to Popular Music,* ed. Paul Oliver. Milton Keynes: Open Univ. Press.

Bedi, Sohinder Singh. 1971. *Folklore of the Punjab.* New Delhi: National Book Trust.

Benjamin, Walter. 1968. "The work of art in the age of mechanical reproduction." In *Illuminations.* New York: Shocken.

Bhargava, Simran. 1991. On a fast track. *India Today,* 15 January, 58–60.

Bhatkhande, Vishnu Narayan. 1954–59. *Kramik Pustak Malika.* Hathras: Sangit Karyalaya.

Bhattacharjea, Ajit. 1990. Bofors, communal frenzy and the puppet. *Mainstream,* 22 December, 34.

Bhattacharya, Mihir. 1989–90. Semi-feudal aesthetics. *Social Scientist* 12(79).

Bilgrami, Akeel. 1991. Cry, the beloved subcontinent. *New Republic,* 10 June, 30–34.

Brahmananda, P. R. The economic record of the Rajiv regime. *Times of India,* 10 November.

Bumiller, Elisabeth. 1990. *May You Be the Mother of a Hundred Sons: A Journey among the Women of India.* New York: Penguin.

Burlingame, Burl. 1991. Jammin' to Jawaiian. *Honolulu Star-Bulletin,* 1 May, E1, E3.

Chandavarkar, Bhaskar. 1987a. Tradition of music in Indian cinema. *Cinema in India,* April, 8–11.

———. 1987b. Now it's the Bombay film song. *Cinema in India,* July-September, 18–23.

———. 1990. The power of the popular film song. *Cinema in India,* April-June, 20–24.

Chandra, Sharmila. 1989. Losing their charm: A traditional art faces extinction. *India Today* 31 December, 187–88.

Chapple, Steve, and Reebee Garofalo. 1973. *Rock 'n' Roll is Here to Pay: The History and Politics of the Music Industry.* Chicago: Nelson-Hall.

Chaudhuri, Nirad. 1966. *The Continent of Circe.* Bombay: Jaico.

Chengappa, Raj. 1987. Sound revolution. *India Today,* 31 July, 112–13.

Chernoff, John. 1979. *African Rhythm and African Sensibility.* Chicago: Univ. of Chicago Press.

Chopra, Anil. 1986. Magnetic tape: To import or not to import. *Playback,* December, 66–67.

———. 1988a. Death wish. *Playback,* March, 17–18.

———. 1988b. Ganpati bappa morya. *Playback,* September, 26–29.

———. 1991. Breaking through. *Playback,* November–December, 6.

Clarke, Paul. 1983. A magic science: Rock music as a recording art. *Popular Music* 3, 195–214.

Cohen, Erik, and Amnon Shiloah. 1985. Major trends of change in Jewish oriental ethnic music in Israel. *Popular Music* 5: 199–224.

Coll, Steve. 1990. India at economic crossroads. *International Herald Tribune,* 28 March, 11.

Collins, John. 1985. *African Pop Roots: The Inside Rhythms of Africa.* London: Foulsham.

Coplan, David. 1985. *In Township Tonight! South Africa's Black City Music and Theatre.* New York: Longman.

Crossette, Barbara. 1991. In India, the star of the video is the candidate. *New York Times,* 30 April, 5.

Das Gupta, Surajeet. 1987. Jatra: Popular Productions. *India Today,* 30 September, 108–09.

de Vries, Fred. 1988. The deadly music pirates. *New African,* May, 32.

Dubashi, Jagganath. 1986. Cassette piracy: High stakes. *India Today,* 31 March, 112.

Durry, Kaokab. 1972. Ghazal: The dying swan. *Lipika,* February, 21–24.

Engleberg, Stephen. 1991. Catching Poland's ear with west's catchy music. *New York Times,* 30 January.

Entwistle, A. W. 1983. Kaila Devi and lamguriya. *Indo-Iranian Journal* 25, 85–101.

———. 1987. *Braj: Centre of Krishna pilgrimage.* Groningen: Egbert Forsten.

Enzensberger, H. M. 1970. Constituents of a theory of the media. *New Left Review* 64:13–36.

Fandy, Mamoun. 1990. The Hawali tapes. *New York Times,* 24 November, 21.

Feld, Steven. 1982. *Sound and Sentiment: Birds, Weeping, Poetics, and Song in Kaluli Expression.* Philadelphia: Univ. of Pennsylvania Press.

Fisher, John. 1991. Improving cassette quality. *Playback,* November–December, 61–63.

Freitag, S., ed. 1989. *Culture and Power in Banaras: Community, Performance, and Environment, 1800–1980.* Berkeley: Univ. of California Press.

Frith, Simon. 1987. "The industrialisation of music," In *Popular Music and Communication,* ed. James Lull. Newbury Park: Sage.

Gamman, Lorraine, and Margaret Marshment, eds. 1989. *The Female Gaze: Women as Viewers of Popular Culture.* Seattle: Real Comet Press.

Garofalo, Reebee. 1987. How autonomous is relative: Popular music, the social formation and cultural struggle. *Popular Music* 6, no. 1: 77–92.

Geertz, Clifford. 1973. *The Interpretation of Cultures.* New York: Basic Books.

Ghosh, Munmun. 1989. Raz ki bat of an oye-oye! *Movie,* October (unpaginated).

Gill, Rena. 1983. Films for development. *Social Change* 13, no. 4 (December): 14–15.

Gopal, Shashi. 1987. For the record. *Playback,* September, 32–33.

Gourlay, Kenneth. 1978. Towards a reassessment of the ethnomusicologist's role. *Ethnomusicology* 22(1): 1–35.

Graham, Ronnie. 1988. *The Da Capo Guide to Contemporary African Music.* New York: Da Capo.

Grierson, George. 1886. Some Bhojpuri folk-songs. *Journal of the Royal Asiatic Society* 18:207–67.

Gronow, Pekka. 1981. Record industry comes to the Orient. *Ethnomusicology* 25(2):251–84.

Hall, Stuart. 1973. "Coding and encoding in television discourse." In *Culture, Media, Language,* ed. S. Hall et al. London: Hutchinson.

Hansen, Kathy. 1989. "The birth of Hindi drama in Banaras, 1868–1885." In *Culture and Power in Banaras,* 62–92. *See* Freitag 1989.

Hartmann, Paul, B. R. Patil, and Anita Dighe. 1989. *The Mass Media and Village Life: An Indian Study.* New Delhi: Sage.

Hein, Norvin. 1972. *The Miracle Plays of Mathura.* Delhi: Oxford Univ. Press.

Henry, Edward O. 1988. *Chant the Names of God: Music and Culture in Bhojpuri-Speaking India*. San Diego: San Diego State Univ. Press.

Heston, Wilma. 1991. "Footpath poets of Peshawar." In *Gender, Genre and Power. See* Appadurai, Korom, and Mills.

Hyderabadi, Akmal. 1982. *Qawwali Amir Khusrau se Shakila Bano tak*. Delhi: Lahore Fine Arts Press.

Ibrahim, Youssef. 1992. Saudi rulers are confronting challenge by Islamic radicals. *New York Times*, 9 March: A1, 7.

Iyengar, Jayanti. 1988. It's super success. *Times of India*, 14 May, 1, 4.

Jairazbhoy, Nazir. 1977. Music in western Rajasthan: Continuity and change. *International Folk Music Council* 9, 50–66.

Jha, Subhash. 1989a. Playin' Mr. Wilson to ol' Bappi. *Times of India*, 11 October.

———. 1989b. Some more of Bappi's 'paap' music. *Times of India*, 8 November.

———. 1990a. Mata's bhajans set to disco beats. *Times of India*, 3 January.

———. 1990b. Numbers for the roadside Romeos. *Times of India*, 31 January.

———. 1990c. There was poetry, passion melody, and no Bappi! *Filmfare*, January (unpaginated).

Joshi, G. N. 1987. Bhakti sangeet of hymn and harmony. *Playback*, October, 28–32.

———. 1988. A concise history of the phonograph industry in India. *Popular Music* 7, no. 2 (May):147–156.

Junghare, Indira. 1983. Songs of the Mahars: An untouchable caste of Maharashtra, India. *Ethnomusicology* 27(2):71–96.

Kakar, Sudhir. 1989. *Intimate Relations: Exploring Indian Sexuality*. New Delhi: Viking.

Kakar, Sudhir, and John Ross. 1986. *Tales of Love, Sex and Danger*. Oxford: Oxford Univ. Press.

Kanjila, Sandip. 1989. Review in *City Scan*, August, 63.

Kaplan, E. Ann. 1987. *Rocking Around the Clock: Music Television, Postmodernism, and Consumer Culture*. New York, Methuen.

Kaye, Lincoln. 1988. Flickering fortunes. *Far Eastern Economic Review*, 1 September, 51.

Keskar, B. V. 1967. *Indian Music: Problems and Prospects*. Bombay: Popular Prakashan.

Khosla, S. N. 1987. Venus in India. *Playback*, July, 25–27.

Kinnear, Michael. 1990. Odeon in India. *International Talking Machine Review*. 77 (Spring):2260–2270.

Kippen, James. 1988. *The Tabla of Lucknow: A Cultural Analysis of a Musical Tradition*. Cambridge: Cambridge Univ. Press.

Kohli, Atul. 1990. *Democracy and Its Discontents: India's Growing Crisis of Governability*. Cambridge: Cambridge Univ. Press.

Koskoff, Ellen. 1987. *Women and Music in Cross-Cultural Perspective*. New York: Greenwood.

Krishen, Pradip. 1981. Introduction. *India International Centre: Quarterly* (March), 3–9.

Kristof, Nicholas. 1991a. A Taiwan pop singer sways the mainland. *New York Times*, 19 February.

―――. 1991b. The end of the golden road. *New York Times Magazine,* 1 December, 52–57, 84–87.

Kumar, Nita. 1988. *The Artisans of Banaras: Popular Culture and Identity, 1880– 1986.* Princeton: Princeton Univ. Press.

Lalitha, S. 1988. The business of bhajans. *Times of India,* 1 October.

Langer, Felicia. 1988. *An Age of Stone.* London: Quartet.

Lazere, Donald, ed. 1987. *American Media and Mass Culture: Left Perspectives.* Berkeley: Univ. of California Press.

Lelyveld, David. n.d. Upon the subdominant: Administering music on All-India Radio. Manuscript.

Levine, Lawrence. 1977. *Black Culture and Black Consciousness.* New York: Oxford Press.

Limón, José. 1983. Texas-Mexican popular music and dancing: Some notes on history and symbolic process. *Latin American Music Review* 4(2):229–46.

Louden, Sarah. 1986. Rajasthani musicians in Delhi: Adaptation in village traditions. M.A. thesis, Univ. of Washington, Seattle.

Lutgendorf, Philip. 1990. Ramayan: The video. *The Drama Review* 126. (Summer): 127–76.

Mahurkar, Uda. 1990. Twisting tradition. *India Today,* 31 October, 167–69.

Mansukhani, G. S. 1982. *Indian Classical Music and Sikh Kirtan.* New Delhi: Oxford and IBH Publishing.

Manuel, Peter. 1985. Formal structure in popular music as a reflection of socioeconomic change. *International Review of the Aesthetics and Sociology of Music* 16(2): 163–80.

―――. 1988a. A historical survey of the Urdu Gazal-song in India. *Asian Music,* 20, no. 1 (Fall-Winter):93–113.

―――. 1988b. *Popular Musics of the Non-Western World: An Introductory Survey,* New York: Oxford Univ. Press.

―――. 1989. *Thumri in Historical and Stylistic Perspectives.* Delhi: Motilal Baarsidas.

―――. 1992. Salsa and the Music Industry: Corporate Control or Grassroots Expression? *Essays on Cuban Music: North American and Cuban Perspectives.* Lanham, MD: Univ. Press of America.

Manuel, Peter, and Randall Baier. 1986. Jaipongan: Indigenous popular music of West Java. *Asian Music* 18, no.1 (Fall-Winter):91–110.

Marcus, Scott. 1987. "The rise of a folk music genre: *Birha.*" In *Culture and Power in Banaras,* 93–113. *See* Freitag 1989.

Marcuse, Herbert. 1964. *One-Dimensional Man.* Boston: Beacon.

Marre, Jeremy, and Hannah Charlton. 1985. *Beats of the Heart: Popular Music of the World.* New York: Pantheon.

Marx, Karl, and Friedrich Engels. [1846] 1964. *The German Ideology.* Moscow.

Mathai, Joseph. 1988. Devotion goes "pop," *The Sunday Observer,* 10 July.

Mattelart, Armand, and Jean-Marie Piemme. 1982. "New technologies, decentralisation and public service," (tr. David Buxton). In *Communication and Class Struggle 2: Liberation, Socialism,* ed. A. Mattelart and Seth Siegelaub. New York: International General, 413–18.

McQuail, Dennis. 1987a. *Mass Communication Theory.* Newbury Park: Sage.

————. 1987b. Review of *Communication Technology: The New Media in Society,* by E. Rogers. *Journal of Communication* 37, no. 4 (Autumn).

Menon, Raghava. 1989. Light music changes scale. *Times of India,* 8 May.

Meyers, Helen. 1991. Indian, East Indian, and West Indian music in Felicity, Trinidad. In *Ethnomusicology and Modern Music History.* Ed. Stephen Blum, Philip Bohlman, and Daniel Neuman. Urbana: Univ. of Illinois Press, 231–41.

Middleton, Richard. 1990. *Studying Popular Music.* Milton Keynes: Open Univ. Press.

Miller, Barbara Stoler. 1982. The divine duality of Radha and Krishna. In *The Divine Consort: Radha and Goddesses of India.* Ed. John S. Hawley and Donna Wulff. Boston: Beacon, 13–26.

Mills, Margaret. 1991. "Gender and verbal performance style in Afghanistan." In *Gender, Genre, and Power. See* Appadurai, Korom, and Mills 1991.

Mishra, V. M. 1970. *Communication and Modernization in Urban Slums.* New York: Asia Publishing House.

Mitra, Ashok. 1986. Bengali pictures retreat from Calcutta's cinema halls. *Far Eastern Economic Review,* 4 September, 39.

Mohideen, Nabeel. 1989. Who's zooming whom? *Times of India,* 23 July, 8.

Mullick, Swapan. 1985. Bengal's changing cultural scenario. *National Centre for the Performing Arts Quarterly Journal* 14(3):29–37.

Muralidharan, Sukumar. 1988. Electronics liberalisation reconsidered. *Economics and Political Weekly,* 13 August, 1661–67.

Nair, Raj. 1986. Pre-recorded cassettes: Caught in a snarl. *Playback,* August, 50–53.

Neuman, Daniel. [1980] 1990. *The Life of Music in North India: The Organization of an Artistic Tradition.* Chicago: Univ. of Chicago Press.

Ojha, Jagdish. 1985. Phonograph and cultural communication in India. Manuscript photocopy. New Delhi: Behavioural Sciences Centre.

Parmar, Shyam. 1977. *Folk Music and Mass Media.* New Delhi: Communication Publishers.

Peña, Manuel. 1985. *The Texas-Mexican Conjunto: History of a Working-Class Music.* Austin: Univ. of Texas.

Pfleiderer, Beatrix, and Lothar Lutze. 1985. *The Hindi Film: Agent and Re-Agent of Cultural Change.* New Delhi: Manohar.

Platts, John. [1884] 1968. *Dictionary of Urdu, Classical Hindi, and English.* Oxford: Oxford Univ. Press.

Pollack, Andrew. 1990. Recording enters a new era and you can't find it on LP. *New York Times,* 1 April, 1, 16.

Pratap, Anita. 1990. Romance and a little rape. *Time,* 13 August, 69.

Purohit, Vinayak. 1988. *Arts of Transitional India: Twentieth Century.* Vol. 2. Bombay: Popular Prakashan.

Racy, Ali Jihad. 1977. Musical change and commercial recording in Egypt, 1904–1932. Ph.D. diss., Univ. of Illinois, Urbana-Champaign.

Rajan, Rajiv. 1989. In small measure. *Advertising and Marketing,* October, 22–24.

Rahman, M. 1987. Filling the void. *India Today,* 30 November, 80–82.

ur-Rahman, Matin. 1982. *Ghazal Gayaki ke Badalte Rang.* Bhopal: Malwa Publishing House.

Ranade, Ashok. 1984. *On Music and Musicians of Hindoostan,* New Delhi: Promilla.

Ranga Rao, V. A. K. 1986. Version recordings: New controversy, old issue. Parts 1, 2. *Playback,* August 26–27, September 29.

Rangoonwalla, Feroze. 1975. *75 Years of Indian Cinema.* New Delhi: Promilla.

Rao, Leela. 1989. Women in Indian films, *Media, Culture and Society* 11(4):443–58.

Ray, Sukumar. 1973. *Music of Eastern India: Vocal Music in Bengali, Oriya, Assamese and Manipuri with Special Emphasis on Bengali.* Calcutta: Firma K. L. Mukhopadhyay.

Reddi, Usha. 1989. Media and culture in Indian society: Conflict or cooperation? *Media, Culture and Society* 11(4):395–414.

Roberge, Gaston. 1985. *Another Cinema for Another Society,* Calcutta: Seagull.

Robinson, Deanna Campbell, Elizabeth Buck, and Marlene Cuthbert. 1991. *Music at the Margins: Popular Music and Global Cultural Diversity.* London: Sage.

Sadiq, Muhammad. 1984. *A History of Urdu Literature.* 2d ed. Delhi: Oxford Univ. Press.

Sarkar, Jayanta. 1989. India's TV Times. *Far Eastern Economic Review,* 26 January, 73–77.

Savur, Sumit. 1989. 1988: An overview. *Playback,* February, 43.

Sayani, Sanjay. 1988. In search of melody. *Playback,* February, 35–37.

Shah, Nalin. 1986. The birth of film song—II. *Playback,* November, 18–19.

———. 1988. Off the record. *Playback,* November, 11.

Shahani, Kumar, Mani Kaul, and Girish Karnad. Comments from the Gallery. *India International Centre Quarterly,* March, 97–123.

Sharma, Premchand. 1983. *Haryana ki Lokdharma Natya Parampara.* Chandigarh: Haryana Sahitya Academy.

el-Shawan Castelo-Branco, Salwa. 1987. Some aspects of the cassette industry in Egypt. *World of Music* 29(2):3–45.

Shetty, Kavitha. 1989. Modern rites. *India Today,* 31 January, 196.

Singer, Milton. 1972. *When a Great Tradition Modernizes: An Anthropological Approach to Indian Civilization.* Chicago: Univ. of Chicago Press.

Singh, Yogendra. 1986. *Modernization of Indian Tradition.* Jaipur: Rawat.

Singhal, Arvind, and Everett Rogers. 1989. *India's Information Revolution.* New Delhi: Sage.

Siriyuvasak, Ubonrat. 1990. Commercialising the sound of the people: *Pleng Luktoong* and the Thai pop music industry. *Popular Music* 9, no. 1 (January):61–78.

Slawek, Stephen. 1986. Kirtan: A study of the sonic manifestations of the divine in the popular Hindu culture of Banaras. Ph.D. diss., Univ. of Illinois, Urbana-Champaign.

Spivak, Gayatri Chakravarti. 1988. "Can the subaltern speak?" In *Marxism and the Interpretation of Culture,* ed. Cary Nelson and Lawrence Grossberg, 271–313. Chicago: Univ. of Illinois Press.

Sreberny-Mohammadi, Annabelle. 1990. Small media for a big revolution: Iran. *International Journal of Politics, Culture, and Society* 3(3):341–72.

Stapleton, Chris, and Chris May. 1987. *African All-Stars: The Pop Music of a Continent.* New York: Quartet.

Sutton, R. Anderson. 1985. Commercial cassette recordings of traditional music in Java: Implications for performers and scholars. *The World of Music* 32(3):23–46.

————. 1991. *Traditions of Gamelan Music in Java: Musical Pluralism and Regional Identity.* Cambridge: Cambridge Univ. Press.

————. Forthcoming. "Interpreting electronic sound technology in the contemporary Javanese soundscape." In *Some Perspectives on Music since 1960,* ed. Graham Hais, Laughton Harris, and Margaret Kartomi. Sidney: Currency Press.

Swamy, Harini. 1991. In the big music bazar. *Times of India,* 21 July, 9.

Tewari, Laxmi. 1974. Folk music of India: Uttar Pradesh. Ph.D. diss. Wesleyan Univ.

————. 1988. Sohar: Childbirth songs of joy. *Asian Folklore Studies* 47(2):257–76.

Thompson, John. 1990. *Ideology and Modern Culture.* Stanford: Stanford Univ. Press.

Tiwari, Alok, and Farzand Ahmed. 1991. Lewd lyrics, *India Today,* 31 March, 163, 166.

Upadhyay, M. 1987. The bhajan samrat. *Playback,* August.

Vatuk, Ved. 1979. *Studies in Indian Folk Traditions.* New Delhi: Manohar.

Wadhera, Prakash. 1986. A mediocre bhajan fare by Hari Om. *The Patriot,* 24 June.

Wallis, Roger, and Krister Malm. 1984. *Big Sounds from Small Peoples: The Music Industry in Small Countries.* New York: Pendragon.

Waterman, Chris. 1990. *Juju: A Social History and Ethnography of an African Popular Music.* Chicago: Univ. of Chicago Press.

Williams, Raymond. 1977. *Marxism and Literature.* Oxford: Oxford Univ. Press.

Williams, Sean. 1990. The urbanization of tembang sunda, an aristocratic musical genre of West Java, Indonesia. Ph.D. diss., Univ. of Washington, Seattle.

Wines, Michael. 1991. C.I.A. joins military move to sap Iraqi confidence. *New York Times,* 19 January, 9.

Wong, Deborah. 1989–90. Thai cassettes and their covers: Two case histories. *Asian Music* 21(1):78–104.

Yadava, J. S. 1986. Mass media and social change in India. *Social Change* 16(2–3):117–124.

Yampolsky, Philip. 1989. "Hati Yang Luka," an Indonesian hit. *Indonesia* 47:1–18.

————. 1987. *Lokananta: A Discography of the National Recording Company of Indonesia, 1957–1985.* Madison: Univ. of Wisconsin, Center for Southeast Asian Studies.

Zindi, Fred. 1985. *Roots Rocking in Zimbabwe.* Zimbabwe: Marubo (?).

Zuzart, Joseph. 1990. Sagarika duplication: Tackling the majors, *Playback,* January–March, 69–71.

Some Recent Parodies in Film Music

Hindi Film Song	Producer	Original Song	Original Composer
Zubie zubie	Bappi Lahiri	*Brother Louie*	Modern Talking
Mere jaise hasina	Bappi Lahiri	*When you are in love with a beautiful woman*	Dr. Hook
Ramba ho samba ho	Bappi Lahiri	(Italian disco hit)	
Krishna dharti pe aaje tu	Bappi Lahiri	*Oh Jesus*	Judas Priest
ABCD	Bappi Lahiri	*Ek do tin*	(Marathi folk song)
Jhopri men charpai	Bappi Lahiri	*Ek do tin*	(Marathi folk song)
One two three	Bappi Lahiri	*Ek do tin*	(Marathi folk song)
Tutuk tutuk	Bappi Lahiri	*Tutuk tutuk*	Milan Singh
Pehli nazar men ho gae	Bappi Lahiri	*O milan*	Bappi Lahiri
De de pyar de	Bappi Lahiri	*Allah megh de*	S. D. Burman
Mausam hai gane ka	Bappi Lahiri	*Love in C Minor*	Cerrone
Hari om Hari	Bappi Lahiri	*One-way ticket*	Corruption
Baaj uthe ghunghru	Bappi Lahiri	*Chor pe mor*	R. D. Burman
Ding dang ding	Bappi Lahiri	*Papa kehte hain*	Laxmikant-Pyarelal
Tauba re tauba	Bappi Lahiri	*Yadon men woh*	Roshan
Pyar bara mushkil hai	Bappi Lahiri	*Lambada*	Kalma
Aya aya	Bappi Lahiri	*Hawa Hawa*	Hassan Jahangir
Han bahi han	Annu Malik		Hassan Jahangir
Billu Badshah	Jagjit Singh		Hassan Jahangir
Mere rang men rangne	Ramlaxman	*The final countdown*	Europe
Ek chhora ek chhori	Laxmikant-Pyarelal	*Ek do tin*	(Marathi folk song)
Ate jate hanste gate	Laxmikant-Pyarelal	*I just called to say . . .*	Stevie Wonder
Purana tera khunta	Laxmikant-Pyarelal	*Come September*	
Pyra ke nam qurban	B. Subhash	*Yad a rahi hai*	Bappi Lahiri

Some Recent Parodies in Film Music (continued)

Hindi Film Song	Producer	Original Song	Original Composer
Baj gai ghanti baj gai	B. Subhash	*De de pyar de*	Bappi Lahiri
Tridev	Kalyanji-Anandji	*Heart*	Pet Shop Boys
Tere liye zamana tere liye	R. D. Burman	*Mama Mia*	Abba

Index